COMMENTARIES

ON THE

TWELVE MINOR PROPHETS

VOL. IV

HABAKKUK, ZEPHANIAH, HAGGAI

THE CALVIN TRANSLATION SOCIETY,

INSTITUTED IN MAY M.DCCC.XLIII.

FOR THE PUBLICATION OF TRANSLATIONS OF THE WORKS OF
JOHN CALVIN.

COMMENTARIES

ON THE

TWELVE MINOR PROPHETS

BY JOHN CALVIN

NOW FIRST TRANSLATED FROM THE ORIGINAL LATIN

BY THE REV. JOHN OWEN,
VICAR OF THRUSSINGTON, LEICESTERSHIRE

VOLUME FOURTH

HABAKKUK, ZEPHANIAH, HAGGAI

WIPF & STOCK · Eugene, Oregon

Wipf and Stock Publishers
199 W 8th Ave, Suite 3
Eugene, OR 97401

Commentaries on the Twelve Minor Prophets, Volume 4
Habakkuk, Zephaniah, Haggai
By Calvin, John and Owen, John
Softcover ISBN-13: 979-8-3852-1618-5
Hardcover ISBN-13: 979-8-3852-1619-2
eBook ISBN-13: 979-8-3852-1620-8
Publication date 2/13/2024
Previously published by Baker Book House, 2005

This edition is a scanned facsimile of the original edition published in 2005.

TRANSLATOR'S PREFACE.

THE present Volume, though it contains the Works of THREE PROPHETS, is yet considerably smaller in size than the preceding Volumes; but the last will more than compensate for this deficiency.

The two first Prophets, HABAKKUK and ZEPHANIAH, lived before the Captivity; and the other, HAGGAI, began his prophetic office about sixteen years after the return of the great body of the people from Babylon by the permission given them by King Cyrus.

It is commonly thought that HABAKKUK prophesied *after* ZEPHANIAH, though placed before him in our Bibles. The reign of JEHOIAKIN is assigned as his age, about 608 years before Christ, while Zephaniah performed his office in the reign of JOSIAH, about 30 years earlier. Like the other prophets he is mainly engaged in reproving the extreme wickedness of the people, on account of which he denounces on them the judgments of God, while he gives occasional intimations of a better state of things, and affords some glimpses of the blessings of the gospel.

In the *first* CHAPTER he begins with a complaint as to the oppression which he witnessed, foretells the dreadful invasion of the CHALDEANS, describes the severity which would be exercised by them, and appeals to God on the subject. In the *second* he waits for an answer, receives it, and predicts the downfal of the Chaldeans, and refers to blessings in reserve for God's people. The *third* contains what is called the "Prayer of Habakkuk," an ode of a singular character, in which he briefly describes, for the encouragement of the faithful, the past interpositions of God on behalf of his people, and concludes with expressing a full and joyful confidence in God, notwithstanding the evils which were coming on the nation.

"The style of HABAKKUK," says Bishop *Lowth,* "is poetical, especially in his Ode, which may justly be deemed one of the most complete of its kind."[1] And in describing the character of this ode he says—"The Prophet indeed embellishes the whole of this poem with a magnificence equal to its commencement, selecting from so great an abundance of wonderful events the grandest, and setting them forth in the most splendid dress, by images and figures, and the most elevated diction; the high sublimity of which he augments and enhances by the elegance of a remarkable conclusion: so that hardly any thing of this kind would be more beautiful or more perfect than this poem, were it not for one or two spots of obscurity which are to be found in it, occasioned, as it seems, by its ancientness."[2]

ZEPHANIAH was in part contemporary with JEREMIAH, that is, during the former portion of the reign of JOSIAH. He

[1] Poeticus est Habbaccuci stylus; sed maximè in Oda, quæ inter absolutissimas in eo genere meritò numerari potest.—*Prœl.* xxi.

[2] Equidem totum hunc locum pari quâ ingressus est magnificentiâ exornat vates; ex tantâ rerum admirandarum copiâ nobilissima quæque seligens, eaque coloribus splendidissimis, imaginibus, figuris, dictione elatissimâ illustrans; quorum summam sublimitatem cumulat et commendat singularis clausulæ elegantiâ: ita ut, nisi una atque altera ei insideret obscuritatis nebula vetustate, ut videtur, inducta, vix quidquam hoc poemate in suo genere extaret luculentius aut perfectius.—*Prœl.* xxviii.

foretells the FALL OF NINEVEH, (ch. ii. 13,) and mentions "the remnant of Baal," (ch. i. 4,) two things which prove that he prophesied during the former half of that king's reign; for NINEVEH was destroyed about the sixteenth year of his reign, and it was after that time that the worship of Baal was demolished by that king.

The sins of THE JEWS and their approaching judgments occupy the *first* Chapter. The *second* contains an exhortation to Repentance, encouraged by a promise of protection during the evils that God would bring on neighbouring nations. In the *third* the Prophet particularizes the sins of JERUSALEM, announces its punishment, and then refers to the future blessings which God would freely confer on His Church.

The style of ZEPHANIAH has been represented as being in some parts prosaic; and *Lowth* says that "he seems to possess nothing remarkable or superior in the arrangement of his matter or in the elegance of his diction."[1] But it is *Henderson's* opinion that "many of the censures that have been passed on his language are either without foundation or much exaggerated." He appears to be as poetic in his ideas as most of the Prophets, and in the manner in which he arranges them, though he deals not much in parallelisms, which constitute a prominent feature in Hebrew poetry.

The matters handled by the Prophet are said by *Marckius* to be "most worthy of God, whether we regard His serious reproofs or His severe threatenings, or His kind warnings, or His gracious promises, which especially appertain to the dispensation of the New Testament. In all these particulars he not only agrees with the other prophets, but also adopts their expressions."[2] He then gives the following examples:—

[1] Is nihil videtur habere singulare aut eximium, in dispositione rerum, vel colore dictionis.—*Præl.* xxi.
[2] Est vaticiniorum ejus argumentum Deo dignissimum, sive serias ejus

Ch. i. 6 compared with Jer. xv. 6.
Ch. i. 15 compared with Joel ii. 1, 2.
Ch. i. 18 compared with Ezek. vii. 19, and Jer. iv. 27.
Ch. ii. 8, 9 compared with Jer. xlviii. 2, and Ezek. xxv. 1.
Ch. iii. 3, 4 compared with Ezek. xxii. 26, 27, 28, &c.

It does not appear at what time HAGGAI returned from exile, though probably at the first return of the Jews under ZERUBBABEL, before Christ 536. But he did not commence his prophetic office till about sixteen years after; and he delivered what his Book contains in the space of *three* months. His messages, which are *five*,[1] are very short; and hence some have concluded that they are but summaries of what he had delivered.

Much of this Book is historical, interspersed with what is conveyed in a poetic style. The Prophet, in the *first* Chapter, remonstrates with the people, who were very attentive to their own private concerns, but neglected to build the Lord's Temple; he refers to the judgments with which they had been visited on this account, encourages them to undertake the work, and promises them the favour of God; and then he tells us of his success. In the *second* Chapter he removes an apparent ground of discouragement, the temple then in building being not so splendid as the former, and promises an additional glory to it, evidently referring to the Gospel times. He then warns them against

---

redargutiones, sive severas comminationes, sive amicas monitiones, sive blandas promissiones, ad gratiam N. T. quam maxime protensas, spectemus. In quabus omnibus non tantum quoad rem consentientes alios habet vates, sed et phrases adhibuit.—*Anal. Tseph. Exeg.*

[1] I. Chap. i. 1-11.
II. Chap. i. 12-15.
III. Chap. ii. 1-9.
IV. Chap. ii. 10-19.
V. Chap. ii. 20-23.

relaxing in their work and thinking it enough merely to offer sacrifices, assures them of God's blessing, and concludes with a special promise to Zerubbabel.

What *Lowth* says of this Prophet's style, that "it is altogether prosaic," is not strictly true; for there are some parts highly poetical. See ch. i. 6, and from 8 to 11 inclusive. "The style of HAGGAI," observes *Henderson*, "is not distinguished by any peculiar excellence; yet he is not destitute of pathos and vehemence, when reproving his countrymen for their negligence, exhorting them to the performance of duty."

Though in some instances our COMMENTATOR may not give the precise import of a passage, yet he never advances but what is consistent with Divine Truth, and always useful and practical, and often what betokens a profound acquaintance with the operations of the human mind under the various trials and temptations which we meet with in this life; so that the observations made are ever interesting and instructive. CALVIN never deduces from a passage what is in itself erroneous or unsound, though in all cases he may not deduce what the text may legitimately warrant. There is, therefore, nothing dangerous in what he advances, though it may not be included in the passage explained. But for the most part his application of doctrine is what may be fully justified, and is often very striking, and calculated to instruct and edify.

Some may think that our Author does not always give that full range of meaning to the promises and predictions which he explains. A reason for this may probably be found in the fact, that most of the Commentators who had preceded him had indulged in very great extravagancies on the subject; and a reaction generally drives men to an opposite extreme. But it is very seldom that CALVIN can be justly charged with a fault of this kind; for, entertaining the profoundest veneration for the Word of God, he strictly followed what he conceived the words imported, and what he apprehended to be the general drift of a passage. Possibly, in the estimation of those who possess a very vivid imagination, he may be thought to have kept too closely to what the text and the context require; but in explaining the Divine Oracles, nothing is more to be avoided than to let loose the imagination, and nothing is more necessary than to possess a sound judgment, and to exercise it in the fear of God, and with prayer for His guidance and direction.

J. O.

THRUSSINGTON,
October 1848.

THE

COMMENTARIES OF JOHN CALVIN

ON THE

PROPHET HABAKKUK.

CALVIN'S PREFACE TO HABAKKUK.

Now follows THE PROPHET HABAKKUK;[1] but the time in which he discharged his office of a Teacher is not quite certain. The Hebrews, according to their usual manner, unhesitatingly assert that he prophesied under the king MANASSEH; but this conjecture is not well founded. We are however led to think that this prophecy was announced when the contumacy of the people had become irreclaimable. It is indeed probable, from the complaint which we shall have presently to notice, that the people had previously given many proofs of irremediable wickedness. To me it appears evident that the Prophet was sent, when others had in vain endeavoured to correct the wickedness of the people. But as he denounces an approaching judgment on the CHALDEANS, he seems to have prophesied either under Manasseh or under the other kings before the time of ZEDECHIAH; but we cannot fix the exact time.[2]

---

[1] Who Habakkuk was is uncertain. Some have concluded, from ch. iii. 19, that he was of the tribe of Levi; but the premises do not warrant the conclusion. "He was probably," says *Adam Clarke*, "of the tribe of *Simeon*, and a native of Beth-zacar." The grounds for this probability are not stated.—*Ed.*

[2] *Newcome's* opinion is the following:—

"It seems probable that Habakkuk lived after the taking of Nineveh, as he prophesies of the Chaldeans, and is silent on the subject of the Assyrians. We have also reason to conclude that he prophesied not long before the Jewish captivity. See ch. i. 5; ii. 3; iii. 2, 6-19. He may

The substance of the Book may be thus stated:—In the *first* chapter he complains of the rebellious obstinacy of the people, and deplores the corruptions which then prevailed; he then appears as the herald of God, and warns the Jews of their approaching ruin; he afterwards applies consolation, as God would punish the Chaldeans when their pride became intolerable. In the *second* chapter he exhorts the godly to patience by his own example, and speaks at large of the near ruin of Babylon; and in the *third* chapter, as we shall see, he turns to supplication and prayer.

We shall now come to the words.

therefore be placed in the reign of Jehoiakim, between the years 606 and 598 before Christ."

Henderson agrees with this view.

" Hunc librum canonicum esse constat,—tum 1. quia in Bibliis Hebræis extat; tum 2. quia in N. T. allegatum, Acts xiii. 41; Rom. i. 17; Gal. iii. 11; Heb. x. 38. It appears that this book is canonical,—1. because it is extant in Hebrew; 2. because it is quoted in the New Testament," &c.—*Tarnovius.*

COMMENTARIES

ON

THE PROPHET HABAKKUK.

CHAPTER I.

Lecture One Hundred and Sixth.

1. The burden which Habakkuk the prophet did see.

1. Onus quod vidit Chabakuk Propheta.

THE greater part of interpreters refer this *burden* to the Chaldeans and the monarchy of Babylon; but of this view I do not approve, and a good reason compels me to dissent from their opinion: for as the Prophet addresses the Jews, and without any addition calls his prophecy a burden, there is no doubt but that he refers to them. Besides, their view seems wholly inconsistent, because the Prophet dreads the future devastation of the land, and complains to God for allowing His chosen and elect people to be so cruelly treated. What others think is more correct—that this burden belonged to the Jews.

What the Prophet understood by the word משא, *mesha*, has been elsewhere stated. Habakkuk then reproves here his own nation, and shows that they had in vain disdainfully resisted all God's prophets, for they would at length find that their threatenings would be accomplished. The burden, then, which the Prophet Habakkuk saw, was this— That God, after having exercised long forbearance towards the Jews, would at length be the punisher of their many sins. It now follows—

2. O Lord, how long shall I cry, and thou wilt not hear! *even* cry out unto thee *of* violence, and thou wilt not save!	2. Quousque, Jehova, clamabo, et non exaudies? vociferabor ad te ob violentiam, et non servabis?
3. Why dost thou shew me iniquity, and cause *me* to behold grievance? for spoiling and violence *are* before me: and there are *that* raise up strife and contention.	3. Quare ostendis mihi iniquitatem, et molestiam aspicere facis? et direptio et violentia in conspectu meo? et est qui litem et contentionem excitet.

As I have already reminded you, interpreters think that the Prophet speaks here of future things, as though he had in his view the calamity which he afterwards mentions; but this is too strained a meaning; I therefore doubt not but that the Prophet expostulates here with God for so patiently indulging a reprobate people. For though the Prophets felt a real concern for the safety of the people, there is yet no doubt but that they burned with zeal for the glory of God; and when they saw that they had to contend with refractory men, they were then inflamed with a holy displeasure, and undertook the cause of God; and they implored His aid to bring a remedy when the state of things had become desperate. I therefore consider that the Prophet here solicits God to visit these many sins in which the people had hardened themselves. And hence we conclude that he had previously exercised his office of a teacher; for it would have been otherwise improper for him to begin his work with such a complaint and expostulation. He had then by experience found that the people were extremely perverse. When he saw that there was no hope of amendment, and that the state of things was becoming daily worse, burning with zeal for God, he gave full vent to his feelings. Before, then, he threatens the people with the future vengeance of God, he withdraws himself, as it were, from intercourse with men, and in private addresses God himself.

We must bear this first in mind, that the Prophet relates here the secret colloquy he had with God: but it ought not to be ascribed to an unfeeling disposition, that in these words he wished to hasten God's vengeance against his own kindred; for it behoved the Prophet not only to be solicitous for the salvation of the people, but also to feel a concern for the glory of God, yea, to burn with a holy zeal. As, then, he had in vain laboured for a length of time, I doubt not but that, being as it were far removed from the presence of all witnesses, he here asks God, how long he purposed thus to bear with the wickedness of the people. We now apprehend the design of the Prophet and the import of his words.

But he says first, *How long, Jehovah, shall I cry, and thou hearest not? How long shall I cry to thee for violence,* that is, on account of violence, *and thou savest not?* We hence learn, that the Prophet had often prayed God to correct the people for their wickedness, or to contrive some means to prevent so much licentiousness in sinning. It is indeed probable that the Prophet had prayed as long as there was any hope; but when he saw that things were past recovery, he then prayed more earnestly that God would undertake the office of a judge, and chastise the people. For though the Prophet really condoled with those who perished, and was touched, as I have said, with a serious concern for their public safety, he yet preferred the glory of God: when, therefore, he saw that boldness in sin increased through impunity, and that the Jews in a manner mocked God when they found that they could sin without being punished, he could not endure such unbridled wantonness. Besides, the Prophet may have spoken thus, not only as expressing his own feeling, but what he felt in common with all the godly; as though he had undertaken here a public duty, and uttered a complaint common to all the faithful: for it is probable that all the godly, in so disordered a state of things, mourned alike. *How long,* then, *shall I cry? How long,* he says, *shall I cry on account of violence?* that is, When all things are in disorder, when there is now no regard for equity and justice, but men abandon themselves, as it were with loose reins, unto all kinds of wickedness, how long, Lord, wilt thou take no notice? But in these words the Prophet not only expresses his own feelings, but makes this kind of preface, that the Jews might better understand that the time of vengeance was come; for they were become not only altogether intolerable to God, but also to his servants. God indeed had suspended his judgment, though he had been often solicited to execute it by his Prophet. It hence appears, that their wickedness had made such advances that it would be no wonder if they were now severely chastised by the Lord; for they had by their sins not only provoked him against them, but also all the godly and the faithful.

He afterwards adds, *How long wilt thou show me iniquity, and make me to see trouble?* Here the Prophet briefly relates the cause of his indignation,—that he could not, without great grief, yea, without anguish of mind, behold such evils prevailing among God's chosen people; for they who apply this to the Chaldeans, do so strainedly, and without any necessity, and they have not observed the reason which I have stated—that the Prophet does not here teach the Jews, but prepares them for a coming judgment, as they could not but see that they were justly condemned, since they were proved guilty by the cry and complaints made by all the godly.

Now this passage teaches us, that all who really serve and love God, ought, according to the Prophet's example, to burn with holy indignation whenever they see wickedness reigning without restraint among men, and especially in the Church of God. There is indeed nothing which ought to cause us more grief than to see men raging with profane contempt for God, and no regard had for his law and for divine truth, and all order trodden under foot. When therefore such a confusion appears to us, we must feel roused, if we have in us any spark of religion. If it be objected, that the Prophet exceeded moderation, the obvious answer is this,—that though he freely pours forth his feelings, there was nothing wrong in this before God, at least nothing wrong is imputed to him: for wherefore do we pray, but that each of us may unburden his cares, his griefs, and anxieties, by pouring them into the bosom of God? Since, then, God allows us to deal so familiarly with him, nothing wrong ought to be ascribed to our prayers when we thus freely pour forth our feelings, provided the bridle of obedience keeps us always within due limits, as was the case with the Prophet; for it is certain that he was retained under the influence of real kindness. Jeremiah did indeed pray with unrestrained fervour (Jer. xv. 10): but his case was different from that of our Prophet; for he proceeds not here to an excess, as Jeremiah did when he cursed the day of his birth, and when he expostulated with God for being made a man of contention. But our Prophet undertakes here the defence of justice; for he could not endure the law of God to be made a sport, and men to allow themselves every liberty in sinning.

We now, then, see that the Prophet can be justly excused, though he expostulates here with God, for God does not condemn this freedom in our prayers; but, on the contrary, the end of praying is, that every one of us pour forth, as it is said in the Psalms, his heart before God. As, then, we communicate our cares and sorrows to God, it is no wonder that the Prophet, according to the manner of men, says, *Why dost thou show me iniquity, and make me to see trouble?* Trouble is to be taken here in an active sense, and the verb תביט, *tabith*, has a transitive meaning.[1] Some render it, *Why*

---

[1] Rather, a causative meaning; for so does *Calvin* take it; and *Junius* and *Tremelius, Piscator, Grotius*, and *Newcome*, agree with him: but *Drusius, Marckius, Henderson*, and others, consider it simply in the sense of seeing or beholding, and say with truth, that there is no other instance in which it has, though it be often found, as here, in Hiphil, a causative sense. The context, as *Calvin* says, seems certainly to favour this meaning; and we might suppose that Habakkuk used it in a sense different from others, were it not that he uses it at least twice in this very chapter, verses 5 and 13, simply in the sense of seeing or beholding.

In these two verses there is no need of continuing the interrogatory form throughout, nor is this justified by the original. A strictly literal rendering, such as the following, would be the most appropriate: —

2. How long, Jehovah, have I cried, and thou hearest not?
 I cry aloud to thee, " oppression," and thou savest not:
3. Why showest thou to me iniquity?
 Yea, wickedness is what thou seest;
 Even wasting and oppression are before me;
 Then there is strife, and contention arises.

Some think that there is to be understood a preposition before חמס, which I render "oppression," in the second line; but there is no need of it. The word means outrage, wrong forcibly done, violent injustice. עמל, wicked-

dost thou look on trouble? as though the Prophet indignantly bore the connivance of God. But the context necessarily requires that this verb should be taken in a transitive sense. "Why dost thou show me iniquity?" and then, "*and* makest me to look on violence?" He says afterwards, in the third place, *in my sight is violence*. But I have said, that the word *trouble* is to be taken actively; for the prophet means not that he was worn out with weariness, but that wicked men were troublesome to the good and the innocent, as it is usually the case when a freedom in sinning prevails.

And *why,* he says, *are violence and plunder in my sight? and there is he who excites,* &c.? The verb נשא, *nusha,* means not here to undertake, as some render it; but, on the contrary, to raise. Others render it, "Who supports," but this is frigid. Therefore the translation which I have stated is the most suitable—*And why is there one who excites strife and contention?*

But the Prophet here accuses them only of sins against the second table of the law: he speaks not of the superstitions of people, and of the corrupted worship of God; but he briefly says, that they had no regard for what was just and right: for the stronger any one was, the more he distressed the helpless and the innocent. It was then for this reason that he mentioned iniquity, trouble, plunder, violence, contention, strife. In short, the Prophet here deplores, that there was now no equity and no brotherly kindness among the people, but that robberies, rapines, and tyrannical violence prevailed everywhere. It follows—

4. Therefore the law is slacked, and judgment doth never go forth: for the wicked doth compass about the righteous; therefore wrong judgment proceedeth.	4. Propterea dissolvitur (*vel,* debilitatur) lex, et non egredietur perpetuo judicium (*vel,* non egreditur;) quia impius circumdat justum, propterea egredietur judicium perversum.

The Prophet confirms here what I have already said, and

ness, in the second line of the third verse, in its primary sense, is labour, toil; it means also what produces toil, mischief, wickedness. *Henderson* renders it misery; but it is not so suitable; for it must be something that corresponds with iniquity in the previous line. Wickedness is the word adopted by *Newcome.* ריב, strife, is a verbal contention or quarrel; and מדון, contention, is a judicial contest, or a trial by law. Then in the next verse we see how unjustly this trial was conducted.—*Ed.*

brings an excuse for his zeal; he proves that he was not without reason led to so great a warmth; for he saw that the law of God was trodden as it were under foot; he saw men so hardened in every kind of sin, that all religion and the fear of God had nearly been extinguished. Hence I have already said, that the Prophet was not here impelled by a carnal passion, as it often happens to us, when we defend ourselves from wrongs done to us; for when any one of us is injured, he immediately becomes incensed, while, at the same time, we suffer God's law to be a sport, His whole truth to be despised, and everything that is just to be violated. We are only tender on what concerns us individually, and in the meantime we easily forgive when God is wronged, and His truth despised. But the Prophet shows here that he was not made indignant through a private feeling, but because he could not bear the profanation of God's worship and the violation of His holy law.

He therefore says, that the law was dissolved or weakened, as though he said that God's law had no longer any authority or regard. Let us hence learn to rouse up ourselves, for we are very frigid, when the ungodly openly despise and even mock God. As, then, we are too unconcerned in this respect, let us learn, by the Prophet's example, to stimulate ourselves. For even Paul also shows, in an indirect way, that there is just reason for indignation—'Be ye angry,' he says, 'and sin not,' (Eph. iv. 26); that is, every one ought to regard his own sins, so as to become an enemy to himself; and he ought also to feel indignant whenever he sees God offended.

This rule the Prophet now follows, *Weakened*, he says, *is the law*.[1] We know that when a sinful custom prevails,

---

[1] *Calvin* omits to notice "therefore," עַל־כֵּן, at the beginning of the verse. *Henderson* says, that the connexion is with the second verse: but this can hardly be the case; and certainly what this verse contains is no reason for what is stated in the previous verse. לְכֵן, a similar proposition with this, when followed by כִּי, as the case is here, refers sometimes to what follows and not to what precedes. See Ps. xvi. 10, 11; lxxviii. 21, 22. The meaning of the verse will be elicited, as I can conceive, by the following version:—

    On this account the law fails,
    And judgment goeth not forth to victory,—

there is but little authority in what is taught: nor are human laws only despised when men's audacity breaks through all restraints, but even the very law of God is esteemed as nothing; for they think that everything erroneously done, by the consent of all, is lawful. We now then see that the Prophet felt great anguish of mind, like holy Lot (Gen. xix.), when he saw every regard for God almost extinct in the land, and especially among the chosen people, whom God had above all others consecrated to himself.

He then adds, *judgment goeth not forth perpetually*. Absurdly do many regard this as having been said in the person of foolish men, who think that there is no such thing as divine providence, when things in the world are in a disordered state: but the Prophet simply says, that all justice was suppressed. We have nearly the very same complaint in Is. lix. 4. He then says, that judgment did not go forth perpetually, because the ungodly thought that no account was to be given by them. When, therefore, any one dared to say a word against them, they immediately boiled with rage, and like wild beasts fiercely attacked him. All then were silent, and nearly made dumb, when the ungodly thus prevailed and gathered boldness from the daily practice of licentiousness. Hence, 'Go forth perpetually does not judgment;' that is, "O Lord, things are now past hope, and there appears to be no end to our evils, except thou comest soon and appliest a remedy beyond what our flesh can conceive." *For the wicked*, he says, *surround the righteous;* that is, when there was any one who continued to retain some regard for religion and justice, immediately the wicked rose up against him on every side and surrounded him before and behind; so it happened, that no one dared to oppose the

Because wickedness surrounds the righteous;
Yea, on this account perverted judgment goeth forth.

The expression, לָנֶצַח אֵל, is rendered "never" in our version, and by *Newcome;* but it never means this: "not for ever, or not always," it is rendered in other places. See Ps. ix. 19; lxxiv. 19. But נֶצַח means as a noun, superiority, excellency, strength, victory; and this, according to *Parkhurst*, is what it means here. It seems better to render רֶשַׁע, wickedness, than wicked. It means injustice, the perversion of right, and by this the just man was surrounded or completely beset, so that he had no chance of having justice done to him.—*Ed.*

torrent, though frauds, rapines, outrages, cruelty, and even murders everywhere prevailed; if any righteous men still remained, they dared not come forth into the public, for the wicked beset them on all sides.

He afterwards adds, *Therefore perverted judgment goeth forth.* The Prophet now rises higher, that even the rulers themselves increased the rage for evils, and as it were supplied fuel to their wickedness, as they confounded all distinction between right and wrong: for the Prophet speaks not here of private wrongs which any one might have done, but he speaks of the very rulers, as though he said, "There might have been one remedy, the judges might have checked so great an audacity; but they themselves stretch out their hands to the wicked and help them." Hence the tribunals, which ought to have been sacred, were become as it were dens of thieves. The word מִשְׁפָּט, *meshiphith*, is taken properly in a good sense: Is not judgment then a desirable thing? Yes, but the Prophet says, that it was perverted. It was then by way of concession that judgment is mentioned; for he afterwards adds a word to it, by which he shows that the administration of the laws was evil and injurious: for when any one oppressed had recourse to the assistance of the laws, he was plundered. In short, the Prophet means, that all things in private and in public were corrupt among the people. It now follows—

5. Behold ye among the heathen, and regard, and wonder marvellously: for *I* will work a work in your days, *which* ye will not believe though it be told *you.*

5. Videte in gentibus, et aspicite, et admiramini, admiramini; quia opus operans in diebus vestris, non credetis, quum narratum fuerit.

The Prophet turns his discourse to the Jews, after having related the private colloquy, in which he expostulated with God for having so patiently borne with the obstinate wickedness of the nation. Being now as it were furnished with God's command, (as the case really was,) he performs the office of a herald, and proclaims an approaching destruction. He indeed adopts a preface, which ought to have awakened drowsy and careless minds. He says—*look, see, be astonished, be astonished;* these repetitions do not a little increase the alarm; he twice bids them to see, and he twice exhorts them to be astonished, or to wonder. He then briefly proclaims the judgment of God, which he afterwards more fully describes. We now, then, perceive the object of the Prophet, and the manner in which he proceeds with his subject.

And he bids those among the nations to behold, as though he had said, that they were unworthy to be taught in the school of God; he therefore appointed other masters for them, even the Chaldeans, as we shall presently see. He might have said—"look to God;" but as the Prophet had so long spent his labour in vain and without profit while teaching them, he sets over them the Chaldeans as teachers. Behold, he says, ye teachers among the Gentiles. There is here indeed an implied contrast, as though he said—"God has hitherto often recalled you to himself, and has offered himself to you, but ye have refused to look to him; now then, as he is wearied with exercising patience so long, he appoints for you other teachers; learn now from the Gentiles what ye have hitherto refused to learn from the holy mouth of God himself."

The Greek translators no doubt read בגודים, for their version is—"Behold, ye despisers."[1] But in Hebrew there is no ambiguity as to the word.

He afterwards adds—*And wonder ye, wonder.*[2] By these words the prophets express how dreadful God's judgment

---

[1] This may perhaps be considered one of the *very few* instances in which the *Septuagint* seems to have retained the true reading without the countenance of a single MS.; for the word "despisers" is more suitable to the context. The very same word is found in the 13th verse of this chapter. The omission is very trifling, only of the letter ד, and Paul in quoting this passage, in Acts xiii. 41, retains this word, while in the other clauses he departs from the *Septuagint*, and comes nearer to the Hebrew text. *Pocock* thought that בגוים is a noun from the Arabic בנא, which means to be unjust or injurious; and thus the Hebrew is made the same with the *Septuagint*, and St. Paul, καταφρονηται, despisers—the insolent; but the former supposition seems the more probable—that the letter ד has been omitted. *Dathius* renders the word "*perfidi*—perfidious," and *Newcome* "transgressors."—*Ed.*

[2] This is the proper rendering, and not as in our version. It is not the usual mode in Hebrew to enhance the meaning by connecting two verbs together; but the two verbs here are in the imperative mood, only the first is in Niphal and the other in Kal. *Parkhurst* very properly renders them, *and be ye astonished, wonder,* &c. The repetition, says *Drusius*, is for the sake of emphasis.—*Ed.*

would be, which would astonish the Jews themselves. Had they not been extremely refractory they might have quietly received instruction, for God would have addressed them by his prophets, as though they had been his own children. They might thus, with composed minds, have listened to God speaking to them; but the time was now come when they were to be filled with astonishment. We hence see that the Prophet meant this in a few words—that there would be a new mode of teaching, which would overwhelm the unwilling with astonishment, because they would not endure to be ruled in a gentle manner, when the Lord required nothing from them but to render themselves teachable.

After having said that God's judgment would be dreadful, he adds that it was nigh at hand—*a work*, he says, *will he work in your days*, &c. They had already been often warned of that vengeance, but as they had for a long time disregarded it, they did ever remain sunk in their own self-delusions, like men who are wont to protract time and hunt on every side for some excuse for indulging themselves. So then when the people became hardened against all threatenings, they thought that God would ever bear with them; hence the Prophet expressly declares, that the execution of that which they regarded as a fable was near at hand—*He will work*, he says, *this work in your days*.

He then subjoins—*ye will not believe when it shall be told you*; that is, God will execute such a punishment as will be incredible and exceed all belief. The Prophet no doubt alludes to the want of faith in the people, and indirectly reproves them, as though he said—" Ye have hitherto denied faith to God's word, but ye shall at length find that he hath told the truth; and this ye shall find to your astonishment; for as his word has been counted by you incredible, so also incredible shall be his judgment." In short, the Prophet intimates this—that though the Prophets had been derided by the Jews, and despised as inventors of fables, yet nothing had been said by them which would not be fully accomplished. This reward then was to be paid to all the unbelieving; for God would in the most dreadful manner avenge their impiety, so that they should themselves be astonished and become an astonishment to others. We now perceive what the Prophet meant by saying that the Jews would not believe the work of God when told them, that is, the vengeance which he will presently describe.

This passage is quoted by Paul, and is applied to the punishment then awaiting the Jews; for Paul, after having offered Christ to them, and seeing that many of them regarded the preaching of Gospel with scorn, added these words—"see," he said, "and be astonished, for God will work a work in your days which ye shall not believe." Paul at the same time made a suitable application of the Prophet's words; for as God had once threatened his people by his Prophet Habakkuk, so he was still like himself; and since had so severely vindicated the contempt of his law as to his ancient people, he could not surely bear with the impiety of that people whom he found to have acted so malignantly and so ungratefully, yea so wantonly and perversely, as to reject his grace; for this was the last remedy for the Jews. No wonder then that Paul set before them this vengeance, when the Jews of his time persisted through their unbelief to reject Christ. Now follows the explanation—

6. For, lo, I raise up the Chaldeans, *that* bitter and hasty nation, which shall march through the breadth of the land, to possess the dwelling-places *that are* not their's.

6. Quia ecce ego excito Chaldæos, gentem asperam, et præcipitem, quæ incedet per latitudines terræ, ad possidendum tabernacula non sua.

This verse is added by the Prophet as an explanation; for it was not enough to speak generally of God's work, without reminding them that their destruction by the Chaldeans was nigh at hand. He does not indeed in this verse explain what would be the character of that judgment which he had mentioned in the last verse; but he will do this in what follows. Now the Prophets differ from Moses in this respect, for they show, as it were by the finger, what he threatened generally, and they declare the special judgments of God; as it is indeed evident from the demonstrative adverb, "Behold." How necessary this was, we may gather from the perverseness of that people; for how distinctly soever the Prophets showed to them God's judgments, so that they saw them with their eyes, yet so great was their insensibility, that they despised denunciations so apparent. What, then, would have been done, if the Prophets had only said in general, 'God will not spare you!' This, then, is the reason why the Prophet, having spoken of God's terrible vengeance, now declares in express terms, that the Chaldeans were already armed by Him to execute His judgment. The rest we leave for to-morrow.

PRAYER.

Grant, Almighty God, that as our sins cry continually to heaven, each of us may turn to repentance, and by condemning ourselves of our own accord may anticipate thy judgment, and thus stir up ourselves to repentance, that being received into favour, we may find thee, whom we have provoked to take vengeance, to be indeed our Father: and may we be so preserved by thee in this world, that having at length put off all our vices, we may attain to that perfection of purity, to which thou invitest us: and thus lead us more and more to thyself by thy Spirit, and separate us from the corruptions of this world, that we may glorify thee before men, and be at last made partakers of that celestial glory which has been purchased for us by the blood of thy only-begotten Son. Amen.

Lecture One Hundred and Seventh.

IN the lecture of yesterday the Prophet began to show from whom the Jews were to expect the vengeance of God, even from the Chaldeans, who would come, not by their own instinct, but by the hidden impulse of God. God indeed testifies that he should be the author of this war, and that the Chaldeans would fight, as it were, under his auspices. *I am he*, he says, *who excites*, &c. Then by calling the Chaldeans *a bitter and hasty nation*, he intended seriously to terrify the Jews, who had heedlessly despised all threatenings.[1] It was not indeed a subject of praise to the Chaldeans, that they were bitter and impetuous: but the Lord could turn these vices to a good purpose, inasmuch as he elicits light from darkness. When, therefore, we read that the Chaldeans were bitter, and also hasty, God thus intimates that he can employ the vices of men in executing his judgments, and yet contract hence no spot nor blemish; for we cannot possibly pollute him with our filth, as he scatters it far away by the brightness of his justice and equity.

He afterwards adds, *They shall march through the latitudes[2] of the earth, to possess habitations not their own.* He means that there would be no obstacles in the way of the Chaldeans, but that they would spread themselves over the whole earth, and occupy regions far remote. For they who fear, dare not thus disperse themselves, but, on the contrary, they advance cautiously with a collected army; but those, who have already obtained victory, march on to lay waste the land. This is what the Prophet says the Chaldeans would do.

The meaning is—that they would not come to carry on an uncertain warfare, but that they would enjoy a victory; for they would by an impetuous course fill the land, so as to occupy tents or habitations not their own. It was indeed a matter of blame in the Chaldeans, that they thus made inroads on their own neighbours: but, as I have said, God intended only to fill the Jews with terror, because he found that all threatenings were despised. He therefore meant to show how terrible the Chaldeans would be, and he confirms the same in the next verse.

[1] "Bitter" rendered "cruel" by *Drusius*. To be "bitter" in mind means passively, to be grieved, or distressed, or discontented, 1 Sam. xxii. 2; and actively, to be revengeful, cruel, or inhuman, Jud. xviii. 25.—"Hasty" signifies to be rash, inconsiderate, or soon excited and made angry. It is obvious that the order is reversed; what follows is mentioned first, and then what precedes it; for to be hasty in entertaining anger is first, and then follows cruelty in executing it. A similar order is found in the next verse; the worst feature is mentioned first, that the nation would be "terrible;" and then what is less, that it would be "fearful." This is what is often done by the writers both of the Old and New Testament.—*Ed.*

[2] The word, מֶרְחֲבֵי, means "breadths" or broad places, or wide regions, as *Henderson* renders it.—*Ed.*

7. They *are* terrible and dreadful: their judgment and their dignity shall proceed of themselves.

7. Terribilis et metuenda ipsa, ab ipsa judicium ejus (*pro* jure *ponitur hoc nomen*,) et exultatio (*vel,* dignitas) ejus egredietur.

By saying that the Chaldeans would be terrible and dreadful, he praises not their virtues; but, as I have already reminded you, he shows that they would be prepared to do his service by executing his vengeance: and he so regulated his judgment, that he used their cruelty for a good purpose. Thus we see that the worst of men are in God's hand, as Satan is, who is their head; and yet that God is not implicated in their wickedness, as some insane men maintain; for they say—That if God governs the world by his providence, he becomes thus the author of sin, and men's sins are to be ascribed to him. But Scripture teaches us far otherwise,—that the wicked are led here and there by the hidden power of God, and that yet the fault is in them, when they do anything in a deceitful and cruel manner, and that God ever remains just, whatever use he may make of instruments, yea, the very worst.

But when the Prophet adds, that *its judgment would be from the nation itself,* he means that the Chaldeans would act according to their own will. When any one indeed obeys laws, and willingly submits to them, he will freely allow either judges or umpires in case of a dispute; but he who will have all things done according to his own purpose repudiates all judges. The Prophet therefore means, that the Chaldeans would be their own judges, so that the Jews or others would complain in vain for any wrongs done to them. "They shall be," he says, "their own judges, and shall execute judgment, for they will not accept any arbitrators." The word *judgment,* taken in a good sense, is put here for law (*jus*); as though he said, "Whatever the Chaldeans will claim for themselves, theirs shall it be; for no one will dare to interfere, and they will not submit to the will of others; but their power shall be for law, and their sword for a tribunal." We now understand the Prophet's meaning; and we must ever bear in mind what I have already said,—That God had no participation in these vices; but it was necessary that the stubbornness of an irreclaimable people should be thus corrected, or at least broken down. The Lord in the meantime could use such instruments in such a way as to preserve some moderation in his judgments. It follows—

| 8. Their horses also are swifter than the leopards, and are more fierce than the evening wolves: and their horsemen shall spread themselves, and their horsemen shall come from far; they shall fly as the eagle *that* hasteth to eat. | 8. Et velociores pardis equi ejus, et acutiores lupis vespertinis: et multiplicati sunt equites ejus, et equites ejus è longinquo venient; volabunt quasi aquila festinans ad comedendum (*vel*, ad cibum.) |

The design of these figurative expressions is the same. The Prophet had spoken of the cruelty of those enemies whom the Jews despised: he now adds, that they would be so active as to surpass in velocity both leopards and eagles, or to be at least equal to them. He then says first, that their horses would be swifter than leopards. The Jews might have eluded his threatenings, or at least have cherished their insensibility by a vain confidence, as we see how this vice prevails in the world; for they might have thought thus within themselves, "The Chaldeans are far away, and the danger of which the Prophet speaks cannot be so near at hand." Hence he declares that their horses would be swifter than leopards.

He then adds, that *they would be fiercer than the evening wolves.* The wolf is a rapacious animal; and when he ranges about all the day in vain seeking what he may devour, then in the evening hunger kindles his rage. There is, therefore, nothing more dreadful than hungry wolves. But, as I have said, except they find some prey about the evening, they become the more furious. We shall meet with the same simile in Zeph. iii. We now see the drift of the Prophet's words.

He adds that *their horsemen would be numerous.*[1] He

---

[1] *Multiplices,* various: but this is not the meaning of the verb פָּשׁ; it signifies to range at large, or to spread far and wide. The whole verse may be thus rendered,—
    And swifter than leopards shall be its horses,
    And more eager than the wolves of the evening;

now sets forth their power, lest the Jews should have recourse to vain hopes, because they might obtain some help either from the Egyptians or other neighbours. The Prophet shows that all such hopes would be wholly vain; for had they gathered auxiliaries from all quarters, still the Chaldeans would exceed them in power and number.

He afterwards says, that *their horsemen would come from a distance.* Though they should have a long journey, yet weariness would not hinder and delay them in coming from a remote part. The toil of travelling would not weaken them, until they reached Judea. How so? Because it will fly, he says, (he speaks throughout of the nation itself,) *as an eagle hastening to devour.* This metaphor is also most suitable to the present purpose; for it signifies, that wherever the Chaldeans saw a prey, they would instantly come, as an eagle to any carcass it may observe. Let the distance be what it may, as soon as it sees a prey, it takes a precipitate flight, and is soon present to devour; for the rapidity of eagles, as it is well known, is astonishing.

We now see that what we learn from the Prophet's words is substantially this,—that God's judgment ought to have been feared, because he purposed to employ the Chaldeans as his servants, whose cruel disposition and inhumanity would be dreadful: he also shows that the Chaldeans would be far superior in power and number; and in third place he makes it known, that they would possess an astonishing rapidity, and that though length of journey might be deemed a hinderance, they would yet be like eagles, which come like an arrow from heaven to earth, whenever a prey is observed by them. And eagles are not only rapid in their flight, but

Spread far and wide shall its horsemen;
Yea, its horsemen from far shall come,
And fly as an eagle hastening to devour.

The horsemen are represented as sweeping the whole country, spreading themselves in all directions; and when espying a prey at a distance, they are said to fly to it like an eagle. The idea of being "numerous" or "abundant," as *Junius* and *Tremelius* render the verb, is derived from the Rabbins, and is not sanctioned by examples in Scripture. The rendering of the Septuagint is ἐξιππάσονται, shall ride forth, and of *Jerome, diffundentur*, shall spread themselves. There is no occasion to borrow a meaning from Arabic, as *Henderson* does, and to render it "spread proudly along." *Newcome* follows our common version.—*Ed.*

they possess also sharpness of sight; for we know that the eyes of eagles are remarkably keen and strong: and it is said that they cast away their young, if they find that they cannot look steadily at the sun; for they regard them as spurious. The Prophet then intimates that the Chaldeans would from a distance observe their prey: as the eagles, who are endued with incredible quickness of sight, see from mid air every carcass lying on the ground; so also would the Chaldeans quickly discover a prey, and come upon it in an instant. Let us proceed.

9. They shall come all for violence: their faces shall sup up *as* the east wind, and they shall gather the captivity as the sand.	9. Tota (*semper de ipsa gente loquitur, hoc est.* totus ipse populus) ad prædam veniet; occursus vultus ipsorum (*jam in plurali numero loquitur*) ventus orientalis, et colliget quasi arenam captivitatem.

By saying that they would come to the prey, he means that they would have no trouble or labour, for they would be victorious before they had any contest, or had any war with their enemies. The meaning then is, that the Chaldeans would not come to spend much time in warfare, as when there is a strong power to resist; but that they would only come for the booty, for the Jews would be frightened, and instantly submit themselves. And by these words the Prophet intimates, that there would be neither strength nor courage in a people so refractory: for God thus debilitates the hearts of those who fiercely resist his word. Whenever, then, men become strong against God, he so melts their hearts, that they cannot resist their fellow-mortals; and thus he mocks their confidence, or rather their madness. Lest then the Jews should still harbour any hope from the chance of war, the Prophet says that the Chaldeans would only come for the prey, for all would become subject to them.

He afterwards adds, that *the meeting of their faces would be like the oriental wind.* The word גִּמֵּה, *gime,* means what is opposite; and its derivative signifies meeting or opposition (*occursus.*) We indeed know that the east wind was very injurious to the land of Judea, that it dried up vegetation, yea, that it consumed as it were the whole produce of the earth. The violence of that wind was also very great. Hence whenever the Prophets wished to express a violent impetuosity, they added this comparison of the east wind. It was therefore the same as though the Prophet had said—that the Jews would now in vain flatter themselves; for as soon as they perceived the blowing of the east wind, they would flee away, knowing that they would be wholly unable to stand against it.[1]

Hence follows what is added by the Prophet, *He shall gather the captivity like the sand;* that is, the king of Babylon shall without any trouble subdue all the people, and collect captives innumerable as the sand; for by the sand of the sea is meant an immense number of men. In short, the Prophet shows that the Jews were already conquered; because their striving and their contest had been with God, whom they had so often and so obstinately provoked; and also, because God had chosen for himself such servants as excelled in quickness, and power, and cruelty. This is the sum of the whole. He afterwards adds—

[1] This clause has been variously interpreted. The *Targum, Vulgate,* and *Symmachus,* countenance the view given here. There is no help from the Septuagint, as no sense is given. The word מגמת, only found here, is rendered by *Symmachus,* πρόσωψις, sight, aspect. Targum explains it by a word which signifies "front." *Henderson* and *Lee* regard this as its meaning. Others, as *Newcome* and *Drusius* render it, supping up, or absorption, and derive it from גמא, to drink up, to absorb; and they regard the idea to be, that the very presence of the Chaldeans would absorb every thing like a scorching wind. But "the supping up of their faces shall be as the east wind," which is *Newcome's* version, is an odd phrase. The last word has ה affixed to it, which is never the case when it means the east wind. It is by all admitted, that "towards the east" is its proper construction. Hence the most probable rendering of this passage is, "The aspect of their faces shall be towards the east;" and with this corresponds what follows, that they should "gather captives as the sand;" that is, that they might carry them away to the place where they turned their faces.

The version of *Henderson*, which is essentially that of *Symmachus*, is the following,—
The aspect of their faces is like the east wind.
He owns the difficulty as to the last word, and views it here as in an irregular form. *Dathius* gives this paraphrase,—
It will have its face direct towards the east.
He says that the word קדים, by itself never means the pestilential wind from the east; but that when it means this, it has another word attached to it.—*Ed.*

10. And they shall scoff at the kings, and the princes shall be a scorn unto them: they shall deride every strong hold; for they shall heap dust, and take it.	10. Et ipse reges ridebit, et principes subsannatio ei; ipse omnem munitionem subsannabit; congregabit pulverem et capiet eam.

The Prophet concludes the subject which he has been hitherto pursuing. He says that the Chaldeans would not come to engage in a doubtful war, but only to triumph over conquered nations. We indeed know that the Jews, though not excelling either in number or in riches, were yet so proud, that they looked down, as it were, with contempt on other nations, and we also know, that they vainly trusted in vain helps; for as they were in confederacy with the Egyptians, they thought themselves to be beyond the reach of danger. Hence the Prophet says, that kings and princes would be only a sport to the Chaldeans, and their fortresses would be only a derision to them. How so? For *they will gather dust*, he says; that is, will make a mound of the dust of the earth, and will thus penetrate into all fortified cities.

In short the Prophet intended to cut off every hope from the Jews, that they might humble themselves before God; or he intended to take away every excuse if they repented not, as it indeed happened; for we know that they did not repent notwithstanding these warnings, until vengeance at length fully overtook them. He then adds—

11. Then shall *his* mind change, and he shall pass over, and offend, *imputing* this his power unto his god.	11. Tunc mutabit spiritum, et transgredietur, et impiè aget: hæc virtus ejus deo ipsius.

The Prophet now begins to give some comfort to the faithful, lest they should succumb under so grievous evils. He has hitherto directed his discourse to that irreclaimable people, but he now turns to the remnant; for there were always among them some of the faithful, though few, whom God never neglected; yea, for their sake often he sent his prophets; for though the multitude derived no benefit, yet the faithful understood that God did not threaten in vain, and were thus retained in his fear. This was the reason why the prophets were wont, after having spoken generally, to come down to the faithful, and as it were to comfort them apart and privately. And this difference ought to be noticed, as we have said elsewhere; for when the prophets denounce God's wrath, the discourse then is directed indiscriminately to the whole body of the people; but when they add promises, it is then as though they called the faithful to a private conference, and spake in their ear what had been committed to them by the Lord. The truth might have been useful to all, had they returned to a right mind; but as almost the whole people had hardened themselves in their vices, and as Satan had rendered stupid the minds and hearts of nearly all, it behoved the Prophet to have a special regard to the chosen of God. We now then apprehend his design.

And he says—*now he will change his spirit*. He bids the faithful to entertain hope, because the Chaldeans, after having poured forth all their fury, will be punished by the Lord for their arrogance, for it will be intolerable. This may indeed seem frigid to ungodly men; for what wonder is it that the Chaldeans, after having obtained so many victories, should grow haughty and exult in their success, as is commonly the case? But as this is a fixed principle with us, that men's pride becomes intolerable to God when they extremely exult and preserve no moderation—this is a very powerful argument—that is, that whosoever thus raises his horns shall suddenly be laid prostrate by the Lord. And Scripture also ever sets this before us, that God beats down supercilious pride, and does this that we may know that destruction is nigh all the ungodly, when they thus grow violently mad, and know not that they are mortals. It was then for this reason that the Prophet mentions what he says here; it was that the faithful might hope for some end to the violence of their enemies, for God would check their pride when they should transgress. But he says—*then He will change his spirit;* not that there was before any humility in the Chaldeans, but that success inebriated them, yea, and deprived them of all reason. And it is a common thing that a person who has fortune as it were in his hand, forgets himself, and thinks himself no longer a mortal. Great kings do indeed confess that they are men; but we see how madness lays hold on them; for, as I have said, being deluded by prosperity, they deem themselves to be nothing less than gods.

The Prophet refers here to the king of Babylon and all his people. He will change, he says, his spirit; that is, success will take away from him whatever reason and moderation he had. Now since the proud betray themselves and their disposition when fortune smiles on them, let us learn to form our judgment of men according to this experiment. If we would judge rightly of any man we must see how he bears good and bad fortune; for it may be that he who has borne adversity with a patient, calm and resigned mind, will disappoint us in prosperity, and will so elate himself as to be wholly another man. The Prophet then does not without reason speak of a change of spirit; for though the Chaldeans were before proud, they were not so extremely haughty as when their pride passed all bounds, after their many victories. He will change then his spirit; not that the Chaldeans were another kind of people, but that the Lord thus discovered their madness which was before hid.

He then adds—*he will pass over.* The Prophet intended to express that when the Lord suffered the Chaldeans to rule far and wide, a way was thus opened for his judgments, which is far different from the judgment of the flesh. For the more power men acquire the more boldness they assume; and it seemed to tend to the establishing of their power that they knew how to use their success. But the Lord, as I have said, was secretly preparing a way to destroy them, when they thus became proud and passed all bounds; hence the Prophet does not simply condemn the haughtiness and pride of the Chaldeans, but shows that a way is already open, as it were, for God's judgment, that he might destroy them, inasmuch as they would render themselves intolerable.

He afterwards adds—*and shall act impiously.* The verb אשם, *ashem,* I refer to the end of the verse—where he ascribes his power to his own god. And the Prophet adds this explanation, in order that the Jews might know what kind of sin would be the sin of the king of Babylon. He then charges him with sacrilege, because he would think that he had become the conqueror of Judea through the kindness of his idol, so that he would make nothing of the power and glory of the true God. Since then the Babylonian would transfer God's glory to his own idol, his own ruin would be thus made ripe; for the Lord would undertake his own cause, and execute vengeance on such a sacrilege; for he speaks here no doubt of the Babylonian, and according to his view, when he says—

This his strength is that of his god; but were any inclined to explain this of the true God, as some do, he would make a harsh and a forced construction; for the Babylonians did not worship the true God, but were devoted, as it is well known, to their own superstitions. The Prophet then no doubt makes known here to the faithful the pride with which the Babylonians would become elated, and thus provoke God's wrath against themselves; and also the sacrilegious boasting in which they would indulge, ascribing the victories given them to their own idols, which could not be done without daring reproach to the true God.[1] It now follows—

12. Art thou not from everlasting, O Lord my God, mine Holy One? we shall not die. O Lord, thou hast ordained them for judgment; and, O mighty God, thou hast established them for correction.

12. Annon tu ab initio, (vel, jampridem,) Jehova, Deus meus? sanctus meus, non moriemur; Jehova, ad judicium posuisti eum; et fortis, ad castigationem fundasti eum.

[1] The foregoing verse is one on which no satisfactory explanation has been given. The one adopted here has been materially followed by *Vatablus*, *Drusius* and *Dathius*, except as to the last clause. As to the first part of the verse *Henderson* gives the best sense, for it corresponds with the preceding context. He gives the idea of "renewing" instead of "changing" to חלף, and "courage" to רוח, (see Jos. ii. 11; v. 1;) and of "passing onward" to עבר, and not of "passing over," *i. e.* bounds or moderation, which it seems not to have, when used, as here, intransitively. The passing here is evidently what is referred to in verse 6, as the renewing of courage would arise from the success mentioned in verse 10.

The best exposition of the last clause is what *Grotius* has suggested, and has been followed by *Marckius* and *Dathius*—that the Chaldeans made their own strength their God; (see verse 16;) the rendering then would be this,—

Then will it renew courage,
And pass through, and become guilty;—

The Prophet now exulting, according to what all the faithful feel, shows the effect of what he has just mentioned; for as ungodly men wantonly rise up against God, and, while Satan renders them insane, throw out swelling words of vanity, as though they could by speaking confound earth and heaven; so also the faithful derive a holy confidence from God's word, and set themselves against them, and overcome their ferocity by the magnanimity and firmness of their own minds, so that they can intrepidly boast that they are happy and blessed even in the greatest miseries.

This then is what the prophet means when he adds—*Art not thou our God?* The question is much more emphatical than if he had simply declared that the true God was worshipped in Judea, and would therefore be the protector of that nation; for when the Prophet puts a question, he means, according to what is commonly understood in Hebrew, that the thing admits of no doubt. "What! art not thou our God?" We hence see that there is a contrast between the wicked and impious boastings in which the profane indulge, and the holy confidence which the faithful have, who exult in their God. But that the discourse is addressed to God rather than to the ungodly is not done without reason, for it would have been useless to contend with the wicked. This is indeed sometimes necessary, for when the reprobate openly reproach God we cannot restrain ourselves; nor is it right that we refrain from testifying that we regard all their slanders as of no account; but we cannot so courageously oppose their audacity as when we have the matter first settled between us and God, and be able to say with the Prophet—"Thou art our God." Whosoever then would boldly contend with the ungodly must

---

This its strength being its god, *or literally*,
This its strength for its god.

There is an inconsistency in our version, and also in *Calvin*, as to this passage, from verse 6 to the end of this verse. The number is changed. The "bitter nation," mentioned in verse 6, is meant throughout; and we ought to adopt the plural number throughout, as *Newcome* does, or, according to *Henderson*, the singular. There is no change of person, as some suppose, at the beginning of verse 10; for הוא, there, and הוא in verse 6 is the same—the "bitter nation."—*Ed.*

first have to do with God, and confirm and ratify as it were that compact which God has proposed to us, even that we are his people, and that he in his turn will be always our God. As then God thus covenants with us, our faith must be really made firm, and then let us go forth and contend against all the ungodly. This is the order which the Prophet observes here, and what is to be observed by us—*Art not thou our God?*

He also adds—*long since,* מִקֶּדֶם, *mekodam,* by which word the Prophet invites the attention of the faithful to the covenant which God had made, not yesterday nor the day before that, with his people, but many ages before, even 400 years before he redeemed their fathers from Egypt. Since then the favour of God to the Jews had been confirmed for so long a time, it is not without reason that the Prophet says here—*Thou art our God from the beginning;* that is, "the religion which we embrace has been delivered to us by thy hands, and we know that thou art its author; for our faith recumbs not on the opinion of men, but is sustained by thy word. Since, then, we have found so often and in so many ways, and for so many years, that thou art our God, there is now no room for doubt."[1]

He then subjoins—*we shall not die.* What the Jews say of this place, that it had been corrected by the scribes, seems

[1] Most commentators agree with our version in connecting "from the beginning," or "from eternity," with Jehovah, and not as *Calvin* seems to do, with "God." His view is evidently the most consonant with the design of the passage, and countenanced by the Septuagint, for Jehovah is rendered κυριε, in the vocative case. To assert the eternity of God seems not to be necessary here; but to say that he had been from old times the God of Israel is what is suitable to the context. The Prophet in saying "my God," identifies himself with the people; for he says afterwards, "we shall not die." Viewed in this light the former part of the verse may be thus rendered,—

Art not thou from of old, O Jehovah, my God!
My holy one, we shall not die.

The reason for which he calls him "holy" will appear from what the next verse contains. The Prophet seems to sustain himself by two considerations—that Jehovah was the God of Israel, and that he was a holy God. When he says "we shall not die," he means, no doubt, as *Marckius* observes, that the people as a nation would not be destroyed, for he had prophesied of their subjugation and captivity by the Chaldeans. What he had in view was the Church of God, respecting which promises had been made.—*Ed.*

not to me probable; for the reason they give is very frivolous. They suppose that it was written לא תמות, *la tamut*, Thou diest not, and that the letter נ, *nun*, had been introduced, "we shall not die," because the expression offended those scribes, as though the Prophet compared God to men, and ascribed to him a precarious immortality; but they would have been very foolish critics. I therefore think that the word was written by the Prophet as we now read it, *Thou art our God, we shall not die.* Some explain this as a prayer—"let us not die;" and the future is often taken in this sense in Hebrew; but this exposition is not suitable to the present passage; for the Prophet, as I have already said, rises up here as a conqueror, and disperses as mists all those foolish boastings of which he had been speaking, as though he said—"we shall not die, for we are under the protection of God."

I have already explained why he turns his discourse to God: but this is yet the conclusion of the argument,—that as God had adopted that people, and received them into favour, and testified that he would be their defender, the Prophet confidently draws this inference,—that this people cannot perish, for they are preserved by God. No power of the world, nor any of its defences, can indeed afford us this security; for whatever forces may all mortals bring either to protect or help us, they shall all perish together with us. Hence, the protection of God alone is that which can deliver us from the danger of death. We now perceive why the Prophet joins together these two things, "Thou art our God," and "We shall not die:" nor can indeed the one be separated from the other; for when we are under the protection of God, we must necessarily continue safe and safe for ever; not that we shall be free from evils, but that the Lord will deliver us from thousand deaths, and ever preserve our life in safety. When only he affords us a taste of eternal salvation, some spark of life will ever continue in our hearts, until he shows to us, when at length redeemed, as I have already said, from thousand deaths, the perfection of that blessed life, which is now promised to us, but as yet is looked for, and therefore hid under the custody of hope.

PRAYER.

Grant, Almighty God, that since thou settest around us so many terrors, we may know that we ought to be roused, and to resist the sloth and tardiness of our flesh, so that thou mayest fortify us by a different confidence: and may we so recumb on thine aid, that we may boldly triumph over our enemies, and never doubt, but that thou wilt at length give us the victory over all the assaults of Satan and of the wicked; and may we also so look to thee, that our faith may wholly rest on that eternal and immutable covenant, which has been confirmed for us by the blood of thy only Son, until we shall at length be united to him who is our head, after having passed through all the miseries of the present life, and having been gathered into that eternal inheritance, which thy Son has purchased for us by his own blood. Amen.

Lecture One Hundred and Eighth.

WE began yesterday to explain the words of the Prophet, by which he encouraged himself and the faithful, and obtained support under circumstances bordering on despair; for he turned to God, when he saw the wicked, not only elated with prosperity, but also pouring forth blasphemies against the living God. The Prophet then says, that those who are under God's protection shall not perish. Of this he felt assured within himself. The declaration, as I have said, is much more striking, as the Prophet turns all his thoughts towards God, than if he had publicly and loudly declared what he testified, as it were, in a private conference.

But it was not without reason that he said, "Thou, my God, my holy one;" as though he had said, "I trust in thee, inasmuch as I am one of thy chosen people." He does not indeed speak here in his own private name, but includes with himself the whole Church; for this privilege belonged to all the children of Abraham, as they had been set apart by the gratuitous adoption of God, and were a royal priesthood. This is the reason why the Prophet says, *Thou, my God, my holy one.* For the Jews were wont thus to call God, because they had been chosen from the rest of the world. And their holiness was, that God had deigned to take them as his people, having rejected others, while yet there was by nature no difference between them.[1]

There is, moreover, much weight in the words which follow, *Jehovah! for judgment hast thou set him.* This temptation ever occurs to us, whenever we strive to put our trust in God—"What does this mean? for God now forsakes us, and exposes us to the caprice of the wicked: they are allowed to do what they please, and God interferes not. How, then, can we cherish hope under these perplexities?" The Prophet now sets up a shield against this temptation—"Thou," he says, "hast appointed him for judgment." For he ascribes it to God's providence, that the Assyrians had with so much wantonness wasted the land, or would waste it when they came; for he speaks of things yet future—"Thou," he says, "hast appointed him for judgment."

This is a truth much needed: for Satan darkens, as with clouds, the favour of God, when any adversity happens to us, and when God himself thus proves our faith. But adversities are as it were clouds, excluding us from seeing God's favour, as the light of the sun appears not to us when the sky is darkened. If, indeed, the mass of evils be so great and so thick, that our minds are overwhelmed, they are not clouds, but the thick darkness of night. In that case our faith cannot stand firm, except the providence of God comes to our view, so that we may know, in the midst of such confusion, why he permits so much liberty to the wicked, and also how their attempts may turn out, and what may be the issue. Except then we be fully persuaded, that God by his secret providence regulates all these confusions, Satan will a hundred times a day, yea every moment, shake that confidence which ought to repose in God. We now see how

---

[1] It seems that *Calvin* regarded "my holy one," as equivalent to "my sanctifier;" he who had separated the people from others to be his own. The primary meaning of קדש is no doubt to separate a thing from a common use to a sacred one; but whether in this connexion it has this meaning is not quite certain. "The holy one of Israel" is a phrase several times used by Isaiah, see ch. xxx. 11; xliii. 3, &c. The sentence here may be rendered, "God of my holiness," or "My God, my holiness."—*Ed.*

opportunely the Prophet adds this clause. He had said, "Art not thou our God? we shall not die." He now subjoins this by way of anticipation, " The Assyrians indeed do lay waste thy land as with an unbridled wantonness, they plunder thy people, and with impunity slay the innocent; but, O Lord, this is not done but by thy permission: Thou overrulest all these confused proceedings, nor is all this done by thee without a cause. Thou, Jehovah, *hast for judgment appointed him.*—Judgment is to be taken for chastisement.

But the Prophet repeats the same thing, *and, being strong, thou hast for correction established him.* Some render צוּר, *tsur*, strong, in the accusative case, and give a twofold explanation. One party apply the term to the Jews, who were to be subdued by hard means, since they were so refractory; and hence they think that the Jews are called strong, because they were like stones. Others give this meaning, *Thou hast made him strong to correct;* that is, Thou hast given him strength, by which he will chastise us. But as this is one of God's titles, I doubt not but that the two clauses correspond. He now, then, gives this name to God. Having given him his name as an eternal God, *Thou, Jehovah,* &c.; he now calls him *strong.* He puts צוּר, *tsur*, to correspond with Jehovah; and then to *correct*, to correspond with *judgment.* We hence see how well the whole context agrees, and how the words answer, the one to the other. Then it is, *Thou, strong one, hast established him to correct.* But why does the Prophet call him *strong?* though this title, as I have said, is commonly ascribed to God, yet the Prophet, I have no doubt, had regard to the circumstances at the time. It is indeed difficult to retain this truth,—that the world is ruled by the secret counsel of God, when things are turned upside down: for the profane then clamour against God, and charge him with listlessness; and others cry out, that all things are thus changed fortuitously and at random; and hence they call fortune blind. It is then difficult, as I have said, to retain a fast hold on this truth. The Prophet, therefore, in order to support his own weakness, sets before himself this title of God, *Thou, the strong God,* or the *rock,* &c.; for צוּר, *tsur*, means properly a rock, but it is to be taken here for God of strength. Why? "Behold, we indeed see revolutions, which not only make our faith to totter, but also dissipate as it were all our thoughts: but how much soever the world revolve in confusion, yet God is a rock; His purpose fails not, nor wavers; but remains ever firm." We now then see why the Prophet calls God strong.[1]

"Thou the strong one," he says, "hast established him." He expresses more by the word *established*, than in the first clause: for he prepared himself with firmness against continued evils, in case God (as it might be easily conjectured) would not give immediate relief to his people, but add calamities to calamities. Should God then join evils to evils, the Prophet prepares himself for perseverance; "Thou," he says, "the strong one hast established him;" that is, "Though the Assyrian should not only like a whirlwind or a violent tempest rush upon us, but also continue to oppress us, as though he were a pestilence attached to the land, or some fixed mountain, yet thou, Lord, hast established him." For what purpose? *to correct.* But the Prophet could not have said this, had he not known that God justly chastised his people. Not only for his own sake did he say this; but he intended also, by his own example, to lead the faithful to make the same holy and pious confession.

The two clauses of this sentence then are these, that though the Assyrian would rage with unbridled wantonness, like a cruel wild beast, he would yet be restrained by the hidden power of God, to whom it peculiarly belongs to overrule by his secret providence the confusions of this world. This is one thing. The Prophet also ascribes justice to God's power, and thus confesses his own guilt and that of the people; for the Lord would justly use so severe a

---

[1] Many agree in this view, *Drusius, Piscator, Marckius, Henderson,* &c. The Septuagint afford no help. The rendering of *Symmachus* is κραταιὸν, strong, and of *Aquila*, στεριὸν, firm; then it would be, "and strong (or firm) for correction hast thou established him." *Grotius*, and also *Newcome*, adopt this meaning,

And thou hast founded them *as* a rock to chasten *us.*

This is, no doubt, the easiest and most natural construction. See Ezek. iii. 9. God rendered the Chaldean nation firm, and strong, and resolute, to punish the Jews.—*Ed.*

scourge, because the people needed such a correction. Let us now go on—

13. *Thou art* of purer eyes than to behold evil, and canst not look on iniquity: wherefore lookest thou upon them that deal treacherously, *and* holdest thy tongue when the wicked devoureth *the man that is* more righteous than he?

13. Mundus es oculis, ne videas malum, et aspicere ad molestiam non potes (non poteris, *ad verbum;*) quare aspicis transgressores? dissimulas quum impius devorat justiorem se?

The Prophet here expostulates with God, not as at the beginning of the chapter; for he does not here, with a holy and calm mind, undertake the defence of God's glory, but complains of injuries, as men do when oppressed, who go to the judge and implore his protection. This complaint, then, is to be distinguished from the former one; for at the beginning of the chapter the Prophet did not plead his own cause or that of the people; but zeal for God's glory roused him, so that he in a manner asked God to take vengeance on so great an obstinacy in wickedness; but he now comes down and expresses the feelings of men; for he speaks of the thoughts and sorrows of those who had suffered injuries under the tyranny of their enemies.

And he says, O God, *thou art pure in eyes, thou lookest not on evil.* Some render the verb טהור, *theur,* in the imperative mood, *clear the eyes;* but they are mistaken; for the verse contains two parts, the one contrary to the other. The Prophet reasons from the nature of God, and then he states what is of an opposite character. Thou, God, he says, *art pure in eyes;* hence thou canst not look on evil; it is not consistent with thy nature to pass by the vices of men, for every iniquity is hateful to thee. Thus the Prophet sets before himself the nature of God. Then he adds, that experience is opposed to this; for the wicked, he says, exult; and while they miserably oppress the innocent, no one affords any help. How is this, except that God sleeps in heaven, and neglects the affairs of men? We now then understand the Prophet's meaning in this verse.[1]

---

[1] Adjectives and participles in Hebrew commonly take a plural form, but not always, as evidently in the present case; for the word for "pure,"

By saying that God is *pure in eyes*, he assumes what ought to be deemed certain and indubitable by all men of piety. But as God's justice does not always appear, the Prophet has a struggle; and he shows that he in a manner vacillated, for he did not see in the state of things before him what yet his piety dictated to him, that is, that God was just and upright. It is indeed true, that the second part of the verse borders on blasphemy: for though the Prophet ever thought honourably and reverently of God, yet he murmurs here, and indirectly charges God with too much tardiness, as he connived at things, while he saw the just shamefully oppressed by the wicked. But we must notice the order which the Prophet keeps. For by saying that God is *pure in eyes*, he no doubt restrains himself. As there was danger lest this temptation should carry him too far, he meets it in time, and includes himself, in a manner, within this boundary—that we ought to retain a full conviction of God's justice. The same order is observed by Jeremiah when he says, 'I know, Lord, that thou art just, but how is it that the ungodly do thus pervert all equity? and thou either takest no notice, or dost not apply any remedy. I would therefore freely contend with thee.' The

though singular, will admit of a better construction with "eyes" than in any other way; and so *Grotius* renders the clause, " Purer are thine eyes," &c.; which is better than our version, followed by *Newcome* and *Henderson*. The whole passage will thus read better:—

    Purer *are thine* eyes than to behold evil,
    And to look on wickedness thou art not able :
    Why *then* lookest thou on the perfidious,
    And art still when the wicked swallows up
    One more righteous than himself?
    And makest man to be like the fish of the sea,
    Like the reptile which has no ruler?

"Evil" means here wrong, injustice; the corresponding clause is "the wicked" swallowing up or oppressing his better. The Jews were bad, but better than the Chaldeans. "Wickedness," עָמָל, is such a mischief as is done through treachery: hence in the next line, which, according to the style of the Prophets, corresponds with this, "the perfidious" are mentioned, improperly rendered "plunderers" by *Henderson*, and "transgressors" by *Newcome*. The Chaldeans had been the allies of the Jews.

With respect to the reptile or the crawling fish, such as keep to the bottom of the waters, why is it said to be without a ruler? Is it more insulated and less gregarious, so to speak, than other fish? If so, "without a ruler" has an obvious meaning.—*Ed*.

Prophet does not immediately break out into such an expression as this, "O Lord, I will contend with thee in judgment:" but before he mentions his complaint, knowing that his feelings were strongly excited, he makes a kind of preface, and in a manner restrains himself, that he might check that extreme ardour which might have otherwise carried him beyond due bounds; "Thou art just, O Lord," he says. In a similar manner does our Prophet speak here, *Thou art pure in eyes, so as not to behold evil; and thou canst not look on trouble.*

Since, he says, *thou canst not look on trouble,* we find that he confirms himself in that truth—that the justice of God cannot be separated from his very nature: and by saying, לא תוכל, *la tucal,* "thou canst not," it is the same as though he had said, "Thou, O Lord, art just, because thou art God; and God, because thou art just." For these two things cannot be separated, as both the eternity, and the very being of God, cannot stand without his justice. We hence see how strenuously the Prophet struggled against his own impetuosity, so that he might not too much indulge himself in the complaint, which immediately follows.

For he then asks, according to the common judgment of the flesh, *Why dost thou look on, when the ungodly devours one more just than himself?* The Prophet here does not divest God of his power, but speaks in doubt, and contends not so much with God as with himself. A profane man would have said, "There is no God, there is no providence," or, "He cares not for the world, he takes his pleasure in heaven." But the Prophet says, "Thou seest, Lord." Hence he ascribes to God what peculiarly belongs to him—that he does not neglect the world which he has created. At the same time he here inclines two ways, and alternates; *Why doest thou look on, when the ungodly devours one more just than himself?* He says not that the world revolves by chance, nor that God takes his delight and ease in heaven, as the Epicureans hold; but he confesses that the world is seen by God, and that he exercises care over the affairs of men: notwithstanding, as he could not see his way clear in a state of things so confused, he argues the point rather with himself than with God. We now see the import of this sentence. The Prophet, however, proceeds—

14. And makest men as the fishes of the sea, as the creeping things, *that have* no ruler over them?
15. They take up all of them with the angle, they catch them in their net, and gather them in their drag: therefore they rejoice and are glad.

14. Facis hominem quasi pisces maris, quasi reptile, quod caret duce (*ad verbum*, non est dux in illo.)
15. Totum hamo suo attrahet, colliget in sagenam suam, et congregabit in rete suum; propterea gaudebit et exultabit (*hoc est*, gaudet et exultat.)

He goes on, as it has been said, in his complaint; and by a comparison he shows that the judgment would be such as though God turned away from men, so as not to check the violence of the wicked, nor oppose his hand to their wantonness, in order to restrain them. Since, then, every one would oppress another as he exceeded him in power, and would with increased insolence rise up against the miserable and the poor, the Prophet compares man to the fish of the sea,—" What can this mean?" he says. " For men have been created after God's image: why then does not some justice appear among them? When one devours another, and even one man oppresses almost the whole world, what can be the meaning of this? God seems to sport with human affairs. For if he regards men as his children, why does he not defend them by his power? But we see one man (for he speaks of the Assyrian king) so enraged and so cruel, as though the rest of the world were like fish or reptiles." *Thou makest men*, he says, *like reptiles or fishes;* and then he adds, *He draws up the whole by his hook, he collects them into his drag, he gathers them into his net, he exults.*[1]

---

[1] The construction of this verse can only be understood by a reference to the preceding verse; where two things are mentioned, the fish of the sea and the reptile: as it is customary with the Prophets, the first clause in this verse refers to the reptile, and the second to the fish; every reptile was raised up by a hook, and the fish were enclosed in a net, or collected by a drag. The reptile, רמש, is in the singular number, and used in a collective sense, and כלה, every one, at the beginning of this verse, is in the same number. This entirely removes the difficulty which critics have felt, and made them to propose emendations. The verse then would read thus:—

Every one (*i.e.* every reptile) by a hook he raises up;

We now see what the Prophet means—that God would, as it were, close his eyes, while the Assyrians wantonly laid waste the whole world: and when this tyranny should reach the holy land, what else could the faithful think but that they were forsaken by God? And there is nothing, as I have already said, more monstrous, than that iniquitous tyranny should thus prevail among men; for they have all, from the least to the greatest, been created after God's image. God then ought to exercise peculiar care in preserving mankind; his paternal love and solicitude ought in this respect to appear evident: but when men are thus destroyed with impunity, and one oppresses almost all the rest, there seems indeed to be no divine providence. For how will it be that he will care for either birds, or oxen, or asses, or trees, or plants, when he will thus forsake men, and bring no aid in so confused a state? We now understand the drift of what the Prophet says.

But yet he does not, as I have already said, take away from God his power, nor does he here rail against fortune, as many cavillers do. *Thou makest men*, he says: he ascribes to God what cannot be taken from him,—that he governs the world. But as to God's justice, he hesitates, and appeals to God. Though the Prophet seems here to rush headlong like insane men; yet if we consider all things, we shall see that he strenuously contended with his temptations, and even in these words some sparks at least of faith will shine forth, which are sufficient to show to us the great firmness of the Prophet. For this especially is

> He draws them out (*i.e.* the fish) by his net,
> And collects them by his drag;
> He therefore rejoices and exults.

To "gather them *into* the net" can hardly be sense; nor is "*in* the net" much better. The drawing out and the collecting were evidently *by* the net and the drag; the preposition, ב, has very commonly this meaning, as ἰν in Greek.

The representation here is, that every means would be employed: men being compared to fishes, some are set forth as creeping along the bottom, and others as swimming at large at all depths; and then the fisherman, the Chaldean comes, and draws out the first by a fishing-hook, and the rest by a net and a drag; so that he takes them all.—*Ed.*

worthy of being noticed,—that the Prophet turns himself to God. The Epicureans, when they clamour against God, for the most part, seek the ear of the multitude; and so they speak evil of God and withdraw themselves at a distance from him; for they do not think that he exercises any care over the world. But the Prophet continually addresses God. He knew then that God was the governor of all things. He also desires to be extricated from thoughts so thorny and perplexing; and from whom does he seek relief? From God himself. When the profane wantonly deride God, they indulge themselves, and seek nothing else but to become hardened in their own impious conjectures: but the Prophet comes to God himself, "How does this happen, O Lord?" As though he had said,

"Thou seest how I am distracted, and also held fast bound—distracted by many absurd thoughts, so that I am almost confounded, and held fast bound by great perplexities, from which I cannot extricate myself. Do thou, O Lord, unfold to me these knots, and concentrate my scattered thoughts, that I may understand what is true, and what I am to believe; and especially remove from me this doubt, lest it should shake my faith; O Lord, grant that I may at length know and fully understand how thou art just, and overrulest, consistently with perfect equity, those things which seem to be so confused."

It also happens sometimes that the ungodly, as it were, openly revile God, a satanic rage having taken possession on them. But the case was far different with the Prophet; for finding himself overwhelmed and his mind not able to sustain him under so heavy trials, he sought relief, and as we have said, applied to God himself.

By saying, *He therefore rejoices and exults,* he increases the indignity; for though the Lord may for a time permit the wicked to oppress the innocent, yet when he finds them glorying in their vices and triumphing, so great a wantonness ought the more to kindle his vengeance. That the Lord then should still withhold himself, seems indeed very strange. But the Prophet proceeds—

| 16. Therefore they sacrifice unto their net, and burn incense unto their drag; because by them their portion *is* fat, and their meat plenteous. | 16. Propterea sacrificabit sagenæ suæ, et suffitum offeret reti suo, quia in illis pinguis portio ejus, et cibus ejus lautus. |

The Prophet confirms the closing sentence of the last verse; for he explains what that joy was of which he had spoken, even the joy by which the wicked, as it were, designedly provoke God against themselves. It is indeed an abominable thing when the ungodly take delight in their vices; but it is still more atrocious when they deride God himself. Such, then, is the account now added by the Prophet, as though he had said, "Not only do the ungodly felicitate themselves while thou sparest them, or for a time bearest with them; but they now rise up against thee and deride all thy majesty, and openly blaspheme against heaven itself; for they sacrifice to their own net, and offer incense to their drag." By this metaphor the Prophet intimates, that the wicked do not only become hardened when they succeed in their vices, but that they also ascribe to themselves the praise of justice; for they consider that to be rightly done which has been attended with success. They thus dethrone God, and put themselves in his place. We now then see the Prophet's meaning.

But this passage discovers to us the secret impiety of all those who do not serve God sincerely and with an honest mind. There is indeed imprinted on the hearts of men a certain conviction respecting the existence of a God; for none are so barbarous as not to have some sense of religion: and thus all are rendered inexcusable, as they carry in their hearts a law which is sufficient to make them a thousand times guilty. But at the same time the ungodly, and those who are not illuminated by faith, bury this knowledge, for they are enveloped in themselves: and when some recollection of God creeps in, they are at first impressed, and ascribe some honour to him; but this is evanescent, for they soon suppress it as much as they can; yea they even strive to extinguish (though they cannot) this knowledge and whatever light they have from heaven. This is what the Prophet now graphically sets forth in the person of the

Assyrian king. He had before said, "This power is that of his God." He had complained that the Assyrians would give to their idols what was peculiar to God alone, and thus deprive him of his right: but he says now, that they would *sacrifice to their own drag, and offer incense to their net.* This is a very different thing: for how could they sacrifice to their idols, if they ascribed to their drag whatever victories they had gained? Now, by the words drag and net, the Prophet means their efforts, strength, forces, power, counsels, and policies as they call them, and whatever else there be which profane men arrogate to themselves. But what is it to sacrifice to their own net? The Assyrian did this, because he thought that he surpassed all others in craftiness; because he thought himself so courageous as not to hesitate to make war with all nations, regarding himself well prepared with forces and justified in his proceedings; and because he became successful and omitted nothing calculated to ensure victory. Thus the Assyrian, as I have said, regarded as nothing his idols; for he put himself in the place of all the gods. But if it be asked whence came his success, we must answer, that the Assyrian ought to have ascribed it all to the one true God: but he thought that he prospered through his own valour. If we refer to counsel, it is certain that God is he who governs the counsels and minds of men; but the Assyrian thought that he gained everything by his own skill. If, again, we speak of strength, whence was it? and of courage, whence was it, but from God? but the Assyrian appropriated all these things to himself. What regard, then, had he for God? We see how he now takes away all honour even from his own idols, and attributes everything to himself.

But this sin, as I have already said, belongs to all the ungodly; for where God's Spirit does not reign, there is no humility, and men ever swell with inward pride, until God thoroughly cleanse them. It is then necessary that God should empty us by his special grace, that we may not be filled with this satanic pride, which is innate, and which cannot by any means be shaken off by us, until the Lord regenerates us by his Spirit. And this may be seen especially in all the kings of this world. They indeed confess that kings rule through God's grace; and then when they gain any victory, supplications are made, vows are paid. But were any one to say to those conquerors, "God had mercy on you," the answer would be, "What! was then my preparation nothing? did I not provide many things beforehand? did I not attain the friendship of many? did I not form confederacies? did I not foresee such and such disadvantages? did I not opportunely provide a remedy?" In a word, they sacrifice apparently to God, but afterwards they have a regard mainly to their drag and their net, and make nothing of God. Well would it be were these things not so evident. But since the Spirit of God sets before us a lively image of the fact, let us learn what true humility is, and that we then only have this, when we think that we are nothing, and can do nothing, and that it is God alone who not only supports and continues us in life, but also governs us by his Spirit, and that it is he who sustains our hearts, gives courage, and then blesses us, so as to render prosperous what we may undertake. Let us hence learn that God cannot be really glorified, except when men wholly empty themselves.

He then adds, *because in (or by) them is his fat portion and his rich meat.* Though some render בראה *berae, choice* meat, and others, *fat* meat, I yet prefer the meaning of *rich*: His meat then will be rich.[1] The Prophet intimates here that men are so blinded by prosperity that they sacrifice to themselves, and hence the more deserving of reproof is their ingratitude; for the more liberally God deals with us the more reason, no doubt, there is why we ought to glorify him. But when men, well supplied and fully satisfied, thus swell with pride and sacrifice to themselves, is not their impiety in this manner more completely discovered? But the

---

[1] "His fat portion and rich meat" were the people whom he conquered. The words verbatim are these,—
    For through them abundant is his portion,
    And his meat well-fed.
The comparison of the drag and net is continued; by which is signified military strength and power. See Is. x. 13.—*Ed.*

Prophet not only proves that the Assyrians abused God's bounty, but he shows in their person what is the disposition of the whole world. For when men accumulate great wealth, and pile up a great heap from the property of others, they become more and more blinded. We hence see that we ought justly to fear the evil of prosperity, lest our fatness should so increase that we can see nothing; for the eyes are dimmed by excessive fatness. Let this then be ever remembered by us. The Prophet then concludes his discourse: but as one verse of the first chapter only remains, I shall briefly notice it.

17. Shall they therefore empty their net, and not spare continually to slay the nations?   17. An propterea extendet[1] sagenam suam, et assiduus erit ad occidendas gentes, ut non parcat (*alii vertunt,* annon *negativè; atqui debuisset* esse הלא על־כן)?

This is an affirmative question, "Shall they therefore;" which, however, requires a negative answer. Then all interpreters are mistaken; for they think that the Prophet here complains, that he presently extends his net after having made a capture, but he rather means, "Is he ever to extend his net?" that is, "How long, O Lord, wilt thou permit the Assyrians to proceed to new plunders, so as to be like the hunter, who after having taken a boar or a stag, is more eager, and immediately renews his hunting; or like the fisherman, who having filled his little ship, with more avidity pursues his vocation? Wilt thou, Lord, he says, suffer the Assyrians to become more assiduous in their work of destruction?" And he shows how unworthy they were of God's forbearance, for they slew the nations. "I speak not here," he says, "either of fish or of any other animal, nor do I speak of this or that man, but I speak of many nations.

---

[1] The verb is יריק, a hiphil form, and means, to evacuate, to empty, to empty out, and this is the sense in which it is taken here by *Drusius, Marckius, Newcome,* and *Henderson.* But the verb means also to draw out, *i. e.* a sword, Ex. xv. 9, Lev. xxvi. 33, and to draw forth, *i. e.* an army, Gen. xiv. 14, and this is the meaning given to it by *Grotius, Junius,* and the Septuagint. To draw forth, to extend, or to expand, seems most in accordance with the drift of the passage. To empty his net, and that for the sake of filling it again, which must be what is implied, is rather a far-fetched notion.—*Ed.*

As these slaughters are thus carried on through the whole world, how long, Lord, shall they be unpunished? for they will never cease." We now see the purport of the Prophet's complaint; but we shall find in the next lecture how he recovers himself.

PRAYER.

Grant, Almighty God, that as it cannot be but that, owing to the infirmity of our flesh, we must be shaken and tossed here and there by the many turbulent commotions of this world,—O grant, that our faith may be sustained by this support—that thou art the governor of the world, and that men were not only once created by thee, but are also preserved by thy hand, and that thou art also a just judge, so that we may duly restrain ourselves; and though we must often have to bear many insults, let us yet never fail, until our faith shall become victorious over all trials, and until we, having passed through continued succession of contests, shall at length reach that celestial rest, which Christ thy Son has obtained for us. Amen.

CHAPTER II.

Lecture One Hundred and Ninth.

1. I will stand upon my watch, and set me upon the tower, and will watch to see what he will say unto me, and what I shall answer when I am reproved.

1. Super speculam meam stabo, et statuam me super arcem, et speculabor ad videndum quid loquatur mecum, et quid respondeam ad increpationem meam.

WE have seen in the first chapter what the Prophet said in the name of all the faithful. It was indeed a hard struggle, when all things were in a perplexed state and no outlet appeared. The faithful might have thought that all things happened by chance, that there was no divine providence; and even the Prophet uttered complaints of this kind. He now begins to recover himself from his perplexities; and he ever speaks in the person of the godly, or of the whole Church. For what is done by some interpreters, who confine what is said to the prophetic office, I do not approve; and it may be easy from the context to learn, that the Prophet does not speak according to his private feeling, but that he represents the feelings of all the godly. So then we ought to connect this verse with the complaints, which we have before noticed; for the Prophet, finding himself sinking, and as it were overwhelmed in the deepest abyss, raises himself up above the judgment and reason of men, and comes nearer to God, that he might see from on high the things which take place on earth, and not judge according to the understanding of his own flesh, but by the light of the Holy Spirit. For the tower of which he speaks is patience arising from hope. If indeed we would struggle perseveringly to the last, and at length obtain the victory over all trials and conflicts, we must rise above the world.

Some understand by *tower* and *citadel* the Word of God: and this may in some measure be allowed, though not in every respect suitable. If we more fully weigh the reason for the metaphor, we shall be at no loss to know that the tower is the recess of the mind, where we withdraw ourselves from the world; for we find how disposed we are all to entertain distrust. When, therefore, we follow our own inclination, various temptations immediately lay hold on us; nor can we even for a moment exercise hope in God: and many things are also suggested to us, which take away and deprive us of all confidence: we become also involved in variety of thoughts, for when Satan finds men wandering in their imaginations and blending many things together, he so entangles them that they cannot by any means come nigh to God. If then we would cherish faith in our hearts, we must rise above all these difficulties and hindrances. And the Prophet by tower means this, that he extricated himself from the thoughts of the flesh; for there would have been no end nor termination to his doubts, had he tried to form a judgment according to his own understanding; *I will stand,* he says, *on my tower,*[1] *and I will set myself on the citadel.*

---

[1] On my watch-tower, משמרתי; the word means commonly the office, or the act of watching, but here it means evidently the place; the verb

In short, the sentence carries this meaning—that the Prophet renounced the judgment of men, and broke through all those snares by which Satan entangles us and prevents us to rise above the earth.

He then adds, *I will watch to see what he may say to me,* that is, I will be there vigilant; for by watching he means vigilance and waiting, as though he had said, " Though no hope should soon appear, I shall not despond; nor shall I forsake my station; but I shall remain constantly in that tower, to which I wish now to ascend: *I will watch then to see what he may say to me."* The reference is evidently to God; for the opinion of those is not probable, who apply this " saying" to the ministers of Satan. For the Prophet says first, ' I will see what he may say to me,' and then he adds, ' and what I shall answer.' They who explain the words ' what he may say,' as referring to the wicked who might oppose him for the purpose of shaking his faith, overlook the words of the Prophet, for he speaks here in the singular number; and as there is no name expressed, the Prophet no doubt meant God. But were the words capable of admitting this explanation, yet the very drift of the argument shows, that the passage has the meaning which I have attached to it. For how could the faithful answer the calumnies by which their faith was assailed, when the profane opprobriously mocked and derided them—how could they satisfactorily disprove such blasphemies, did they not first attend to what God might say to them? For we cannot confute the devil and his ministers, except we be instructed

---

"stand" and the corresponding word מְצוּר. fortress, or citadel, in the next line, prove clearly that this is its meaning here. The metaphor is taken from the practice of ascending a high tower, when any messenger was expected with news. That any locality is meant here is supported by nothing in the passage. The Prophet puts himself in an attitude of waiting for an answer from God to the complaints which he had made : and the metaphor of "tower and citadel" is most beautifully applied by *Calvin,* and in a very instructive and striking manner. I give this version—

> On my watch-tower will I stand,
> And I will set myself on a citadel;
> That I may look out to see what he will say to me,
> And what I shall answer to the reproof given to me;
> *Literally,* to my reproof.—*Ed.*

by the word of God. We hence see that the Prophet observes the best order in what he states, when he says in the first place, 'I will see what God may say to me;' and in the second place, 'I shall then be taught to answer to my chiding;'[1] that is, "If the wicked deride my faith, I shall be able boldly to confute them; for the Lord will suggest to me such things as may enable me to give a full answer." We now perceive the simple and real meaning of this verse. It remains for us to accommodate the doctrine to our own use.

It must be first observed, that there is no remedy, when such trials as those mentioned by the Prophet in the first chapter meet us, except we learn to raise up our minds above the world. For if we contend with Satan, according to our own view of things, he will a hundred times overwhelm us, and we can never be able to resist him. Let us therefore know, that here is shown to us the right way of fighting with him, when our minds are agitated with unbelief, when doubts respecting God's providence creep in, when things are so confused in this world as to involve us in darkness, so that no light appears: we must bid adieu to our own reason; for all our thoughts are nothing worth,

---

[1] That is, to the chiding, rebuke, or reproof, given to me. Both *Newcome* and *Henderson* give a version of this line, which is nearly the same, but seems incongruous, though *Grotius* agrees with them. The version of the former is as follows:—
And what I should reply to my arguing *with him*.
The latter renders the line thus:—
And what I shall reply in regard to my argument.
The phrase is, על־תוכחתי upon, (to, says *Drusius*) my reproof, or rebuke, or chiding. This is the current meaning of the word, see 2 Kings xix. 3; Prov. x. 17; xii. 1; Is. xxxvii. 3. He calls it "my," because given him, either by his enemies, as *Calvin* thinks, or by God, as some others suppose. The view of *Piscator* and *Junius* is, that it is the reproof or correction he administered to the people in ch. i. 2-12. He was waiting to know what he might have to give as a reply in defence of that reproof, "And what I may reply as to my reproof," *i. e.* the reproof given by him. In this case, the preceding clause, "What he may or will say to me," refers to his complaint respecting the Chaldeans. This is altogether consistent with the mode in which the Prophets usually write: reversing the order, they take up first the last subject, and then refer to the first. He then waited to know two things, how to solve his difficulties respecting the conduct of the Chaldeans, and how to reply to his own people for the severe rebuke he gave them. There is much in this view to recommend it.—*Ed.*

when we seek, according to our own reason, to form a judgment. Until then the faithful ascend to their tower and stand in their citadel, of which the Prophet here speaks, their temptations will drive them here and there, and sink them as it were in a bottomless gulf. But that we may more fully understand the meaning, we must know, that there is here an implied contrast between the tower and the citadel, which the Prophet mentions, and a station on earth. As long then as we judge according to our own perceptions, we walk on the earth; and while we do so, many clouds arise, and Satan scatters ashes in our eyes, and wholly darkens our judgment, and thus it happens, that we lie down altogether confounded. It is hence wholly necessary, as we have before said, that we should tread our reason under foot, and come nigh to God himself.

We have said, that the tower is the recess of the mind; but how can we ascend to it? even by following the word of the Lord. For we creep on the earth; nay, we find that our flesh ever draws us downward: except then the truth from above becomes to us as it were wings, or a ladder, or a vehicle, we cannot rise up one foot; but, on the contrary, we shall seek refuges on the earth rather than ascend into heaven. But let the word of God become our ladder, or our vehicle, or our wings, and, however difficult the ascent may be, we shall yet be able to fly upward, provided God's word be allowed to have its own authority. We hence see how unsuitable is the view of those interpreters, who think that the tower and the citadel is the word of God; for it is by God's word, as I have already said, that we are raised up to this citadel, that is, to the safeguard of hope; where we may remain safe and secure while looking down from this eminence on those things which disturb us and darken all our senses as long as we lie on the earth. This is one thing.

Then the repetition is not without its use; for the Prophet says, *On my tower will I stand, on the citadel will I set myself.* He does not repeat in other words the same thing, because it is obscure; but in order to remind the faithful, that though they are inclined to sloth, they must yet strive to extricate themselves. And we soon find how slothful we become, except each of us stirs up himself. For when any perplexity takes hold on our minds, we soon succumb to despair. This, then, is the reason why the Prophet, after having spoken of the tower, again mentions the citadel.

But when he says, *I will watch to see,* he refers to perseverance; for it is not enough to open our eyes once, and by one look to observe what happens to us; but it is necessary to continue our attention. This constant attention is, then, what the Prophet means by watching; for we are not so clear-sighted as immediately to comprehend what is useful to be known. And then, though we may once see what is necessary, yet a new temptation can obliterate that view. It thus happens, that all our observations become evanescent, except we continue to watch, that is, except we persevere in our attention, so that we may ever return to God, whenever the devil raises new storms, and whenever he darkens the heavens with clouds to prevent us to see God. We hence see how emphatical is what the Prophet says here, *I will watch to see.* The Prophet evidently compares the faithful to watchmen, who, though they hear nothing, yet do not sleep; and if they hear any noise once or twice, they do not immediately sound an alarm, but wait and attend. As, then, they who keep watch ought to remain quiet, that they may not disturb others, and that they may duly perform their office; so it behoves the faithful to be also tranquil and quiet, and wait patiently for God during times of perplexity and confusion.

Let us now inquire what is the purpose of this watching: *I will watch to see,* he says, *what he may say to me.* There seems to be an impropriety in the expression; for we do not properly see what is said. But the Prophet connects together here two metaphors. To speak strictly correct, he ought to have said, " I will continue attentive to hear what he may say;" but he says, *I will watch to see what he may say.* The metaphor is found correctly used in Psal. lxxxv. 8, " I will hear what God may say; for he will speak peace to his people." There also it is a metaphor, for the Prophet speaks not of natural hearing: " I will hear what God may speak,"

—what does that hearing mean? It means this, "I will quietly wait until God shows his favour, which is now hid; for he will speak peace to his people;" that is, the Lord will never forget his own Church. But the Prophet, as I have said, joins together here two metaphors; for to speak, or to say, means no other thing than that God testifies to our hearts, that though the reason for his purpose does not immediately appear to us, yet all things are wisely ruled, and that nothing is better than to submit to his will. But when he says, "I will see, and I will watch what he may say," the metaphor seems incongruous, and yet there appears a reason for it; for the Prophet intended to remind us, that we ought to employ all our senses for this end,—to be wholly attentive to God's word. For though one may be resolved to hear God, we yet find that many temptations immediately distract us. It is not then enough to become teachable, and to apply our ears to hear his voice, except also our eyes be connected with them, so that we may be altogether attentive.

We hence see the object of the Prophet; for he meant to express the greatest attention, as though he had said, that the faithful would ever wander in their thoughts, except they carefully concentrated both their eyes and their ears, and all their senses, on God, and continually restrained themselves, lest vagrant speculations or imaginations should lead them astray. And further, the Prophet teaches us, that we ought to have such reverence for God's word as to deem it sufficient for us to hear his voice. Let this, then, be our understanding, to obey God speaking to us, and reverently to embrace his word, so that he may deliver us from all troubles, and also keep our minds in peace and tranquillity.

God's speaking, then, is opposed to all the obstreperous clamours of Satan, which he never ceases to sound in our ears. For as soon as any temptation takes place, Satan suggests many things to us, and those of various kinds:—
"What will you do? what advice will you take? see whether God is propitious to you from whom you expect help. How can you dare to trust that God will assist you? How can he

extricate you? What will be the issue?" As Satan then disturbs us in various ways, the Prophet shows that the word of God alone is sufficient for us. All, then, who indulge themselves in their own counsels, deserve to be forsaken by God, and to be left by him to be driven up and down, and here and there, by Satan; for the only unfailing security for the faithful is to acquiesce in God's word.

But this appears still more clear from what is expressed at the close of the verse, when the Prophet adds, *and what I may answer to the reproof given me;* for he shows that he would be furnished with the best weapons to sustain and repel all assaults, provided he patiently attended to God speaking to him, and fully embraced his word: "Then," he says, "I shall have what I may answer to all reproofs, when the Lord shall speak to me." By "reproofs," he means not only the blasphemies by which the wicked shake his faith, but also all those turbulent feelings by which Satan secretly labours to subvert his faith. For not only the ungodly deride us and mock at our simplicity, as though we presumptuously and foolishly trusted in God, and were thus over-credulous; but we also reprove ourselves inwardly, and disturb ourselves by various internal contentions; for whatever comes to our mind that is in opposition to God's word, is properly a chiding or a reproof, as it is the same thing as if one accused himself, as though he had not found God to be faithful. We now, then, see that the word reproof extends farther than to those outward blasphemies by which the unbelieving are wont to assail the children of God; for, as we have already said, though no one attempted to try our faith, yet every one is a tempter to himself; for the devil never ceases to agitate our minds. When, therefore, the Prophet says, *what I may answer to reproof,* he means, that he would be sufficiently fortified against all the assaults of Satan, both secret and external, when he heard what God might say to him.

We may also gather from the whole verse, that we can form no judgment of God's providence, except by the light of celestial truth. It is hence no wonder that many fall away under trials, yea, almost the whole world; for few there are who ascend into the citadel of which the Prophet speaks, and who are willing to hear God speaking to them. Hence, presumption and arrogance blind the minds of men, so that they either speak evil of God who addresses them, or accuse fortune, or maintain that there is nothing certain : thus they murmur within themselves, and arrogate to themselves more than they ought, and never submit to God's word. Let us proceed,—

2. And the Lord answered me, and said, Write the vision, and make *it* plain upon tables, that he may run that readeth it. 3. For the vision *is* yet for an appointed time, but at the end it shall speak, and not lie : though it tarry, wait for it; because it will surely come, it will not tarry.	2. Et respondit mihi Jehova et dixit, Scribe visionem, et explana super tabulas, ut currat legens in ea : 3. Quia adhuc visio ad tempus statutum, et loquetur ad finem, et non mentietur ; si moram fecerit, expecta eam ; quia veniendo veniet, et non tardabit.

The Prophet now shows by his own example that there is no fear but that God will give help in time, provided we bring our minds to a state of spiritual tranquillity, and constantly look up to him : for the event which the Prophet relates, proves that there is no danger that God will frustrate their hope and patience, who lift up their minds to heaven, and continue steadily in that attitude. *Answer me*, he says, *did Jehovah, and said.* There is no doubt but that the Prophet accommodates here his own example to the common instruction of the whole Church. Hence, by testifying that an answer was given him by God, he intimates that we ought to entertain a cheerful hope, that the Lord, when he finds us stationed in our watch-tower, will in due season convey to us the consolation which he sees we need.

But he afterwards comes to the discharge of his prophetic office ; for he was bid to write the vision on tables, and to write it in large letters, that it might be read, and that any one, passing by quickly, might be able by one glance to see what was written : and by this second part he shows still more clearly that he treated of a common truth, which belonged to the whole body of the Church ; for it was not for his own sake that he was bid to write, but for the edification of all.

Write, then, *the vision*, and *make it plain ;* for באר, *bar*, properly means, to declare plainly.[1] Unfold it then, he says, *on tables, that he may run who reads it;* that is, that the writing may not cause the readers to stop. Write it in large characters, that any one, in running by, may see what is written. Then he adds, *for the vision shall be for an appointed time.*

This is a remarkable passage; for we are taught here that we are not to deal with God in too limited a manner, but room must be given for hope; for the Lord does not immediately execute what he declares by his mouth; but his purpose is to prove our patience, and the obedience of our faith. Hence he says, *the vision is for a time,* and a fixed time: for מוֹעֵד, *muod,* means a time which has been determined by agreement. But as it is God who foreappoints the time, the constituted time, of which the Prophet speaks, depends on his will and power. *The vision, then, shall be for a time.* He reproves here that immoderate ardour which takes hold on us, when we are anxious that God should immediately accomplish what he promises. The Prophet then shows that God so speaks as to be at liberty to defer the execution of his promise until it seems good to him.

At the end, he says, *it will speak.*[2] In a word, the Prophet intimates, that honour is to be given to God's word, that we ought to be fully persuaded that God speaks what is true, and be so satisfied with his promises as though what is promised were really possessed by us. *At the end,* then,

---

[1] The word means, to open, or make open. It was to be written in open and plain letters, and on tables or tablets. These were either of wood or stone, made smooth. The Septuagint render the word πυξίον, a smooth plank of boxwood, and give the whole sentence thus: " Write the vision, and openly (or plainly—σαφῶς,) on boxwood." See Deut. xxvii. 8. So *Junius* takes the word as an adverb, *perspicue*, perspicuously.—*Ed.*

[2] It is not a common word that is used: יָפֵחַ, " it will breathe." When transitively, it signifies, to breathe out or forth, and is rendered often in our version, to speak; see Prov. vi. 19; xii. 17. The idea here seems to be the restoration, as it were, of a suspended life. The vision was to be for a time like a body without any symptom of life: but " it will breathe," he says, " at last," or at the end; that is, it will live, and manifest life and vigour. This breathing, or this life, would be its accomplishment. Corresponding with this idea is ἀνατιλῖ, " it will rise," by the Septuagint.—*Ed.*

it will speak and it will not lie.[1] Here the Prophet means, that fulfilment would take place, so that experience would at length prove, that God had not spoken in vain, nor for the sake of deceiving; but yet that there was need of patience; for, as it has been said, God intends not to indulge our fervid and importunate desires by an immediate fulfilment, but his design is to hold us in suspense. And this is the true sacrifice of praise, when we restrain ourselves, and remain firm in the persuasion that God cannot deceive nor lie, though he may seem for a time to trifle with us. *It will not*, then, *lie*.

He afterwards adds, *If it will delay, wait for it*. He again expresses still more clearly the true character of faith, —that it does not break forth immediately into complaints, when God connives at things, when he suffers us to be oppressed by the wicked, when he does not immediately succour us; in a word, when he does not without delay fulfil what he has promised in his word. If, then, *it delays, wait for it*. He again repeats the same thing, *coming it will come;* that is, however it may be, God, who is not only true, but truth itself, will accomplish his own promises. The fulfilment, then, of the promise will take place in due time.

But we must notice the contrariety, *If it will delay; it will come, it will not delay*. The two clauses seem to be contrary the one to the other. But delay, mentioned first, has a reference to our haste. It is a common proverb, "Even quickness is delay to desire." We indeed make such haste in all our desires, that the Lord, when he delays one moment, seems to be too slow. Thus it may come easily to our mind to expostulate with him on the ground of slowness. God, then, is said on this account to delay in his promises; and his promises also as to their accomplishment may be said to be delayed. But if we have regard to the counsel of God, there is never any delay; for he knows all

---

[1] כזב, its primary meaning, is to fail, Isa. lviii. 11; and to fail, in a moral sense, is to lie, and also to deceive; and the latter meaning is attached to it here by *Drusius, Piscator*, and *Grotius, non fallet*, it will not deceive, *i. e.* disappoint.—*Ed.*

the points of time, and in slowness itself he always hastens, however this may be not comprehended by the flesh. We now, then, apprehend what the Prophet means.[1]

He is now bidden to *write the vision, and to explain it on tables.* Many confine this to the coming of Christ; but I rather think that the Prophet ascribes the name of vision to the doctrine or admonition, which he immediately subjoins. It is indeed true, that the faithful under the law could not have cherished hope in God without having their eyes and their minds directed to Christ: but it is one thing to take a passage in a restricted sense as applying to Christ himself, and another thing to set forth those promises which refer to the preservation of the Church. As far then as the promises of God in Christ are yea and amen, no vision could have been given to the Fathers, which could have raised their minds, and supported them in the hope of salvation, without Christ having been brought before them. But the Prophet here intimates generally, that a command was given to him to supply the hearts of the godly with this support, that they were, as we shall hereafter more clearly see, to wait for God. The vision, then, is nothing else than an

---

[1] What is here said is very true; but the words are not the same in Hebrew. The first signifies delay, יתמהמה rendered "linger" in Gen. xix. 16; xliii. 10. The other verb, יאחר, means, to put off, to postpone: and the sense is, that the vision will not be *after* the appointed time. So the two lines may be thus rendered:—

    If it will delay, wait for it,
    For coming it will come, it will not be postponed;

or, be after, *i. e.* the appointed time.

Dr. Wheeler, quoted by *Newcome*, gives the right idea, by the following paraphrase:—

    It shall not be later than its season.

Both *Jerome* and *Marckius* have found a grammatical difficulty in this verse from a mistake as to the gender of חזון, vision; and they had been evidently led astray by the Septuagint; in which the gender is changed, and the phrase, "wait for it," is rendered, "wait for him," ὑπόμεινον αὐτόν; and so as to what follows, "for he that cometh (ἐρχόμενος) shall come." But חזון. is the masculine gender; it is elsewhere connected with verbs in that gender. See 1 Sam. iii. 1; Ezek. xii. 22. Indeed the whole tenor of the passage admits not of any other construction. It is probable that this mistake made *Eusebius* and *Augustine* to apply this verse to Christ, and some to Nebuchadnezzar, in a typical sense.—*Ed.*

admonition, which will be found in the next and the following verses.

He uses two words, to *write* and to *explain;* which some pervert rather than rightly distinguish: for as the Prophets were wont to write, and also to set forth the summaries or the heads of their discourses, they think that it was a command to Habakkuk to write, that he might leave on record to posterity what he had said; and then to publish what he taught as an edict, that it might be seen by the people passing by, not only for a day or for a few days. But I do not think that the Prophet speaks with so much refinement: I therefore consider that to write and to explain on tables mean the same thing. And what is added, *that he may run who reads it,* is to be understood as I have already explained it; for God intended to set forth this declaration as memorable and worthy of special notice. It was not usual with the Prophets to write in long and large characters; but the Prophet mentions here something peculiar, because the declaration was worthy of being especially observed. What is similar to this is said in Isaiah viii. 1, 'Write on a table with a man's pen.' By a man's pen is to be understood common writing, such as is comprehended by the rudest and the most ignorant. To the same purpose is what God bids here his servant Habakkuk to do. *Write,* he says— how? Not as Prophecies are wont to be written, for the Prophets set before the people the heads of their discourses; but write, he says, so that he who runs may read, and that though he may be inattentive, he may yet see what is written; for the table itself will plainly show what it contains.

We now see that the Prophet commends, by a peculiar eulogy, what he immediately subjoins. Hence this passage ought to awaken all our powers, as God himself testifies that he announces what is worthy of being remembered: for he speaks not of a common truth; but his purpose was to reveal something great and unusually excellent; as he bids it, as I have already said, to be written in large characters, so that those who run might read it.

And by saying that *the vision is yet for a time,* he shows, as I have briefly explained, what great reverence is due to heavenly truth. For to wish God to conform to our rule is extremely preposterous and unreasonable: and there is no place for faith, if we expect God to fulfil immediately what he promises. It is hence the trial of faith to acquiesce in God's word, when its accomplishment does in no way appear. As then the Prophet teaches us, that *the vision is yet for a time,* he reminds us that we have no faith, except we are satisfied with God's word alone, and suspend our desires until the seasonable time comes, that which God himself has appointed. *The vision,* then, *yet* shall be. But we are inclined to reduce, as it were, to nothing the power of God, except he accomplishes what he has said: "Yet, yet," says the Prophet, "the vision shall be;" that is, "Though God does not stretch forth his hand, still let what he has spoken be sufficient for you: let then the vision itself be enough for you; let it be deemed worthy of credit, so that the word of God may on its own account be believed; and let it not be tried according to the common rule; for men charge God with falsehood, except he immediately yields to their desires. Let then the vision itself be counted sufficiently solid and firm, until the suitable time shall come." And the word מוֹעֵד, *muod,* ought to be noticed; for the Prophet does not speak simply of time, but, as I have already said, he points out a certain and a preordained time. When men make an agreement, they on both sides fix the day: but it would be the highest presumption in us to require that God should appoint the day according to our will. It belongs, then, to him to appoint the times, and so to govern all things, that we may approve of whatever he does.

He afterwards says, *And it will speak at the end, and it will not lie.* The same is the import of the expression, *it will speak at the end;* that is, men are very perverse, if they wish God to close his mouth, and if they wish to deny faith to his word, except he instantly fulfils what he speaks. *It will* then *speak;* that is, let this liberty of speaking be allowed to God. And there is always an implied contrast between the voice of God and its accomplishment; for we are to acquiesce in God's word, though he may conceal his hand: though he may afford no proof of his power, yet the

Prophet commands this honour to be given to his word. *The vision, then, will speak at the end.*

He now expresses more clearly what he had before said of the preordained time; and thus he meets the objections which Satan is wont to suggest to us: "How long will that time be delayed? Thou indeed namest it as the preordained time; but when will that day come?" "The Lord," he says, "will speak at the end;" that is, "Though the Lord protracts time, and though day after day we seem to live on vain promises, yet let God speak, that is, let him have this honour from you, and be ye persuaded that he is true, that he cannot disappoint you; and in the meantime wait for his power; wait, so that ye may yet remain quiet, resting on his word, and let all your thoughts be confined within this stronghold—that it is enough that God has spoken. The rest we shall defer until to-morrow.

PRAYER.

Grant, Almighty God, that as thou seest us labouring under so much weakness, yea, with our minds so blinded that our faith falters at the smallest perplexities, and almost fails altogether,— O grant that by the power of thy Spirit we may be raised up above this world, and learn more and more to renounce our own counsels, and so to come to thee, that we may stand fixed in our watch-tower, ever hoping, through thy power, for whatever thou hast promised to us, though thou shouldst not immediately make it manifest to us that thou hast faithfully spoken; and may we thus give full proof of our faith and patience, and proceed in the course of our warfare, until at length we ascend, above all watch-towers, into that blessed rest, where we shall no more watch with an attentive mind, but see, face to face, in thine image, whatever can be wished, and whatever is needful for our perfect happiness, through Christ our Lord. Amen.

Lecture One Hundred and Tenth.

THE Prophet taught us yesterday, that we ought to allow God his right of speaking to us, and of sustaining us by his own word, until the ripe time shall come, when he shall really fulfil what he has promised. Then an exhortation follows, added at the close of the verse—that we are to exercise patience; and the Apostle also, referring to this passage in Heb. x. 38, makes a similar application. He indeed quotes what we shall find in the next verse, 'The just by his faith shall live;' but he had in view the whole context; and at the same time he reminds us of the Prophet's object here in exalting the authority of God's word. The exhortation, then, is briefly this—that though God may keep us in suspense, we yet ought not to cast away hope, for he knows when it is expedient for us that he should stretch forth his hand. And as there are two clauses, as I said yesterday, which seem at first sight to be inconsistent the one with the other, the Prophet very fitly joins them together, and considers them to be in perfect harmony; for though God may appear to delay, yet he is not slower than what is necessary and expedient. Let us then be fully persuaded that there is in God prudence and wisdom enough to assist us as soon as it may be needful. The Prophet now reminds us that it is no wonder if God seems to us to delay, for we are too hasty in our desires. Let therefore this fervour be restrained, so that we may subject our feelings to the providence and purpose of God. Let us now proceed—

4. Behold, his soul *which* is lifted up is not upright in him: but the just shall live by his faith.

4. Ecce exaltatio, (*vel*, qui se munit, *ut alii vertunt*,) non recta est anima ejus in ipso: justus autem in fide sua vivet.

This verse stands connected with the last, for the Prophet means to show that nothing is better than to rely on God's word, how much soever may various temptations assault our souls. We hence see that nothing new is said here, but that the former doctrine is confirmed—that our salvation is rendered safe and certain through God's promise alone, and that therefore we ought not to seek any other haven, where we might securely sustain all the onsets of Satan and of the world. But he sets the two clauses the one opposed to the other: every man who would fortify himself would ever be subject to various changes, and never attain a quiet mind;

then comes the other clause—that man cannot otherwise obtain rest than by faith.

But the former part is variously explained. Some interpreters think the word עפלה, *ophle*, to be a noun, and render it elevation, which is not unsuitable; and indeed I hesitate not to regard this as its real meaning, for the Hebrews call a citadel עופל, *ouphel*, rightly deriving it from עפל, *ophel*, to ascend. What some others maintain, that it signifies to strengthen, is not well founded. Some again give this explanation—that the unbelieving seek a stronghold for themselves, that they may fortify themselves; and this makes but little difference as to the thing itself. But interpreters vary, and differ as to the meaning of the sentence; for some substitute the predicate for the subject, and the subject for the predicate, and elicit this meaning from the Prophet's words—"Every one whose mind is not at ease seeks a fortress, where he may safely rest and strengthen himself;" and others give this view—"He who is proud, or who thinks himself well fortified, shall ever be of an unquiet mind." And this latter meaning is what I approve, only that I retain the import of the word עפלה, *ophle*, as though it was said—"where there is an elation of mind there is no tranquillity."

Let us see first what their view is who give the other explanation. They say that the unbelieving, being obstinate and perverted in their minds, ever seek where they may be in safety, for they are full of suspicions, and having no regard to God they resort to the world for those remedies, by which they may escape evils and dangers. This is their view. But the Prophet, as I have already said, does here, on the contrary, denounce punishment on the unbelieving, as though he had said—"This reward, which they have deserved, shall be repaid to them—that they shall always torment themselves." The contrast will thus be more obvious; and when we say that God punishes the unbelieving, when he suffers them to be driven here and there, and also harasses their minds with various tormenting thoughts, a more fruitful doctrine is elicited. When therefore the Prophet says that there is no calmness of mind possessed by those who deem themselves well fortified, he intimates that they are their own executioners, for they seek for themselves many troubles, many sorrows, many anxieties, and contrive and mingle together many designs and purposes; now they think of one thing, then they turn to another; for the Hebrews say that the soul is made right when we acquiesce in a thing and continue in a tranquil state of mind; but when confused thoughts distract us, then they say that our soul is not right in us. We now perceive the real meaning of the Prophet.

Behold, he says: by this demonstrative particle he intimates that what he teaches us may be clearly seen if we attend to daily events. The meaning then is, that a proof of this fact exists evidently in the common life of men—that he who fortifies himself, and is also elated with self-confidence, never finds a tranquil haven, for some new suspicion or fear ever disturbs his mind. Hence it comes that the soul entangles itself in various cares and anxieties. This is the reward, as I have said, which is allotted by God's just judgment to the unbelieving; for God, as he testifies by Isaiah, offers to us rest; and they who reject this invaluable benefit, freely offered to them by God, deserve that they should not only be tormented in one way, but be also harassed by endless agitations, and that they should also vex and torment themselves. It is indeed true that he who is fortified may also acquiesce in God's word; but the word עפלה, *ophle*, refers to the state of the mind. Whosoever, then, swells with vain confidence, when he finds that he has many auxiliaries according to the flesh, shall ever be agitated, and will at length find that there is nowhere rest, except the mind recumbs on God's grace alone. We now understand the import of this clause.[1]

---

[1] Most authors agree in the main with *Calvin* in his exposition of this clause. The whole verse is quoted by Paul in Heb. x. 38, nearly *verbatim* from the Septuagint; only he inverts the clauses, and leaves out the pronoun "my," connected with "faith." But this clause, as quoted by him, is materially different from the Hebrew text as it now exists, though the chief difference relates to the word עפלה, rendered elation, or pride, by *Calvin* and many others. Two MSS. give another reading; one has עולפה, and the other, עלפה, which means to swoon, or to faint, or to fail.

It follows, *but the just shall live by his faith.* The Prophet, I have no doubt, does here place faith in opposition to all those defences by which men so blind themselves as to neglect God, and to seek no aid from him. As men therefore rely on what the earth affords, depending on their fallacious supports, the Prophet here ascribes life to faith. But faith, as it is well known, and as we shall presently show more at large, depends on God alone. That we may then live by faith, the Prophet intimates that we must willingly give up all those defences which are wont to disappoint us.

This reading would essentially harmonize the passage, and the context evidently favours it, as well as the antithesis in the verse itself. As to the rest of the clause the *meaning* is same with the Septuagint version, as cited by Paul, though the words are different; and there are other examples in which the apostle did not alter that version, though varying in words, when the sense was preserved. To say that man's soul is not right in him amounts to the same thing as to say that God is not pleased with him. There is indeed one MS. which has נפשי, "my soul," and not "his soul;" and then ישרה is often rendered ἀρίσκειν, to please, by the Septuagint. See Num. xxiii. 27; 2 Chr. xxx. 4. There would in this case be a complete identity of words as well as of meaning.

What especially countenances these readings is, that the alteration would agree better with the preceding verse. There is an exhortation to wait for the vision, *i.e.* its fulfilment. To refer to pride in this connexion seems not suitable; but to mention fainting or failing through unbelief is quite appropriate; and then as a contrast to this state of mind, the latter clause is added. Adopting the main alteration, עלפה instead of עפלה, (only a transposition of two letters,) I would render the verse thus—

Behold the fainting! not right is his soul within him;
But the righteous, by his faith shall he live.

The word for "fainting" is in the feminine gender, either on account of the word "soul" in what follows, or איש is understood, the "man of fainting," instances of which are adduced by *Henderson* on this verse, though he retains the word of the present text; as אני תפלה, "I am prayer," instead of "I am a man of prayer."—Ps. cix. 4; see Jer. l. 31, 32; Dan. ix. 23.

Now not only the antithesis is here complete, but the *order* also in which it occurs corresponds with what is often the style of the Prophets; the first part of the first clause corresponds with the last part of the second, and the last of the former with the first of the latter; and not according to Dr. *Henderson,* who represents the clauses as regularly antithetic. See a similar instance in ch. i. 13, and also in the first verse of this chapter. The man who faints, and he who lives by faith, form the contrast; and the addition "by faith" in the latter clause implies the fainting to be through want of faith, or through unbelief. Then the soul that is not right stands in contrast with the righteous, or the just in the second line. Thus every thing in the verse itself, and in its connexion with what precedes it, is in favour of what has been proposed. And *Grotius* and *Newcome* seemed disposed to adopt this reading.—*Ed.*

He then who finds that he is deprived of all protection, will live by his faith, provided he seeks in God alone what he wants, and leaving the world, fixes his mind on heaven.

As אמונה, *amunat*, is in Hebrew truth, so some regard it as meaning integrity; as though the Prophet had said, that the just man has more safety in his faithfulness and pure conscience, than there is to the children of this world in all those munitions in which they glory. But in this case they frigidly extenuate the Prophet's declaration; for they understand not what that righteousness of faith is from which our salvation proceeds. It is indeed certain that the Prophet understands by the word אמונת, *amunat*, that faith which strips us of all arrogance, and leads us naked and needy to God, that we may seek salvation from him alone, which would otherwise be far removed from us.

Now many confine the first part to Nebuchadnezzar, but this is not suitable. The Prophet indeed speaks to the end of the chapter of Babylon and its ruin; but here he makes a distinction between the children of God, who cast all their cares on him, and the unbelieving, who cannot go forth beyond the world, where they seek to be made secure, and gather hence their defences in which they confide. And this is especially worthy of being observed, for it helps us much to understand the meaning of the Prophet; if this part—" Behold the proud, his soul is not right in him," be applied to Nebuchadnezzar, the other part will lose much of its import; but if we consider that the Prophet, as it were, in these two tablets, shows what it is to glory in our own powers or in earthly aids, then what it is to repose on God alone will appear much more clear, and this truth will with more force penetrate into our minds; for we know how much such comparisons illustrate a subject which would be otherwise obscure or less evident. For if the Prophet had only declared that our faith is the cause of life and salvation, it might indeed be understood; but as we are disposed to entertain worldly hopes, the former truth would not have been sufficient to correct this evil, and to free our minds from all vain confidence. But when he affirms that all the unbelieving are deceived, while they fortify or elate themselves, because God will ever confound them, and that though no one disturbs them outwardly, they will yet be their own tormentors, as they have nothing that is right, nothing that is certain; when therefore all this is said to us, it is as though God drew us forcibly to himself, while seeing us deluded by the allurements of Satan, and seeing us too inclined to be taken with deceptions, which would at length lead us to destruction.

We now, then, perceive why Habakkuk has put these two things in opposition the one to the other—that the defences of this world are not only evanescent, but also bring always with them many tormenting fears—and then, that the just lives by his faith. And hence also is found a confirmation of what I have already touched upon, that faith is not to be taken here for man's integrity, but for that faith which sets man before God emptied of all good things, so that he seeks what he needs from his gratuitous goodness: for all the unbelieving try to fortify themselves; and thus they strengthen themselves, thinking that anything in which they trust is sufficient for them. But what does the just do? He brings nothing before God except faith: then he brings nothing of his own, because faith borrows, as it were, through favour, what is not in man's possession. He, then, who lives by faith, has no life in himself; but because he wants it, he flies for it to God alone. The Prophet also puts the verb in the future tense, in order to show the perpetuity of this life: for the unbelieving glory in a shadowy life; but the Lord will at last discover their folly, and they themselves shall really know that they have been deceived. But as God never disappoints the hope of his people, the Prophet promises here a perpetual life to the faithful.

Let us now come to Paul, who has applied the Prophet's testimony for the purpose of teaching us that salvation is not by works, but by the mercy of God alone, and therefore by faith. Paul *seems* to have misapplied the Prophet's words, and to have used them beyond what they import; for the Prophet speaks here of the state of the present life, and he has not previously spoken of the celestial life, but exhorted, as we have seen, the faithful to patience, and at the same time testified that God would be their deliverer; and now he adds, *the just shall live by faith*, though he may be destitute of all help, and though he may be exposed to all the assaults of fortune, and of the wicked, and of the devil. What has this to do, some one may say, with the eternal salvation of the soul? It seems, then, that Paul has with too much refinement introduced this testimony into his discussion respecting gratuitous justification by faith. But this principle ought ever to be remembered—that whatever benefits the Lord confers on the faithful in this life, are intended to confirm them in the hope of the eternal inheritance; for however liberally God may deal with us, our condition would yet be indeed miserable, were our hope confined to this earthly life. As God then would raise up our minds to the hopes of eternal salvation whenever he aids us in this world, and declares himself to be our Father; hence, when the Prophet says that the faithful shall live, he certainly does not confine this life to so narrow limits, that God will only defend us for a day or two, or for a few years; but he proceeds much farther, and says, that we shall be made really and truly happy; for though this whole world may perish or be exposed to various changes, yet the faithful shall continue in permanent and real safety. Hence, when Habakkuk promises life in future to the faithful, he no doubt overleaps the boundaries of this world, and sets before the faithful a better life than that which they have here, which is accompanied with many sorrows, and proves itself by its shortness to be unworthy of being much desired.

We now perceive that Paul wisely and suitably accommodates to his subject the Prophet's words—that the just lives by faith; for there is no salvation for the soul except through God's mercy.

Quoting this place in Rom. i. 17, he says that the righteousness of God is in the Gospel revealed from faith to faith, and then adds, "As it is written, The just shall live by faith." Paul very rightly connects these things together—that righteousness is made known in the Gospel—and that it comes to us by faith only; for he there contends that men cannot obtain righteousness by the law, or by the works of the law; it follows that it is revealed in the Gospel alone: how does he prove this? By the testimony of the Prophet Habakkuk—"If by faith the just lives, then he is just by faith; if he is just by faith, then he is not so by the works of the law." And Paul assumes this principle, to which I have before referred—that men are emptied of all works, when they produce their faith before God: for as long as man possesses anything of his own, he does not please God by faith alone, but also by his own worthiness.

If then faith alone obtains grace, the law must necessarily be relinquished, as the apostle also explains more clearly in the third chapter of the Epistle to the Galatians: 'That righteousness,' he says, 'is not by the works of the law, is evident; for it is written, The just shall live by faith, and the law is not of faith.' Paul assumes that these, even faith and law, are contrary, the one to the other; contrary as to the work of justifying. The law indeed agrees with the gospel; nay, it contains in itself the gospel. And Paul has solved this question in the first chapter of the Epistle to the Romans, by saying, that the law cannot assist us to attain righteousness, but that it is offered to us in the gospel, and that it receives a testimony from the law and the Prophets. Though then there is a complete concord between the law and the gospel, as God, who is not inconsistent with himself, is the author of both; yet as to justification, the law accords not with the gospel, any more than light with darkness: for the law promises life to those who serve God; and the promise is conditional, dependent on the merits of works. The gospel also does indeed promise righteousness under condition; but it has no respect to the merits of works. What then? It is only this, that they who are condemned and lost are to embrace the favour offered to them in Christ.

We now then see how, by the testimony of our Prophet, Paul rightly confirms his own doctrine, that eternal salvation is to be attained by faith only; for we are destitute of all merits by works, and are constrained to stand naked and needy before God; and then the Lord justifies us freely.

But that this may be more evident, let us first consider

why men must come altogether naked before God; for were there any worthiness in them, the Lord would by no means deprive them of such an honour. Why then does the Lord justify us freely, except that he may thereby appear just? He has indeed no need of this glory, as though he could not himself be glorified except by doing wrong to men. But we obtain righteousness by faith alone for this reason, because God finds nothing in us which he can approve, or what may avail to obtain righteousness. Since it is so, we then see that to be true which the Holy Spirit everywhere declares respecting the character of men. Men indeed glory in a foolish conceit as to their own righteousness: but all philosophic virtues, as they call them, which men think they possess through free-will, are mere fumes; nay, they are the delusions of the devil, by which he bewitches the minds of men, so that they come not to God, but, on the contrary, precipitate themselves into the lowest deep, where they seek to exalt themselves beyond measure. However this may be, let us be fully convinced, that in man there is not even a particle either of rectitude or of righteousness; and that whatever men may try to do of themselves, is an abomination before God. This is one thing.

Now after God has stretched forth his hand to his elect, it is still necessary that they should confess their own want and nakedness, as to justification; for though they have been regenerated by the Spirit of God, yet in many things they are deficient, and thus in innumerable ways they become exposed to eternal death in the sight of God; so that they have in themselves no righteousness. The Papists differ from us in the first place, imagining as they do, that there are certain preparations necessary; for that false notion about free-will cannot be eradicated from their hearts. As then they will have man to be endued with free-will, they always connect with it some power, as though they could obtain grace by their own doings. They indeed confess that man of himself can do nothing, except by the helping grace of God; but in the meantime they blend, as I have said, their own fictitious preparations. Others confess, that until God anticipates us by his grace, there is no power whatever in free-will; but afterwards they suppose that free-will concurs with God's grace, as it would be by itself inefficient, except received by our consent. Thus they always reserve for men some worthiness; but a greater difference exists as to the second subject: for after we have been regenerated through God's grace, the Papists imagine that we are justified by the merits of works. They confess, that until God anticipates us by his grace, we are condemned and cannot attain salvation except through the assisting grace of God; but as soon as God works in us, we are then, they say, able to attain righteousness by our own works.

But we object and say, that the faithful, after having been regenerated by the Spirit of God, do not fulfil the law: they allow this to be true, but say that they might if they would, for that God has commanded nothing which is above what men are capable of doing. And this also is a most pernicious error. They are at the same time forced to confess, that experience itself teaches us that no man is wholly free from sin: then some guilt always remains. But they say, that if we kept half the law, we could obtain righteousness by that half. Hence, if one by adultery offended God and thus becomes exposed to eternal death, and yet abstains from theft, he is just, they say, because he is no thief. He is an adulterer, it is true; but he is yet just in part, because he keeps a part of the law; and they call this partial righteousness. But God has not promised salvation to men, except they fully and really fulfil whatever he has commanded in his law. For it is not said, "He that fulfils a part of the law shall live;" but he who shall do these things shall live in them. Moses does not point out two or three commandments, but includes the whole law (Lev. xviii. 5.) There is also a declaration made by James, ' He who has forbidden to commit adultery, has also forbidden to steal: whosoever then transgresses the law in one particular, is a transgressor of the whole law' (James ii. 8, 11): he is then excluded from any hope of righteousness. We hence see that the Papists are most grossly mistaken, who imagine, that men, when they keep the law only in part, are just.

Were there indeed any one found who strictly kept God's

law, he could not be counted just, except by virtue of a promise. And here also the Papists stumble, and are at the same time inconsistent with themselves; for they confess that merits do not obtain righteousness for men by their own intrinsic worth, but only by the covenant of the law. But as soon as they have said this, they immediately forget themselves, and say what is contrary, like men carried away by passion. Were then the Papists to join together these two things—that there is no righteousness except by covenant, and that there is a partial righteousness—they would see that they are inconsistent: for where is this partial righteousness? If we are not righteous except according to the covenant of the law, then we are not righteous except through a full and perfect observance of the law. This is certain.

They go astray still more grievously as to the remission of sins; for as it is well known, they obtrude their own satisfactions, and thus seek to expiate the sins of men by their own merits, as though the sacrifice of Christ was not sufficient for that purpose. Hence it is that they will not allow that we are gratuitously justified by faith; for they cannot be brought to acknowledge a free remission of sins; and except the remission of sins be gratuitous, we must confess that righteousness is not by faith alone, but also by merits. But the whole Scripture proves that expiation is nowhere else to be sought, except through the sacrifice of Christ alone. This error, then, of the Papists is extremely gross and false. They further err in pleading for the merits of works; for they boast of their own inventions, the works of supererogation, or as they call them, satisfactions. And these meritorious works, under the Papacy, are gross errors and worthless superstitions, and yet they toil in them and macerate themselves, nay, they almost wear out themselves. If they mutter many short prayers, if they run to altars and to various churches, if they buy masses, in a word, if they accumulate all these fictitious acts of worship, they think that they merit righteousness before God. Thus they forget their own saying, that righteousness is by covenant; for if it be by covenant, it is certain that God does not promise it to fictitious works, which men of themselves invent and contrive. It then follows, that what men bring to God, devised by themselves, cannot do anything towards the attainment of righteousness.

There is also another error which must be noticed, for in good works they perceive not those blemishes which justly displease God, so that our works might be deservedly condemned were they strictly examined and tried. The Papists rightly say, that we are not justified by the intrinsic worthiness of works, but afterwards they do not consider how imperfect our works are, for no work proceeds from mortal man which can fully answer to what God's covenant requires. How so? For no work proceeds from the perfect love of God, and where the perfect love of God does not exist, there is corruption there. It hence follows, that all our works are polluted before God; for they flow not except from the impure fountain of the heart. Were any to object and say, that the hearts of men are cleansed by the regeneration of the Spirit, we allow this; but at the same time much filth always remains in our hearts, and it ought to be sufficient for us to know that nothing is pure and genuine before God except where the perfect love of him exists.

As, then, the Papists are blind to all these things, it is no wonder that they with so much hostility contend with us about righteousness, and can by no means allow that the righteousness of faith is gratuitous, for from the beginning this figment about free-will has been resorted to—"if men of themselves come to God, then they are not freely justified." They, then, as I have said, imagine a partial righteousness, they suppose the deficiency to be made up by satisfactions, they have also, as they say, their devotions, that is, their own contrived modes of worship. Thus it comes, that they ever persuade themselves that the righteousness of man, at least in part, is made up by himself or by works. They indeed allow that we are justified by faith, but when it is added, by faith alone, then they begin to be furious; but they consider not that righteousness, if obtained by faith, cannot be by works, for Paul, as I have shown above, reasons from the contrary, when he says, that righteousness, if it be by the works of the law, is not by faith, for faith, as it has been said, strips man of everything, that he may seek of God what he needs. But the Papists, though they think that man has not enough for himself, do not yet acknowledge that he is so needy and miserable, that righteousness must be sought in God alone. But yet sufficiently clear is the doctrine of Paul, and if Paul had never spoken, reason itself is sufficient to convince us that men cannot be justified by faith until they cast away every confidence in their own works, for if righteousness be of faith, then it is of grace alone, and if by grace alone, then it cannot be by works. It is wholly puerile in the Papists to think, that it is partly by grace and partly by the merits of works; for as salvation cannot be divided, so righteousness cannot be divided, by which we attain salvation itself. As, then, faith acquires for us favour before God, and by this favour we are counted just, so all works must necessarily fall to the ground, when righteousness is ascribed to faith.

PRAYER.

Grant, Almighty God, that as the corruption of our flesh ever leads us to pride and vain confidence, we may be illuminated by thy word, so as to understand how great and how grievous is our poverty, and be thus taught wholly to deny ourselves, and so to present ourselves naked before thee, that we may not hope for righteousness or for salvation from any other source than from thy mercy alone, nor seek any rest but only in Christ; and may we cleave to thee by the sacred and inviolable bond of faith, that we may boldly despise all those empty boastings by which the ungodly exult over us, and that we may also so cast ourselves down in true humility, that thereby we may be carried upward above all heavens, and become partakers of that eternal life which thine only-begotten Son has purchased for us by his own blood. Amen.

Lecture One Hundred and Eleventh.

WE yesterday compared this passage of Habakkuk with the interpretation of Paul, who draws this inference, that we are justified by faith without the works of the law, because the Prophet teaches us that we are to live by faith, for the way of life and of righteousness is the same, inasmuch as life is not to be otherwise sought by us than through the paternal favour of God. This then is our life—to be united to God; but this union with God cannot be hoped for by us while he imputes sins to us; for as he is just and cannot deny himself, iniquity must be ever hated by him. Then as long as he regards us as sinners, he must necessarily hold us as hateful to him. Where the hatred of God is, there is death and ruin. It then follows, that we can have no hope of life until we be reconciled to God, and there is no other way by which God can restore us to favour, but by regarding and counting us as just. It hence follows, that Paul reasons correctly, when he leads us from life to righteousness; for they are two things which are connected and inseparable.

Hence the error of the Papists comes to light, who think that to be justified is nothing else but to be renewed in righteousness, in order that we may lead a pious and a holy life. Hence their righteousness is a quality. But Paul's view is very different, for he connects our justification and salvation together, inasmuch as God cannot be propitious to us without being reconciled to us. And how is this done? even by not imputing to us our sins. Hence they speak correctly and truly express what the Holy Spirit everywhere teaches us, who call it imputative righteousness, for they thus show that it is not a quality, but, on the contrary, a relative righteousness, and therefore we said yesterday that he who lives by faith derives life from another, and that every one who is just by faith, is just through what is not in himself, even through the gratuitous mercy of God.

We now then see how suitably Paul joins righteousness with life, and adduces the Prophet's testimony to prove gratuitous justification, who affirms that we are to live by faith. But it is no wonder that the Papists go in so many ways astray in this instance, for they even differ with us in the meaning of the word faith. Hence it is that they so obstinately deny that we are justified by faith alone. They are forced, as we have said yesterday, to admit the righteousness of faith; but the exclusive particle they cannot endure;

for they imagine that it is a moulded faith that justifies, and this moulded or formed faith is piety, or the fear of God. And by calling faith unformed they seem to think that we can embrace the promises of God without the fruit of regeneration, which is very absurd, as though faith were not the peculiar gift of the Spirit, and a pledge of our adoption. But these are principles of which the Papists are wholly ignorant; for they are given up to a reprobate mind, so that they stumble at the very first elements of religion.

But it is sufficient for us, in order to understand this passage, to know that we live by faith; for our life is a shadow or a passing cloud; and hence our only remedy is to seek life from God alone. And how does God communicate this life to us? even by gratuitous promises which we embrace by faith; hence salvation is by faith. Now, salvation cannot be ascribed to faith and to works too; for faith refers the praise for life and salvation to God alone, and works show that something is due to man. Faith, then, as to justification, entirely excludes all works, so that they come to no account before God; and hence I have said that salvation is by faith; for we are accepted of God by gratuitous remission of sins. The union of God with us is true and real salvation; but no one can be united to God without righteousness, and there is found in us no righteousness; hence God himself freely imputes it to us; and as we are justified freely, so our salvation is said to be gratuitous.

I will not now repeat what may be said of justification by faith; for it is better to proceed with the Prophet's subject, only it may be necessary to add two things to what has been said. The Prophet testified to the men of his age that salvation is by faith; it then follows that they had regard to Christ; for without relying on a mediator they could not have trusted in God. For as our righteousness is said to be the remission of sins, so a sacrifice must necessarily intervene, by which God is pacified, so as not to impute our sins. They had indeed their sacrifices according to the law; but these were to direct their minds to Christ; for they were by no means acceptable to God, except through that Mediator on whom our faith at this day is founded. There is also another thing: the Prophet, by distinctly expressing that the just live by faith, clearly shows, that through the whole course of this life we cannot be deemed just in any other way than by a gratuitous imputation. He does not say that the children of Adam, born in a state exposed to eternal death, do recover life by faith; but that the just, who are now endued with the true fear of God, live by faith; and thus refuted is the romance about initial justification. Let us now then proceed—

5. Yea also, because he transgresseth by wine, *he is* a proud man, neither keepeth at home, who enlargeth his desire as hell, and *is* as death, and cannot be satisfied, but gathereth unto him all nations, and heapeth unto him all people.

5. Quanto magis (*vel* etiam certè) vino transgrediens vir superbus, et non habitabit, qui dilatat quasi sepulchrum animam suam, et est similis morti, (ipse quasi mors, *ad verbum*,) et non satiabitur (non satiatur, *significat actum continuum*,) et colliget ad se omnes gentes, et coacervabit ad se omnes populos.

The Prophet has taught us that a tranquil state of mind cannot be otherwise had than by recumbing on the grace of God alone; and that they who elate themselves, and fly in the air, and feed on the wind, procure for themselves many sorrows and inquietudes. But he now comes to the king of Babylon, and also to his kingdom; for in my judgment he speaks not only of the king, but includes also that tyrannical empire with its people, and represents them as a great company of robbers. He then says in short, that though the Babylonians, like drunken men, hurried here and there without any control, yet God's vengeance, by which they were to be brought to nothing, was nigh at hand. Whatever therefore the Prophet subjoins to the end of the chapter tends to confirm his doctrine, which we have already explained—that the just shall live by faith. We cannot indeed be fully convinced of this except we hold firmly this principle—that God cares for us, and that the whole world is governed by his providence; so that it cannot be but that he will at length check the wicked, and punish their sins, and deliver the innocent who call upon him. Unless this be our conviction, there can be no benefit derived from our faith; we might indeed be a hundred times deceived; for experience teaches us that the hopes of men, as long as they are fixed on the earth, are vain and delusive, as they are only mere imaginations. Except then God governs the world there is no salvation to the faithful; for God in that case would delude them with vain promises, and they would flatter themselves with an empty prospect, or hope for that which is not. Hence the Prophet shows how it is that the just shall live by faith; and that is because the Lord will defend all who call upon him, and that inasmuch as he is the just Judge of all the world, he will finally execute judgment on all the wicked, though for a time they act wantonly, and think that they shall escape punishment, because God does not execute upon them immediate vengeance. We now perceive the design of the Prophet.

As to the words, these two particles, אף כי, *aph ki*, when joined together, amplify the meaning; and some render them—"how much more;" others take them as a simple affirmative, and render them "truly." I approve of a middle course, and render them "yea, truly;" (*Etiam certè;*) and they are so taken as I think, in Gen. iii. 1, Satan thus asked the woman—yea, truly! *Est-ce pour vrai?* for the question is that of one doubting, and yet it refers to what is certain, —" How comes it that God should interdict the eating of the fruit? yea, is it so truly? can it be so? So it is in this place, *yea, truly*, says the Prophet. That it is an amplification may be gathered from the context. He had said before that they who elevate themselves, or seem to themselves to be well fortified, are fearful in their minds, and driven backwards and forwards. He now advances another step— that when men are borne along by unrestrained wantonness, and promise themselves all things, as though there was no God, they surpass even the drunken, being hurried on by blind cupidity. When therefore men thus abandon themselves, can they escape the judgment of God? Far less bearable is such a madness than that simple arrogance of which he had spoken in the last verse. Thus then are the two verses connected together,—" Yea, truly, he who in his pride is like a drunken man, and restrains not himself, and who is even like to wild beasts or to the grave, devouring whatever meets them—he surely will not at length be endured by God." Vengeance, then, is nigh to all the proud, who are cruelly furious, passing all bounds and without any fear. But interpreters differ as to the import of the words which follow. Some render בוגד, *bugad*, to deceive, and it means so in some places; and they render the clause thus—"Wine deceives a proud man, and he will not dwell." This is indeed true, but the meaning is strained; I therefore prefer to follow the commonly received interpretation—that the proud man transgresses as it were through wine. At the same time I do not agree with others as to the expression "transgressing as through wine." Some give this version—"Man addicted to wine or to drunkenness transgresses;" and then they add—"a proud man will not inhabit;" but they pervert the sentence, and mangle the words of the Prophet; for his words are—*By wine transgressing the proud man:* he does not say that a man addicted to wine transgresses; but he compares the proud to drunken men, who, forgetting all reason and shame, abandon themselves unto all that is disgraceful; for the drunken distinguishes nothing, and becomes like a brute animal, so that he shuns nothing that is base and unbecoming. This is the reason why the Prophet compares proud men to the drunken, who transgress through wine, that is, who observe no moderation, but indulge themselves in excesses. We now then understand the real meaning of the Prophet, which many have not perceived.[1]

[1] Though the general meaning of the beginning of this verse is what most critics agree in, yet the construction is difficult. The only difference as to the meaning is, whether the proud man is said to be given to wine, or is compared to such an one, or to wine itself. *Newcome* takes the first, and gives this version—

  Moreover, as a mighty man transgresseth through wine,
  He is proud, and remaineth not at rest.

Henderson, agreeing with *Grotius* and *Mede*, takes the latter sense, and renders the lines as follows:—

  Moreover wine is treacherous;
  The haughty man stayeth not at home.

This is rather a paraphrase than a version; but this is the meaning of which the words are most capable. The two first particles need not be connected according to what *Calvin* proposes. Then the distich may be thus rendered—

  And truly, as wine is treacherous,
  So is the proud man, and he will not rest.

As to the word *inhabiting* I take it in a metaphorical sense, as signifying to rest or to continue in the same place. The drunken are borne along by a certain excitement; so they do not restrain themselves, for they have no power over their feet or their hands: but as wine excites them, so they ramble here and there like insane persons. As then such an unruly temper lays hold on and bewilders drunken men, so the Prophet very aptly says that the proud man never rests.

And the reason follows, (provided the meaning be approved,) *because he enlarges as the grave his soul he is like to death.* This is then the insatiableness which he had mentioned—that the proud cannot be satisfied, and therefore include heaven and earth and sea within the compass of their desires. Since then they thus run here and there, it is no wonder that the Prophet says that they do not rest. *He enlarges* then *as the grave his soul;* and then he adds—*he heaps together*, or congregates, or collects *to himself all nations, and accumulates to himself all people;* that is, the proud man keeps within no moderate limits; for though he were able to make one heap of all nations, he would yet think that not enough, like Alexander, who wept because he had not then enjoyed the empire of the whole world; and had he enjoyed it his tears would not have been dried; for he had heard that, according to the opinion of Democritus, there were many worlds. What did he mean? even this—" Were I to obtain the empire of the world, I should

---

Then follows a delineation of his character—
  Because he enlarges as the grave his desire,
  And he is like death and cannot be satisfied;
  For he gathers to himself all the nations,
  And collects to himself all the people.

As to wine being treacherous, see Prov. xxx. 1. Wine is pleasant to the taste and inviting in its colour, but degrading, when taken immoderately, in its effects; so a proud and arrogant man is at first glittering and plausible, and splendid in his appearance, but afterwards cruel and oppressive. This seems to be the most obvious similitude, as contained in the passage.

Parkhurst renders the two first lines as follows—
  Yea, *as* when wine deceiveth a man,
  So he is proud, and is not at rest.

He interprets "proud," as meaning "intoxicated with power and dominion," and refers to Dan. iv. 30.—*Ed.*

still be poor; for if there are more worlds I should still wish to devour them all." These proud men surpass every kind of drunkenness.

We now apprehend the meaning of the words; and though they contain a general truth, yet the Prophet no doubt applies them to the king of Babylon and to all the Chaldeans; for as it has been said, he includes the whole nation. He shows then here, that the Chaldeans were much worse and less excusable than those who with great fierceness elated themselves, for their rage carried them farther, as they wished to swallow up the whole world. But in order to express this more fully, he says that they were like drunken men; and he no doubt indirectly derides here the counsels of princes, who think themselves to be very wise, when either by deceit they oppress their neighbours, or by artful means seize for themselves on the lands of others, or by some contrivance, or even by force of arms, take possession of them. As princes take wonderful delight in their iniquities, so the Prophet says that they are like drunken men *who transgress by wine*, that is, who are completely overcome by excessive drinking; and at the same time he shows the cause of this drunkenness by mentioning the words גבר יהיר, " proud man." As then they are proud, so all their crafts are like the freaks of drunkenness, that is, furious, as when a man is deprived of reason by wine. Having thus spoken of the Babylonians he immediately adds—

6. Shall not all these take up a parable against him, and a taunting proverb against him, and say, Woe to him that increaseth *that which is* not his! how long? and to him that ladeth himself with thick clay.

6. Annon ipsi omnes super eum parabolam (*vel* apophthegma) tollent? et dicterium ænigmaticum (*vel* ænigmatum; *alii* מליצה vertunt interpretationem; *sed dicemus de vocibus*) ei (*vel* super eum,) et dicet, Væ qui multiplicat non sua (*vel* ex non suis, *qui sese locupletat ex alieno*); quousque? et qui accumulat (*vel* aggravat) super se densum lutum.

Now at length the Prophet denounces punishment on the Babylonian king and the Chaldeans; for the Lord would render them a sport to all. But some think that a punishment is also expressed in the preceding verse, such as awaits violent robbers, who devour the whole world. But I, on the contrary, think that the Prophet spoke before of proud cruelty, and simply showed what a destructive evil it is, being an insatiable cupidity; and now, as I have stated, he comes to its punishment; and he says first, that all the people who had been collected as it were into a heap, would take up a parable or a taunt, in order to scoff at the king of Babylon. When therefore the Chaldeans should possess the empire of almost the whole world, and subject to their power all their neighbouring nations, all these would at length take up against them parables and taunts; and what would be said everywhere would be this—*Woe to him who increases and enriches himself by things not his own. How long?* that is, Is this to be perpetual? All then who thus increase themselves *heap on* themselves *thick clay*, by which they shall at last be overthrown.

With regard to the words, משל, *meshil*, is a short saying or a pithy sentence, and worthy to be remembered, as we have noticed elsewhere. Some render it parable. As to the word מליצה, *melitse*, it probably signifies a scoff or a taunt, by which any one is reproved; for it comes from לוץ, *luts*, which means to laugh at one or to deride him. It is indeed true, that the Hebrews call a rhetorician or an interpreter מליץ, *melits;* and hence some render מליצה, *melitse*, interpretation; but it is not suitable to this passage; for the Prophet speaks here of taunts that would be cast against the king of Babylon. For as he had as with an open mouth swallowed up all, so also all would eagerly prick him with their goads, and disdainfully deride him. The word he afterwards adds חידות, *chidut*, is to be read, I have no doubt, in the genitive case.[1] I therefore do not approve of adding

---

[1] This can hardly be allowed; for in this case the final letter of the previous word must have been ת and not ה. It is a word evidently in apposition, designating the character of the proverb and the taunt, they being enigmas, conveyed in a highly figurative language. The whole verse may be thus rendered—

    Shall not these, all of them,
    Raise against him a proverb and a taunt—
    Enigmas for him;
    Yea, say will *every one*—
    " Woe to him who multiplies *what is* not his own! how long!
    " And to him who accumulates on himself thick clay!"

a copulative, as many do, and read thus—"a taunt and an enigma." This word comes from the verb חוּד, *chud*, which is to speak enigmatically; hence חִידוֹת, *chidut*, are enigmas, or metaphors, or obscure sentences; and we know that when we wish to touch a man to the quick, there is more sharpness when we use an obscure word, which contains a metaphor or ambiguity, or something of this kind. It is not therefore without reason that the Prophet calls taunts, enigmas, חִידוֹת, *chidut*, that is, obscure words, which bite or prick men sharply, as it were with goads. Hence in all scoffs a figurative language ought to be used; and except the expression be ambiguous or alliterative, or, in short, contain such metaphors as it is not necessary to recite here, there would be in it no beauty, no aptness. When therefore men wish to form biting taunts, they obscure what might be plainly said by some indirect metaphor; and this is the reason why the Prophet speaks here of a taunt that is enigmatical, for it is on that account more severe.

And he shall say. There is a change of number in this verb, but it does not obscure the sense.¹ The particle הוֹי may be rendered "woe;" or it may be an exclamation, as when one is attracted by some particular sight, *ça ça or sus*; and so it is taken often by the Hebrews, and the context seems to favour this meaning, for "woe" would be frigid. When the Prophets pronounce a curse on the wicked, it is no doubt a dreadful threat; but what is found here is a taunt, by which the whole world would deride those haughty tyrants who thought that they ought to have been worshipped as gods. Ho! they say, where is he who *multiplies himself by what belongs to another?* and then, *How long*

To render the last word עבטיט, (or עב טיט, apart, as given by ten MSS.,) "pledges," as it is done by *Newcome* and *Henderson*, does not comport at all with the rest of the passage. The Septuagint favour the common explanation, and also the *Vulgate*, and most commentators.—*Ed.*

¹ It is rendered impersonally by *Jerome* "et dicetur—and it shall be said." *Junius* introduces a question, and supposes the just, who lives by faith to be referred to—"And shall not he, *i. e.* the just, say?" But *Marckius* considers that God is the speaker—"And he, *i. e.* God, shall say." But the most obvious construction is, that each one of the nations previously mentioned is introduced as speaking—"Unusquisque illorum—every one of them," is understood, says *Piscator.*—*Ed.*

is this to be? even *such accumulate on themselves thick clay;* that is, they sink themselves in deep caverns, and heap on themselves mountains, by which they become overwhelmed. We now understand the meaning of the Prophet's words.

What seems here to be the singing of triumph before the victory is no matter of wonder; for our faith, as it is well known, depends not on the judgment of the flesh, nor regards what is openly evident; but it is a vision of hidden things, as it is called in Heb. xi. 1, and the substance of things not seen. As then the firmness of faith is the same, though what it apprehends is remote, and as faith ceases not to see things hidden,—for through the mirror of God's word it ascends above heaven and earth, and penetrates into the spiritual kingdom of God,—as faith, then, possesses a view so distant, it is not to be wondered that the Prophet here boldly triumphs over the Babylonians, and now prescribes a derisive song for all nations, that the proud, who had previously with so much cruelty exalted themselves, might be scoffed at and derided.

But were any to ask, whether it be right to assail even the wicked with scoffs and railleries, the question is unsuitable here; for the Prophet does not here refer to what is lawful for the faithful to do, but speaks only of what is commonly done by men: and we know that it is almost natural to men, that when those whom they had feared and dared not to blame as long as they were in power, are overthrown, they break forth against them not only with many complaints and accusations, but also with wanton rudeness. As, then, it usually happens, that all triumph over fallen tyrants, and throw forth their taunts, and all seek in this way to bite, the Prophet describes this regular course of things. It is not, however, to be doubted, but that he composed this song according to the nature of the case, when he says, that they were men who multiplied their own by what belonged to others; that is, that they gathered the wealth of others. It is indeed true, that many things are commonly spread abroad, for which there is no reason nor justice; but as some principles of equity and justice remain in the hearts of men, the consent of all nations is as it were the voice of nature, or the testimony of that equity which is engraven on the hearts of men, and which they can never obliterate. Such is the reason for this saying; for Habakkuk, by introducing the people as the speakers, propounded, as it were, the common law of nature, in which all agree; and that is,—that whosoever enriches himself by another's wealth, shall at length fall, and that when one accumulates great riches, these will become like a heap to cover and overwhelm him. And if any one of us will consult his own mind, he will find that this is engraven on his very nature.

How, then, does it happen, that many should yet labour to get for themselves the wealth of others, and strive for nothing else through their whole life, but to spoil others that they may enrich themselves? It hence appears that men's minds are deprived of reason by sottishness, whenever they thus addict themselves to unjust gain, or when they give themselves loose reins to commit frauds, robberies, and plunders. And thus we perceive that the Prophet had not without reason represented all the proud and the cruel as drunken.

Then follow the words, עד־מתי, *od-mati, how long?* This also is the dictate of nature; that is, that an end will some time be to unjust plunders, though God may not immediately check plunderers and wicked men, who proceed and effect their purposes by force and slaughters, and frauds and evil-doings. In the mean time the Prophet also intimates, that tyrants and their cruelty cannot be endured without great weariness and sorrow; for indignity on account of evil deeds kindles within the breasts of all, so that they become wearied when they see that wicked men are not soon restrained. Hence almost the whole world sound forth these words, How long, how long? When any one disturbs the whole world by his ambition and avarice, or everywhere commits plunders, or oppresses miserable nations,—when he distresses the innocent, all cry out, How long? And this cry, proceeding as it does from the feeling of nature and the dictate of justice, is at length heard by the Lord. For how comes it that all, being touched with weariness, cry out, How long? except that they know that this confusion of order and justice is not to be endured? And this feeling, is it not implanted in us by the Lord? It is then the same as though God heard himself, when he hears the cries and groanings of those who cannot bear injustice.

But let us in the meantime see that no one of us should have to say the same thing to himself, which he brings forward against others. For when any avaricious man proceeds through right or wrong, as they say, when an ambitious man, by unfair means, advances himself, we instantly cry, How long? and when any tyrant violently oppresses helpless men, we always say, How long? Though every one says this as to others, yet no one as to himself. Let us therefore take heed that, when we reprove injustice in others, we come without delay to ourselves, and be impartial judges. Self-love so blinds us, that we seek to absolve ourselves from that fault which we freely condemn in others. In general things men are always more correct in their judgment, that is, in matters in which they themselves are not concerned; but as soon as they come to themselves, they become blind, and all rectitude vanishes, and all judgment is gone. Let us then know, that this song is set forth here by the Prophet, drawn, as it were, from the common feeling of nature, in order that every one of us may put a restraint on himself when he discharges the office of a judge in condemning others, and that he may also condemn himself, and restrain his desires, when he finds them advancing beyond just bounds.

We must also observe what he subjoins,—that the avaricious *accumulate on themselves thick clay.* This at first may appear incredible; but the subject itself plainly shows what the Prophet teaches here, provided our minds are not so blinded as not to see plain things. Hardly indeed an avaricious man can be found who is not a burden to himself, and to whom his wealth is not a source of trouble. Every one who has accumulated much, when he comes to old age, is afraid to use what he has got, being ever solicitous lest he should lose any thing; and then, as he thinks nothing is sufficient, the more he possesses the more grasping he becomes, and frugality is the name given to that sordid, and, so to speak, that servile restraint within which the rich confine themselves. In short, when any one forms a judgment of all the avaricious of this world, and is himself free from all avarice, having a free and unbiassed mind, he will easily apprehend what the Prophet says here,—that all the wealth of this world is nothing else but a heap of clay, as when any one puts himself of his own accord under a great heap which he had collected together.

Some refer this to the walls of Babylon, which were built of baked bricks, as it is well known; but this is too farfetched. Others think that the Prophet speaks of the last end of us all; for they who possess the greatest riches, being at last thrown into the grave, are covered with earth: but this also is not suitable here, any more than when they apply it to Nebuchadnezzar, that is, to that sottishness by which he had inebriated himself almost through his whole life; or when others apply it to Belshazzar, his grandson, because when he drank from the sacred vessels of the temple, he uttered slanders and blasphemies against God. These explanations are by no means suitable; for the Prophet does not here speak of the person of the king alone, but, as it has been said, he, on the contrary, summons to judgment the whole nation, which had given itself up to plunders and frauds and other evil deeds.

Then a general truth is to be drawn from this expression —that all the avaricious, the more they heap together, the more they lade themselves, and, as it were, bury themselves under a great load. Whence is this? Because riches, acquired by frauds and plunders, are nothing else than a heavy and cumbrous lump of earth: for God returns on the heads of those who thus seek to enrich themselves, whatever they have plundered from others. Had they been contented with some moderate portion, they might have lived cheerfully and happily, as we see to be the case with all the godly; who though they possess but little, are yet cheerful, for they live in hope, and know that their supplies are in God's hand, and expect everything from his blessing. Hence, then, their cheerfulness, because they have no anxious fears. But they who inebriate themselves with riches, find that they carry a useless burden, under which they lie down, as it were, sunk and buried.

PRAYER.

Grant, Almighty God, that as thou deignest so far to condescend as to sustain the care of this life, and to supply us with whatever is needful for our pilgrimage—O grant that we may learn to rely on thee, and so to trust to thy blessing, as to abstain not only from all plunder and other evil deeds, but also from every unlawful coveting; and to continue in thy fear, and so to learn also to bear our poverty on the earth, that being content with those spiritual riches which thou offerest to us in thy gospel, and of which thou makest us now partakers, we may ever cheerfully aspire after that fulness of all blessings which we shall enjoy when at length we shall reach the celestial kingdom, and be perfectly united to thee, through Christ our Lord. Amen.

Lecture One Hundred and Twelfth.

7. Shall they not rise up suddenly that shall bite thee, and awake that shall vex thee, and thou shalt be for booties unto them?	7. Annon repentè consurgent qui te mordeant, et evigilabunt qui te exagitent, et eris in conculcationes ipsis?

THE Prophet proceeds with the subject which we have already begun to explain; for he introduces here the common taunts against the king of Babylon and the whole tyrannical empire, by which many nations had been cruelly oppressed. He therefore says that enemies, who should *bite him*,[1] would

---

[1] This is rendered by *Henderson*, "that have lent thee on usury;" but incorrectly, as the corresponding clause is found in the following, and not, as he says, in the preceding line. The literal version is as follows,—
  Shall not suddenly arise thy biters,
  And awake thy tormentors,
  And thou become for spoils to them?
Now, the two corresponding words are "biters" and "tormentors;" and the idea of lending on usury cannot be admitted; and the common meaning of the word נשך, is to bite, and means lending on usury only in Hiphil. What the Septuagint give is δακνοντες—biters.
Here is an instance of the peculiar manner of the Prophets, and also of the writers of the New Testament; the most obvious act is mentioned first, "arise," and then what is previous to it, "awake." There is also a similar difference in "biters" and "tormentors," or those who vex and harass: to torment or vex is not so great an evil as to bite, as it were, like a serpent; for such is the biting meant here.—*Ed.*

suddenly and unexpectedly *rise up*. Some expound this of worms, but not rightly: for God not only inflicted punishment on the king when dead, but he intended also that there should be on earth an evident and a memorable proof of his vengeance on the Babylonians, by which it might be made known to all that their cruelty could not be suffered to go unpunished.

The words, *Shall not they rise suddenly*, are emphatical, both as to the question and as to the word, פֶּתַע, *peto*, suddenly. We indeed know that interrogations are more common in Hebrew than in Greek and Latin, and that they are stronger and more forcible. Our Prophet then speaks of what was indubitable. He adds, *suddenly;* for the Babylonians, relying on their own power, did not think that any evil was nigh them; and if any one dared to rise up against them, this could not have been so sudden, but they could have in time resisted and driven far away every danger. They indeed ruled far and wide; and we know that the wicked often sleep when they find themselves fortified on all sides. But the Prophet declares here that evil was nigh them, which would suddenly overwhelm them. It now follows—

| 8. Because thou hast spoiled many nations, all the remnant of the people shall spoil thee; because of men's blood, and *for* the violence of the land, of the city, and of all that dwell therein. | 8. Quia tu spoliasti gentes multas, spoliabunt te omnes reliquiæ populorum propter sanguines hominis et violentiam terræ, urbis et omnium habitantium in ea. |

The Prophet here expresses more clearly why the Babylonians were to be so severely dealt with by God. He shows that it would be a just reward that they should be plundered in their turn, who had previously given themselves up to plunder, violence, and cruelty. Since, then, they had exercised so much inhumanity towards all people, the Prophet intimates here that God could not be deemed as treating them cruelly, by inflicting on them so severe a punishment: he also confirms the former truth, and recalls the attention of the faithful to the judgment of God, as a main principle to be remembered; for when things in the world are in a state of confusion, we despond, and all hope vanishes, except this comes to our mind—that as God is the judge of the world it cannot be otherwise, but that at length all the wicked must appear before his tribunal, and give there an account of all their deeds; and Scripture, also, is wont to set God before us as a judge, whenever the purpose is to allay our troubles. The Prophet now does the same thing: for he says, that robbers should soon come upon the Babylonians, who would plunder them; for God, the judge of the world, would not at last suffer so many plunders to be unpunished.

But it was everywhere known that the Babylonians had, beyond all bounds and moderation, given themselves up to plunder, so that they spared no nations. Hence he says, *because thou hast plundered many nations;* and on this he enlarges; because the Babylonians had not only done wrongs to a few men, or to one people, but had marched through many countries. As, then, they had taken to themselves so much liberty in doing evil, the Prophet draws this conclusion—that they could not escape the hand of God, but that they were at length to find by experience that there was a God in heaven, who would repay them for their wrongs.

He says also, *Spoil thee shall the remnant of all people.* This admits of two expositions; it may mean, that the people, who had been plundered by the Chaldeans, would take revenge on them: and he calls them a remnant, because they were not entire; but yet he intimates that they would be sufficient to take vengeance on the Babylonians. This view may be admitted, and yet we may suppose, that the Prophet takes in other nations, who had never been plundered; as though he had said—" Thou hast indeed spoiled many nations; but there are other nations in the world whom thy cruelty could not have reached. All the people then who remain in the world shall strive to outdo one another in attacking thee; and canst thou be strong enough to resist so great a power?" Either of these views may be admitted; that is, that in the wasted and plundered countries there would be still a remnant who would take vengeance,—or that the world contained other people who would willingly undertake this cause and execute vengeance on the Babylonians; for God would by his secret influence fulfil by their means his purpose of punishing them.

He then adds, *on account of man's blood;* that is, because thou hast shed innocent blood, and because thou hast committed many plunders; for thou hast not only injured a few men, but thy daringness and cruelty have also extended to many nations. He indeed mentions the *earth,* and also the *city.* Some confine these words to the land of Judea and to Jerusalem, but not rightly; for the Prophet speaks here generally; and to the land, he joins cities and their inhabitants.[1]

But this verse contains a truth which applies to all times. Let us then learn, during the licentious success of tyrants, to raise up our minds to heaven's tribunal, and to nourish our patience with this confidence, that the Lord, who is the judge of the world, will recompense these cruel and bloody robbers, and that the more licentious they are, the heavier judgment is nigh them; for the Lord will awaken and raise up as many to execute vengeance as there are men in the world, who by shedding blood will inflict punishment, though they may not intend to fulfil his purpose. God can indeed (as it has been often observed) execute his judgments in a wonderful and sudden manner. Let us hence also learn to restrain our evil desires; for none shall go unpunished who will allow themselves to injure their brethren; though they may seem to be unpunished for a time, yet God, who is ever the same, will at length return on their heads whatever they have devised against others, as we shall presently see again. He now adds—

[1] So *Grotius, Drusius,* and *Henderson* regard the passage: the land, and the city, are supposed to have been used poetically for lands and cities. The word rendered "violence," חמס, means an unjust or wrong act done by force, an outrage, a violent injustice: hence *Grotius* rightly renders it here, " direptionem—robbing, pillaging, or plundering." While *Newcome* and others apply the passage to Judea and Jerusalem, the Septuagint version would lead us to suppose that Babylon was intended. The view taken here would be the most probable, were it not that the words are repeated at the end of ver. 17; and there clearly they refer to the land of Judea and Jerusalem.—*Ed.*

9. Woe to him that coveteth an evil covetousness to his house, that he may set his nest on high, that he may be delivered from the power of evil!

9. Væ concupiscenti concupiscentiam malam domui suæ, ut ponat in excelso nidum suum, quò se eripiat è manu (*id est*, è potestate) infortunii (mali, *ad verbum*.)

Habakkuk proceeds in exciting the king of Babylon by taunts; which were not scurrilous jests, but contained serious threatenings; for, as it has been already said, the Prophet here introduces indeed the common people, but in that multitude we are to recognise the innumerable heralds of God's vengeance: and hence he says, *Woe to him who coveteth*, &c.; or we may say, Ho! for it is a particle of exclamation, as it has been said: Ho! thou, he says, who covetest an evil covetousness to thy house, and settest on high thy nest; but what shall happen? The next verse declares the punishment.

The clause, *Woe to him who covets an evil covetousness to his house*, may be read by itself,—that this cupidity shall be injurious to his house; as though he had said, "Thou indeed wouldest provide for thy house by accumulating great riches; but thy house shall find this to be evil and ruinous. So the word רעה, *roe*, evil, might be referred to the house; but the verse is best connected by reading the whole together; that is, that the Babylonians not only provided for themselves, while they with avidity plundered and collected much wealth from all quarters; but that they wished also to make provisions for their sons and grandsons: and we also see, that avarice has this object in view; for they who are anxiously bent on the accumulation of riches do not only regard what is needful for themselves to pass through life, but also wish to leave their heirs rich. Since then the avaricious are desirous of enriching for ever their houses, the Prophet, deriding this madness, says, *Woe to him who covets an evil covetousness to his house;* that is, who wishes not only to abound and be satiated himself, but also to supply his posterity with abundance.

He adds another vice, which is almost ever connected with the former—*that he may set*, he says, *his nest on high;* for the avaricious have a regard to this—to fortify themselves; for as an evil conscience is always fearful, many dangers come across their minds—" This may happen to me," and then, " My wealth will procure for me the hatred and envy of many. If then some danger be at hand, I shall be able to redeem my life many times;" and he also adds, " Were I satisfied with a moderate portion, many would become my rivals; but when my treasures surpass what is common, then I shall be as it were beyond the reach of men; and when others envy one another, I shall escape." So the avaricious think within themselves when they are ardently bent on accumulating riches, and form for themselves a great heap like a nest; for they think that they are raised above the world, and are exempt from the common lot of men, when surrounded by their riches.

We now then see what the Prophet means: *Woe*, he says, *to him who wickedly and intemperately covets*. And why does he so do? To enrich his posterity. And then he adds, to him who covets that *he may set his nest on high;* that is, that he may by wealth fortify himself, that he may be able to drive away every danger, and be thus exempt from every evil and trouble. And he adds, *that he may deliver himself from the power of evil;* he expresses now more clearly what I have said—that the rich are inebriated with false confidence, when they surpass all others; for they think not themselves to be mortals, but imagine that they have another life, as though they had a world of their own, free from all dangers. But while the avaricious thus elevate themselves by a proud confidence, the Prophet derides their madness. He then subjoins their punishment—

10. Thou hast consulted shame to thy house by cutting off many people, and hast sinned *against* thy soul.	10. Consultasti in ignominiam domui tuæ (*vel*, conflasti tuo consilio probrum et dedecus domui tuæ) excidendo populos multos; et peccasti in animam tuam.

The Prophet again confirms the truth, that those who count themselves happy, imagining that they are like God, busy themselves in vain; for God will turn to shame whatever they think to be their glory, derived from their riches. The avaricious indeed wish, as it appears from the last verse, to prepare splendour for their posterity, and they think to render illustrious their race by their wealth; for this is deemed to be nobility, that the richer any one is the more he excels, as he thinks, in dignity, and the more is he to be esteemed by all. Since, then, this is the object of almost all the avaricious, the Prophet here reminds them, that they are greatly deceived; for the Lord will not only frustrate their hopes, but will also convert their glory into shame. Hence he says, that they consult shame to their family.

He includes in the word *consult*, all the industry, diligence, skill, care, and labour displayed by the avaricious. We indeed see how very sagacious they are; for if they smell any gain at a distance, they draw it to themselves, night and day they form new designs, that they may circumvent this person and plunder that person, and accumulate into their heap whatever money they can find, and also that they may join fields to fields, build great palaces, and secure great revenues. This is the reason why the Prophet says, that they *consult shame*. What is the object of all their designs? for they are, as we have said, very sharp and keen-sighted, they are also industrious, and torment themselves day and night with continual labour; for what purpose are all these things? even for this, that their posterity may be eminent, that their nobility may be in the mouth of all, and spread far and wide. But the Prophet shows that they labour in vain; for God will turn to shame whatever they in their great wisdom contrived for the honour of their families. The more provident then the avaricious are, the more foolish they are, for they consult nothing but disgrace to their posterity.

He adds, *though thou cuttest off many people*. This seems to have been expressed for the sake of anticipating an objection; for it might have seemed incredible that the Babylonians should form designs disgraceful to their posterity, when their fame was so eminent, and Babylon itself was like an idol, and the king was everywhere regarded with great reverence and also fear. Since then the Babylonians had made such advances, who could have thought it possible that what the Prophet declares here should take place? But, as I have already said, he meets these objections, and says, "Though the Babylonians shall conquer many enemies, and overthrow strong people, yet this will be of no advantage to them; nay, even that will turn out to their disgrace which they think will be to their glory."

To the same purpose is what he adds, *thou hast sinned against thy soul.* Some give this version, "Thou hast sinned licentiously" or immoderately; others, "Thy soul has sinned," but these pervert the Prophet's meaning; for what he intended was nothing else but the evils which the avaricious and the cruel bring on themselves, and which will return on their own heads. When therefore the Babylonians contrived ruin for the whole world, the Prophet predicts that an end, very different from what they thought, would be to them: *thou hast sinned,* he says, *against thine own soul;*[1] that is, the evil which thou didst prepare to bring on others, shall be made by God to fall on thine own head.

And this kind of declaration ought to be carefully noticed; that is, that the ungodly, while they trouble all, and harass all, while they torment one, plunder another, oppress another, do always sin against their own souls; that is, they do not cause so much loss and sorrow to others as to themselves: for the Lord will make the evil they intend for others to return on themselves. He does not speak here of guilt, but of punishment, when he says, "Thou hast sinned against thy soul;" that is, thou shalt receive the reward due to all thy sins. We now then see what the Prophet means. It now follows—

11. For the stone shall cry out of the wall, and the beam out of the timber shall answer it.	11. Quia lapis ex muro clamabit, et lignum ex tabulato (*ad verbum est,* ex ligno,) respondebit ei.

[1] Literally, "sinning thy soul." We have in Prov. viii. 36, הֹטְאִי, "my sinner," rendered no doubt correctly, "he that sinneth against me." So here "sinning thy soul," means "sinning against thy soul." See the same words in Prov. xx. 2. In Num. xvi. 38, the preposition ב is before "souls." "Thy soul hath sinned," as given by the Septuagint, and adopted by *Newcome,* does not convey the meaning; for to sin against our souls, is to injure ourselves so as to bring down judgment, as in the case mentioned in Num. xvi. 38, while the other phrase conveys only the idea of doing what is wrong.—*Ed.*

12. Woe to him that buildeth a town with blood, and stablisheth a city by iniquity!
13. Behold, *is it* not of the Lord of hosts that the people shall labour in the very fire, and the people shall weary themselves for very vanity?

12. Væ ædificanti urbem in sanguinibus, et paranti civitatem in iniquitate.
13. Annon ecce à Jehova exercituum? ideo laborabunt populi in igne et gentes in vanitate (*hoc est*, frustra fatigabuntur.)

There is here introduced by the Prophet a new personification. He had before prepared a common song, which would be in the mouth of all. He now ascribes speech to stones and wood, of which buildings are formed. *The stone,* he says, *shall cry from the wall, and the wood from the chamber;* that is, there is no part of the building that will not cry out that it was built by plunder, by cruelty, and, in a word, by evil deeds. The Prophet not only ascribes speech to wood and stone, but he makes them also respond one to the other as in a chorus, as in lyrics there are voices which take up the song in turns. *The stone,* he says, *shall cry from the wall,* and *the wood shall respond to it from the chamber;*[1] as though he said, "There will be a striking harmony in every part of the building; for the wall will begin and will utter its song, 'Behold I have been built by blood and by iniquity;' and the wood will utter the same, and will cry, 'Woe;' but all in due order; there will be no confused noise, but as music has distinct sounds, so also the stones will respond to the wood and the wood to the stones, so that there may be, as they say, corresponding voices."

The stone, then, *from the wall shall cry, and the wood shall answer*—what will it answer?—*Woe to him who builds a city*

---

[1] The word rendered here "wood," *lignum,* is כפיס, and only found here. The Septuagint has κάνθαρος, a beetle,—*Sym.* σύνδεσμος, bond, tie, or joint,—*Theod.* ἔνδεσμος, bandage or jointing. The context shows that it must be something connected with wood-building. *Parkhurst* says, that it is a verb in Syriac, and means to connect, to fasten together, and he renders it a beam or a rafter, which would exactly suit this place. The word, מעץ, "from the wood," evidently means the wood-building or woodwork. So that *tabulatum*, a story or a chamber in a building, as rendered by *Calvin,* is not amiss. Perhaps the best version would be,—
  And the beam from the wood-work answers it.
Bochart says, that כפיס, in Rabbinical writings, means a brick, and that it was usual formerly, as it was in this country not long ago, to build with bricks and wood or timber together; and *Henderson* has adopted this meaning, but the other is more satisfactory.—*Ed.*

by blood, and who adorns *his city by iniquity.* By blood and by iniquity he understands the same thing; for though the avaricious do not kill innocent men, they yet suck their blood, and what else is this but to kill them by degrees, by a slow tormenting process? For it is easier at once to undergo death than to pine away in want, as it happens to helpless men when spoiled and deprived of all their property. Wherever there is wanton plundering, there is murder committed in the sight of God; for as it has been said, he who spares not the helpless, but drinks up their blood, doubtless sins no less than if he were to kill them.

But if this personification seems to any one strange, he must consider how incredible seemed to be what the Prophet here teaches, and how difficult it was to produce a conviction on the subject. We indeed confess that God is the judge of the world; nay, there is no one who does not anticipate his judgment by condemning avarice and cruelty; the very name of avarice is infamous and hated by all: the same may be said of cruelty. But yet when we see the avaricious in splendour and in esteem, we are astounded, and no one is able to foresee by faith what the Prophet here declares. Since, then, our dulness is so great, or rather our sottishness, it is no wonder that the Prophet should here set before us the stones and the wood, as though he said, "When all prophecies and all warnings become frigid, and God himself obtains no credit, while openly declaring what he will do, and when his servants consume their labour in vain by warning and crying, let now the stones come forth, and be teachers to you who will not give ear to the voice of God himself, and let the wood also cry out in its turn." This, then, is the reason why the Prophet introduces here mute things as the speakers, even to awaken our insensibility.

Then he adds, *Shall it not be, behold, from Jehovah of hosts?* Some give a wrong version, "Is not this," as though הנה, *ene,* were put here instead of a pronoun demonstrative; but they extenuate and obscure the beauty of the expression; nay, they pervert the meaning of the Prophet: for when he says, הנה, *ene,* behold, he refers not to what he had said, nor specifies any particular thing, and yet he shows, as it were by the finger, the judgment of God, which he bids us to expect; as though he said, "Shall not God at length have his turn, when the avaricious and the cruel have obtained their triumphs in the world, and darkened the minds and thoughts of all, as though no account were to be given by them before the tribunal of God? Shall not God sometime show that it is his time to interpose?" When, therefore, he says, *Shall it not be, behold, from Jehovah?* it is an indefinite mode of speaking; he does not say, This or that shall be from the God of hosts; but, *Shall it not be, behold, from Jehovah of hosts?* that is, God seems now indeed to rest, and on this account men indulge themselves with greater boldness; but he will not always remain still, Shall not God then come forth, who seems now to be unconcerned? Something there will at length be from the God of hosts. And the demonstrative particle confirms the same thing: *Behold*, he says, as though he would show to the faithful as in a picture the tribunal of God, which cannot be seen by us now but by faith. He says, *Behold, will not there be something* from the God of *hosts?* that is, Will not God at length stretch forth his hand, to show that he is not unconcerned, but that he cares for the affairs of men? In a word, by this mode of speaking is pointed out to us the change, which we are to hope for, inasmuch as it cannot be soon realized.

Hence he concludes, *The people*, then, *labour in the fire, and the people weary themselves in vain.* To labour in the fire means the same thing as to take in hand an unprofitable work, the fruit of which is immediately consumed. Some say that people labour in the fire, because Babylon had been built by a great number of men, and at length perished by fire; but this explanation seems far-fetched. I take a simpler view—that *people labour in the fire*, like him who performs a work, and a fire is put under it and consumes it; or like him, who with great labour polishes his own work, and a fire is prepared, which destroys it while in the hands of the artificer. For it is certain that the Prophet repeats the same thing in another form, when he says,

בְּדֵי־רִיק, *bedi-rik*, with vanity, or for vanity. We now then apprehend his object.

We may here collect a useful doctrine—that not only the fruit of labour shall be lost by all who seek by wicked means to enrich themselves, but also, that were the whole world favourable and subservient to them, the whole would yet be useless; as it happened to the king of Babylon, though he had many people ready to obey him. But the Prophet derides all those great preparations; for God had fire at hand to consume whatever they had so eagerly contrived, who wished to spend all their labour to please one man. He at length adds—

14. For the earth shall be filled with the knowledge of the glory of the Lord, as the waters cover the sea.	14. Quia replebitur terra cognitione gloriæ Jehovæ, sicuti aquæ operiunt mare.

The Prophet briefly teaches us here, that so remarkable would be God's judgment on the Babylonians, that his name would thereby be celebrated through the whole world. But there is in this verse an implied contrast; for God appeared not in his own glory when the Jews were led away into exile; the temple being demolished and the whole city destroyed; and also when the whole eastern region was ex-

---

[1] The construction of the first line of this verse, as given by *Calvin*, is stiff and unnatural. There is no doubt but that הנה is a pronoun in the plural number, and so it has been taken by the Septuagint, ταυτα, these things, and such is the rendering of the Syriac and Arabic versions. No improvement, perhaps, can be made on *Newcome's* rendering of this verse,—
    Are not these things from Jehovah *God* of hosts,
    That people should labour for the fire,
    And nations should weary themselves for a vain thing?
The intimation is, that all the buildings erected by blood and prepared by iniquity, were destined for the fire. "For the fire," בדי אש, literally is, for the supply of fire, as *Parkhurst* renders the phrase: then it is, for the supply of emptiness or vacuity, בדי ריק.

The two last lines, with some variety, are found in Jer. li. 58, and applied to Babylon. In Jeremiah, "for a vain thing" is in the first line, and "for the fire" is in the second. Jeremiah puts the less evil first, and the greatest last; but Habakkuk's usual manner is the reverse, which has been before noticed, and we find an instance in the preceding verse, where he mentions "blood" first, and in the next line "iniquity."

That the destination of Babylon for the fire is here meant, seems evident from the following verse. See Jer. li. 25.—*Ed.*

posed to rapine and plunder. When therefore the Babylonians were, after the Assyrians, swallowing up all their neighbours, the glory of God did not then shine, nor was it conspicuous in the world. The Jews themselves had become mute; for their miseries had, as it were, stupified them; their mouths were at least closed, so that they could not from the heart bless God, while he was so severely afflicting them. And then, in that manifold confusion of all things, the profane thought that all things here take place fortuitously, and that there is no divine providence. God then was at that time hid: hence the Prophet says, *Filled shall be the earth with the knowledge of* God; that is, God will again become known, when by stretching forth his hand he will execute vengeance on the Babylonians; then will the Jews, as well as other nations, acknowledge that the world is governed by God's providence, as it had been once created by him.

We now understand the Prophet's meaning, and why he says, that the earth would be filled with the knowledge of God's glory; for the glory of God previously disappeared from the world, with regard to the perceptions of men; but it shone forth again, when God himself had erected his tribunal by overthrowing Babylon, and thereby proved that there is no power among men which he cannot control. We have the same sentence in Isaiah xi. 9.[1] The Prophet there

---

[1] The idea is nearly the same, though not the words. The verse in Isaiah is literally this—
    For fill the earth shall the knowledge of Jehovah,
    Like the waters spreading over the sea.
The verb rendered "cover" here and in Isaiah is, כסה, which means first to spread, and in the second place to cover, as the effect of spreading. It is followed here by על, over, and by ל, over, in Isaiah; and so spreading must be the idea included in the verb. The comparison in Isaiah is between knowledge and waters, and the earth and the sea. Hence the common version does not properly present the comparison. The verb מלא, is used in a passive and active sense. See Gen. vi. 13, and Gen. i. 22; xxiv. 16. This verse may be rendered in *Welsh* word for word, without changing the order in one instance:—
    Canys llenwa y ddaear wybodaeth o Jehova,
    Vel y dyvroedd dros y mor yn ymdaenu.
"The knowledge of Jehovah," דעה את־יהוה, is not an instance of a genitive case by juxtaposition, which is common both in Hebrew and in Welsh;

speaks indeed of the kingdom of Christ; for when Christ was openly made known to the world, the knowledge of God's glory at the same time filled the earth; for God then appeared in his own living image. But yet our Prophet uses a proper language, when he says that the earth shall then be filled with the knowledge of God's glory, when he should execute vengeance on the Babylonians. Hence incorrectly have some applied this to the preaching of the gospel, as though Habakkuk made a transition from the ruin of Babylon to the general judgment: this is a strained exposition. It is indeed a well-known mode of speaking, and often occurs in the Psalms, that the power, grace, and truth of God are made known through the world, when he delivers his people and restrains the ungodly. The same mode the Prophet now adopts; and he compares this fulness of knowledge to the waters of the sea, because the sea, as we know, is so deep, that there is no measuring of its waters. So Habakkuk intimates, that the glory of God would be so much known that it would not only fill the world, but in a manner overflow it: as the waters of the sea by their vast quantity cover the deep, so the glory of God would fill heaven and earth, so as to have no limits. If, at the same time, there be a wish to extend this sentence to the coming of Christ, I do not object: for we know that the grace of redemption flowed in a perpetual stream until Christ appeared in the world. But the Prophet, I have no doubt, sets forth here the greatness of God's power in the destruction of Babylon.[1]

for את here must be a preposition, "from," for it is sometimes used for מאת. It is a knowledge that was to come from Jehovah, and not a knowledge of Jehovah.—*Ed.*

[1] There is no reason to doubt but that this is the meaning of the sentence here: and it is a striking instance of the variety of meaning which belongs to similar expressions, when differently connected. The glory of God is manifested by judgments as well as by mercies. In Isaiah it is "the knowledge of or from Jehovah;" here the expression is, "the knowledge of the glory of Jehovah." By "the knowledge of Jehovah" is to be understood the revelation made by the gospel. But by "the knowledge of his glory" is meant evidently the display of his power in destroying Babylon, as power is often signified by glory.—*Ed.*

PRAYER.

Grant, Almighty God, that as we are so inclined to do wrong, that every one is naturally disposed to consider his own private advantage—O grant that we may confine ourselves by that restraint which thou layest on us by thy Prophets, so that we may not allow our coveting to break forth so as to commit wrong or iniquity, but confine ourselves within the limits of what is just, and abstain from what belongs to others: may we also so learn to console ourselves in all our distresses, that though we may be unjustly oppressed by the wicked, we may yet rely on thy providence and righteous judgment, and patiently wait until thou deliverest us, and makest it manifest that whatever the wicked devise for our ruin, so cleaves to themselves as to return and recoil at length on their own heads; and may we so fight under the banner of the Cross, as to possess our souls in patience, until we at length shall attain that blessed life which is laid up in heaven for us, through our Lord Jesus Christ. Amen.

Lecture One Hundred and Thirteenth.

15. Woe unto him that giveth his neighbour drink, that puttest thy bottle to *him*, and makest *him* drunken also, that thou mayest look on their nakedness!

16. Thou art filled with shame for glory: drink thou also, and let thy foreskin be uncovered: the cup of the Lord's right hand shall be turned unto thee, and shameful spewing *shall be* on thy glory.

15. Væ qui potat socium suum (*vel,* amicum;) conjungis (conjungens) calorem tuum (*vel,* utrem tuum; *alii vertunt,* adhibes venenum tuum, *vel,* iram tuam; *alii,* intendens iram;) atque etiam inebrias, ut aspicias super nuditates eorum (*id est,* verenda.)

16. Saturatus es ignominia ex gloria (*vel,* pro gloria;) bibe etiam tu et disco-operire (*vel,* sopiares;) fundetur super te calix dexteræ Jehovæ, et vomitus ignominiæ super gloriam tuam.

This passage, in which the Prophet condemns the king of Babylon for his usual practice of rendering drunk his friends, is frigidly interpreted by most expounders. It has been already often said how bold the Jews are in contriving what is fabulous; when nothing certain occurs to them, they divine this or that without any discrimination or shame. Hence they say, that Nebuchadnezzar was given to excess, and led all whom he could into a participation of the same vice. They also think that his associates were captive kings, as though he bid them for the sake of sport to be brought to his table, and by drinking to their health, forced them to intoxication, that he might laugh at them when they made themselves base and ridiculous. But all this is groundless; for there is no history that relates any such thing. It is, however, easy to see that another matter is here treated of by the Prophet; for he does not speak of the king only, but he refers to the whole empire. I therefore doubt not but that this whole discourse, in which the Babylonian king is condemned for making drunk his associates or friends, is metaphorical or allegorical. But before I proceed further on the subject, I shall say something as to the words; for the meaning of the Prophet will thereby be made more evident.

Woe, he says, *to him who gives his friend drink;* then he adds, מספח חמתך, *mesephech chemetak*, "who joinest thy bottle." חמה, *cheme*, is taken in Hebrew for a bottle; and we know, and it is sufficiently evident from Scripture, that the Jews used bottles of skin, as there are casks and larger vessels with us. Since, then, they put their wine into bottles, these were often taken for their cups, as it is in our language, when one says, *Des flacons, des bouteilles.* Hence some give this explanation—that the king of Babylon brought forth his flagons, that he might force to intoxication, by excessive drinking, those who could not and dared not to resist his will. But others render חמה, *cheme*, wrath, with a preposition understood: and in order that nothing may be understood, some render the participle, מספה, "displaying," that is, "his fury." But as חמה, *cheme*, means to be hot, we may, therefore, properly give this version, " Uniting thy heat;" that is, "It is not enough for thee to inebriate others, except thou implicatest them with thyself." We now perceive the meaning of this phrase. He adds, *And thou also dost inebriate.* We may hence learn that the Prophet had no other thing in view, but to show that the king of Babylon sought for himself many associates in his intemperance or excess: at the same time he takes, as I have said, excess in a metaphorical sense. I shall presently explain more fully what all this means; but now we only expound the words. *And thou,* he says, *dost also inebriate :* the particle אַף, as it is well known, is laid down for the sake of amplifying. After having said, *Thou unitest thy heat;* that is, thou exhalest thine intemperance, so that others also contract the same heat with thyself, he immediately adds, *Thou inebriatest them.* It follows, *that their nakedness may be made open ;* that is, that they may disclose themselves with shame. The following verse I shall defer until we shall see more clearly what the Prophet had in view.[1]

As I have already said the Prophet charges the Babylonian king with having implicated neighbouring kings in his own evil desires, and with having in a manner inebriated

---

[1] The rendering of this verse has been various, though most agree as to its import. *Grotius, Marckius,* and *Henderson,* take nearly the same view of its meaning as *Calvin,* regarding it as metaphorical. But *Marckius* thinks that the drunkenness which the king of Babylon produced, means the evils which he inflicted on other nations. To make a nation drunk was to subdue and oppress it. See Is. li. 17, 22 ; Jer. xxv. 15, 16, 27, 28 ; li. 7, 39, 57. This view is confirmed by the following verse, where the king of Babylon is threatened with a similar judgment ; he was also to drink of the cup of Jehovah's right hand. As he made other nations drunk, so the Lord threatens him with a like visitation.

The verse will admit of a much simpler rendering than what has been commonly offered, such as the following :—

    Woe to him who makes his neighbour to drink,
    Who adds his bottle, and also strong drink,
    In order that he may look on their nakedness.

To render חמה, wrath, or heat, or gall, or poison, as some have done, is to introduce an idea foreign to the context, and the word is often found to signify the bottle of skin in which wine was kept. *Newcome* renders it "flagon." By mentioning bottle, abundance of wine was probably intended, and to this abundance was added the strong drink, שכר, intoxicating liquor. It is commonly rendered as though it were a verb in Hiphil; but it is not so. It means here no doubt, as in other places, strong drink. This line is only an amplification, as we find often in the Prophets, of the preceding line.

Though there is no MS. which has "his" instead of "thy" connected with "bottle," yet the preceding and the following lines seem to require it ; and this is the reading of *Symmachus* and of the *Vulgate.* The change of persons, it is true, is very common in the Prophets, but not in such a way as we find here, the third person being adopted both in the preceding and in the following line.

The idea of drinking as a judgment may have arisen from the cup of malediction given to criminals before their execution. See also Ps. lxxv. 8. Babylon is in Jer. li. 7, represented as "a golden cup" in God's hand to make the nations drunken. It was "golden" to signify an outward appearance that was plausible and alluring. So the mystic Babylon is said to have a golden cup, which was full of all abominations, Rev. xvii. 4.—*Ed.*

them. He indeed compares the insatiable avarice of that king to intemperance; for as it is the object of drunken men not to drink what may suffice them, but to glut themselves with wine, so also when avarice is dominant in the hearts of men, they are seized with a certain kind of fury, like a person who has an immoderate love for wine. This is the reason for the metaphor; for the Babylonian king, when he thirsted for the blood of men, and also for wealth and kingdoms, led into the same kind of madness many other kings; for he could not have succeeded except he had allured the favour of many others, and deceived them with vain expectations. As a person who gives himself up to drinking wishes to have associates, so Habakkuk lays the same thing to the charge of the king of Babylon; for being himself addicted to insatiable avarice, he procured associates to be as it were his guests, and quaffed wine to them, that is, excited their cupidity, that they might join him in his wars; for each hoped for a part of the spoil after victory. Since, then, he had thus blinded many kings, they are said to have been inebriated by him. We indeed know that such allurements infatuate the minds and hearts of men; for there is no intoxication that stultifies men more than that eager appetite by which they devour both lands and seas.

We now then apprehend what the Prophet meant—that the Babylonian king not only burnt with his own avarice, but kindled also, as it were, a flame in others, like drunken men who excite one another. As then he had thus inflamed all the neighbouring kings to rush headlong without any consideration and without any shame, like a person suffocated and overcome by excessive drinking; so the Prophet designates this inflaming as quaffing wine to them.

And this metaphor ought to be carefully observed; for we see at this day as in a mirror what the Prophet teaches here. For all the great princes, when they devise any plans of their own, send their ambassadors here and there, and seek to involve with themselves other cities and princes; and as no one is willing to endanger himself without reason, they set forth many fallacious allurements. And when any city fears a neighbouring prince, it will seek to fortify itself by a new protection; so a treaty, when offered, becomes like a snare to it. And then when any inferior prince wishes to enlarge his borders, or to revenge himself, he willingly puts on arms, nay, anxiously, that he may be able, by the help of a greater, to effect his purpose, which he could not otherwise accomplish. Thus we see that dukes and counts, as they are called, and free cities, are daily inebriated. They who are chief kings, abounding in wine, that is, full of many vain promises, give to drink, as it were with full flagons, bidding wine to be brought forth on a well furnished table— " I will make thine enemy to give way to thee, and thou shalt compel him according to thy wish, and when I shall obtain the victory a part of the spoil shall be allotted to thee; I desire nothing but the glory. With regard to you, the free cities, see, ye tremble continually; now if you lie under my shadow, it will be the best security for you." Such quaffing is to be found at this day almost throughout the whole of Europe.

Then the Prophet does not without reason commemorate this vice in the king of Babylon—that he made those associates drunk whom he had bound to himself by perfidious treaties; for as it has been said, there is no intoxication so dangerous as this madness; that is, when any one promises this or that to himself, and imagines what does not exist. Hence he not only says, that the Babylonian king gave drink to his friends, but also that he *joined his bottles;* as though he had said that he was very liberal, nay, prodigal, while seeking associates in his intemperance; for if one condition did not suffice, another was added—" Behold, my king is prepared; but if he is not enough another will be joined with him." They thus then join together their heat. If we take חמה, *cheme,* for a bottle, then to join together their bottles would mean, that they accumulated promises until they inebriated those whom they sought to deceive. But if the other interpretation be more approved, which I am disposed to follow, then the meaning would be—*They join together their own heat,* that is, they implicate others with themselves; as they burn themselves with insatiable cupidity, so they spread this ardour far and wide, so that the desires of many become united.

He afterwards adds—*that thou mayest see their nakedness.* It was not indeed an object to the king of Babylon to disclose the reproach of all those whom he had induced to take part in his wars; but we know that great kings are wont to neglect their friends, to whom at first they promise every thing. When a king wishes to entice to himself a free city or an inferior prince, he will say—" See, I seek nothing but to be thy friend." We indeed see how shamefully they perjure themselves; nor is it enough for them to utter these perjuries in their courts; but not many years pass away before our great kings make public their abominable perjuries; and it appears immediately afterwards that they thus seek, without any shame, to mock both God and all mankind. After testifying that they seek nothing except to defend by their protection what is right and just, and to resist the tyranny and pride of others, they immediately draw back when anything adverse afterwards happens, and the city, which had hoped everything from so liberal a king, is afterwards forced to submit and to agree with its enemies, and to manage matters anyhow; thus its *nakedness is disclosed.* In the same manner also are inferior princes deprived of their power. And to whom is this to be imputed but to the principal author? For when any one, for the sake of ambition or avarice, leads others to inconvenience or to danger, he may justly and correctly be said to disclose their nakedness. We now apprehend the Prophet's real meaning, which interpreters have not understood. I come now to the next verse—

He says that he is *satiated with shame instead of glory.* Some give this rendering—" Thou art satiated with shame more than glory;" but this does not suit the passage; for the Prophet does not mean that the Babylonian king was satiated with his own reproach, but rather with that of others. Secondly, the particle מ, *mem,* is not put here in a comparative sense, but the clause is on the contrary to be understood thus—" By thy glory, or, on account of thy glory, thou art satiated with shame." It must also in the third place be observed, that punishment is not what the Prophet describes in these words; for it immediately follows שתה גם אתה, *shite gam ate,* "drink thou also." He comes now to punishment. By saying, then, that the king of Babylon was satiated with shame on account of glory, it is the same as though he had said, that while he was intent on increasing his own glory he brought all others to shame. It is indeed the common game of great kings, as it has been said, to enlarge their own power at the expense and loss of others. They would, indeed, if they could, render their friends safe; but when any one loses ground in their favour they neglect him. We see how at this day great kings, raising great armies, shed innocent blood. When a slaughter is made in war they express their grief, but it is only on account of their own glory or advantage. They will in words profess that they sympathize with the miserable men who faithfully spent their life for them, but they have for them no real concern. As, then, great kings draw human blood, and care nothing when many perish for their sake, the Prophet justly says, That the king of Babylon was satiated with shame on account of glory; that is, that while he was seeking his own glory he was satiated with the reproaches of many; for many perished on his account, many had been robbed of their power, or were afterwards to be robbed—for the Prophet refers not here to what had taken place, but he speaks of things future; and the past tense of verbs was intended to express certainty; and we know that this was a common mode of speaking with the Prophets.[1]

He now adds—*drink thou also.* We hence see that the king of Babylon was secure as long as he remained un-

---

[1] The view presented here of the first clause of the verse is striking, and such as the words may admit. But most commentators attach to them another meaning. *Newcome's* version is—
    Thou art filled with shame instead of glory.
Henderson's rendering is—
    Thou art filled with shame, not with glory.
The verb being in the past tense seems to favour *Calvin's* view—" Thou hast been satiated with shame from glory," that is, thou hast been filled to satiety with the shame occasioned to others, arising from the pursuit of thine own glory. And then, as *Calvin* justly observes, his punishment is denounced—" Drink thou also."—*Ed.*

touched, though his alliance and friendship had proved ruinous to many. As long then as his kingdom flourished, the king of Babylon cared but little for the losses of others. Hence the Prophet says—" Thou shalt also drink; thou thinkest that others only shall be punished, as though thou wert not exposed to God's judgment; but thou shalt come in thy turn and drink;"—in what way? He speaks here allegorically of the vengeance which was nigh the king of Babylon—" Thou, also," he says, " shalt drink and become a reproach," or, shalt be uncovered.

The word עָרֵל, *orel*, means in Hebrew the foreskin; and the foreskinned, or uncircumcised, was the name given to the profane and the base, or the contaminated; and hence many give this rendering—" Thou also shalt become ignominious;" but others express more clearly the Prophet's meaning by this version—" Thou shalt be uncovered." Yet their opinion is not amiss who think that there is here a change of letters, that הֵעָרֵל, *eorel*, is put for הֵרָעֵל, *erol*; and רָעֵל, *rol*, means to be cast asleep; and it well suits a drunken man to say that he is stupified. But as the Prophet had spoken of nakedness, I retain the word as it is; and thus the two clauses will correspond—*Then thou shalt drink and be uncovered.*

Then follows the explanation—*Poured forth*[1] *into thee shall be the cup of Jehovah's right hand;* that is, "the Lord shall in his time be thy cup-bearer; as thou hast inebriated many nations, and under the pretence of friendship hast defrauded those who, being bound to thee by treaties, have been ruined; so the Lord will now recompense thee with the reward which thou hast deserved: As thou hast been a cup-bearer to others, so the Lord will now become thy cup-bearer, and will inebriate thee, but after another manner." We indeed know what the Scripture everywhere means by the cup of God's hand—even vengeance of every kind. God strikes some with giddiness and precipitates them, when deprived of all humanity, into a state of mad-

[1] The verb תִּסּוֹב, loosely expressed here, is very correctly rendered by *Henderson* " shall come round;" and this is the idea which *Calvin* suggests in the following explanation.—*Ed.*

ness; others he infatuates by insensibility; some he deprives of all understanding, so that they perceive nothing aright; against others he rouses up enemies, who treat them with cruelty. Hence the Lord is said to extend his cup to the wicked whenever he takes vengeance on them.

Therefore he adds—*the reproach of spewing shall be on thy glory.* The word קִיקָלוֹן, *kikolun*, is a compound.[1] We have already seen that קָלוֹן, *kolun*, is shame; and now he speaks of shameful spewing. And this may be referred to the king of Babylon—that he himself would shamefully spew out what he had before intemperately swallowed down; or it might be fitly applied to his enemies—that they would spew in the face of the king of Babylon.

The end of which Habakkuk speaks, awaits all tyrants, who disturb the world by their cupidity. Ambition does indeed so infatuate them, that they neither spare human blood, nor hesitate to endanger their nearest and most friendly associates. Since then an insatiable thirst for glory thus inflames them, the Prophet justly allots to them this reward—that they shall receive filthy and shameful spewing instead of that glory, in seeking which they observed no limits. Let us now proceed—

17. For the violence of Lebanon shall cover thee, and the spoil of beasts, *which* made them afraid, because of men's blood, and for the violence of the land, of the city, and of all that dwell therein.	17. Quia violentia Libani operiet te et prædatio animalium, quæ terruit ea (*vel*, quæ contrivit,) propter sanguines hominis et violentiam terræ, urbis et omnium habitantium in ea.

We may hence easily learn, that the Prophet has not been speaking of drunkenness, but that his discourse, as we have explained, was metaphorical; for here follows a reason, why

---

[1] It is commonly derived from קִי, a contraction of קִיא, a vomit or spewing, and קָלוֹן, shame. Compounds are no common things in Hebrew; and these are found separate in nine MSS. The *Septuagint* have ἀτιμία, reproach only; and the *Vulgate*, "vomitus ignominiæ—the spewing of shame." *Newcome* renders it "foul shame," and *Henderson* "great ignominy," regarding it as a reduplicate noun for קִלְקָלוֹן. But as drunkenness is the metaphor used, "shameful spewing," or the spewing of shame or of reproach is most suitable to the passage.—*Ed.*

he had denounced such a punishment on the king of Babylon, and that was, because he had exercised violence, not only against all nations indiscriminately, but also against the chosen people of God. He had before only set forth in general the cruelty with which the king of Babylon had destroyed many nations; but he now speaks distinctly of the Jews, in order to show that God would in a peculiar manner be the avenger of that cruelty which the Chaldeans had employed towards the Jews, because the Lord had taken that people under his own protection. Since then the king of Babylon had assailed the children of God, who had been adopted by him, and whose defender he was, he denounces upon him here a special punishment. We thus see that this discourse is properly addressed to the Jews; for he intended to bring them some consolation in their extreme evils, so that they might strengthen their patience; for they were thereby made to see that the wrongs done to them were come to a reckoning before God.

By *Libanus* then we are to understand either Judea or the temple; for Libanus, as it is well known, was not far from the temple; and it is elsewhere found in the same sense. But if any extends this to the land of Judea, the meaning will be the same; there will be but little or no difference as to the subject that is handled. *Because the violence* then *of Libanus shall overwhelm thee.*

Then come the words, *the pillaging of beasts.* Interpreters think that the Chaldeans and Assyrians are here called בהמות, *bemut*, beasts, as they had been savage and cruel, like wild beasts, in laying waste Judea; but I rather understand by the beasts of Libanus those which inhabited that forest. The Prophet exaggerates the cruelty of the king of Babylon by this consideration, that he had been an enemy to brute beasts; and I consider the pronoun relative אשר, *asher*, which, to be understood before the verb יחיתן, *ichiten*, which may be taken to mean, to tear, or to frighten. Some give this rendering, "The plundering of beasts shall tear them;" as though he had said, "The Babylonians are indeed like savage beasts, but they shall be torn by their own plunderings:" but another sense will be more suitable—

that the plundering of beasts, which terrified them, shall overwhelm thee; for the same verb, יכס, *icas*, shall cover or overwhelm the king of Babylon, is to be repeated here. He adds at last the clause, which was explained yesterday. We now perceive the meaning of the Prophet to be—that the king of Babylon would be justly plundered, because he had destroyed the holy land and iniquitously attacked God's chosen people, and had also carried on his depredations through almost the whole of the eastern world.[1] It now follows—

18. What profiteth the graven image that the maker thereof hath graven it; the molten image, and a teacher of lies, that the maker of his work trusteth therein, to make dumb idols?	18. Quid prodest sculptile? quia sculpsit illud fictor ejus conflatile et doctorem mendacii; quia confidit fictor figmento suo, ut faciat idola muta.

The Prophet now advances farther, and shows that whatever he had predicted of the future ruin of Babylon and of its monarchy, proceeded from the true God, from the God of Israel: for it would not have been sufficient to hold, that some deity existed in heaven, who ruled human affairs, so that it could not be, but that tyrants would have to suffer punishment for their cruelty. We indeed know that such

---

[1] It is commonly agreed, that Libanus here means either the temple or the land of Judah; most probably the last, according to the opinion of *Jerome*, *Drusius*, and others. The "violence," or outrage, of Libanus, means the violence *done* to it, as *Newcome* and others render the clause. The next line is more difficult: if the verb be retained as it is, we must either adopt what *Calvin* has proposed, and after him *Drusius*, or take the ו at the beginning as a particle of comparision, according to what is done by *Henderson*, "As the destruction of beasts terrifieth them." But to preserve the parallelism of the two lines, it would be better to adopt the correction of all the early versions, *Sept. Arab. Syr.* and also of the *Chald. par.*; which substitute ך for ו, and make the verb to be יחיתך: and there are two MSS. which have חתי. In this case the rendering would be the following—

    Because the violence done to Libanus shall overwhelm thee,
    And the depredation done to the beasts shall rend thee;
      On account of the blood of men, and of violence to the land,
        To the city, and to all who dwelt in it.

The reason men are called "beasts" is because Libanus is mentioned, which was inhabited by beasts; and in the two following lines the statement is more clear, and according to the order usually observed, "the depredation done to beasts" is "the blood of men;" and "the violence to Libanus" is "violence to the land." And then, as it is often the case in the Prophets, there is an addition made to the two last lines, "To the city," &c.—*Ed.*

sayings as these were everywhere common among heathen nations—that justice sits with Jupiter—that there is a Nemesis—that there is Divine vengeance. Since then such a conviction had ever been imprinted on the hearts of men, it would have been a frigid and almost an empty doctrine, had not the Prophet introduced the God of Israel. This is the reason why he now derides all idols, and claims for God the government of the whole world, and clearly shows that he speaks of the Jews, because they worshipped no imaginary gods, as the heathen nations, but plainly understood him to be the creator of heaven and earth, who revealed himself to Abraham, who gave his law by the hand of Moses. We now perceive the Prophet's design.

As then the king of Babylon did himself worship his own gods, the Prophet dissipates that vain confidence, by which he might be deceived and deceive others. Hence he says, *What avails the graven image?* He speaks here contemptuously of images formed by men's hands. And he adds a reason, *because the maker has graven it,* he says. Interpreters give a sense that is very jejune, as though the Prophet had said, "What avails a graven image, when it is graven or melted by its artificer?" But the Prophet shows here the reason why the worship of idols is useless, and that is, because these gods are made of dead materials. And then he says, "What deity can the artificer produce?" We hence see that a reason is given in these words, and therefore we may more clearly render them thus—" What avails the graven image, when the framer has graven it?" that is, since the graven image has its origin from the hand and skill of man, what can it avail? He then adds, *he has formed a molten image;* that is, though the artificer has given form to the metal, or to the wood, or to the stone, yet he could not have changed its nature. He has indeed given it a certain external appearance; but were any one to ask what it is, the answer would surely be, "It is a graven image." Since then its nature is not changed by the work of man, it evidently appears, how stupid and mad must all those be who put their trust in graven images.[1]

[1] Rightly to understand this verse, it is necessary to remember that the

He then adds, *and a teacher of falsehood.* He added this clause, because men previously entertain false notions, and dare not to form a judgment on the matter itself. For, how comes it that a piece of wood or a stone is called a god? Had any one asked the sages at Rome or at Athens, or in other cities, who thought all other nations barbarous, What is that? on seeing a Jupiter made of silver, or of wood, or of stone, the answer would have been, " It is Jupiter, it is God." But how could this be? It is a stone, a piece of wood, or of silver. They would yet have asserted that it was God. Whence came this madness? Even from this, because men were bewitched, so that seeing they saw not; they wilfully closed their eyes, and resolved to be blind, being unwilling to understand. This is the reason why the Prophet, by way of anticipation, says, *the artificer has formed*—what has he formed? *a graven image and a teacher of falsehood.* The material remains the same, but a false notion prevails, for men think idols to be gods. How come they to think so? It is no doubt the teaching of falsehood, a mere illusion. He then confirms the same thing; *the fashioner,* or the artificer, he says, *trusts in his own work,* or in what he has formed. How is this? Must they not be void of sense and reason who trust in lifeless things? " The workman," as Isaiah says, " will take his instruments, will form an idol, and then he will bow the knee, and call it his god; yet it is the work of his own hands."

graven and the molten image was the same; it was first graven and then covered with some metal, either of gold or of silver. See Note on Mic. i. 7, vol. iii. p. 167.

This verse, as given in our version and in that of *Newcome,* presents hardly a meaning; and *Henderson* is not justified in the peculiar sense he gives to the particle כי, taking it as a relative pronoun. The rendering of *Calvin* gives an evident and a striking sense. The verse may be thus literally rendered—

  18. What avails the graven image?—
   For its graver has formed it,—
   The molten image and the teacher of falsehood?
   For trust in it does the former of its form,
   After having made dumb idols.

The last line shows that the singular number before used is to be taken in a collective sense: and the preposition ל before an infinitive has sometimes the meaning of " after." See Ex. xix. 1, " When he has made," &c., is the rendering of *Grotius.—Ed.*

What! art not thou thyself a god? thou knowest thine own frailty, and yet thou createst new gods! Even in this manner does the Prophet confirm what he had previously said,—that men are extremely stupid, nay, that they are seized with monstrous sottishness, when they ascribe a kind of deity to wood, or to a stone, or to metal. How so? because they are, he says, false imaginations.

And he adds, *that he may make dumb idols*. He again repeats what he had said,—that the nature of the material is not changed by men's workmanship, when they form to themselves gods either from wood or from stone. How so? because they cannot speak. To the same purpose is what immediately follows; the next verse must therefore be added. We shall afterwards say something more on the general subject.

| 19. Woe unto him that saith to the wood, Awake; to the dumb stone, Arise, it shall teach! Behold, it *is* laid over with gold and silver, and *there is* no breath at all in the midst of it. | 19. Væ qui dicit ligno, Expergiscere; excitare, lapidi muto (mortuo,) ipse docebit: Ecce, ipse (*vel* ipsum *lignum, si referamus ad lignum*; ipse *ergo*) opertus est auro et argento; et nullus spiritus in medio ejus. |

He pursues, as I have said, the same subject, and sharply inveighs against the sottishness of men, that they call on wood and stone, as though there were some hidden power in them. *They say to the wood, Awake;* for they implored help from their idols. *Shall it teach?* Some render it thus as a question; but I take it in a simpler form, "It will teach;" that is, "It is a wonder that ye are so wilfully foolish; for were God to send to you no Prophet, were there no one to instruct you, yet the wood and the stone would be sufficient teachers to you: ask your idols, that is, ascertain rightly what is in them. Doubtless, the god that is made of wood or of stone, sufficiently declares by his silence that he is no god. For there is no motion in wood and stone. Where there is no vigour and no life, is it not right to feel assured, that there is no deity? There are, indeed, many creatures endued with feeling and motion; but the God who gives power, and motion, and feeling to the whole world, and to all its parts, does he not surpass in these respects all his creatures? Since, then, wood and stone are silent, they are teachers sufficient for you, provided ye be apt scholars."

We hence see how the Prophet in this way amplifies the insensibility of men; for they did not perceive what was quite manifest. The design of what follows is the same. *Behold, it is covered over with gold and silver;* that is, it is made splendid: for idolaters think that their gods are better when adorned with gold and silver; but yet *there is no breath in the midst of them.* " Look," he says, " within; look within, and ye shall see that they are dead."[1] The rest we shall dilate on to-morrow.

PRAYER.

Grant, Almighty God, that as there is in us so little of right judgment, and as our minds are blind even at mid-day,—O grant, that thy Spirit may always shine in us, and that being attentive to the light of thy word, we may also keep to the right way through the whole course of our pilgrimage, and subject to thee both ourselves and every action of our life, so that we may not be led by any allurements into the same ruin with the ungodly, who would deceive and entrap us, and who lie in wait on every side; but that being ruled by the counsel of thy Spirit, we may beware of all their intrigues: and may we, especially as to our spiritual life, be so given up to thee alone, as ever to keep ourselves far away from the defilements of all people, and so remain in the pure worship of thy majesty, that the ungodly may never draw us away into the same delusions with themselves, by which Satan so mightily deceives them; but may we follow Him as our leader whom thou wouldst have to be our ruler, even Christ thy Son, until he at length gathers us all into that celestial kingdom which he has purchased for us by his own blood. Amen.

---

[1] With the exception of the clause, "It will teach," there is a general agreement in the mode of rendering this verse. " Shall it teach," is *Newcome's* version. *Henderson* considers it to be ironical, " It teach!" *Grotius* agrees with *Calvin,* " It will itself teach thee," that is, that it is deaf, and no god. I regard the verse as capable of a simpler and more literal rendering, as follows:—

19. Woe to him who saith to the wood, " Awake, Arise;"
   To the dumb stone, " It will teach :"
   Behold, it is covered with gold and silver!
   Yet there is no breath within it.

The two verbs, " Awake, Arise," stand connected with " wood," and they are so given in the Septuagint; and there is a striking contrast between the dumb stone and teaching.—*Ed.*

Lecture One Hundred and Fourteenth.

WE said yesterday, that the Prophet speaks now of idols, that he might deprive the king of Babylon of his vain confidence: for though heathens claim everything to themselves and to their own powers, yet their superstition in some measure dementates them. Hence the Prophet shows, that that tyrant in vain trusted in his idols, since they were things of nought. But the reasons by which he refutes idolatry ought to be noticed: he says, that the artificers, who formed gods, were not able to change the nature of the material, for the wood remained wood, and stone continued to be stone, and that the workmen and artificers in forming it did nothing more than make a molten image. The material then remained still the same. As to the image itself, the Prophet says, that it was mere falsehood and deception; yea, that gods made of wood or of silver, or of any other material, were instructors and teachers of falsehood, for they allured simple souls: and Satan spread his snares before men, when he set before their eyes these visible figures, and persuaded them that they contained something divine. Then this reasoning of the Prophet ought to be carefully observed; for he reminds us, that fictitious gods are made of lifeless and perishable materials, and that images are only the juggleries of Satan.

That saying of Gregory is common among the Papists, that images are the books of the ignorant; for such was his answer to Serenus, bishop of Marseilles, who turned out images from all the churches (Lib. 9, Epist. 9.) He said that he approved of his object, in wishing to correct the superstition which prevailed among the people, but that he had done what was not right in wholly taking away images, the books of the ignorant. But let us consider whether more faith is due to Gregory, a man embued with many errors, (as that age was very corrupt), or to the Prophet Habakkuk, and also to Jeremiah, who announces nearly the same sentiment. Though, then, there is some speciousness in idols, yet the Prophet here reminds us that they are nothing but the impostures of Satan; for they teach falsehood. The reason also that is given is deserving of notice— that the workmen put their hope in what they themselves have formed. And it is indeed a thing most preposterous, that a mortal man should form his own god, and then imagine that something divine is enclosed in the very form, for deity is not in the material. The material is disregarded when unformed; but not so when it attains a beautiful shape. While the tree grows, while it produces flowers and fruit, it is deemed, as it really is, a dead thing; but when a piece of it is formed in the figure of a man, it is believed to be a god! But it is extremely absurd to suppose that the hand of the artificer gives deity to a dead material; for the wood is dead, and nothing is perceived but the shape given to it by man. Since, then, the artificer trusts in what he has formed, it is what seems beyond anything strange. It is hence quite evident, that men are wholly demented by the devil, when they worship their own workmanship.

But now, in order to press the matter more fully on idolaters, the Prophet upbraids them for calling on the wood and on the stone to awake. It is certain, that when idolaters bow the knee before what they have themselves formed, they still imagine that there are celestial gods; but when before a figure of wood or stone they call upon God, it is the same thing as though they expected help from the wood and stone; for the question is not here what idolaters imagine, but the thing itself is to be regarded; and this is what the Prophet most fully and plainly condemns. Since, then, the superstitious are wont to address their prayers to wood and stone, he says, that they make to themselves gods, to whom they sacrifice. And the Prophet rightly refers in express terms to this kind of service; for the chief sacrifice which God bids to be offered to him, and demands from us, is to call on him; for we thus testify that life and all things belonging to salvation are found alone in him. Since, then, the majesty of God appears especially from having this testimony borne to him, that he is the fountain of life and of all blessings, every one who prostrates himself before a stone or wood, and implores the aid of a visible god, transfers, no doubt, the glory of the eternal God to a dead piece of wood or to a stone. If, then, we wish to be free from every superstition, let us remember this truth, that then only we have the only true God, when we direct our prayers and supplications to him alone, or, in a word, when we call on him alone. When we have recourse to dead idols, God is deprived of his own right. We may call him God a hundred times, but we give him an empty title, and one of no value, except we pray to him alone.

The Prophet, in the last place, derides the madness of men, by saying that the very idols teach: for, as it was said yesterday, the clause is not to be read as a question, as some do; but in order more sharply to reprove the stupidity of men, the Prophet says, "Doubtless the very figures themselves, except ye are wholly senseless, will teach you." He had before said, it is true, that they were the teachers of falsehood and vanity; but he speaks now of another kind of teaching, that if men wisely attended to the thing itself, they might soon learn from a mere view of their gods, that they were most palpably the deceits of Satan; for if any one looked on the idols with a clear eye, he would see that they were a dead material, and would see that great wrong is done to God by transforming him into a likeness of what is dead.

We now understand the Prophet's meaning, when he says, That idols themselves are sufficient, and more than sufficient teachers, when men are teachable, and lend an attentive ear. He means not, as it was said yesterday, that idols teach fallaciously to the destruction of men, while something divine is ascribed to them; but he says that they teach, if any one of a sane mind, and free from error, comes to view the idol, and forms a judgment of the thing itself. But superstition occupies the minds of men; and hence it is that all become the scholars of Satan, and no one applies his mind to understand the doctrine he mentions here. In short, idols teach naturally, and they teach through the artifice and delusion of Satan. They teach naturally; for by their silence they show that they are not gods, inasmuch as there is no strength in them. They teach, also, by the artifice of the devil; for they are made to claim a kind of divinity, and thus dazzle the minds of men, who are already corrupted by their own delusions. To the first teaching, of which the Prophet now speaks, none apply their minds; for almost all renounce nature wholly: this only lays hold on them—that idols are gods; for they make an image of the heavenly and eternal God, from whom we are at a great distance, and who does not otherwise descend to us, except through visible representations!

The same truth the Prophet confirms when he says, that though these gods are covered over with gold and silver, *there is no breath in them*, or in the midst of them. In short, he means that they are mere masks; for no divinity can be without life. As then idols are dead things, it follows that they are the most palpable impostures of Satan, by which he fascinates the minds of men, when they thus devote themselves to dead things.

Moreover, whatever is here said against idols, most certainly applies to the superstitions of popery. They deny that they give divine honours to their idols; but let us consider what the Prophet says. They indeed sacrifice to gold and silver, and then bend their knees before their images, and do not think that God is near them, except in these figures. Let them show, then, that the Prophet reasons here foolishly, or let them be held guilty according to the declaration, as it were, of the Holy Spirit, when they thus present their prayers before idols. It now follows—

20. But the Lord *is* in his holy temple: let all the earth keep silence before him.	20. Jehova autem in templo sanctitatis suæ (*id est*, in templo sancto suo:) sileat à facie ejus omnis terra.

After having taught us that the Babylonians were deceived in expecting any help from their idols, and were deluded by Satan, Habakkuk now recalls the attention of the faithful to the only true God; for it would not have been enough to take away from the Babylonians the false confidence which they had in their idols, except the Israelites, on the other hand, trusting in the grace of the true God, were fully persuaded that God was on their side, as he had taken them under his protection.

And we ought carefully to observe this order; for we see that many boldly deride all the superstitions which prevail in the world, and at the same time daringly and with cyclopic fury despise the true God. How many are at this day either Epicureans or Lucianians, who prate jestingly and scoffingly against the superstitions of the papacy, but in the meantime they are not influenced by any fear of God? If, however, we are to choose one of two evils, superstition is more tolerable than that gross impiety which obliterates every thought of a God. It is indeed true, that the more the superstitious toil in their delusions, the more they provoke God's wrath against them; for they transfer his glory to dead things; but yet they retain this principle—that honour and worship are due to God: but the profane, in whom there is no religion whatever, not only change God from what he is, but also strive as far as they can to reduce him to nothing. Hence I have said, that the order which the Prophet observes here ought to be maintained. For, after having overturned the false illusions of the devil, by which he deludes the superstitious, by setting before them a mere shadow in the place of the true God, he now sets up the true worship of the only true God. Then the Prophet has hitherto been endeavouring to subvert superstitions, but he now builds up: for except God, when idols are pulled down, ascends his own tribunal, and shines there as supreme according to his right, it would be better, at least it would be more tolerable, as I have said, that superstitions should be left entire.

He now says that God *is in his own temple* or palace: this word is often taken for heaven, but is applied to the sanctuary. Many consider that the reference is made to heaven; as though the Prophet had said, that the true God, who is the artificer and creator of heaven and earth, is not to be seen in a visible form, nor covered over with gold and silver, nor represented by wood or stone; but that he rules in heaven, and fills heaven with his infinite glory: and this view is by no means unsuitable. But as he here specially addresses the Jews, it seems to me more probable that he speaks of the temple, where God then designed to be worshipped, and sacrifices to be offered to him: for it would not have been sufficient to set God, the creator of heaven and earth, in opposition to the superstitions of all the nations; but it was also necessary to introduce the contrast between the God of Israel and all those gods who then had obtained a name and reputation in the world, as they had been formed by the will of men. The God of Israel was indeed the creator of heaven and earth; but he had made himself known by his law, he had revealed himself to men, so that his majesty was not hidden; for when we speak of God, we are lost except he comes to us, and in a manner exhibits himself to us; for the capacity of our understanding is not so great that it can penetrate above all heavens. Hence the majesty of God is in itself incomprehensible to us; but he makes himself known by his works and by his word. Now as the Israelites worshipped, and surely knew that they worshipped the only true God, the Prophet here rightly confirms them in the hope they derived from the teaching of the law—that God was their Father, inasmuch as he had adopted them. If any prefer to take the word for heaven, I do not object; and that meaning, as I have said, is not unsuitable. But as the Prophet seems to me to have a special view to his own people, to whom he was appointed a teacher, it is more probable that the word, temple or palace, is here to be understood of the sanctuary.

If any raises the objection that there is then no difference between the God of Israel and the gods of the Gentiles, for he also dwells in an earthly habitation, the answer is obviously this—that though God is said to dwell between the cherubim, he has not been represented by an image, as though he had anything like to wood or stone, or possessed any likeness to human bodies. All these delusions were banished from the Temple; for he commanded his worshippers to look up to heaven. There was an intervening veil, that the people might understand that they could not otherwise come to God than through that celestial model, the antitypes of which they saw in the altar of incense, in the altar on which they sacrificed, in the table of the shewbread, in short, in all other services of the Temple. And there is another difference to be noticed; for though there was there the golden altar, though there was there the ark of the covenant, and the altar on which the victims were immolated, yet inscribed on all these typical representations was the word of God, by which alone true religion was to be distinguished from all false inventions. For whatever specious appearance of reason may therefore be in fictitious modes of worship, men have no authority to render them lawful; but so much reverence is due to the only true word of God, that it ought to overrule all other reasons. And besides, this word, as I have hinted already, did not retain the Jews in these delusions, but elevated their minds to heaven. We now then see that there was a wide difference between the Temple which was at Jerusalem, and the temples which the superstitious had then built for themselves throughout the world; for God ruled over the Jews, so that they could not have been deluded. And at this day, where the word of God shines among us, we can follow it with safety. And, further, God did spiritually draw to himself his own servants, though he employed, on account of their ignorance, certain outward elements. Hence the Prophet justly says, that God was in his palace or his Temple; for the Israelites knew of a certainty that they did not worship a fictitious God, since in his law he had revealed himself to them, and had chosen the sanctuary, where he intended to be worshipped in a typical, and yet in a spiritual manner.

He then adds, *Let all the earth be silent before him.* Habakkuk, no doubt, commends the power of God, that the Israelites might proceed with alacrity in their religious course, knowing it to be a sufficient security to be under the protection of the only true God, and that they might not seek after the superstitions of the nations, nor be carried here and there, as it often happens, by vain desires. *Keep silence,* then, he says, *let all the earth.* He shows that though the Israelites might be far inferior to the Babylonians and other nations, and be far unequal to them in strength, military art, forces, and, in short, in all things of this kind, yet they would be always safe under the guardianship of God; for the Lord was able to control whatever power there might be in the world.

We now see what the Prophet had in view: for he does not here simply exhort all people to worship God, but shows, that though men may grow mad against him, he yet can easily by his hand subjugate them; for after all the tumults made by kings and their people, the Lord can, by one breath of his mouth, dissipate all their attempts, however furious they may be. This, then, is the silence of which the Prophet now speaks. But there is another kind of silence, and that is, when we willingly submit to God; for silence in this respect is nothing else but submission: and we submit to God, when we bring not our own inventions and imaginations, but suffer ourselves to be taught by his word. We also submit to him, when we murmur not against his power or his judgments, when we humble ourselves under his powerful hand, and do not fiercely resist him, as those do who indulge their own lusts. This is indeed, as I have said, a voluntary submission: but the Prophet here shows that there is power in God to lay prostrate the whole world, and to tread it under his feet, whenever it may please him; so that the faithful have nothing to fear, for they know that their salvation is secured; for though the whole world were leagued against them, it yet cannot resist God. Now follows a prayer:—

CHAPTER III.

1. A prayer of Habakkuk the prophet upon Shigionoth.

1. Precatio Chabakuk Prophetæ super ignorantiis (*vel*, super canticis, *aut* instrumentis musicis.)

THERE is no doubt but that the Prophet dictated this form of prayer for his people, before they were led into exile, that they might always exercise themselves in the study of religion. We indeed know that God cannot be rightly and from the heart worshipped but in faith. Hence, in order to confine the dispersed Israelites within due limits, so that they might not fall away from true religion, the Prophet here sets before them the materials of faith, and stimulates them to prayer: and we know, that our faith cannot be supported in a better way than by the exercise of prayer.

Let us then bear in mind, that the way of fostering true religion, prescribed here to the miserable Israelites while dispersed in their exile, was to look up to God daily, that they might strengthen their faith; for they could not have otherwise continued in their obedience to God. They would, indeed, have wholly fallen away into the superstitions of the Gentiles, had not the memory of the covenant, which the Lord had made with them, remained firm in their hearts: and we shall presently see that the Prophet lays much stress upon this circumstance.

He calls it his own prayer,[1] not because he used it himself privately, or composed it for himself, but that the prayer might have some authority among the people; for they knew that a form of prayer dictated for them by the mouth of a Prophet, was the same as though the Spirit itself was to show them how they were to pray to God. The name, then, of Habakkuk is added to it, not because he used it himself, but that the people might be more encouraged to pray, when they knew that the Holy Spirit, through the Prophet, had become their guide and teacher.

There is some difficulty connected with the word שגינות, *sheginut*. The verb שגג, *shegag*, or שגה, *shege*, means, to act inconsiderately; and from שגה, *shege*, is derived שגיון, *shegiun*. Many render it, ignorance; some, delight. Some think it to be the beginning of a song; others suppose it to be a common melody; and others, a musical instrument. Thus interpreters differ. In the seventh Psalm David, no

---

[1] The more correct rendering here would be, "A Prayer (or rather, An Intercession) by Habakkuk the Prophet;" that is, It was a prayer composed by him. The preposition ל before Habakkuk, as often before David in the Psalms, would be better rendered in this way, than by "of;" for the meaning is, not that it was his prayer, that is, one offered up by him, but that it was composed by him. "A Psalm of David," ought to be, "A Psalm by David."—*Ed.*

doubt, calls either a song or some musical instrument by the word שִׁגְיוֹן, *shegiun*. Yet some think that David bears testimony there to his own innocency; and that, as he was not conscious of having done wrong, his own innocency is alone signified by the title: but this is a strained view. The word is taken in this place, almost by common consent, for ignorances: and we know that the Hebrews denominate by ignorances all errors or falls which are not grievous, and such things as happen through inadvertence; and by this word they do not extenuate their faults, but acknowledge themselves to be inconsiderate when they offend. Then שִׁגְיוֹן, *shegiun*, is no excusable ignorance, which men lay hold on as a pretext; but an error of folly and presumption, when men are not sufficiently attentive to the word of God. But perhaps the word שִׁגְיֹנוֹת, *sheginut*, being here in the plural number, ought to be taken for musical instruments. Yet as I would not willingly depart from a received opinion, and as there is no necessity in this case to constrain us to depart from it, let us follow what has been already said,— that the Prophet dictates here for his people a form of prayer for ignorances, that is, that they could not otherwise hope for God's forgiveness than by seeking his favour.[1] And how can we be reconciled to God, except by his not imputing to us our sins?

But the Prophet, by asking for the pardon of ignorances, does not omit more grievous sins; but intimates that though

---

[1] This explanation, adopted by *Calvin*, is derived originally from *Aquila* and *Symmachus*, who rendered the phrase, ἐπὶ ἀγνοημάτων,—respecting oversights or errors: and they have been followed by *Jerome*, *Vulgate*, &c. The prior version of the *Septuagint* is, μετ' ᾠδῆς,—with an ode. That this prayer is composed in metre, is evident from the word, "Selah," and from the conclusion of the chapter. The most probable meaning of the word is what *Drusius* has suggested, and adopted by *Grotius*, *Marckius*, and *Henderson*, and that is, that it refers to a peculiar metre, a kind of composition, which from its irregularity is called *erratica cantio*, an erratic verse. "The prayer of Habakkuk," says *Drusius*, "was to be sung according to the odes which they called *Sigionoth*." To the same purpose is what *Grotius* says, that is, it is "a song according to the notes of an ancient ode which began with this word." It is derived from שָׁגָה, to go astray, to wander, that is, in this instance, from the regular metre of an ode. It is an erratic ode, that is, one containing varieties. It may be thus paraphrastically expressed, "According to the notes of the irregular ode;" or, as it is in the margin of our Bibles, "According to variable songs or tunes."—*Ed.*

their conscience does not reprove men, they are yet not on that account innocent and without guilt; for they often inconsiderately fall, and their faults are not to be excused for inadvertence. It is, then, the same thing as though the Prophet reminded his own people, that there was no remedy for them in adversity but by fleeing to God, and fleeing as suppliants, in order to solicit his forgiveness; and that they were not only to acknowledge their more grievous sins, but also to confess that they were in many respects guilty; for they might have fallen through error a thousand times, as we are inconsiderate almost through the whole course of our life. We now, then, perceive what this word means, and why the Prophet spoke rather of ignorances than of other sins. But I shall not proceed farther now, as there is some other business.

PRAYER.

Grant, Almighty God, that as thou hast deigned to make thyself known to us by thy word, and as thou elevatest us to thyself in a way suitable to the ignorance of our minds,—O grant, that we may not continue fixed in our stupidity, but that we may put off all superstitions, and also renounce all the thoughts of our flesh, and seek thee in the right way; and may we suffer ourselves to be so ruled by thy word, that we may purely and from the heart call upon thee, and so rely on thine infinite power, that we may not fear to despise the whole world, and every adversity on the earth, until, having finished our warfare, we shall at length be gathered into that blessed rest, which thine only-begotten Son has procured for us by his own blood.—Amen.

Lecture One Hundred and Fifteenth.

2. O Lord, I have heard thy speech, *and* was afraid: O Lord, revive thy work in the midst of the years, in the midst of the years make known; in wrath remember mercy.

2. Jehova, audivi vocem tuam (auditum tuum, *ad verbum*, שָׁמְעֲךָ ;[1]) Jehova, opus tuum in medio annorum vivifica illud (*sed relativum pronomen abundat;*) in medio annorum notum fac; in irâ misericordiæ recorderis.

THE Prophet says here, in the name of the whole people,

---

[1] The verb, "territus sum,—I feared," has been omitted. It is even omitted in the French version.—*Ed.*

that he was terrified by the voice of God, for so I understand the word, though in many places it means report, as some also explain it in this place. But as the preaching of the Gospel is called in Isa. liii., שְׁמֻעָה, *shemoe*, report, it seems to me more suitable to the present passage to render it the voice of God; for the general sentiment, that the faithful were terrified at the report of God, would be frigid. It ought rather to be applied to the Prophecies which have been already explained: and doubtless Habakkuk did not intend here to speak only in general of God's power; but, as we have seen in the last lecture, he humbly confesses the sins of the people, and then prays for forgiveness. It is then not to be doubted but that he says here, that he was terrified by the voice of God, that is, when he heard him threatening punishment so grievous. He then adds, *Revive thy work in the middle of the years, and make it known.* At last, by way of anticipation, he subjoins, that *God would remember his mercy,* though justly offended by the sins of the people.

But by saying, that he feared the voice of God, he makes a confession, or gives an evidence of repentance; for we cannot from the heart seek pardon, unless we be first made humble. When a sinner is not displeased with himself, and confesses not his guilt, he is not deserving of mercy. We then see why the Prophet speaks here of fear; and that is, that he might thus obtain for himself and for others the favour of God; for as soon as a sinner willingly condemns himself, and does not do this formally, but seriously from the heart, he is already reconciled to God; for God bids us in this way to anticipate his judgment. This is one thing. But if it be asked, for what purpose the Prophet heard God's voice; the obvious answer is,—that as it is not the private prayer of one person, but of the whole Church, he prescribes here to the faithful the way by which they were to obtain favour from God, and turn him to mercy; and that is, by dreading his threatenings and by acknowledging that whatever God threatened by his Prophets was near at hand.

Then follows the second clause, *Jehovah! in the middle*

of the years revive thy work. By the work of God he means the condition of his people or of the Church. For though God is the creator of heaven and earth, he would yet have his own Church to be acknowledged to be, as it were, his peculiar workmanship, and a special monument of his power, wisdom, justice, and goodness. Hence, by way of eminence, he calls here the condition of the elect people the work of God; for the seed of Abraham was not only a part of the human race, but was the holy and peculiar possession of God. Since, then, the Israelites were set apart by the Lord, they are rightly called his work; as we read in another place, " The work of thine hands thou wilt not despise," Ps. cxxxviii. 8. And God often says, " This is my planting," " This is the work of my hands," when he speaks of his Church.

By *the middle of the years*, he means the middle course, as it were, of the people's life. For from the time when God chose the race of Abraham to the coming of Christ, was the whole course, as it were, of their life, when we compare the people to a man; for the fulness of their age was at the coming of Christ. If, then, that people had been destroyed, it would have been the same as though death were to snatch away a person in the flower of his age. Hence the Prophet prays God not to take away the life of his people in the middle of their course; for Christ having not come, the people had not attained maturity, nor arrived at manhood. *In the middle,* then, *of the years thy work revive;* that is, " Though we seem destined to death, yet restore us." *Make it known,* he says, in the middle of the years; that is, " Show it to be in reality thy work."[1]

[1] The view given of " the middle of the years," is ingenious and striking; but the common interpretation is, that " the years" of calamity, allotted to the Jews, are meant. The Septuagint version of this verse is so extremely wide of the original, that none can account for the differences. There are no various readings of any moment; and the literal rendering of this verse, and of the former part of the following, I consider to be this,—
    2. O Jehovah! I have heard thy report;
       I feared, O Jehovah!
       Thy work! in the midst of the years revive it;
       In the midst of the years make it known;
       In anger remember mercy:

We now apprehend the real meaning of the Prophet. After having confessed that the Israelites justly trembled at God's voice, as they saw themselves deservedly given up to perdition, he then appeals to the mercy of God, and prays God to revive his own work. He brings forward here nothing but the favour of adoption: thus he confesses that there was no reason why God should forgive his people, except that he had been pleased freely to adopt them and to choose them as his peculiar people; for on this account it is that God is wont to show his favour towards us even to the last. As, then, this people had been once chosen by God, the Prophet records this adoption, and prays God to continue and fulfil to the end what he had begun. With regard to the half course of life, the comparison ought to be observed; for we see that the race of Abraham was not chosen for a short time, but until Christ the Redeemer was manifested. Now we have this in common with the ancient people, that God adopts us, that he may at length bring us into the inheritance of eternal life. Until, then, the work of our salvation is completed, we are, as it were, running our course. We may therefore adopt this form of prayer, which is prescribed for us by the Holy Spirit,—that God would not forsake his own work in the middle of our course.

What he now subjoins—*in wrath remember mercy*, is intended to anticipate an objection; for this thought might have occurred to the faithful—"there is no ground for us to hope pardon from God, whom we have so grievously provoked, nor is there any reason for us to rely any more on the covenant which we have so perfidiously violated." The Prophet

> 3. May God from Teman come,
> And the Holy One from mount Paran. Selah.

It is called " thy report," as it was a report which came from God; the allusion is to the threatenings in chap. i. " The report from thee," would convey the sense. The third line is a prayer; and so are the following lines, though all the verbs are in the future tense, while that for "revive" is in the imperative mood. The third verse ought to end with the word " Selah." What follows in the other part and in the subsequent verses, is a relation of what took place when God had formerly interfered in behalf of Israel; while here, and in the latter part of the preceding verse, the Prophet expresses a prayer to God in reference to his people, and borrows his language from the past interpositions of God.—*Ed.*

meets this objection, and he flees to the gracious favour of God, however much he perceived that the people would have to suffer the just punishment of their sins, such as they deserved. He then confesses that God was justly angry with his people, and yet that the hope of salvation was not on that account closed up, for the Lord had promised to be propitious. Since God then is not inexorable towards his people—nay, while he chastises them he ceases not to be a father; hence the Prophet connects here the mercy of God with his wrath.

We have elsewhere said that the word wrath is not to be taken according to its strict sense, when the faithful or the elect are spoken of; for God does not chastise them because he hates them; nay, on the contrary, he thereby manifests the care he has for their salvation. Hence the scourges by which God chastises his children are testimonies of his love. But the Scripture represents the judgment with which God visits his people as wrath, not towards their persons but towards their sins. Though then God shows love to his chosen, yet he testifies when he punishes their sins that iniquity is hated by him. When God then comes forth as it were as a judge, and shows that sins displease him, he is said to be angry with the faithful; and there is also in this a reference to the perceptions of men; for we cannot, when God chastises us, do otherwise than feel the accusations of our own conscience. Hence then is this hatred; for when our conscience condemns us we must necessarily acknowledge God to be angry with us, that is with respect to us. When therefore we provoke God's wrath by our sins we feel him to be angry with us; but yet the Prophet connects together things which seem wholly contrary—even that God *would remember mercy in wrath;* that is, that he would show himself displeased with them in such a way as to afford to the faithful at the same time some taste of his favour and mercy by finding him to be propitious to them.

We now then perceive how the Prophet had joined the last clause to the foregoing. Whenever, then, the judgment of the flesh would lead us to despair, let us ever set up against it this truth—that God is in such a way angry that he never forgets his mercy—that is, in his dealings with his elect. It follows—

3. God came from Teman, and the Holy One from mount Paran. Selah. His glory covered the heavens, and the earth was full of his praise.

3. Deus de Theman veniet, et Sanctus è monte Paran. Selach.[1] Operuit cœlos decor (*vel*, gloria) ejus; laude ejus plena est terra.

This verse interpreters explain in two ways. Some construe the verb in the future tense in the past time—"God went forth from Teman, and the holy one from mount Paran;" for a verb in the past tense follows. But others consider it to be in the optative mood—"May God come, or go forth, from Teman, and the holy one from mount Paran;" as though the Prophet prayed God to come as the defender of his people from mount Sinai, where the law was promulgated and the covenant ratified, which God had formerly made with Abraham and his posterity. I rather subscribe to their opinion who think that the manifestation of God, by which he had testified that he was the guardian of that people, is repeated by the Prophet. As, then, God had so made known his glory on mount Sinai, that it was evident that that nation was under his protection, so the Prophet, with the view of strengthening himself and others, records what was well known among the whole people—that is,

---

[1] The word סלה is found 70 times, as *Parkhurst* says, in the Psalms, and thrice in this chapter. "It was most probably," he adds, "a *note of music*, or a direction to the singers in the temple service to *raise* their voices or instruments where it is inserted." The opinion of *Gesenius* is the same, it being a direction, as he says, "to repeat the preceding verse in a *louder* strain." It is always rendered by the Septuagint Διαψαλμα, which means a variation in singing.

Some have rendered the word pause, but it cannot be so considered, for it occurs at the *end* of at least three of the Psalms. There seems to be no regularity in its adoption. In some of the Psalms it occurs once, in some twice, in others thrice, and in one psalm four times.

Calvin has not referred, in his comment, to the latter part of this verse, which, according to his Latin, may be thus translated,—

Cover the heavens did his glory;
With his praise full was the earth.

Both glory and praise here are to be taken as signifying their manifestations. The reference is made to the displays of divine majesty on mount Sinai. The original may be thus rendered—

Cover the heavens did his shining,
And his lustre filled the earth.—*Ed.*

that the law was given on mount Sinai, which was a testimony of singular favour; for God then by a new pledge testified, that the covenant formerly made with Abraham was firm and inviolable. The reason why Habakkuk does not mention mount Sinai, but Teman and Paran, seems to some to be this—because these mountains were nearer the Holy Land, though this view, I fear, will appear too refined; I therefore take this simple view—that instead of mentioning mount Sinai, he paraphrastically designates it by mount Paran and the desert of Teman. Some suppose these to be two mountains; but I know not whether Teman ought to be understood only as a mountain; it seems on the contrary to have been some large tract of country. It was a common thing among the Jews to add this name when they spoke of the south, as many nations were wont to give to winds the names of some neighbouring places; so when the Jews wished to designate a wind from Africa, they called it Teman. "It is a Teman wind;" and so when they spoke of the south, they said Teman.

However this may be, it is certain that the desert of Teman was nigh to Sinai, and also that mount Paran was connected with that desert. As then they were places towards the south, and nigh to mount Sinai, where the law had been proclaimed, the Prophet records here, in order to strengthen the faith of the whole people, that God had not in vain gone forth once from Teman, and there appeared in his celestial power; for God then openly showed, that he took under his guardianship the children of Abraham, and that the covenant which he had formerly made with him was not vain or of no effect. Since, then, God had testified this in so remarkable and wonderful a manner, the Prophet brings forward here that history which tended especially to confirm the faith of the godly—" God went forth once from Teman, and the holy one from mount Paran."

For it was not God's will that the memory of that manifestation should be obliterated; but he had once appeared with·glory so magnificent, that the people might feel assured that they would ever be safe, for they were protected by God's hand, and that full of power, as the fathers had once known by manifest and visible evidences; and hence the Prophet represents God's going forth from mount Paran as a continued act, as though he rendered himself visible chiefly from that place. Nor is this representation new; for we see, in many other places, a living picture, as it were, set before the eyes of the faithful, in order to strengthen them in their adversity, and to make them assured that they shall be safe through God's presence. The Lord, indeed, did not daily fulminate from heaven, nor were there such visible indications of his presence as on mount Sinai; but it behoved the people to feel assured that he was the same God who had given to their fathers such clear evidence of his power, and that he is also at this time, and to the end of the world, endued with the same power, though it be not rendered visible.

We now then apprehend the design of the Prophet: *God then came from Teman, and the holy one from mount Paran.* We must also observe, that the minds of the godly were recalled to the spectacle on mount Sinai, when they were drawn away into exile, or when they were in the power of their enemies. They might indeed have then supposed, that they were wholly forsaken. Obliterated then must have been the memory of that history, had not this remedy been introduced. It is, therefore, the same as though the Prophet had said—" Though God now hides his power, and gives no evidence of his favour, yet think not that he formerly appeared in vain to your fathers as one clothed with so great a power, when the law was proclaimed on mount Sinai. It follows—

4. And *his* brightness was as the light; he had horns *coming* out of his hand: and there *was* the hiding of his power.

4. Et splendor quasi lux fuit; cornua è manu ejus ei, et ibi absconsio fortitudinis ejus.

He confirms the declaration which I have explained—that God, when he intended his presence to be made known to his people, gave evidences of his wonderful power, capable of awakening the minds of all. He then says, that the brightness was like light. By the word אוֹר, *aur,* is doubtless meant the light, which diffuses itself through the whole world, and proceeds from the sun. Then he says, that the brightness which appeared on mount Sinai was equal to the light of the sun, capable of filling the whole world. He adds, that *horns were to him from the hand.* Some render it, splendour; but קֶרֶן, *coren,* properly means a horn, and קַרְנַיִם, *corenim,* is here in the dual number: it is therefore more probable, that the Prophet ascribes horns to God, carried in both hands; and it more corresponds with what immediately follows, that " there was the hiding of his strength," or that " there was his power hidden." They who render the word, splendours, think that what had been said is repeated, that is, that the brightness was like light; but they are mistaken, for we may collect from the verse that two different things are expressed by the Prophet: he first speaks of the visible form of God; and then he adds his power, designating it metaphorically by horns, which is common in Scripture. Indeed this mode of speaking occurs often. He then says, that God came armed with power, when he gave the law to his people; for he bore horns in his hands, where his strength was hid.[1]

As to the word *hiding,* some indeed give this refined view, that God then put forth his strength, which was before hidden. But this is a very strained explanation. To me it seems evident, that the Prophet in the first place says, that God's glory was conspicuous, capable of irradiating the

---

[1] That קרן means to irradiate or to shine, is clear from Ex. xxxiv. 29, 30, 35; " for shine did the skin of his face," כי קרן עור.פני. Most critics consider that the noun here, though in this sense in no other instance, means rays or beams of light; and this corresponds with the description given elsewhere of God's appearance on mount Sinai. *Drusius, Marckius, Newcome,* and *Henderson,* render it "rays." The line then would literally be—
    Rays from his hand *were* to him.
or, to retain the English idiom,
    He had rays from his hand.
To render the line, " Rays streamed from his hand," is to give a paraphrase.

The objection of *Calvin* as to the next line, seems not valid; for the hiding of strength may refer to the hand, or to the place, Sinai, whether we render the previous word, rays or horns;—to the place, if we retain our present reading, עֻזֹּה, " of its strength;" but to the hand, if we adopt the reading of *many* copies, עֻזּוֹ, " of his strength," which is perhaps the most accordant with the passage.—*Ed.*

whole world like the light of the sun; and he then adds, that this splendour was connected with power, for God carried horns in both his hands, where his strength was hid: and he says, that it was hid, because God did not intend to make known his power indiscriminately throughout the world, but peculiarly to his own people; as it is also said in Ps. xxxi. 20, that "the greatness of his goodness is laid up for the faithful alone, who fear and reverence him." As then it is said, that the goodness of God is laid up for the faithful, for they enjoy it as children and members of the household; so also the power of God is said to be laid up, because he testifies that he is armed with power to defend his Church, that he may render safe the children of Abraham, whom he has taken under his protection. It afterwards follows—

5. Before him went the pestilence, and burning coals went forth at his feet.

5. Coram facie ejus ambulavit pestis, et egredietur carbo ignitus (*vel*, ustio) ad pedes ejus.

The Prophet repeats here, that God came armed to defend his people, when he went forth from Teman; for he connects with it here the deliverance of the people. He does not indeed speak only of the promulgation of the law, but encourages all the godly to confidence; for God, who had once redeemed their fathers from Egypt, remained ever like himself, and was endued with the same power.

And he says, that *before God's face walked the pestilence;* this is to be referred to the Egyptians; and that *ignited coal proceeded from his feet.* Some render רשף, *reshoph*, exile; but its etymology requires it to be rendered burning or ignited coal, and there is no necessity to give it another meaning.[1]

---

[1] Most agree in the view given of this verse, only there is some shade of difference as to the word רשף; but though *Calvin* renders it *carbo ignitus*—ignited coal, yet in his exposition he seems to regard it with many others as a burning disease. In the six other instances in which the word occurs, it certainly has not this sense, except it be in Deut. xxxii. 24, which is doubtful. It signifies not a burning coal, but a glowing fire, burning, or lightening. Compare Exod. ix. 23, 25, with Ps. lxxviii. 48; where it designates the fires or lightnings produced by thunder, which accompanied

The import of the whole is—that God had put to flight all the enemies of his people; for we know that the Egyptians were smitten with various plagues, and that the army of Pharaoh was drowned in the Red Sea. Hence, the Prophet says, that God had so appeared from Teman, that the pestilence went before him, and then the ignited coal; in short, that the pestilence and ignited coal were God's officers, which were ready to perform his commands: as when a king or a judge, having attendants, commands them to put this man in prison, and to punish another in a different way; so the Prophet, giving us a representation of God, says, that all kinds of evils were ready to obey his orders, and to destroy his and their enemies. He does not then intend here to terrify the faithful in mentioning the pestilence and the ignited coal; but, on the contrary, to set before their eyes evidences of God's power, by which he could deliver them from the hand of their enemies, as he had formerly delivered their fathers from Egypt. By God's feet, he then means his going forth or his presence; for I do not approve of what some have said, that ignited coals followed, when pestilence had preceded; for both clauses are given in the same way. It follows—

6. He stood, and measured the earth: he beheld, and drove asunder the nations; and the everlasting mountains were scattered, the perpetual hills did bow: his ways *are* everlasting.	6. Stetit et mensus est terram; aspexit et dissolvit gentes; et afflicti sunt montes æterni; incurvati sunt colles seculi; itinera seculi ei.

He says that God possessed every power to subdue the earth to himself, and that he could at his will destroy it, yea, dissolve mountains as well as nations. Some of the

---

the hail. Lightning would be its most proper rendering here; for instead of referring this verse to the plagues in Egypt, it may be considered as a continuation of what is contained in the foregoing verse; and the *Septuagint* and *Theodotion* have rendered דבר in the preceding clause, not pestilence, but word—λόγος, its most usual meaning. This makes the whole to comport to what we read of God's appearance on mount Sinai. See Exod. xix. 16; Deut. xxxiii. 2. The version then would be this—
    From before him proceeded the word (*i. e.* the law;)
    And forth came lightning at his feet.
Most of the ideas in this, and in the two preceding verses, seem to be similar to those we find in Deut. xxxiii. 2, 3.—*Ed.*

Jews understood this of the ark, which stood at that time in Gilead. They then suppose that the Prophet meant this in short—that when God chose a place for the ark of the covenant in Gilgal, that he determined then what he would do, and that he then in his secret counsel divided the land, so that each should have his portion by lot. This, it is true, was accomplished shortly after, for Joshua, as we know, divided it by lot between the tribes. But what the Jews affirm of the ark seems to me strained and frigid. Habakkuk, on the contrary, means by the word *stand*, that God was openly conspicuous, like him who assumes an erect posture, so that he is seen at a distance. In this sense we are to take the expression that God stood.

The measuring of the earth is not to be confined to Judea, but is to be extended to the whole world. God, he says, has *measured the earth.* To measure the earth is what properly belongs to a sovereign king; and it is done that he may assign to each his portion. Except God, then, had a sovereign right over the earth and the whole world, Habakkuk would not have ascribed to him this office; and this we learn from the verse itself, for he immediately subjoins, that the *nations, as it were, melted away, that the mountains were destroyed, that the hills were bowed down.*

We hence see that by earth we are not to understand Judea only, but the whole world; as though he had said, that when God appeared on mount Sinai, he made it fully evident that the earth was under his power and authority, so that he could determine whatever he pleased, and prescribe limits to all nations. For he does not speak of God here as having, like a surveyor, a measuring line; but he says, that he measured the earth as one capable even then of changing the boundaries of the whole world; nay, he intimates that it was he himself who had at first created the earth and assigned it to men. It is indeed true that the nations did not then melt away, nor were the mountains demolished, nor the hills bowed down; but the Prophet simply means, that God's power then appeared, which was capable of shaking the whole world.

But he calls these *the mountains of eternity and the hills of ages*, which had been from the beginning fixed on their own foundations. For if an earthquake happens on a plain, it seems less wonderful; and then if any of those mountains cleave, which are not so firmly fixed, it may be on account of some hollow places; for when the winds fill the caverns, they are forced to burst, and they cleave the mountains and the earth. But the Prophet relates an unusual thing, and wholly different from the ordinary course of nature—that the mountains of eternity, which had been from the beginning, and had remained without any change, were thus demolished and bowed down. In short, the Prophet intended by all means to raise up to confidence the minds of the godly, so that they should become fully persuaded that God's power to deliver them would be the same as that which their fathers had formerly experienced; for there is no other support under adverse, and especially under despairing circumstances, than that the faithful should know that they are still under the protection of that God who has adopted them. This is the reason why the Prophet amplifies, in so striking a manner, on the subject of God's power.

And hence also he subjoins, that *the ways of ages* are those of God. Some render the clause, "the ways of the world." The word, עוֹלָם, *oulam*, however, means properly an age, or perpetual time. The Prophet, I have no doubt, means by ways of ages, the wonderful means which God is wont to adopt for the defence of his Church; for we are ever wont to reduce God's works to our own understanding, while it is his purpose to perfect, in a manner that is wonderful, the work of our salvation. Hence the Prophet bids the faithful here to raise upwards their thoughts, and to conceive something greater of God's power than what they can naturally comprehend. If we take the ways of eternity in this sense, then they are to be understood as in opposition to those means which are known and usual. They are his daily ways, when the sun rises and sets, when the spring succeeds the winter, when the earth produces fruit; though even these are so many miracles, yet they are his common ways. But God has *ways of eternity*, that is he has means unknown to us by which he can deliver us from death, whenever it may please him.

But yet, if any prefer taking the *ways of eternity* as signifying the continued power of God, which has ever appeared from the beginning, the sense would be appropriate and not less useful: for it especially avails to confirm our faith, when we consider that God's power has ever been the same from the creation of heaven and earth, that it has never been lessened or undergone any change. Since, then, God has successively manifested his power through all ages, we ought hence to learn that we have no reason to despair, though he may for a time conceal his hand; for he is not on that account deprived of his right. He ever retains the sovereignty of the world. We ought, then, to be attentive to the ways of ages, that is, to the demonstration of that power, which was manifested in the creation of the world, and still continues to be manifested.[1] It follows—

7. I saw the tents of Cushan in affliction: *and* the curtains of the land of Midian did tremble.	7. Pro iniquitate (*vel*, pro nihilo, *alii vertunt*) vidi tentoria Chusan (*vel*, Æthiopiæ;) contremiscent cortinæ (*vel*, pelles) terræ Madian.

The Prophet relates here, no doubt, whatever might bring comfort to the miserable Jews, as they thought themselves rejected and in a manner alienated from God. Hence the Prophet mentions here other deliverances, which were clear evidences of God's constant favour towards his chosen

---

[1] This verse is explained in a very striking manner, but the version is not so strictly correct. It may be thus rendered:—
    6. He stood, and measured the earth;
       He looked, and agitated the nations;
       And burst themselves open did the perpetual mountains,
       Bend down did the hills of ages;
       The goings of ages were his.
"The perpetual mountains" are literally "the mountains of perpetuity," which had remained the same from the beginning. "The hills of ages" might be rendered the hills of antiquity or of old time, עולם, an indefinite past time. "The goings of ages," are God's proceedings, that is, in his works, and may therefore be rendered "deeds;" and they are said to be deeds "of ages," *i.e.* of old time, with reference probably to the creation of the world: for he who makes perennial mountains to burst, and perpetual hills to bend downwards, must be their first creator.—*Ed*.

people. He had hitherto spoken of their redemption, and he will presently return to the same subject: but he introduces here other histories; as though he had said, that it was not only at one time that God had testified how much he loved the race of Abraham, and how inviolable was the covenant he had made; but that he had given the same testimonies at various times: for as he had also defended his people against other enemies, the conclusion was obvious, that God's hand was thus made manifest, that the children of Abraham might know that they were not deceived, when they were adopted by him.

Hence Habakkuk mentions the *tents of Chusan* as another evidence of God's power in preserving his people, and the *curtains of Madian;* for we know how wonderful was the work, when the Jews were delivered by the hand of Gideon; and the same was the case with respect to the king of Chusan.

We now, then, understand the design of the Prophet: for as he knew that the time was near when the Jews might succumb to despair in their great adversities, he reminds them of the evidences of God's favour and power, which had been given to their fathers, that they might entertain firm hope in time to come, and be fully persuaded that God would be their deliverer, as he had been formerly to their fathers.

PRAYER.

Grant, Almighty God, that as we have a continual contest with powerful enemies, we may know that we are defended by thine hand, and that even thou art fighting for us when we are at rest; so that we may boldly contend under thy protection, and never be wearied, nor yield to Satan and the wicked, or to any temptations; but firmly proceed in the course of our warfare: and however much thou mayest often humble us, so as to make us to tremble under thine awful judgment, may we yet never cease to entertain firm hope, since thou hast once promised to be to us an eternal Father in thine eternal and only-begotten Son; but being confirmed by the invincible constancy of faith, may we so submit ourselves to thee, as to bear all our afflictions patiently, until thou gatherest us at length into that blessed rest, which has been procured for us by the blood of thine own Son. Amen.

Lecture One Hundred and Sixteenth.

We said yesterday that the Prophet spoke of the king of Chusan and of the Madianites, in order to strengthen the minds of the godly, and to set before their eyes the continued aid of God, so that they might venture to feel assured that he would not act otherwise towards the Church to the end of the world, than what he had done from the beginning. The meaning, then, is sufficiently evident. We must now consider the words.

Some understand by the word, אן, *aun*, nothing, or vanity; as though the Prophet had said, that the tents of Chusan had been reduced to nothing: but another sense is more probable; *I have seen the tents of Chusan on account of his iniquity;*[1] that is, the reward which God had repaid, for the iniquity of the king of Chusan had been made manifest. The Prophet says that he had seen it, because it was evident and known to all. We now perceive what is meant —that God had been a just judge against the army of Chusan; for as they had unjustly assailed the Israelites, so a just reward was rendered to them. The account of this we have in Judg. iii. Chusan, the king of Mesopotamia, had well-nigh destroyed the Israelites, when the Lord put him to flight with all his forces. Some render the words, "The tents of Ethiopia," as though it was written Chus; but this is strained, and contrary to the rules of grammar;

---

[1] The word אן not only means iniquity, but also what iniquity produces, labour, trouble, affliction; and this latter meaning, as allowed by *Newc me* and *Henderson*, is most suitable to it here. The word is so taken in Gen. xxxv. 18; Deut. xxvi. 14; Hos. ix. 4. Besides, this meaning makes a correspondence between this and the following line, as will be seen by the following version—

    Under trouble have I seen the tents of Cushan,
    Tremble did the curtains of the land of Madian.

The "curtains" were those used in forming tents, and are used here to designate them. The most obvious reference here is to Cushan, mentioned in Judg. iii. 8, 10, as *Calvin* states; yet some consider that it stands for *Cush*, as *Lotan*, in Gen. xxvi. 20, is put for *Lot:* and some, as *Gesenius*, say, that the African *Cush* is meant, and others, as *Henderson*, think, that it is the Arabian *Cush*, especially as *Madian* is also mentioned. Still the events recorded in Judges, nearly connected together, favour the opinion adopted by *Calvin.—Ed.*

and besides, the following clause confirms what I have said; for the Prophet mentions the slaughter with which God destroyed the Madianites, who had also nearly overwhelmed the miserable people. He says that *their curtains trembled,* or their dwellings: for God, without the hand or sword of men, drove them into such madness, that they slew one another, as the sacred history testifies. See Judg. vi. and vii. It now follows—

8. Was the Lord displeased against the rivers? *wás* thine anger against the rivers? *was* thy wrath against the sea, that thou didst ride upon thine horses *and* thy chariots of salvation?	8. An contra fluvios iratus es, Jehova? an contra fluvios indignatio tua? an contra mare furor tuus (*vel*, ira tua)? quia equitasti super equos tuos; quadrigæ tuæ salus.

The Prophet here applies the histories to which he has already referred, for the purpose of strengthening the hope of the faithful; so that they might know these to be so many proofs and pledges of God's favour towards them, and that they might thus cheerfully look for his aid, and not succumb to temptation in their adversities. When he asks, was God angry with the rivers and the sea, he no doubt intended in this way to awaken the thoughts of the faithful, that they might consider the design of God in the works which he had already mentioned; for it would have been unreasonable that God should show his wrath against rivers and the sea; why should he be angry with lifeless elements? The Prophet then shows that God had another end in view when he dried the sea, when he stopped the course of Jordan, and when he gave other evidences of his power. Doubtless God did not regard the sea and the rivers; for that would have been unreasonable. It then follows that these changes were testimonies of God's favour towards his Church: and hence the Prophet subjoins, that God *rode on his horses,* and that his *chariots were for salvation* to his people.[1] We now perceive the Prophet's meaning, which

---

[1] The two first lines present a difficulty in their construction. The most literal is this rendering of *Junius*—
  Did against rivers kindle, O Jehovah—
  Against rivers, thy wrath?
Our language will admit of a similar construction in another form, by inverting the order—

interpreters have not understood, or at least have not explained.

We now, then, see why the Prophet puts these questions: and a question has much more force when it refers to what is in no way doubtful. What! can God be angry with rivers? Who can imagine God to be so unreasonable as to disturb the sea and to change the nature of things, when a certain order has been established by his own command? Why should he dry the sea, except he had something in view, even the deliverance of his Church? except he intended to save his people from extreme danger, by stretching forth his hand to the Israelites, when they thought themselves utterly lost? He therefore denies, that when God dried the Red Sea, and when he stopped the flowing of Jordan, he had put forth his power against the sea or against the river, as though he was angry with them. The design of God, says the Prophet, was quite another; for God *rode on his horses*, that is, he intended to show that all the elements were under his command, and that for the salvation of his people. That God, then, might be the redeemer of his Church, he constrained Jordan to turn back its course, he constrained the Red Sea to make a passage for his miserable captives, who would have otherwise been exposed to the slaughter of their enemies. There was indeed no hope of saving Israel, without a passage being suddenly opened to them through the Red Sea.

> Did thy wrath against rivers, O Jehovah,
> Did it kindle against rivers?

Some connect the two last lines of the verse with the previous one, thus—

> Was thine indignation against the sea,
> When thou didst ride on thy horses,
> On thy chariots of salvation?

But *Calvin* considers them rather as an answer to the previous questions, or as explanatory; and they may be thus rendered—

> When thou didst ride on thy horses,
> Thy chariots were *those* of salvation.

It is observed by *Henderson*, that "there is no necessity for our understanding either the angels or thunder and lightning by 'horses' and 'chariots.' They are," he adds, "merely figurative expressions, designed to carry out the metaphor adopted from military operations." Or it may be, that the horses and chariots of the Israelites are here meant, as in the 11th verse, the arrows and spears of the people are spoken of as those of God.—*Ed.*

Hence all these miracles were designed to show that God had become the redeemer of his Church, and had put forth his power for the salvation of those whom he had taken under his protection: and it is easy from this fact to conclude, that the same help ought to be expected from God by posterity; for God was not induced by some sudden impulse to change the nature of things, but exhibited a proof of his favour: and his grace is perpetual, and flows in an even course, though not according to the apprehension of men; for it suffers some interruptions, because God exercises the faithful under the cross; yet his goodness never ceases. It hence follows that the faithful are to entertain hope; for God, when he pleases, and when he sees it expedient, will really show the same power which was formerly exhibited to the fathers. It now follows—

9. Thy bow was made quite naked, *according* to the oaths of the tribes, *even thy* word. Selah. Thou didst cleave the earth with rivers.

9. Nudando nudatus fuit (*vel,* manifestatione manifestus fuit) arcus tuus; juramenta Tribuum, sermo: Selach: fluviis scindes terram.

The Prophet explains the same thing more clearly in this verse—that the power of God was formerly manifested for no other reason but that the children of Abraham might be taught to expect from him a continued deliverance: for he says that *the bow* of God *was made bare.* By the "bow," he means also the sword and other weapons; as though he had said, that God was then armed, as we have found declared before. God therefore was then furnished with weapons, and marched to the battle, having undertaken the cause of his chosen people, that he might defend them against the wicked. Since it was so, we hence see that these miracles were not to avail only for one period, but were intended perpetually to encourage the faithful to look ever for the aid of God, even in the midst of death; for he can find escapes, though they may not appear to us.

We now see the import of the text; but he emphatically adds, *The oaths of the tribes;* for hereby he more fully confirms that God had not then assisted the children of Abraham, so as to discard them afterwards; but that he had really proved how true he was in his promises; for by the oaths of (or to) the tribes he means the covenant that God had made not only with Abraham, but also with his posterity for ever. He puts oaths in the plural number, because God had not only once promised to be a God to Abraham and to his seed, but had often repeated the same promise, in order that faith might be rendered more certain, inasmuch as we have need of more than one thing to confirm us. For we see how our infirmity always vacillates, unless God supplies us with many props. As, then, God had often confirmed his servant Abraham, the Prophet speaks here of his oaths: but then as to the substance, the oath of God is the same; which was, that he had taken the race of Abraham under his protection, and promised that they should be to him a peculiar people, and, especially, that he had united the people under one head; for except Christ had been introduced, that covenant of God would not have been ratified nor valid. As, then, God had once included every thing, when he said to Abraham, "I am God Almighty, and I shall be a God to you and to your children;" it is certain that nothing was added when God afterwards confirmed the faith of Abraham: but yet the Prophet does not without reason use the plural number; it was done, that the faithful might recumb with less fear on God's promise, seeing that it had been so often and by so many words confirmed.

He calls them too *the oaths to the tribes:* for though God had spoken to Abraham and afterwards to Moses, yet the promise was deposited in the hands of Abraham, and of the patriarchs, and afterwards in those of Moses, that the people might understand that it belonged equally to them; for it would have been no great matter to promise what we read of to a few men only. But Abraham was as it were the depository; and it was a certain solemn stipulation made with his whole race. We hence see why the Prophet here mentions the tribes rather than Abraham, or the patriarchs, or Moses. He had indeed a special regard to those of his own time, in order to confirm them, that they might not doubt but that God would extend to them also the same power. How so? Because God had formerly wrought in a wonderful manner for the deliverance of his people. Why? That he might prove himself to be true and faithful. In what respect? Because he had said, that he would be the protector of his people; and he did not adopt a few men only, but the whole race of Abraham. Since it was so, why should not his posterity hope for that which they knew was promised to their fathers? for the truth of God can never fail. Though many ages had passed away, the faith of his people ought to have remained certain, for God intended to show himself to be the same as he had been formerly known by their fathers.

He afterwards adds אמר, *amer*, which means a word or speech; but it is to be taken here for a fixed and an irrevocable word. The word, אמר, *amer*, he says; that is, as they say, the word and the deed: for when we say, that words are given, we often understand that those who liberally promise are false men, and that we are only trifled with and disappointed when we place confidence in them. But the term, word, is sometimes taken in a good sense. "This is the word," we often say, when we intend to remove every doubt. We now then perceive what the Prophet meant by adding אמר, *amer*, the word. "O Lord, thou hast not given mere words to thy people; but what has proceeded from thy mouth has been found to be true and valid. Such, therefore, is thy faithfulness in thy promises, that we ought not to entertain the least doubt as to the event. As soon as thou givest to us any hope, we ought to feel assured of its accomplishment, as though it were not a word but the exhibition of the thing itself." In short, by this term the Prophet commends the faithfulness of God, lest we should harbour doubts as to his promises.[1]

---

[1] This clause has been variously explained: the interpretation here given has been mostly adopted. In the Barberinean manuscript the whole of this prayer is given in many respects different from the present received text of the Septuagint, and this clause is thus found in it—ἐχέρτασας βολίδας τῆς φαρέτρας αὐτοῦ—Thou hast satiated the arrows (or darts) of his quiver. It is evident that this idea falls in more with the preceding clause than any other; and the Hebrew will admit of a sense bordering on this with less alteration than any other that has been offered. No version has been

He then says, that *by rivers had been cleft the earth.* He refers, I doubt not, to the history we read in Num. xiv; for the Lord, when the people were nearly dead through thirst, drew forth water from the rock, and caused a river to flow wherever the people journeyed. As then he had cleft the earth to make a perpetual course for the stream, and thus supplied the people in dry places with abundance of water, the Prophet says here, that the *earth had been cleft by rivers or streams.* It was indeed but one river; but he amplifies, and justly so, that remarkable work of God. He afterwards adds—

10. The mountains saw thee, *and* they trembled: the overflowing of the water passed by: the deep uttered his voice, *and* lifted up his hands on high.

10. Viderunt me, timuerunt montes; inundatio (*vel,* gurges) aquarum transivit; dedit abyssus vocem suam; in altum manus suas sustulit (*vel,* altitudo, רוֹם; *potest tam in casu nominandi legi quàm in accusativo.*)

Habakkuk proceeds with the history of the people's redemption. We have said what his object was, even this—

given without supposing something to be understood. *Newcome* says, that sixteen MSS. read שׂבעת; by leaving out the ו, it may be a verb in Kal in the past tense, as rendered above, and writers might have easily put down אמר for אזור. Then the line in Hebrew would be,

שׁבעת מטות אזור :
"Thou hast filled with arrows the girdle."

It is a description of one equipped for battle; his bow was made ready, and he had filled his girdle, that is, his military girdle, with arrows: for this girdle the preceding Greek version introduced the quiver, in which arrows were commonly carried. The word מטות, means rods or staves, that is, of arrows, as we may take it here. This is the most satisfactory solution of the difficulties connected with this line, of which there have been, as *Henderson* says, more than a hundred interpretations.

The last clause of the verse is thus rendered by *Newcome,*—
Thou didst cleave the streams of the land;
and by *Henderson,*—
Thou didst cleave the earth into rivers.

The words will not admit the first version; the genitive case in Hebrew is always by juxtaposition; here "streams" and "earth" are separated by the verb. The other version contains hardly a meaning. The most literal rendering is that given by *Calvin,* and it affords the best sense. The words will admit of the following, which is materially the same,—
By streams didst thou cleave the earth.

The allusion evidently is to the streams of that water which miraculously issued from the smitten rock, and followed the Israelites in the wilderness. —*Ed.*

that the people, though in an extreme state of calamity, might yet entertain hope of God's favour; for he became not a Redeemer to the race of Abraham for one time, but that he might continue the same favour to them to the end.

He says that *mountains had seen and grieved.* Some explain this allegorically of kings, and say, that they grieved when envy preyed on them: but this view is too strained. The Prophet, I have no doubt, means simply, that the mountains obeyed God, so as to open a way for his people. At the same time, the verb חול, *chul,* signifies not only to grieve, but also to bring forth, and then to fall and to abide in the same place. We might then with no less propriety read thus—*see thee did the mountains, and were still,* or fell down; that is, they were subservient to thy command, and did not intercept the way of thy people. I think the real meaning of the Prophet to be, that God had formerly imprinted on all the elements evident marks of his paternal favour, so that the posterity of Abraham might ever confide in him as their deliverer in all their distresses: and even the context requires this meaning; for he subjoins—

The stream or the inundation *of waters,* &c.: and this second part cannot be explained allegorically. We then see, that the import of the words is—That God removed all obstacles, so that neither mountains, nor waters, nor sea, nor rivers, intercepted the passage of the people. He says now, that the inundation of waters had passed away. This applies both to Jordan and to the Red Sea; for God separated the Red Sea, so that the waters stood apart, contrary to the laws of nature, and the same thing happened to Jordan; for the flowing of the water was stayed, and a way was opened, so that the people passed over dryshod into the land of Canaan. Thus took place what is said by the Prophet, *the stream of waters passed away.* We indeed know that such is the abundance of waters in the sea and in the rivers, that they cannot be dried up: when therefore waters disappear, it is what is beyond the course of nature. The Prophet, therefore, records this miracle, that the faithful might know, that though the whole world were resisting, their salvation would still be certain; for the Lord can surmount whatever impediments there may be.

He then ascribes life to waters; for he says, that *the abyss gave its voice,* and also, that *the deep lifted up its hands;* or that the abyss with uplifted hands was ready to obey God. It is a striking personification; for though the abyss is void of intelligence, and it cannot speak, yet the Prophet says, that the abyss with its voice and uplifted hands testified its obedience, when God would have his people to pass through to the promised land. When anxious to testify our obedience, we do this both with our voice and in our gesture. When any one is willing to do what is commanded, he says, "Here I am," or "I promise to do this." As, then, servants respond to orders, so the Prophet says, that a voice was uttered by the abyss. The abyss indeed uttered no voice; but the event itself surpassed all voices. Now when a whole people meet together, they raise their hands; for their consent cannot be understood except by the outstretching of the hands, and hence came the word hand-extending, $\chi\epsilon\iota\rho\sigma\tau o\nu i a$. This similitude the Prophet now takes, and says, that the abyss raised up its hands; that is, showed its consent by this gesture. As when men declare by this sign that they will do what they are bidden; so also the abyss lifted up its hands. If we read, The deep raised up its hands, the sense will be the same.[1] Let us proceed—

| 11. The sun *and* moon stood still in their habitation: at the light of thine arrows they went, *and* at the shining of thy glittering spear. | 11. Sol, luna stetit in habitaculo, ad lucem sagittarum tuarum ambulabunt, ad splendorem fulguris hastæ tuæ. |

[1] Most critics have overlooked the peculiar construction of this verse; but it presents a striking instance of the order in which the Prophets often arrange their ideas. There are two things referred to—the mountains and the waters—and the first verb regards both; the nominative case being anticipated, and the first of the two last lines refers to the waters, and the last to the mountains. This is the literal version,—
They saw thee,—in pain were the mountains,
The flood of waters passed away:
Utter did the deep its voice,
The height its hands lifted up.
To construe רוֹם adverbially, "on high," does not so well comport with the character of the Hebrew language; and it evidently here refers to the "mountains," as the "deep" refers to the waters.—*Ed.*

Here the Prophet refers to another history; for we know that when Joshua fought, and when the day was not long enough to slay the enemies, the day was prolonged according to his prayer, (Josh. x. 12.) He seems indeed to have authoritatively commanded the sun to stay its course: but there is no doubt, but that having been answered as to his prayer, when he expressed this, he commanded the sun, as he did, through the secret impulse of the Holy Spirit: and we know that the sun would not have stopped in its course, except the moon also was stayed. There must indeed have been the same action as to these two luminaries.

Hence Habakkuk says, that the *sun and moon stood still in their habitation;* that is, that the sun then rested as it were in its dwelling. When it was hastening in its course, it then stood still for the benefit of God's people. *The sun then and the moon stood,*—How? *At the light of thy arrows shall they walk.* Some refer this to the pillar of fire, as though the Prophet had said, that the Israelites walked by that light, by which God guided them: but I doubt not but that this is said of the sun. The whole sentence is thus connected—that the sun and moon walked, not as from the beginning, but at the light of God's arrows; that is, when instead of God's command, which the sun had received from the beginning as its direction, the sun had God's arrows, which guided it, retarded its course, or restrained the velocity which it had before. There is then an implied contrast between the progress of the sun which it had by nature to that day, and that new direction, when the sun was retained, that it might give place to the arrows of God, and to the sword and the spear; for by the arrows and the spear he means nothing else but the weapons of the elect people; for we know, that when that people fought under the protection of God, they were armed as it were from above. As then it is said of Gideon, "The sword of God and of Gideon;" so also in this place the Prophet calls whatever armour the people of Israel had, the arrows of God and his spear; for that people could not move—no, not a finger's breadth—without the command of God. The sun then was wont before to regard the ordinary command, of which we read in

Genesis; but it was then directed for another purpose: for it had regard to the arrows of God flying on the earth as lightning; and it had regard to the arrows, as though it stood astonished and dared not to advance. Why? because it behoved it to submit to God while he was carrying on war.[1] We now then perceive how much kindness is included in these words.

What, therefore, we have already referred to, ought to be borne in mind—that in this place there is no frigid narrative, but such things are brought before the faithful as avail to confirm their hope, that they may feel assured, that the power of God is sufficient for the purpose of delivering them; for it was for this end that he formerly wrought so many miracles. It follows—

| 12. Thou didst march through the land in indignation, thou didst thrash the heathen in anger. | 12. In ira calcasti terram (*vel*, ambulasti super terram; צָעַד *enim significat ambulare;*) in ira (*est tamen aliud nomen, ergo vertamus uno loco*, indignationem, *vel*, furorem,—in furore) triturasti gentes (*vel*, triturabis.) |

The Prophet relates here the entrance of the people into the land of Canaan, that the faithful might know that their fathers would not have obtained so many victories had not God put forth the power and strength of his hand. Hence he says, that God himself *had trampled on the land in anger.* For how could the Israelites have dared to attack so many

---

[1] There is much beauty and force in this explanation: and accordant with it is the version of *Henderson*. But that of *Newcome* is somewhat different—

    The sun *and* the moon stood still *in their* habitation:
    By *their* light thine arrows went abroad;
    By *their* brightness, the lightning of thy spear.

To avoid the insertion of so many words in italics, which are not in the original, I would render the verse thus—

    The sun! the moon!—it stood,—she remained stationary,
    For light to thine arrows *which* went forth,
    For brightness to the flashing of thy spear.

The genitive case is often to be rendered as a dative, as in Jer. xxxi. 35, לְאוֹר לַיְלָה, "for the light of the night;" that is, "for light to the night." There are twelve MSS. which have "and," וְ, before "moon:" but it is not wanted, the verb "stood" being singular; and it is followed, as I conceive, by another verb in the singular number, and in the feminine gender, while "stood" is in the masculine, and refers to the moon, and the last refers to the sun, which is sometimes feminine, while moon is ever masculine. The verb זָבַל is not properly to dwell, but to continue fixed, or to remain stationary. The order in our language would be this—

    The sun remained stationary, the moon stood.—*Ed.*

nations, who had lately come forth from so miserable a bondage? They had indeed been in the desert for forty years; but they were always trembling and fearful, and we also know that they were weak and feeble. How then was it, that they overcame most powerful kings? that they made war with nations accustomed to war? Doubtless God himself *trod down the land in his wrath,* and also *threshed the nations:* as it is said in Ps. xliv. 5, " It was not by their own sword that they got the land of Canaan; neither their own power, nor their own hand saved them; but the Lord showed favour to them, and became their Deliverer." Justly then does the Prophet ascribe this to God, that he himself walked over the land; for otherwise the Israelites would never have dared to move a foot. Doubtless, they could never have been settled in that land, had not God gone before them. Hence when God did tread on the land in his anger, then it became a quiet habitation to the children of Abraham; warlike nations were then easily and without much trouble conquered by the Israelites, though they were previously very weak.

We now see, that the Prophet sets forth here before the eyes of the people their entrance into the land, that they might know that God did not in vain put to flight so many nations at one time; but that the land of Canaan might be the perpetual inheritance of his chosen people.

The Prophet changes often the tenses of the verbs, inconsistently with the common usage of the Hebrew language; but it must be observed, that he so refers to those histories, as though God were continually carrying on his operations; and as though his presence was to be looked for in adversities, the same as what he had granted formerly to the fathers. Hence the change of tenses does not obscure the sense, but, on the contrary, shows to us the design of the Prophet, and helps us to understand the meaning. It follows at length—

13. Thou wentest forth for the salvation of thy people, *even* for salvation with thine anointed; thou woundedst the head out of the house of the wicked, by discovering the foundation unto the neck. Selah.

13. Egressus es in salutem populi tui, in salutem cum Christo tuo; transfodisti caput è domo impii, nudando fundamentum usque ad collum. Selah.

The Prophet applies again to the present state of the people what he had before recorded—that God went forth with his Christ for the salvation of his people. Some consider that there is understood a particle of comparison, and repeat the verb twice, " As thou didst then go forth for the deliverance of thy people, so now wilt thou go forth for the deliverance of thy people with thy Christ." But this repetition is strained. I therefore take the words of the Prophet simply as they are—that God went forth for the deliverance of his people. But when God's people are spoken of, their gratuitous adoption must ever be remembered. How was it that the children of Abraham became the peculiar people of God? Did this proceed from any worthiness? Did it come to them naturally? None of these things can be alleged. Though then they differed in nothing from other nations, yet God was pleased to choose them to be a people to himself. By the title, the people of God, is therefore intimated their adoption. Now this adoption was not temporary or momentary, but was to continue to the end. Hence it was easy for the faithful to draw this conclusion—that they were to hope from God the same help as what he had formerly granted to the fathers.

Thou wentest forth, he says, *for the salvation, for the salvation of thy people.* He repeats the word salvation, and not without reason; for he wished to call attention to this point, as when he had said before—that God had not in vain manifested, by so many miracles, his power, as though he were angry with the sea and with rivers, but had respect to the preservation of his people. Since then the salvation of the Church has ever been the design of God in working miracles, why should the faithful be now cast down, when for a time they were oppressed by adversities? for God ever remains the same: and why should they despond, especially since that ancient deliverance, and also those many deliverances, of which he had hitherto spoken, are so many evidences of his everlasting covenant. These indeed ought to be connected with the word of God; that is, with that promise, according to which he had received the children of Abraham into favour for the purpose of protecting them to the end. "For salvation, for salvation," says the Prophet, and that of his elect people.

He adds, *with thy Christ*. This clause still more confirms what Habakkuk had in view—that God had been from the beginning the deliverer of his people in the person of the Mediator. When God, therefore, delivered his people from the hand of Pharaoh, when he made a way for them to pass through the Red Sea, when he redeemed them by doing wonders, when he subdued before them the most powerful nations, when he changed the laws of nature in their behalf—all these things he did through the Mediator. For God could never have been propitious either to Abraham himself or to his posterity, had it not been for the intervention of a Mediator. Since then it has ever been the office of the Mediator to preserve in safety the Church of God, the Prophet takes it now for granted, that Christ was now manifested in much clearer light than formerly; for David was his lively image, as well as his successors. God then gave a living representation of his Christ when he erected a kingdom in the person of David; and he promised that this kingdom should endure as long as the sun and moon should shine in the heavens. Since, then, there were in the time of Habakkuk clearer prophecies than in past times respecting the eternity of this kingdom, ought not the people to have taken courage, and to have known of a certainty that God would be their Deliverer, when Christ should come? We now then apprehend the meaning of the Prophet.[1] But

---

[1] However true is what is said here, it seems not to be the doctrine of this text. The version of *Aquila* and the *Vulgate* have been followed as to the second clause of the verse. The *Septuagint* read, τοῦ σῶσαι τὸν χριστόν σου—to save thy Christ; or, according to Alex. cod., "thy Christs—τοὺς χριστούς σου;" or, according to Barb. MS., "thine elect—τοὺς ἐκλεκτούς σου." Five Hebrew MSS. have מְשִׁיחֶיךָ, "thine anointed ones." But if we retain the present text, there is no difficulty; for it refers to the "people" in the preceding line; or it may refer to Joshua and his successors, the singular being used, as it is often done by the Prophets, in the collective sense. The particle אֵת before it is not often used as a preposition; and the word ישע may better be taken here as a verb, according to the *Septuagint*, than as a noun, though as a verb it most commonly occurs in *Hiphil*: but see 1 Samuel xxiii. 5; 2 Samuel viii. 6. The following would then be the version—

    Go forth didst thou to save thy people,
    To save thine anointed:

I cannot now go farther; I shall defer the subject until to-morrow.

PRAYER.

Grant, Almighty God, that as thou hast so often and in such various ways testified formerly how much care and solicitude thou hast for the salvation of those who rely and call on thee,—O grant, that we at this day may experience the same: and though thy face is justly hid from us, may we yet never hesitate to flee to thee, since thou hast made a covenant through thy Son, which is founded in thine infinite mercy. Grant then, that we, being humbled in true penitence, may so surrender ourselves to thy Son, that we may be led to thee, and find thee to be no less a Father to us than to the faithful of old, as thou everywhere testifiest to us in thy word, until at length being freed from all troubles and dangers, we come to that blessed rest which thy Son has purchased for us by his own blood. Amen.

Lecture One Hundred and Seventeenth.

We explained yesterday why the Prophet says that God went forth for the salvation of the elect people with his Christ. His purpose was to confirm still more the faithful in the hope of their deliverance; for God is not only the same, and never changes his purpose, but the same Mediator also performs his office, through whom the people were formerly preserved. We must also notice this difference, to which I referred yesterday; for as God had then more clearly manifested Christ, with more cheerfulness it behoved the faithful to go on, as they had so remarkable a pledge of God's favour, inasmuch as God had promised that the kingdom of God would be for ever.

> Thou didst smite the head from the house of the wicked,
> Emptying out the foundation even to the neck.

The reference in the two last lines is evidently to the rooting out of the Canaanites, and not, as *Newcome* thinks, to the destruction of the first-born in Egypt. The singular is poetically used for the plural: "head," instead of heads, or chiefs, &c. The last line seems to be a proverbial saying, signifying an entire demolition, the very foundation being dug up, though so deep as to reach up to man's neck. There is no MS. nor version to countenance צור, "rock," which *Houbigant* and *Newcome* adopt.—*Ed.*

He adds, that *wounded was the head from the house of the wicked;* that is, that there was no power which had not been laid prostrate by God for the sake of his people; and we know that all the great kings were formerly destroyed, in order that favour might be shown to God's people. The other comparison seems different, and yet its object is the same—that God *had made bare the foundation to the neck;* that is, that he had destroyed from the roots his enemies; for by foundation he means, in a metaphorical sense, whatever stability there was in these enemies, and that this was torn up and overthrown to the very neck, that is, to the very summit; for the body of men, we know, is covered from the neck to the feet. And he says that their houses, that is their families, were made bare to the neck, for the Lord had destroyed them all from the bottom to the top. We now understand what the Prophet meant.

As to the word סלה, *selah*, I have hitherto said nothing; but I shall now briefly refer to what the Hebrew interpreters think. Some explain it by לעולם, *laoulam*, "for ever;" and by עד ועד, *od uod*, "yet and yet;" as though, when this word is inserted, the Holy Spirit pronounced what is to be for ever. Others render it by אמן, *amen*, as though God testified that what is said is true and indubitable. But as it never occurs except in this song and in the Psalms, and does not always comport with what they say, that is, that it denotes certainty or perpetuity, I prefer embracing the opinion of those who think that it refers to singing, and not to things. And what they add is also probable, if we regard its etymology, for the word means to raise or to elevate; and it was therefore put down to remind the singers to raise their voice. But as it is a thing of no great importance, it is enough shortly to state what others think. Let us now go on—

14. Thou didst strike through with his staves the head of his villages: they came out as a whirlwind to scatter me: their rejoicing *was* as to devour the poor secretly.

14. Perforasti baculis ejus caput villarum ejus; prosilierunt instar turbinis ad dispellendum me; exultatio eorum sicut ad vorandum pauperem in abscondito.

At the beginning of this verse the Prophet pursues the

same subject—that God had wounded all the enemies of his people; and he says that the head of villages or towns had been wounded, though some think that פְּרָזִים, *perezim*, mean rather the inhabitants of towns; for the Hebrews call fortified towns or villages פְּרָזוֹת, *perezut*, and the word is commonly found in the feminine gender; but as it is here a masculine noun, it is thought that it means the inhabitants. At the same time this does not much affect the subject; for the Prophet simply means, that not only kings had been overthrown by God's hand, but also all the provinces under their authority; as though he had said that God's vengeance, when his purpose was to defend his people, advanced through all the villages and through every region, so that not a corner was safe.[1] But we must also notice what follows—*with his rods.* The Prophet means that the wicked had been smitten by their own sword. Though the word rods is put here, it is yet to be taken for all kinds of instruments or weapons; it is the same as though it was said that they had been wounded by their own hands.[2]

We now perceive the import of this clause—that God not only put forth his strength when he purposed to crush the enemies of his people, but that he had also smitten them with infatuation and madness, so that they destroyed themselves by their own hands. And this was done, as in the case of the Madianites, who, either by turning their swords against one another, fell by mutual wounds, or by slaying themselves, perished by their own hands. (Judg. vii. 2.) We indeed often read of the wicked that they ensnared themselves, fell into the pit which they had made, and, in short, perished through their own artifices; and the Prophet says here that the enemies of the Church had fallen, through

---

[1] The Keri and many MSS. read פְּרָזָיו. "his villages;" but there is no need of this change, for the singular is used throughout instead of the plural, until we come to the two following lines; and this proves that the singular is to be taken in a collective sense. *Henderson* renders it "captains," contrary to the meaning of the word in other parts. It means an open unfortified village, as it were scattered, and without any boundaries.—*Ed.*

[2] *Newcome* and some others, without any authority, read "thy rod;" but conjecture, without some solid reason, cannot be allowed.—*Ed.*

God's singular kindness, though no one rose up against them; for they had transfixed or wounded themselves by their own staff. Some read—"Thou hast cursed his sceptres and the head of his villages;" but the interpretation which I have given is much more appropriate.

He adds, that they *came like a whirlwind.* It is indeed a verb in the future tense; but the sentence must be thus rendered—"When they rushed as a whirlwind to cast me down, when their exultation was to devour the poor in their hiding-places." It is indeed only a single verb, but it comes from סער, *sor,* which means a whirlwind, and we cannot render it otherwise than by a paraphrase. They rushed, he says, like a whirlwind. The Prophet here enlarges on the subject of God's power, for he had checked the enemies of his people when they rushed on with so much impetuosity. Had their advance been slow God might have frustrated their attempts without a miracle, but as their own madness rendered them precipitate, and made them to be like a whirlwind, God's power was more clearly known in restraining such violence. We now understand the import of what is here said; for the Prophet's special object is not to complain of the violent and impetuous rage of enemies, but to exalt the power of God in checking the violent assaults of of those enemies whom he saw raging against his people.

He subjoins, *their exultation was to devour the poor.* He intimates that there was nothing in the world capable of resisting the wicked, had not God brought miraculous help from heaven; for when they came to devour the poor, they came not to wage war, but to devour the prey like wild beasts. Then he says, *to devour the poor in secret.* He means, that the people of God had no strength to resist, except help beyond all hope came from heaven.[1]

The import of the whole is—that when the miserable Israelites were without any protection, and exposed to the

---

[1] "To devour the poor in secret" seems to have an allusion to the practice of wild beasts, who take their prey to their dens to devour it there. The poor here, as in many other places, mean the helpless, such as are destitute of aid or of power to resist their enemies. The line may be thus rendered—
Their joy *was,* as it were, to devour the helpless in secret.—*Ed.*

rage and cruelty of their enemies, they had been miraculously helped; for the Lord destroyed their enemies by their own swords; and that when they came, as it were to enjoy a victory, to take the prey, they were laid prostrate by the hand of God: hence his power shone forth more brightly. It follows—

15. Thou didst walk through the sea with thine horses, *through* the heap of great waters.

15. Viam fecisti in mari equis tuis per acervum aquarum magnarum.

Some read, "Thou hast trodden thy horses in the sea;" but it is a solecism, that is quite evident. Others, "Thou hast trodden in the sea by thy horses." But what need is there of seeking such strained explanations, since the verb דרך, *darek*, means to go or to march? The Prophet's meaning is by no means doubtful—that God would make a way for himself in the sea, and on his own horses. How? even when *great waters were gathered into a mass*. The Prophet again refers to the history of the passage through the Red Sea; for it was a work of God, as it has been said, worthy of being remembered above all other works: it is therefore no wonder that the Prophet dwells so much in setting forth this great miracle. *Thou* then *didst make a way for thy horses*—where? *in the sea;* which was contrary to nature. And then he adds, *The heap of waters:* for the waters had been gathered together, and a firm and thick mass appeared, which was not according to nature; for we know that water is a fluid, and that hardly a drop of water can stand without flowing.[1] How then was it that he stopped the course of Jordan, and that the Red Sea was divided? These were

[1] The word is חמר, which many have rendered *acervus*—heap; but there is no clear instance in which it has such a meaning. It is without a preposition, and the *Septuagint* render it by a participle, ταρασσοντας, which agrees with "horses." It is singular in Hebrew, and, if a participle, it agrees with the nominative case to the preceding verb, דרכת, "thou didst guide" or direct. The two lines might then be rendered thus,—
 Thou didst guide through the sea thy horses,
 Disturbing mighty waters.
Both *Marckius* and *Henderson* think that the passage through the Red Sea is not what is meant; but the subjugation of the Canaanites, conveyed in a language derived from that event.—*Ed.*

evidences of God's incomprehensible power, and rightly ought these to have added courage to the faithful, knowing, as they ought to have done, that nothing could have opposed their salvation, which God was not able easily to remove, whenever it pleased him. It follows—

16. When I heard, my belly trembled; my lips quivered at the voice: rottenness entered into my bones, and I trembled in myself, that I might rest in the day of trouble: when he cometh up unto the people, he will invade them with his troops.

16. Audivi, et contremuit (*vel*, tumultuatus est) venter meus; ad vocem trepidarunt labia mea; ingressa est putredo in ossa mea; et apud me tumultuatus sum (*ad verbum*, tumultuabitur; *sed diximus heri de temporibus verborum*,) ut requiescam in die afflictionis, ad ascendendum ad populum, excidet eum (*vel*, colliget se.)

Those interpreters are mistaken in my view, who connect the verb, "I have heard," with the last verse, as though the Prophet had said, that he had conceived dread from those evidences of God's power: for the Prophet had no occasion to fear in regarding God as armed with unexpected power for the salvation of his people; there was no reason for such a thing. Hence these things do not agree together. But he returns again to that dread which he had entertained on account of God's voice in those terrific threatenings which we before referred to. We must always bear in mind the Prophet's design—that his object was to humble the faithful, that they might suppliantly acknowledge to God their sins and solicit his forgiveness. His purpose also was to animate them with strong hope, that they might nevertheless look for deliverance. He had already said at the beginning, "Lord, I have heard thy voice; I feared." He now repeats the same thing: for if he had spoken only of that terrific voice, the faithful might have been overwhelmed with despair; he therefore wished opportunely to prevent this evil, by interposing what might have comforted them. For this reason he recited these histories, by which God had proved that he was armed with invincible power to save his Church. Having done this, he applies his general doctrine to present circumstances, and says, "I have heard." What had he heard? even those judgments with which God had determined to visit the contumacy of his people. Since, then,

God had threatened his people with a horrible destruction, the Prophet says now, that he had heard and trembled, so that he had been confounded. He speaks in the singular number; but this was done, as we have said, because he represented the whole people, as was the case before (which escaped my notice) when he said, his enemies came like whirlwind to cast him down; for certainly he did not then speak of himself but of the ancient people. As, then, the Prophet here undertakes the cause of the whole Church, he speaks as though he were the collective body of the people: and so he says that he had heard; but the faithful speak here as with one mouth, that they had *heard*, and that their *inside trembled*.

Some read, "I was dismayed, or I feared, and my inside trembled at his voice." He takes קוֹל, *kul*, voice, not for report, but, as it has been said, for threatenings. The faithful, then, declare here, that they dreaded the voice of God, before he had executed his judgments, or before he inflicted the punishment which he had threatened. He says, *quiver did my lips*. The verb צלל, *tsalel*, means sometimes to tingle, and so some render it here, "Tingle did my lips;" but this is not suitable, and more tolerable is the rendering of others, "Palpitate did my lips." The Hebrews say that what is meant is that motion in the lips which fear or trembling produces. I therefore render the words, "quiver did my lips;" as when one says in our language, *Mes levres ont barbaté;* that is, when the whole body shakes with trembling, not only a noise is made by the clashing of the teeth, but an agitation is also observed in the lips.

Enter, he says, *did rottenness into my bones and within myself I made a noise*, (it is the verb רגז, *regaz*, again,) or I trembled. No doubt the Prophet describes here the dread, which could not have been otherwise than produced by the dreadful vengeance of God. It hence follows that he does not treat here of those miracles which were, on the contrary, calculated to afford an occasion of rejoicing both to the Prophet and to the whole of the chosen people; but that the vengeance of God, such as had been predicted, is described here.

He now adds, *That I may rest in the day of affliction*.[1] There seems to be here an inconsistency—that the Prophet was affected with grief even to rottenness, that he trembled throughout his members with dread, and now that all this availed to produce rest. But we must inquire how rest is to be obtained through these trepidations, and dreads, and tremblings. We indeed know that the more hardened the wicked become against God, the more grievous ruin they ever procure for themselves. But there is no way of obtaining rest, except for a time we tremble within ourselves, that is, except God's judgment awakens us, yea, and reduces us almost to nothing. Whosoever therefore securely slumbers,

---

[1] The word אשר, which *Calvin* renders *ut*, "that," has occasioned great trouble to critics. *Marckius* reads *qui*—" who," "Who shall rest," &c.; *Henderson*, "yet," "Yet I shall have rest," &c. But it is never found as an adversative. The construction of this line and the following is very difficult; and many have been the forms in which they have been rendered. The verb נוח means not only to *rest* from action or labour, but also to *rest* in the sense of remaining or continuing. See 2 Kings ii. 15, and Is. ii. 2. And were it taken in this latter sense here, there would be a consistency in the whole passage. The Prophet describes first the dread which seized him on hearing the report of God's vengeance; and then in the two last lines he accounts for his consternation, because he should remain to witness this vengeance; and he proceeds in verse 17 to set forth the effects of it, and in verse 18 he states that he would still rejoice in the God of his salvation. The three verses may be thus rendered,—

16. I heard,—and tremble did my bowels;
 At the voice my lips quivered;
 Enter does rottenness into my bones,
 And on my own account I tremble;
 Because I shall remain to the day of distress,
 To *his* coming up to the people, *who* shall invade us.
17. For the fig-tree shall not shoot forth,
 And no produce *shall be* on the vines;
 Fail shall the fruit of the olive,
 And the fields, none shall yield food;
 Cut off from the fold shall be the sheep,
 And no ox *shall be* in the stalls:
18. But as for me, in Jehovah will I rejoice,
 I will exult in the God of my salvation.

"On my own account," or for myself, תחתי: the preposition, תחת, is often taken in this sense; See 2 Sam. xix. 21, Prov. xxx. 21. "Invade us" or assault us, or them, the people, יגודנו; for נו is either us or him, but in our language them, for so we speak of people. "And the fields, none," &c. There are instances of לא, as here, in which it may be rendered "none" and "nothing." See Ezek. xx. 38, Job vi. 21, viii. 9. "In the God," &c.; it may be rendered, "In my God, my Saviour," as it is in the *Septuagint* and the *Vulgate*.—*Ed.*

will be confounded in the day of affliction; but he who in time anticipates the wrath of God, and is touched with fear, as soon as he hears that God the judge is at hand, provides for himself the most secure rest in the day of affliction. We now then see, that the right way of seeking rest is set forth here by the Prophet, when he says, that he had been confounded, and that rottenness had entered into his bones—that he could have no comfort, except he pined away as one half-dead: and the design of the Prophet, as I have already said, was to exhort the faithful to repentance. But we cannot truly and from the heart repent, until our sins become displeasing to us: and the hatred of sin proceeds from the fear of God, and that sorrow which Paul regards as the mother of repentance. (2 Cor. vii. 10.)

This exhortation is also very necessary for us in the present day. We see how inclined we are by nature to indifference; and when God brings before us our sins, and then sets before us his wrath, we are not moved; and when we entertain any fear, it soon vanishes. Let us, then, know that no rest can be to us in the day of distress, except we tremble within ourselves, except dread lays hold on all our faculties, and except all our soul becomes almost rotten. And hence it is said in Ps. iv. 4, "Tremble, and ye shall not sin." And Paul also shows that the true and profitable way of being angry is, when one is angry with his sins (Eph. iv. 26,) and when we tremble within ourselves. In the same manner does the Prophet describe the beginnings of repentance, when he says, that the faithful trembled in their bowels, and were so shaken within, that even their lips quivered, and, in short, (and this is the sum of the whole,) that all their senses felt consternation and fear.

He says, *When he shall ascend:* he speaks, no doubt, of the Chaldeans; *When therefore the enemy shall ascend against the people, that he may cut them off:* for גדה or גוד, g*a*de or g*u*d, means to cut off, and it means also to gather, and so some render it, "that he may gather them:" but the other meaning is better, "when the enemy shall ascend, that he may cut them off." If one would have the word God to be understood, I do not object: for the Prophet does not otherwise speak of the Chaldeans than as the ministers and executioners of God's wrath.

In short, he intimates, that they who had been moved and really terrified by God's vengeance, would be in a quiet state when God executed his judgments. How so? because they would calmly submit to the rod, and look for a happy deliverance from their evils; for their minds would be seasonably prepared for patience, and then the Lord would also console them, as it is said in Ps. li. 17, that he despises not contrite hearts. When, therefore, the faithful are in a suitable time humbled, and when they thus anticipate the judgment of God, they then find a rest prepared for them in his bosom. It follows—

| 17. Although the fig-tree shall not blossom, neither *shall* fruit *be* in the vines; the labour of the olive shall fail, and the fields shall yield no meat; the flock shall be cut off from the fold, and *there shall be* no herd in the stalls: | 17. Quia ficus non florebit, et nullus erit fructus in vineis; fraudabit opus olivæ, et agri non producent cibum (*ad verbum,* non faciet cibum; *est mutatio numeri, sed esset asperior illa translatio;* Agri *igitur* non producent cibum: *porro hac voce comprehendi triticum, legumina, et quæ ad victum pertinent, satis liquet;*) excissum est ab ovili pecus, et nullus bos in stabulis: |
| 18. Yet I will rejoice in the Lord, I will joy in the God of my salvation. | 18. Ego autem in Jehovâ exultabo, lætabor in Deo salutis meæ. |

The Prophet declares now at large what that rest would be of which he had spoken; it would be even this—that he would not cease to rejoice in God, even in the greatest afflictions. He indeed foresees how grievous the impending punishment would be, and he warns also and arouses the faithful, that they might perceive the approaching judgment of God. He says, *Flourish shall not the fig, and no fruit shall be on the vines; fail shall the olive.* First, the fig shall not flourish; then, the fields shall produce nothing; and lastly, the cattle and the sheep shall fail. Though the figs produce fruit without flowering, it is not yet an improper use of פרח, *perech,* which means strictly to bud.[1] He means that the desolation of the land was nigh at hand, and

[1] The verb means to *break forth* either in buds, or germs, or shoots, and so to germinate, or to blossom. It is rendered by the Septuagint καρποφορήσει, shall bear fruit.—*Ed.*

that the people would be reduced to extreme poverty. But it was an instance of rare virtue, to be able to rejoice in the Lord, when occasions of sorrow met him on every side.

The Prophet then teaches us what advantage it is to the faithful seasonably to submit to God, and to entertain serious fear when he threatens them, and when he summons them to judgment; and he shows that though they might perish a hundred times, they would yet not perish, for the Lord would ever supply them with occasions of joy, and would also cherish this joy within, so as to enable them to rise above all their adversities. Though, then, the land was threatened with famine, and though no food would be supplied to them, they would yet be able always to rejoice in the God of their salvation; for they would know him to be their Father, though for a time he severely chastised them. This is a delineation of that rest of which he made mention before.

The import of the whole is—"Though neither the figs, nor the vines, nor the olives, produce any fruit, and though the field be barren, though no food be given, yet I *will rejoice in my God;*" that is, our joy shall not depend on outward prosperity; for though the Lord may afflict us in an extreme degree, there will yet be always some consolation to sustain our minds, that they may not succumb under evils so grievous; for we are fully persuaded, that our salvation is in God's hand, and that he is its faithful guardian. We shall, therefore, rest quietly, though heaven and earth were rolled together, and all places were full of confusion; yea, though God fulminated from heaven, we shall yet be in a tranquil state of mind, looking for his gratuitous salvation.

We now perceive more clearly, that the sorrow produced by the sense of our guilt is recommended to us on account of its advantage; for nothing is worse than to provoke God's wrath to destroy us; and nothing is better than to anticipate it, so that the Lord himself may comfort us. We shall not always escape, for he may apparently treat us with severity; but though we may not be exempt from punishment, yet while he intends to humble us, he will give us reasons to rejoice: and then in his own time he will mitigate his severity, and by the effects will show himself propitious to us. Nevertheless, during the time when want or famine, or any other affliction, is to be borne, he will render us joyful with this one consolation, for, relying on his promises, we shall look for him as the God of our salvation. Hence, on one side Habakkuk sets the desolation of the land; and on the other, the inward joy which the faithful never fail to possess, for they are upheld by the perpetual favour of God. And thus he warns, as I have said, the children of God, that they might be prepared to bear want and famine, and calmly to submit to God's chastisements; for had he not exhorted them as he did, they might have failed a hundred times.

We may hence gather a most useful doctrine,—That whenever signs of God's wrath meet us in outward things, this remedy remains to us—to consider what God is to us inwardly; for the inward joy, which faith brings to us, can overcome all fears, terrors, sorrows and anxieties.

But we must notice what follows, *In the God of my salvation:* for sorrow would soon absorb all our thoughts, except God were present as our preserver. But how does he appear as such to the faithful? even when they estimate not his love by external things, but strengthen themselves by embracing the promise of his mercy, and never doubt but that he will be propitious to them; for it is impossible but that he will remember mercy even while he is angry. It follows—

19. The Lord God *is* my strength, and he will make my feet like hinds' *feet,* and he will make me to walk upon mine high places. To the chief singer on my stringed instruments.

19. Jehova Dominus fortitudo mea, et ponet pedes meos quasi cervarum, et super excelsa mea ambulare me faciet. Prefecto in Neginothai (*vel,* in pulsationibus meis, *vel,* musicis instrumentis.)

He confirms the same truth,—that he sought no strength but in God alone. But there is an implied contrast between God and those supports on which men usually lean. There is indeed no one, who is not of a cheerful mind, when he possesses all necessary things, when no danger, no fear is impending: we are then courageous when all things smile on us. But the Prophet, by calling God his strength, sets him in opposition to all other supports; for he wishes to encourage the faithful to persevere in their hope, however grievously God might afflict them. His meaning then is,— that even when evils impetuously rage against us, when we vacillate and are ready to fall every moment, God ought then to be our strength; for the aid which he has promised for our support is all-sufficient. We hence see that the Prophet entertained firm hope, and by his example animated the faithful, provided they had God propitious, however might all other things fail them.

He will make, he says, *my feet like those of hinds.* I am inclined to refer this to their return to their own country, though some give this explanation,—"God will give the swiftest feet to his servants, so that they may pass over all obstacles to destroy their enemies;" but as they might think in their exile that their return was closed up against them, the Prophet introduces this most apt similitude, that God would give his people *feet like those of hinds,* so that they could climb the precipices of mountains, and dread no difficulties: *He will* then, he says, *give me the feet of hinds, and make me to tread on my high places.* Some think that this was said with regard to Judea, which is, as it is well known, mountainous; but I take the expression more simply in this way,—that God would make his faithful people to advance boldly and without fear along high places: for they who fear hide themselves and dare not to raise up the head, nor proceed openly along public roads; but the Prophet says, *God will make me to tread on my high places.*

He at last adds, *To the leader on my beatings.* The first word some are wont to render conqueror. This inscription, To the leader, למנצח *lamenetsech,* frequently occurs in the Psalms. To the conqueror, is the version of some; but it means, I have no doubt, the leader of the singers. Interpreters think that God is signified here by this title, for he presides over all the songs of the godly: and it may not inaptly be applied to him as the leader of the singers, as though the Prophet had said,—"God will be a strength to me; though I am weak in myself, I shall yet be strong in him; and he will enable me to surmount all obstacles, and I shall proceed boldly, who am now like one half-dead; and he will thus become the occasion of my song, and be the leader of the singers engaged in celebrating his praises, when he shall deliver from death his people in so wonderful a manner." We hence see that the connection is not unsuitable, when he says, that there would be strength for him in God; and particularly as giving of thanks belonged to the leader or the chief singer, in order that God's aid might be celebrated, not only privately but at the accustomed sacrifices, as was usually the case under the law. Those who explain it as denoting the beginning of a song, are extremely frigid and jejune in what they advance; I shall therefore pass it by.

He adds, *on my beatings*. This word, נגינות, *neginoth*, I have already explained in my work on the Psalms. Some think that it signifies a melody, others render it beatings (*pulsationes*) or notes (*modos;*) and others consider that musical instruments are meant.[1] I affirm nothing in a doubtful matter: and it is enough to bear in mind what we have said,—that the Prophet promises here to God a continual thanksgiving, when the faithful were redeemed, for not only each one would acknowledge that they had been saved by God's hand, but all would assemble together in the Temple, and there testify their gratitude, and not only with their voices confess God as their Deliverer, but also with instruments of music, as we know it to have been the usual custom under the Law.

PRAYER.

Grant, Almighty God, that as we cease not daily to provoke thy wrath against us, and as the hardness and obstinacy of our flesh

---

[1] No satisfactory conjectures have been made by any as to the *my* added to this word. Hezekiah says at the end of his prayer, Is. xxxviii. 20, ונגינותי נגן, " and my neginoth will we sing," or play, &c. Our version makes this *my* to refer to the ode or song he made to be played on the neginoth, supposed to have been a stringed instrument. In this case "my neginoth" means the song he made for the neginoth. Then we might render the words,—

For the leader; my song on the stringed instruments.—*Ed.*

is so great, that it is necessary for us to be in various ways afflicted,—O grant, that we may patiently bear thy chastisements, and under a deep feeling of sorrow flee to thy mercy; and may we in the meantime persevere in the hope of that mercy, which thou hast promised, and which has been once exhibited towards us in Christ, so that we may not depend on the earthly blessings of this perishable life, but relying on thy word may proceed in the course of our calling, until we shall at length be gathered into that blessed rest, which is laid up for us in heaven, through Christ our Lord. Amen.

THE
COMMENTARIES OF JOHN CALVIN

ON THE

PROPHET ZEPHANIAH.

CALVIN'S PREFACE TO ZEPHANIAH.

ZEPHANIAH is placed the last of the Minor Prophets who performed their office before the Babylonian Captivity; and the inscription shows that he exercised his office of teaching at the same time with JEREMIAH, about thirty years before the city was destroyed, the Temple pulled down, and the people led into exile. JEREMIAH, it is true, followed his vocation even after the death of JOSIAH, while ZEPHANIAH prophesied only during his reign.

The substance of his Book is this: He first denounces utter destruction on a people who were so perverse, that there was no hope of their repentance;—he then moderates his threatenings, by denouncing God's judgments on their enemies, THE ASSYRIANS, as well as others, who had treated with cruelty the Church of God; for it was no small consolation, when the Jews heard that they were so regarded by God, that he would undertake their cause and avenge their wrongs. He afterwards repeats again his reproofs, and shortly mentions the sins which then prevailed among the elect people of God; and, at the same time, he turns his discourse to the faithful, and exhorts them to patience, setting before them the hope of favour, provided they ever looked to the Lord; and provided they relied on the gratuitous covenant which he made with Abraham, and doubted not but that he would be a Father to them, and also looked, with a tranquil mind, for that redemption which had been promised to them. This is the sum of the whole Book.

COMMENTARIES

ON

THE PROPHET ZEPHANIAH.

CHAPTER I.

Lecture One Hundred and Eighteenth.

1. The word of the Lord which came unto Zephaniah the son of Cushi, the son of Gedaliah, the son of Amariah, the son of Hizkiah, in the days of Josiah the son of Amon, king of Judah.

1. Sermo Jehovæ, qui fuit ad Zephaniam, filium Chusi, filii Gedoliæ, filii Amariæ, filii Chizkiæ, in diebus Josiæ, filii Amon, regis Jehudah.

ZEPHANIAH first mentions the time in which he prophesied; it was under the king Josiah. The reason why he puts down the name of his father Amon does not appear to me. The Prophet would not, as a mark of honour, have made public a descent that was disgraceful and infamous. Amon was the son of Manasseh, an impious and wicked king; and he was nothing better than his father. We hence see that his name is recorded, not for the sake of honour, but rather of reproach; and it may have been that the Prophet meant to intimate, what was then well known to all, that the people had become so obdurate in their superstitions, that it was no easy matter to restore them to a sound mind. But we cannot bring forward anything but conjecture; I therefore leave the matter without pretending to decide it.

With regard to the pedigree of the Prophet, I have mentioned elsewhere what the Jews affirm—that when the

Prophet put down the names of their fathers, they themselves had descended from Prophets. But Zephaniah mentions not only his father and grandfather, but also his great-grandfather and his great-great-grandfather; and it is hardly credible that they were all Prophets, and there is not a word respecting them in Scripture. I do not think, as I have said elsewhere, that such a rule is well-founded; but the Jews in this case, according to their manner, deal in trifles; for in things unknown they hesitate not to assert what comes to their minds, though it may not have the least appearance of truth. It is possible that the father, grandfather, the great-grandfather, and the great-great-grandfather of the Prophet, were persons who excelled in piety; but this also is uncertain. What is especially worthy of being noticed is—that he begins by saying that he brought nothing of his own, but faithfully, and, as it were, by the hand, delivered what he had received from God.

With regard, then, to his pedigree, it is a matter of no great moment; but it is of great importance to know that God was the author of his doctrine, and that Zephaniah was his faithful minister, who introduced not his own devices, but was only the announcer of celestial truth. Let us now proceed to the contents—

2. I will utterly consume all *things* from off the land, saith the Lord. 3. I will consume man and beast; I will consume the fowls of the heaven, and the fishes of the sea, and the stumblingblocks with the wicked; and I will cut off man from off the land, saith the Lord.	2. Perdendo perdam (*vel*, colligendo colligam) omnia ex superficie terræ, dicit Jehova. 3. Perdam (*vel*, colligam) hominem et bestiam; perdam autem avem cœlorum, et pisces maris; et offendicula erunt impiis; et excidam hominem è superficie terræ, dicit Jehova.

It might seem at the first view that the Prophet dealt too severely in thus fulminating against his own nation; for he ought to have begun with doctrine, as this appears to be the just order of things. But the Prophet denounces ruin, and shows at the same time why God was so grievously displeased with the people. We must however remember, that the Prophet, living at the same period with Jeremiah, had regard to the stubbornness of the people, who had been already with more than sufficient evidence proved to have been guilty. Hence he darts forth as of a sudden and denounces the wickedness of the people, which had been already exposed; so there was to be no more contention on the subject, for their iniquity had become quite ripe. And no doubt it was ever the object of the Prophets to unite their endeavours so as to assist one another: and this united effort ought ever to be among all the servants of God, that no one may do anything apart, but with joined efforts they may promote the same object, and at the same time strive mutually to confirm the common truth. This is what our Prophet is now doing.

He knew that God would have used various means to restore them, had not the corruption of the people become now past recovery. Having observed that all others had spent their labour in vain, he directly attacks the wicked men who had, as it were designedly, cast aside every fear of God, and shook off every shame. Since, then, it was openly evident that with determined rebellion they resisted God, it was no wonder that the Prophet began with so much severity.

But here a difficulty meets us. He said in the first verse, that he thus spoke under Josiah; but we know that the land was then cleansed from its superstitions. For we learn, that when that pious king attained manhood, he laboured most strenuously to restore the pure worship of God; and when all places were full of wicked superstitions, he not only constrained the tribe of Judah to adopt the true worship of God, but he also stimulated his neighbours who had remained and were dispersed through the land of Israel. Since, then, the pious king had strenuously and courageously promoted the interest of true religion, it seems a wonder that God was still so much displeased. But we must remember, that though Josiah sincerely worshipped God, yet the people were not really changed; for it has often happened, that God roused the chief men and leaders, while few, or hardly any, followed them, but only yielded a feigned obedience. This was no doubt the case in the time of Josiah; the hearts of the people were alienated from God and true religion, so that they chose rather to rot in their filth than to return to the true worship of God. And that this was the case soon appeared by the event; for Josiah did not reign long after he had cleansed the land from its defilements, and Jehoahaz succeeded him; and then the people immediately relapsed into their idolatry; and though for three months only his successor reigned, yet true religion was in that short time abolished. It is hence an obvious conclusion, that the people had ever been wedded to impiety, and that its roots were hidden in their hearts; though they apparently pretended to worship God, and, in order to please the king, embraced the worship divinely prescribed in their law; yet the event proved that it was a mere act of dissimulation, yea, of perfidy. Then after Jehoahaz followed Jehoiakim, and no better was their condition down to the time of Zedekiah; in short, no remedy could be found for their unhealable wound.

It hence plainly appears, that though Josiah made use of all means to revive the true and unadulterated worship of God in Judea, he did not yet gain his object. And we hence clearly learn how hard were the trials he sustained, seeing that he effected nothing, though at great hazard he attempted to restore the worship of God. When he found that he laboured in vain, he no doubt had to contend with great difficulties; and this we know by our own experience. When hope of success shines on us, we easily overcome all troubles, however arduous our work may be; but when we see that we strive in vain, we become dejected; and when we see that our labour succeeds only for a few years, our spirit grows faint. Josiah surmounted these two difficulties; for the perverseness of the people was sufficiently evident, and he was also reminded by two Prophets, Jeremiah and Zephaniah, that the people would still cherish their impious perverseness. When, therefore, he plainly saw that his labour was almost in vain, he might have fainted in the middle of his course, or, as they say, at the starting-place. And since the benefit was so small during his reign, what could he have hoped after his death?

This example ought at this day to be carefully observed:

for though God now appears to the world in full light, yet very few there are who submit themselves to his word; and of this small number fewer still there are who sincerely and without any dissimulation embrace sound doctrine. We indeed see how great is their inconstancy and indifference. For they who pretend great zeal for a time very soon vanish and fall away. Since then the perversity of the world is so great, sufficient to deject the minds of God's servants a hundred times, let us learn to look to Josiah, who in his own time left undone nothing, which might serve to establish the true worship of God; and when he saw that he effected but little and next to nothing, he still persevered, and with firm and invincible greatness of mind proceeded in his course.

We may also derive hence an admonition no less useful— not to regard ours as the golden age, because some portion of men profess the pure worship of God: for many, by no means wicked men, think, that almost all mortals are like angels, as soon as they testify in words their approbation of the gospel: and the sacred name of Reformation is at this day profaned, when any one who shows as it were by a nod only that he is not wholly an enemy to the gospel, is immediately lauded as a person of extraordinary piety. Though then many show some regard for religion, let us yet know that among so large a number there are many hypocrites, and that there is much chaff mixed with the wheat: and that our senses may not deceive us, we may see here, as in a mirror, how difficult it is to restore the world to the obedience of God, and utterly to root up all corruptions, though idols may be taken away and superstitions be abolished. No doubt Josiah had regard to everything calculated to cleanse the Church, and had recourse to the advice of Jeremiah and also of Zephaniah; we yet see that he did not attain the object he wished, for God now became more grievously displeased with his people than under Manasseh, or under Amon. These wicked kings had attempted to extinguish all true religion; they had cruelly raged against all God's servants, so that Jerusalem became almost drenched with innocent blood: and yet God seems here to have manifested greater displeasure under Josiah than during the previous cruelty and so many impieties. But as I have already said, there is no reason why we should despond, though the world by its ingratitude may close up the way against us; and however much may Satan also by this artifice strive to discourage us, let us still perseveringly go on according to the duties of our calling.

But it may be now asked, why God denounces his vengeance on *the beasts of the field, the birds of heaven, and the fishes of the sea;* for how much soever the Jews may have provoked him by their sins, innocent animals ought to have been spared. If a son is not to be punished for the fault of his father, (Ezek. xviii. 4,) but that the soul that has sinned is to die, why did God turn his wrath against fishes and other animals? This seems to have been a hasty and unreasonable infliction. But let this rule be first borne in mind—that it is preposterous in us to estimate God's doings according to our judgment, as froward and proud men do in our day; for they are disposed to judge of God's works with such presumption, that whatever they do not approve, they think it right wholly to condemn. But it behoves us to judge modestly and soberly, and to confess that God's judgments are a deep abyss: and when a reason for them does not appear, we ought reverently and with due humility to look for the day of their full revelation. This is one thing. Then it is meet at the same time to remember, that as animals were created for man's use, they must undergo a lot in common with him: for God made subservient to man both the birds of heaven, and the fishes of the sea, and all other animals. It is then no matter of wonder, that the condemnation of him, who enjoys a sovereignty over the whole earth, should reach to animals. And we know that the world was not made subject to corruption willingly— that is, naturally; but because the contagion from Adam's fall diffused itself through heaven and earth. Hence the sun and the moon, and all the stars, and also all the animals, the earth itself, and the whole world, bear marks of God's wrath, not because they have provoked it through their own fault, but because the whole world is involved in man's curse. The reason then is, because all things were created for the sake of man. Hence there is no ground to conclude, that God acts with too much severity when he executes his vengeance on innocent animals, for he can justly involve in the same ruin with man whatever he has created for his use.

But the reason also is sufficiently plain, why the Prophet speaks here of the beasts of the earth, the fishes of the sea, and the birds of heaven: for we find that men grow torpid, or rather stupid in their own indifference, except they are forcibly roused. It was, therefore, necessary for the Prophet, when he saw the people so hardened in their wickedness, and that he had to do with men past recovery, to set clearly before them these judgments of God, as though he had said—" Ye lie down securely, and indulge yourselves, when God is coming forth prepared for vengeance: but his wrath shall not only proceed against you, but will also lay hold on the harmless animals; for ye shall see a horrible judgment executed on your oxen and asses, on the birds and the fishes. What will become of you when God's wrath shall be thus kindled against the unhappy creatures who have committed no sins? Shall ye indeed escape unpunished?" We now understand why the Prophet does not speak here of men only, but connects with them the beasts of the earth, the fishes of the sea, and the birds of the air.

He says first, *By removing I will remove all things from the face of the land;* he afterwards enumerates particulars: but immediately after he clearly shows, that God would not act rashly and inconsiderately while executing his vengeance, for his sole purpose was to punish the wicked, *There shall be,* he says, *stumblingblocks to the ungodly;*[1] it is the same as though he said—" When I cite to God's tribunal both the

---

[1] This clause stands connected with the preceding words; "the stumblingblocks" were the idols, and they were to be taken away " along with the wicked," according to *Henderson,* and according to the version of *Symmachus,* συν ασιβισι, though *Newcome,* with less accuracy, renders the words thus,—
                And the stumblingblocks of the wicked.

The whole verse is poetical in its language; the collective singular, and not the plural, is used; and the first verb, אסף, in its most common meaning, is very expressive, and denotes the manner of the ruin that awaited

fishes of the sea and the birds of heaven, think not that God's controversy is with these creatures which are void of reason, but they are to sustain a part of God's vengeance, which ye have through your sins deserved." The Prophet then does here briefly show, that what he had before threatened brute creatures with, would come upon them on men's account; for God's design was to execute vengeance on the wicked; and as he saw that they were extremely torpid, he tried to awaken them by manifest tokens, so that they might see God the avenger as it were in a striking picture. And at the same time he also adds, *I will remove man from the face of the land.* He does not speak now of fishes or of other animals, but refers to men only. Hence appears more clearly what I have said—that the Prophet was under the necessity of speaking as he did, owing to the insensibility of the people. He now adds—

4. I will also stretch out mine hand upon Judah, and upon all the inhabitants of Jerusalem; and I will cut off the remnant of Baal from this place, *and* the name of the Chemarims with the priests;	4. Et extendam manum meam super Jehudah, et super omnes incolas Jerusalem; et excidam ex loco hoc reliquias Baal, et nomen cultorum cum sacerdotibus.

The Prophet explains still more clearly why he directed his discourse in the last verse against the beasts of the earth and the birds of heaven, even for this end—that the Jews might understand that God was angry with them. *I will stretch forth,* he says, *my hand on Judah and on Jerusalem.* God, then, by executing his vengeance on animals, intended to exhibit to the Jews, as in a picture, the dreadfulness of his wrath, which yet they despised and regarded as nothing. The stretching forth of God's hand I have elsewhere explained; and it means even this—that he stretches

the Jews. They were "gathered" and led into captivity. The two verses may be thus literally rendered,—

  2. Gathering I will gather everything
   From off the face of the land, saith Jehovah;
  3. I will gather man and beast;
   I will gather the bird of heaven and the fish of the sea,
   And the stumblingblocks together with the wicked;
   And I will cut *them* off, together with man,
   From the face of the land, saith Jehovah.—*Ed.*

forth his hand when he acts in an unusual manner, and employs means beyond what is common. We indeed know that God has no hands, and we also know that he performs all things by his command alone: but as everything seen in the world is called the work of his hands, so he is said to stretch forth his hand when he mentions a work that is remarkable and worthy of being remembered. In a like manner, when I intend to do some slight work, I only move my hand; but when I have some difficult work to do, I prepare myself more carefully, and also stretch forth my arms. This metaphor, then, is intended only for this purpose, to render men more attentive to God's works, when he is set forth as stretching forth his hand.

But he says, *on Judah* and on the inhabitants of *Jerusalem*. The kingdom of Israel had now been abolished, and the ten tribes had been led into exile; and a few only of the lowest and the poorest remained. The Jews thought themselves safe for ever, because they had escaped that calamity. This is the reason why the Prophet declares that God's judgment was impending not only over the kingdom of Judah, but also over the holy city, which thought itself exempt from all such evil, because there were the sacrifices performed, and there was the royal city, and, in short, because God had testified that his habitation was to be there for ever. Since, then, by this vain confidence the inhabitants of Jerusalem deceived themselves and others, Zephaniah specifically addresses them. And as he had before spoken of the wicked, he intended here, no doubt, sharply to reprove the Jews, as though he said by way of anticipation, "There is no reason for you to enquire who are the wicked; for ye yourselves are they, even ye who are the holy people of God and God's chosen inheritance, ye who are the race of Abraham, who flatter yourselves so much on account of your excellency; ye are the wicked, who have not hitherto ceased to provoke the vengeance of God." And at the same time he shows, as it were by the finger, some of their sins, though he mentions others afterwards: but he speaks now of their superstitions.

I will cut off, he says, *the remnants of Baal and the name of Chamerim.* The severity of the Prophet may seem here again to be excessive, for being so incensed against superstitions which had been abolished by the great zeal and singular diligence of the king; but, as we have already intimated, he regarded not so much the king as the people. For though they dared not openly to adulterate God's worship, they yet cherished those corruptions at home to which they had before been accustomed, as we see to be done at this day. For when it is not allowed to worship idols, many mutter their prayers in secret and invoke their idols: and, in short, they are restrained only by the fear of men from manifesting their own impiety; and in the meantime, they retain before God the same abominations. So it was in the time of Josiah; the people were wedded to their corruptions, and this we may easily conclude from the words of Zephaniah: for the remnants of Baal were not seen in the temple, nor in the streets, nor in their chapels, nor in the high places; but their hidden impiety is here discovered by the Spirit of God; and no doubt their sin was the more heinous and less excusable, because the people refused to follow their pious leader. It was indeed the most abominable ingratitude; for when they saw that the right worship was restored to them, they preferred to remain fixed in their own filth, rather than to return to God, even when they had liberty to do so, and also when that pious king extended his hand to them.

As to the word כמרים, *camerim*, it designated either the worshippers of Baal or some such men as our monks at this day: and they are supposed by some to have been thus called, because they were clothed in black vestments; while others think that they derived this name from their fervour, because they were madly devoted to their superstitions, or because they had marks on their foreheads, or because they imposed, as is commonly the case, on the simple by the ardour of their zeal. The name is also found in 2 Kings xxiii. in the account given of Josiah: for it is said there, that the כמרים, *camerim*, were taken away, together with other abominations of superstition. But as Zephaniah connects priests with them, it is probable that they were a kind of people like the monks, who did not themselves offer sacrifices, but were a sort of attendants, who undertook vows and offered prayers in the name of the whole people. For what some think, that they were thus called because they burnt incense, appears not to me probable; for then they must have been priests. They were then inferior to the sacrificers, and occupying a station between them and the people, like the monks and hermits of this day, who deceive foolish men by their sanctity. Such, then, were the Camerim.[1]

But as Josiah could not attain his object, so as immediately to cleanse the land from these pollutions, we need not wonder that at this day we are not able immediately to remove superstitions from the world: but let us in the meantime ever proceed in our course. Let those endued with authority, who bear the sword, that is, all magistrates, perform their office with greater diligence, inasmuch as they see how difficult and protracted is the contest with the ministers of idolatry. Let also the ministers of the gospel earnestly cry against idolatry, and all ungodly ceremonies, and not desist. Though they may not effect as much as they wish, yet let them follow the example of Josiah. If God should in the meantime thunder from heaven, let them not be discouraged, but, on the contrary, know that their labour is approved by

---

[1] The word is found in two other places, 2 Kings xxiii. 5, and Hos. x. 5. In the latter text the priests of the calf of Bethaven are thus called; in the former, they are said to be those who "burnt incense in the high places." From this fact *Parkhurst* concludes, that they were called *Camerim* in contempt by the faithful Jews, because they were *shrivelled* or *scorched*, as the word means, by their fumigating fires.

The "priests," mentioned here were the sacrificers, while the "Camerim" were the incense-burners. There were "altars" (not an altar) reared for Baal in the temple; one, as it seems, for sacrifices, and the other for incense. See 2 Kings xxi. 3. In 2 Chr. xxxiv. 4, 5, the priests and sacrificers are alone mentioned; but in 2 Kings xxiii. 5, where the same things are recorded, the Camerim and incense are alone named. The Prophet in this passage mentions both.

Some, as *Cocceius* and *Henderson*, have been disposed to think that the unfaithful priests of the true God are here meant. But the other view is more consistent with the whole passage. If we retain not the original word, we may thus render the line,—

The name of the incense-burners with the priests;

That is, those who burnt incense and those who offered sacrifices to Baal. —*Ed.*

him, and never doubt of their own safety; for though all were destroyed, their godly efforts would not be in vain, nor fail of a reward before God. Thus, then, ought all God's servants to animate themselves, each in his particular sphere and vocation, whenever they have to contend with superstitions, and with such corruptions as vitiate and adulterate the pure worship of God.

PRAYER.

Grant, Almighty God, that as we are so prone to corruptions, and so easily turn from the right course after having commenced it, and so easily degenerate from the truth once known,—O Grant, that, being strengthened by thy Spirit, we may persevere to the end in the right way which thou showest to us in thy word, and that we may also labour to restore the many who abandon themselves to various errors; and though we may effect nothing, let us not yet be led away after them, but remain firm in the obedience of faith, until having at length finished all these contests, we shall be gathered into that blessed rest which is prepared for us in heaven, through Christ our Lord. Amen.

Lecture One Hundred and Nineteenth.

5. And them that worship the host of heaven upon the housetops; and them that worship *and* that swear by the Lord, and that swear by Malcham;	5. Et super eos qui adorant super tecta militiam cœlorum, et eos qui adorant et jurant per Jehovam, et jurant per regem suum.

ZEPHANIAH pursues the subject contained in the verse I explained yesterday. For as the majority of the people still adhered to their superstitions, though the pure worship of the law had been restored by Josiah, the Prophet threatens here, that God would punish such ingratitude. As then he had spoken in the last verse of the worshippers of Baal and their sacrifices, so now he proceeds farther—that the Lord would execute vengeance on the whole people, who prayed to the host of heaven, or bowed themselves down before the host of heaven. It is well known that those stars are thus called in Scripture to which the Gentiles ascribed, on account of their superior lustre, some sort of divinity. Hence it was, that they worshipped the sun as God, called the moon the queen of heaven, and also paid adoration to the stars. The people, then, did not only sin in worshipping Baal, but were also addicted to many superstitions, as we see to be the case whenever men degenerate from the genuine doctrine of true religion; they then seek out various inventions on all sides, so that they observe no limits and keep within no boundaries.

But he says, that they *worshipped* the stars on their *roofs*. It is probable that they chose this higher place, as interpreters remind us, because they thought that they were more seen by the stars the nearer they were to them. For as men are gross in their ideas they never think God propitious to them except he exhibits some proof or sign of a bodily presence; in short, they always seek God according to their own earthly notions. Since, then, the Jews thought that there were so many Gods as there are stars in heaven, it is no wonder that they ascended to the roofs of their houses, that they might be, as it were, in the sight of their gods, and thus not lose their labour; for the superstitious never think that their devotion is observed by God, unless they have before their eyes, as we have just said, some sign of his presence.

We now then see how this verse stands connected with the last. God declares that he would punish all idolaters; but as the Jews worshipped Baal, the Prophet first condemned that strange religion; and now he adds other devices, to which the Jews perversely devoted themselves; for they worshipped also all the stars, ascribing to them some sort of divinity. Then he mentions all those who *worshipped* and *swore* by *their own king*, and swore by *Jehovah*.

By these last words the Prophet intimates, that the Jews had not so repudiated the law of God but that they boasted that they still worshipped the God who had adopted them, and by whom they had been redeemed, who had commanded the temple to be built for him, and an altar on mount Sion. They then did not openly reject the worship of the true God, but formed such a mixture for themselves, that they joined to the true God their own idols, as we see to be the state of things at this day under the Papacy. It seems a sufficient excuse to foolish men that they retain the name of God; and they confidently boast that the true God is worshipped by them; and yet we see that they mix together with this worship many of the delusions of Satan; for under the Papacy there is no end to their inventions. When any devise some peculiar mode of worship, it is then connected with the rest; and thus they form such a mixture, that from one God, divided into many parts, they bring forth a vast troop of deities. As then at this day the Papists worship God and idols too, so Zephaniah had to condemn the same wickedness among the Jews.

We here learn that God's name was not then wholly obliterated, as though the world had openly fallen away from God; for though they worshipped Jupiter, Mercury, Apollo, and other fictitious gods, they yet professed to worship the only true and eternal God, the Creator of heaven and earth. What then was it that the Prophet condemned? that they were not content with what the law simply and plainly prescribed, but that they devised for themselves various and strange modes of worship; for when men take to themselves such a liberty as this, they no longer worship the true God, how much soever they may pretend to do so, inasmuch as God repudiates all spurious modes of worship, as he testifies especially in Ezek. xx.—"Go ye," he says, "worship your idols." He shows that all kinds of worship are abominable to him whenever men depart in any measure from his pure word. For we must hold this as the main principle—that obedience is more valued by God than all sacrifices. Whenever men run after their own inventions they depart from the true God; for they refuse to render to him what he principally requires, even obedience.

But our Prophet speaks according to the common notions of men; for they pretended to be the true worshippers of God, while they still adhered to their own inventions. They did not, indeed, properly speaking, worship the true God; but as they thought, and openly professed to do this, Zephaniah, making this concession, says—"God will not suffer his own worship to be thus profaned: ye seek to blend it with that of your idols; this he will not endure. Ye worship the true God, and ye worship your idols; but he would have himself to be worshipped alone; and this he deserves. But the partition which ye make is nothing else than the mangling of true worship; and God will not have himself to be thus in part worshipped." We now understand what the Prophet means here; for the Jews covered their abominations with the pretext that their purpose was to worship the God of Abraham: the Prophet does not simply deny this to be done by them, but declares that this worship was useless and disapproved by God; nay, he proceeds farther, and says that this worship, made up of various inventions, was an abominable corruption which God would punish; for he can by no means bear that there should be such an alliance—that idols should be substituted in his place, and that a part of his glory should be transferred to the inventions of men. This is the true meaning.

We hence learn how greatly deceived the Papists are, who think it enough, provided they depart not wholly from the worship of the only true God; for God allows and approves of no worship except when we attend to his voice, and turn not aside either to the left hand or to the right, but acquiesce only in what he has prescribed.

It is nothing strange that he connects swearing with worship, for it is a kind of divine worship. Hence the Scripture, stating a part for the whole, often mentions swearing in this sense, as including the service due to God. But the Prophet pronounces here generally a curse on all the superstitious, who worshipped fictitious gods; and then he adds one kind of worship, and that is swearing. I shall not here speak at large, nor is it necessary, on the subject of swearing. We know that the use of an oath is lawful when God is appealed to as a witness and a judge, on important occasions; for God's name may be interposed when a matter requires proof, and when it is important; but God's name is not to be introduced thoughtlessly. Hence two things are especially required in an oath—that all who swear by his name should present themselves with reverence before his tribunal, and acknowledge him to be the avenger if they take his name falsely or inconsiderately. This is one thing. Then the matter itself, on account of which we swear, must be considered; for if men allow themselves to swear by God's name respecting things which are trifling and frivolous, it is a shameful profanation, and by no means to be borne. For it is a singular favour on the part of God, that he allows us to take his name when there is any controversy among us, and when a confirmation is necessary. As then we thus receive through kindness the name of God, it is surely a great favour; for how great is the sanctity of that name, though it serves even earthly concerns? God then does so far accommodate himself to us, that it is lawful for us to swear by his name. Hence a greater seriousness ought to be observed by us in oaths, so that no one should dare to interpose an oath except when necessity requires; and we should also especially take heed lest God be called a witness to what is false. For how great a sacrilege it is to cover a falsehood with his name, who is the eternal and immutable truth! They then who swear falsely by his name change God, as far as they can, into what he is not. We now sufficiently understand how swearing is a kind of divine worship, because his honour is thereby given to God; for his majesty is, as it were, brought before us, and as it is his peculiar office to know and to discover hidden things, and also to maintain the truth, this his own work is ascribed to him. Now when any one swears by a mortal, or by the sun, or by the moon, or by creatures, he deprives God in part of his own honour.

We hence see that in superstitious oaths there was a clear proof of idolatry. This is the reason why the Prophet here condemns those who did *swear by Jehovah and by Malkom;* that is, who joined their idols with the true and eternal God when they swore. For it is a clear precept of God's law, ' By the name of thy God shalt thou swear.' (Deut. vi. 13.) And when the Prophets speak of the renovation of the Church, they use this form—' Ye shall swear by the name of God;' ' To me shall bend every knee;' ' Every tongue shall swear to me.' What does all this mean? " The whole world shall acknowledge me as the true God; and as every knee shall bow to me, so every one will submit himself to my judgment." We may hence doubtlessly conclude, that God is deprived of his right, whenever we swear by the sun, or by the moon, or by the dead, or by any creatures.

This evil has been common in all ages; and it prevails still at this day under the Papacy. They swear by the Virgin, by angels, and by the dead. They do not think that they thus take away anything from the sovereignty of the only true God; but we see what he declares respecting them. The Papists therefore foolishly excuse themselves, when they swear by their saints: for they cannot elude the charge of sacrilege, which the Holy Spirit has stamped with perpetual infamy, since he has said, that all those are abominable in the sight of God who swear by any other name than his own: and the reason is evident, for the sun, moon, and stars, and also dead or living men, are honoured with the name of God, when they are set up as judges. For they who swear by the sun, do the same as though they said—" The sun is my witness and judge;" that is, " The sun is my God." They who swear by the name of a king, or as profane men swore formerly, " By the genius of their king," ascribe to a mortal what is peculiar to the true God alone. But when any one swears by heaven or the temple, and does not think that there is any divinity in the heavens or in the temple, it is the same as though he swore by God himself, as it appears from Matt. xxiii. 20-22; and Christ, when he forbad us to swear by heaven or by the earth, did not condemn such modes of swearing as inconsistent with his word, but as only useless and vain. At the same time he showed that God's name is profaned by such expressions: ' They who swear by heaven, swear also by him who inhabits heaven; they who swear by the temple, swear also by him who is worshipped in the temple, and to whom sacrifices are offered.' When one swears by his head or by his life, it is a protestation, as though he said—" As my life is dear to me." But they who swear by the saints, either living or dead, ascribe to mortals what is due to God. They who swear by the sun, place a dead created thing on the throne of God himself.

As to the term מלכם, *melkom*, it may be properly rendered, *their king;* for מלך *melak,* as it is well known, means a king; but it is here put in construction, מלכם, *melkom,* their king; *they swear by their own king.*[1] The Prophet, I doubt not, alludes to the word מולך, *molok,* which is derived from the verb, to reign: for though that word was commonly used by all as a proper name, it is yet certain that that false god was so called, as though he was a king: and the Prophet increases the indignity by saying—*They swear by Malkom.* He might have simply said, "They swear by Moloch;" but he says, *They swear by Malkom;* that is, "They forget that I am their king, and transfer my sovereignty to a dead and empty image." God then does here, by an implied contrast, exaggerate the sin of the Jews, as they sought another king for themselves, when they knew that under his protection they always enjoyed a sure and real safety. Let us now proceed—

6. And them that are turned back from the Lord; and *those* that have not sought the Lord, nor enquired for him.

6. Et qui retrò aguntur, ne sequantur Jehovam, (*ad verbum est,* de-post Jehovam,) et qui non quærunt Jehovam, neque investigant eum.

---

[1] It appears that this idol had two names, Moloc and Milcom, or Molcam. It is called Moloc, or Molec, in Lev. xx. 5, and in seven other places; but Milcom in 1 Kings xi. 5, 33; 2 Kings xxiii. 14; as well as here, and also in Jer. xlix. 1, 3, though improperly rendered in our version, "their king." The Ammonites are the people spoken of.

The swearing is here differently expressed: it is *to* (ל) Jehovah; and by (ב) Milcam. To swear *to,* is to make a promise to another by an oath, or, in this instance, to swear allegiance to God: but to swear *by,* is to appeal to another as witness to an engagement. We have the two forms together in Josh. ix. 19. The Jews made a solemn profession of obedience to God, and yet they acknowledged Melcam as God, by appealing to him as a witness to the truth. It is called the abomination of the Ammonites. 1 Kings xi. 33.

The image of this god, according to the Rabbins, was hollow, made of brass, and had seven compartments. In the first, they put flour—in the second, turtles—in the third, an ewe—in the fourth, a ram—in the fifth, a calf—in the sixth, an ox—and in the seventh, a child! All these were burnt together by heating the image in the inside! To drown the cries and noises that might be made, they used drums and other instruments. See מלך in *Parkhurst.* How cruel is superstition! and yet how wedded to it is man by nature! Though the Jews had knowledge of the religion of him who is the God of love and mercy; yet they preferred the religion of savages and barbarians. How strongly does this fact prove man's natural antipathy to God!—*Ed.*

The Prophet seems here to include, as it were, in one bundle, the proud despisers of God, as well as those idolaters of whom he had spoken. It may yet be, that he describes the same persons in different words, and that he means that they were addicted to their own superstitions, because they were unwilling to serve God sincerely and from the heart, and even shunned everything that might lead their attention to true religion. And this view I mostly approve; for what some imagine, that their gross contempt of God is here pointed out, is not sufficiently supported. I therefore rather think that the idolaters are here reproved, that they might not suppose that they could by subterfuges wash away their guilt; for they were wont to cover themselves with the shield of ignorance, when they were overcome, and their impiety was fully proved: "I did not think so; but, on the contrary, my purpose was to worship God." Since, then, the superstitious are wont to hide themselves under the covering of ignorance, the Prophet here defines the idolatry of the people, and briefly shows that it was connected with obstinacy and wickedness.

They did *not seek Jehovah;* but, on the contrary, they turned wilfully away from him, and sought, as it were designedly, to extinguish true religion. Nor was it to be wondered at, that so grievous and severe a sentence was pronounced on them; for they had been taught by the law how God was to be served. How was it, then, that errors so gross had crept in? Doubtless, God had kindled the light of celestial truth, which clearly showed the way of true religion; but as men ever seek to perform some frivolous trifles, the Israelites and the Jews, when they felt ashamed openly and manifestly to reject the true God, laboured at the same time to add many ceremonies, that their impiety might be thus concealed. This is the reason why the Prophet says that they turned back; that is, that they could not be excused on the ground of ignorance, but that they were perfidious and apostates, who had preferred their own idols to the true God; though they knew that he could not be rightly worshipped, but according to the rule prescribed in the law, they yet neglected this, and heaped together many superstitions.

And, doubtless, we shall find that the fountain of all false worship is this—that men are unwilling truly and from the heart to serve God; and, at the same time, they wish to retain some appearance of religion. For there is nothing omitted in the law that is needful for the perfect worship of God: but as God requires in the law a spiritual worship, hence it is that men seek hiding-places, and devise for themselves many ceremonies, that they may turn back from God, and yet pretend that they come to him. While they sedulously labour in their own ceremonies, it is indeed true that the worship of God and religion are continually on their lips: but, as I have said, it is all hypocrisy and deception; for they accumulate ceremonies, that there might be something intervening between God and them. It is not, therefore, without reason that the Prophet here accuses the Jews that they *turned back from Jehovah, and that they sought him not.* How so? For there was no need of a long, or of a difficult, or of a perplexed enquiry; for the Lord had freely offered himself to them. How, then, was it that they were blind in the midst of light, except that they knowingly and wilfully followed their own inventions?[1]

The same is the case at this day with the Papists: for though they may clamour a hundred times that they seek to worship God, it is quite evident that they wilfully go astray; inasmuch as they so delight themselves with their own inventions, that they do not purely and from the heart devote and consecrate themselves to God.

We now, then, see that this verse was added, as an explanation, by the Prophet, that he might deprive the Jews

---

[1] *Calvin* has omitted to notice the last words in the verse, "Nor enquire of him;" which *Henderson*, adopting a modern phraseology, has rendered, "nor apply to him." The reading ought to be, as many MSS. have it, דרשוהו. The verb means to enquire of, to consult, and also to regard or to care for. They did not enquire of God as to his will, or they did not show any regard for him. See Gen. xxv. 22; Ezek. xx. 1; and also Deut. xi. 12; Job iii. 4. To *seek* the Lord is to seek his favour and communion with him; to *enquire* of the Lord is to seek the knowledge of his will in any difficulty.—*Ed.*

of their false plea of ignorance, and show that they sinned wilfully; for they would have been sufficiently taught by the law, had they not adopted their own inventions, which dazzled their eyes and all their senses. It follows—

7. Hold thy peace at the presence of the Lord God: for the day of the Lord is at hand: for the Lord hath prepared a sacrifice, he hath bid his guests.

8. And it shall come to pass in the day of the Lord's sacrifice, that I will punish the princes, and the king's children, and all such as are clothed with strange apparel.

9. In the same day also will I punish all those that leap on the threshold, which fill their masters' houses with violence and deceit.

7. Tace à facie Domini Jehovæ, quia propinquus dies Jehovæ, quia paravit Jehova sacrificium, (vel, ordinavit, הכין,) sanctificavit invitatos suos.

8. Et erit, in die sacrificii Jehovæ tunc visitabo super Principes, et super filios Regis, et super omnes qui induti sunt vestitu extraneo.

9. Et visitabo super omnem qui tripudiat super limen in die illo, qui replent domum dominorum suorum violentia et fraude.

The Prophet confirms here what he has previously taught, when he bids all *to be silent before God;* for this mode of speaking is the same as though he had said, that he did not terrify the Jews in vain, but seriously set before them God's judgment, which they would find by experience to be even more than terrible. He also records some of their sins, that the Jews might know that he did not threaten them for nothing, but that there were just causes why God declared that he would punish them. This is the substance of the whole.

Let us first see what the Prophet means by the word, silence. Something has been said of this on the second chapter of Habakkuk. We said then that by silence is meant submission; and to make the thing more clear, we said that we were to notice the contrast between the silence to which men calmly submit, and the contumacy, which is ever clamorous: for when men seek to be wise of themselves, and acquiesce not in God's word, it is then said, that they are not silent, for they refuse to give a hearing to his word; and when men give loose reins to their own will, they observe no bounds. Until God then obtains authority in the world, all places are full of clamour, and the whole life of men is in a state of confusion, for they run to and fro in their wanderings; and there is no restraint where God is not heard. It is for the same reason that the Prophet now demands silence: but the expression is accommodated to the subject which he handles. To be silent at the presence of God, it is true, is to submit to God's authority; but the connection is to be considered; for Zephaniah saw then that God's judgment was despised and regarded as nothing; and he intimates here that God had so spoken, that the execution was nigh at hand. Hence he says, *Be silent*,[1] that is, "Know ye, that I have not spoken merely for the purpose of terrifying you; but as God is prepared to execute vengeance, of this he now reminds you, that if there be any hope of repentance, ye may in time seek to return into favour with him; if not, that ye may be without excuse."

We now then understand why the Prophet bids them to be *silent before the Lord Jehovah:* and the context is a confirmation of the same view; for the reason is added, *Because the day of Jehovah is nigh.* For profane men ever promise to themselves some respite, and think that they gain much by delay: the Prophet, on the contrary, does now expose to scorn this self-security, and says, that the day of Jehovah was nigh at hand. It is then the same thing as though he had said, that his judgment ought to have been quickly anticipated, and even with fear and trembling.

---

[1] The word is הס, and is evidently an interjection enjoining silence, Hush! or, Silence!

    7. Silence at the presence of the Lord Jehovah!
       For nigh is the day of Jehovah,
       For prepared hath Jehovah a sacrifice,
       Selected hath he his guests!

The passage is remarkably forcible and striking. Jehovah was coming, and everything was prepared, and all were to be silent. And then follows what is no less striking and expressive,—

    8. And it shall be in the day of Jehovah's sacrifice,
       That I will visit the princes and the king's sons,
       And all who wear foreign apparel.
    9. I will also visit, in that day,
       Every one who leaps on the threshold,
       Who fill the house of their master
       By plunder and by fraud.

There is in the last line a metonymy; the act is put for what was acquired by it: they filled the house of their master by spoils gained by plunder or violence, and by fraud or cheating.—*Ed.*

He afterwards employs a metaphor to set forth what he taught,—that God had *prepared a sacrifice*, yea, that he had already *appointed* and *set apart his guests*. By the word, sacrifice, the Prophet reminded them, that the punishment of which he had spoken would be just, and that the glory of God would thereby shine forth. We indeed know how ready the world is to make complaints; when it is pressed by God's hand, it expostulates on account of too much rigour; and many in an open manner give utterance to their blasphemies. As then they own not God's justice in his punishment, the Prophet calls it a sacrifice; and sacrifices, we know, are evidences of divine worship, and he who offers a sacrifice to God, owns him to be just. So also by this kind of speaking Zephaniah intimates that God would not act a cruel part in cutting off the city Jerusalem and its inhabitants; for this would be a sacrifice, according to the language often employed by the Prophets, and especially by Isaiah, who says of Bozrah, 'A sacrifice is prepared in Bozrah,' (Is. xxxiv. 6;) and who says also of Jerusalem itself, 'Oh! Ariel! Ariel!' (Is. xxix. 1,) where Jerusalem itself is represented as the altar; as though he had said, "In all the streets, in the open places, there shall be altars to me; for I will collect together great masses of men, whom I shall slay as a sacrifice to me." For all who were not willing to render worship to God, and who did not freely offer themselves as spiritual victims to him, were to be drawn to the slaughter, and were at the same time called sacrifices. So the executions on the gallows, when the wicked suffer, may be said to be sacrifices to God: for the Lord arms the magistrate with the sword to restrain wickedness, that the wicked may not have such liberty as to banish all equity from the world. The cities also, which, being forcibly taken, are subject to a slaughter, and the fields, where armies are slain, become altars, for God makes the rebellious a sacrifice, because they refuse willingly to offer themselves.

So also in this place the Prophet says, *Jehovah has prepared for himself a sacrifice,*—Where? At Jerusalem, through the whole city, as it has appeared from the quotation from Isaiah; for as they had not rightly sacrificed to

God on Mount Sion, but vitiated his whole worship, God himself declares, that he would become a priest, that he might slay, as he thought right, those beasts, who had obstinately refused his yoke: *And he has prepared his guests.* But I cannot finish to-day.

PRAYER.

Grant, Almighty God, that as we continue in so many ways to provoke against us thy wrath, we may patiently bear the punishment, by which thou wouldest correct our faults, and also anticipate thy judgment: and since thou art pleased to recall us in due time to thyself, let us not turn deaf ears to thy counsels, but so obey and submit ourselves to thee, that we may become partakers of that mercy, which thou offerest to us, provided we seek to be reconciled to thee, and so proceed in thy service, that under the government of Christ thy Son, whom thou hast appointed to be our supreme and only king, we may so strive to be wholly devoted to thee that thou mayest be glorified through our whole life, until we become at length partakers of that celestial glory, which has been procured for us by the blood of thy only-begotten Son. Amen.

Lecture One Hundred and Twentieth.

WE stated yesterday why God compares the slaughter of the wicked to a sacrifice,—because in punishing the ungodly, he shows himself to be the judge of the world: and this slaying is a sacrifice of sweet odour, because it makes known this glory. And he immediately adds, that he had *prepared his guests.* The word he uses is קדש, *kodash,* which means to sanctify, but is often to be taken in a different sense. It may be explained as meaning, that God had prepared his guests: but as there is an express mention made of sacrifice, Zephaniah, I have no doubt, continues the same metaphor. The meaning then is, that the Chaldeans, who were ministers of God's vengeance, were already not only chosen for the purpose of executing it, but were divinely consecrated for that end: and this unwelcome saying was uttered by the Prophet, that he might more sharply touch the feelings of his own nation. The Jews ought indeed to have acknowledged God's judgment even when executed by heathens; but this they would not have done, had they not understood, that these were, in exercising their cruelty, as it were, the priests of God; for the royal priesthood at Jerusalem had been profaned. We now then see why the Prophet says, that those were sanctified by the Lord who had been invited to feed on the flesh of the chosen people, as they were wont to eat of the remainder of their sacrifices on festal days.[1] Let us now proceed.

I yesterday repeated this verse, *And it shall be, on the day of the sacrifice of Jehovah, that I will then visit the Princes, and the sons of the king, and those who are clothed with strange apparel.* The Prophet shows, that he not only threatened the common people, but also the chief leaders, so that he spared not even the king's sons. He attacks then here the principal men among the people; for they were justly led to punishment in the first place, as they had been to others the cause of their errors. We indeed know, that they who excel in dignity give a much greater offence when they abuse their power in promoting what is sinful. Hence it was, that God seemed often to have sent his Prophets to them only. For though the low and the humble in the community were not exempt from punishment, yet it was but reasonable that God should more severely punish their leaders. Hence the Prophet now says, that God would *visit the Princes and the king's sons.*[2] He did not indeed intend

[1] The first idea of the verb קדש, is evidently to set apart, to separate either men or things for a certain purpose. For this meaning *Parkhurst* refers to Lev. xx. 24, compared with ver. 26, and to Deut. xix. 2, 7, compared with Josh. xx. 7. This idea seems the most suitable here, "I have set apart (or selected) my guests." *Newcome* renders it "appointed," and *Henderson*, "consecrated," as *Calvin* does. " Segregavit—set apart," is the version of *Drusius*, and *Junius* has " preparavit—prepared." When the verb is followed by "war," it is rendered "prepare" in our version. See Jer. vi. 4; Joel iii. 9; Mic. iii. 5. The explanation given by *Theodoret* is ἀφωρισι—he separated or selected.—*Ed.*

[2] This was a prophecy: though the king Josiah had no children at this time, yet he had some afterwards; and they proved themselves deserving of the judgment here announced, and it was inflicted on them. *Henderson's* objection, that as Josiah had then no children, the prophecy could not apply to them personally, seems wholly inadmissible: it was a *prophecy*. —*Ed.*

here to flatter obscure men, as though God meant to overlook them: but as the king and his counsellors had more grievously sinned, the more angry was God with them. We also know, that kings and others, who exercise power, are not easily moved, for the splendour of their fortune blinds them; and they think that they are in a manner exempt from laws, because they occupy a higher station. We now then see why the Prophet speaks especially of the princes and the king's sons.

He also adds, *And those who wear foreign apparel.*[1] Some refer this to the worshippers of Baal, or his priests; but the context does not allow us to apply it to any but to courtiers, whose great delight was in apparel: for what Christ says is proved by the experience of all ages to be too true,—that they who wear soft clothing are in king's courts. (Matt. xi. 8.) And it is probable, that courtiers, through a foolish affectation, often changed their clothes; as it is the case with men who seek to appear great, they devise daily some new way for spending money; and though they may be more splendidly clothed than needful, yet they think it almost too sordid to wear the same apparel for a whole month; and that their prodigality may be more evident, they change also the forms of their dress. This affectation prevails far too much at this day in the world. But even then in the age of the Prophet, as it appears, the courtiers and those who had power among the people, often changed their dress, that they might the more display their pomp and attract the admiration of the simple and poor people. And it was not simple ambition, but it brought with it a contempt for others; for the rich in this way upbraided the poor, that they themselves were alone worthy of this superfluity and opulence. It was not enough for them, that they were clothed for their own comfort, and also that ornament and splendour were added; but they would have willingly made bare all others: and as it was a shame to do this, they yet showed, as far as they could, by their superfluous abundance, that they were alone worthy of

---

[1] Or, literally, "the garment of a foreigner or stranger," נכרי. The singular is used poetically for the plural, instead of "the garments of foreigners."—*Ed.*

such display. It was then no wonder that the Lord threatened them with so much severity.

As this vice in course of time had greatly increased, this passage of the Prophet deserves particular notice. And the more luxurious men become and the more they indulge in such varieties, and thus manifest their pride, the more carefully we ought to learn to restrain the desires of our flesh, that they may not leap over the bounds of moderation; and let those who abound in wealth be contented with what is modest and becoming; and let them especially abstain from that absurd affectation, which the Prophet evidently condemns here. It may however have been, that the Jews then sought new and unusual fashions as to their clothes from remote countries, like the French at this day, who delight in the Turkish habit; for they have too much intercourse with Turkey. So also at that time a foolish desire had possessed the hearts of the people, so as to wish to ingratiate themselves with the Chaldeans, and to make friends of them by a likeness in dress. And we may learn this from a passage in Ezekiel, where he compares them to harlots or to foolish lovers (Ezek. xxiii. 2, &c.:) for as lovers paint harlots on walls, and whoremongers and adulterers do the same; so Ezekiel accuses the Jews, that they were so inflamed with a mad desire of making a covenant with the Chaldean nation, that they had their images painted in their chambers. They also no doubt imitated their dress, in order to show that they regarded it a great happiness, if they became their friends and confederates.

Now follows what I repeated also yesterday, *I will visit every one who danceth on the threshold.* Some explain this of the worshippers of Baal, but improperly; for as I have already said, the context will not allow us to understand this except of the servants of princes, who cruelly harassed the people and deprived helpless men of their property, who were not able to resist them. The Prophet then, after having spoken of the chief governors of the kingdom and of the king's sons, now comes to their servants, who, like hunting dogs, were ready to seize everywhere on the prey. They who understand this to be said of the sacrifices of Baal, adduce a passage from sacred history,—that since the image of Dagon had been found on the threshold of the temple, they dared not to tread on the threshold, but leaped over it: but this is too far-fetched. Others also bring expositions of a different kind; but the Prophet, I have no doubt, refers here to the liberty they took in plundering, when he says, that they danced on the threshold, as persons triumphing; for he afterwards adds, that they *filled, by rapine and fraud, the houses* of the princes. To leap or dance then on the threshold is no other thing than to take possession of the houses of other people, and insolently to triumph over them, as it is usually done by conquerors. For he who takes possession of what belongs to another, does not quietly rest there as in his own habitation, but boasts and exults. So also here, the Prophet paints to the life that wantonness, which the servants of princes showed, when they entered into the houses of others. He therefore says, that *they danced*, and said, "This is my house; and who will dare to say a word to the contrary?" Since then the servants of princes took so much liberty, the Prophet here denounces on them the vengeance of God.[1]

He then adds, that they filled their masters' houses by *rapine and fraud*. By rapine and fraud he means the prey gathered, partly by armed force, and partly by deceit and craft; for courtiers have their nets by which they lay in wait for helpless men. But if they cannot obtain by fraud what they hope for, they have recourse to armed force. However this may be, they enrich themselves, sometimes by plundering, and sometimes by fraud. Hence the Prophet mentions both here. It follows—

10. And it shall come to pass in that day, saith the Lord, *that there shall be* the noise of a cry from the fish gate, and an howling from the second, and a great crashing from the hills.	10. Et erit in die illa, dicit Iehova, vox clamoris à porta piscium, et ululatus à secunda (*ad verbum; sed multi intelligunt* scholam,) et contritio magna à collibus.

[1] *Marckius*, following the *Septuagint*, and some of the fathers, *Cyril, Theodoret, Jerome*, &c., think that the thoughtless intruders into the temple are here meant, and such as brought there as sacrifices and gifts the fruits of plunder and fraud. But the passage cannot possibly bear this

He confirms here the same truth, and amplifies and illustrates it by a striking description; for we know how much a lively representation avails to touch the feelings, when the event itself is not only narrated, but placed as it were before our eyes. So the Prophet is not content with plain words, but presents a scene, that the future destruction of Jerusalem might appear in a clearer light. But as I have elsewhere explained this mode of speaking, I shall not dwell on the subject now.

He says, that there would be *the voice of crying from the gate of the fishes.* He names here three places in Jerusalem, and afterwards he adds a fourth. But as we do not understand the situation of the city, sufficient for us is this probable conjecture,—that he refers to parts opposite to one another; as though he had said, that no corner of the city would be in a quiet state, when the Lord roused up war. Let us then suppose it to be triangular, and let the gate of the fishes be one side, and let the second gate or the school be on the other; and let the part nigh the hills form the third side. What some say, that the hills mean palaces, I do not approve of; nor is it consistent with the context: but we ought to bear in mind what I have already stated, that the Prophet here denounces ruin on every part of the city, so that the Jews would in vain seek refuges for themselves; for by running here and there, they would find all places full of crying and howling. *There shall be* then *the voice of crying from the gate of the fishes.* Why the Prophet calls it the gate of the fishes we cannot for certainty say, except that it is a probable conjecture, that either some fish-pond was near it, or that the fish-market was nigh.

As to the word משנה, *meshene,* the majority of interpreters think that it means the place where the priests explained the law and devoted themselves to the study of it; and they adduce a passage from 2 Kings xxii. 14, where it seems, as there is mention made of priests, the word is taken in this sense. But as gates are spoken of here, and as the Hebrews

---

meaning according to the Hebrew text: nor is such a meaning consistent with the context. The view given here is that of *Kimki, Drusius, Newcome* and *Henderson.—Ed.*

often call whatever is second in order by this word, as the second part in buildings and also in towns and in other places, is thus called, we may take it here in this sense, that is, as meaning that gate which was next to the first in general esteem. But as the subject has little to do with the main point, I dismiss it.[1]

He says in the last place, that there *would be a great breach in the hills.* He refers, I have no doubt, to that part of the city which was contiguous to the mountains. However this may be, it was the Prophet's object to include here the whole city, that he might shake off from the Jews all vain confidence, and show that there would be no escape, when the Lord stretched forth his hand to punish their sins. It now follows—

11. Howl, ye inhabitants of Maktesh, for all the merchant people are cut down; all they that bear silver are cut off.	11. Ululate habitatores loci concavi; quia exterminatus est populus mercatorum, excisi sunt omnes onusti pecuniâ.

The Prophet addresses the merchants here who inhabited

---

[1] *Junius, Piscator, Newcome* and *Henderson* think that it means the second city, a part of Jerusalem being so called, as they suppose, in Neh. xi. 9; where our version is considered to be wrong, and the clause ought to be, "and Judah, the son of Jeruiah, was over the second city"—על־העיר משנה. So it is deemed improperly rendered "college" in 2 Kings xxii. 14, and 2 Chron. xxxiv. 22; where it ought to be "in the second city." But the passage in Nehemiah is not decisive on the subject; and our version is countenanced by the former part of the verse, where "Joel" is said to be the "overseer," and "Judah" is mentioned as being next to him, the second in office: and it is so rendered in the *Septuagint*. As to the other text, the word is by itself as here. What *Calvin*, after *Cyril* and *Theodoret*, suggests, is the most probable solution.

The word rendered by *Calvin* "contritio—breach," and by *Henderson*, "destruction," is שבר. As "crying" and "howling" are said to proceed from the other parts, so something similar must have proceeded from "the hills." The word means breaking, and it is often applied to the heart— "a broken heart," Ps. xxxiv. 18; li. 19, &c. It seems to mean here the breaking out into weeping and wailing. The parallelism of the verse would thus be complete,—

    And there shall be in that day, saith Jehovah,
    The voice of crying from the fish-gate,
    And howling from the second *gate*,
    And great wailing from the hills.

Wailing is the breaking out of anguish and pangs. The word is used in Ezek. xxi. 6, for acute pain in the loins, and may be considered as used here metonymically.—*Ed.*

the middle part of the city, and hence thought themselves farther off from all danger and trouble. As then they were concealed as it were in their hiding-places, they thought that no danger was nigh them; and thus security blinded them the more. After having spoken of the king's palace and of the princes and their servants, Zephaniah now turns his discourse to the merchants.

And he calls them the inhabitants of the hollow place, מכתש, *mecatash*. The verb כתש, *catash*, means to be hollow; hence the Hebrews call a hollow place מכתש, *mecatash*. So Solomon calls a mortar by this name, because it is hollow:[1] and we learn also from other parts of scripture that the word means sometimes either a cavern or some low place. But we know that merchants have for the most part their streets on level ground, and it is for their advantage, as they have goods to carry. It may then have been, that at Jerusalem there was a large company of merchants in that part of the city, which was in its situation low. But they who regard it as a proper name, bring nothing either of reason or probability to confirm their opinion: and it is also evident from the context that merchants are here addressed, *for cut off*, he says, *is the mercantile people*. The word כנען, *canon*, means a merchant. Some think that the Jews are here, as often elsewhere, called Canaan, because they were become degenerate, and more like the Canaanites than the holy fathers, from whom they descended.[2] But the Prophet

---

[1] This original meaning of the word is much more probable than what lexicographers generally give. The braying or pounding is evidently derived from the noun, and the noun from the form of the mortar. Most agree that the word here means the *lower* part of the city—the hollow, from the circumstance of being surrounded by hills. The "hills" were those on which a part of the city was built, such as Zion, Moriah and Ophal.—*Ed.*

[2] This opinion has been entertained, because the Jews are so called in Hos. xii. 8. That the word means a trader or merchant is evident from Job xli. 6, (in the Hebrew Bibles, xl. 30;) Is. xxiii. 8; Ezek. xvii. 4. In the last passage it is rendered "traffic" in our version; and it may be so rendered here—"all the people of traffic," or of trade. The version of *Newcome* is, "all the trafficking people." The verse may be thus literally rendered,—

    Howl ye, the inhabitants of the lower part,
    For reduced to silence have been all the people of trade,
    Cut off have been all the laden with silver.

speaks here no doubt of merchants, for an explanation immediately follows, *all who are laden with money*. And he says that merchants were laden with money, because they would not transact business without making payments and counting money, and also, because merchants for the most part engrossed by their gainful arts a great portion of the wealth of the world.

We now then understand what the Prophet means: He threatens howling to the merchants, who were concealed in their hidden places, for they occupied that part of the city, as I have already said, which was below the hills; and he then makes use of the word כנען, *canon*, a trafficker; and lastly he speaks of their wealth, as it is probable that they became rich through frauds and most dishonest means, and shows that their money would be useless to them, for they would find in it no defence, when the Lord extended his hand to punish them. It now follows—

12. And it shall come to pass at that time, *that* I will search Jerusalem with candles, and punish the men that are settled on their lees: that say in their heart, The Lord will not do good, neither will he do evil.

12. Et erit in tempore illo, scrutabor Ierusalem in lucernis, et visitabo super homines, qui congelati sunt in fæcibus suis, et dicunt in cordibus suis, Neque benefaciet Iehova, neque malefaciet.

The Prophet addresses here generally the despisers of God, who were become hardened in their wickedness. But before he openly names them, he says that the visitation would be such, that God would search every corner, so that no place would remain unexplored. For to visit with candles, or to search with candles, is so to examine all hidden places or coverts, that nothing may escape. When one intends to plunder a city, he first enters into the houses, and takes away whatever he finds; but when he thinks that there are some hidden treasures, he descends into the secret cells; and

---

They are called to howl, as though their calamity had already taken place, a mode of speaking often used by the Prophets. That the event was future is clear from the context, especially from the next verse. "Reduced to silence"—נדמה, is literally the meaning, not "destroyed;" and appropriate is the term, as people of trade create much bustle and noise. "The laden with silver," may be rendered, as *Newcome* does, "the bearers of silver:" and silver is here for money.—*Ed.*

then if there be no light there, he lights a candle, and carefully looks here and there, that he may not overlook anything. By this comparison then God intimates, that Jerusalem would be so plundered, that nothing whatever would remain. Hence he says, *I will search it with candles.* We indeed know that nothing is hid from God; but it is evident, that he is constrained to borrow comparisons from the common practice of men, because he could not otherwise express what is necessary for us to know. The world indeed deal with God as men do with one another; for they think that he can be deceived by their craftiness. He therefore laughs to scorn this folly, and says, that he would have candles to search out whatever was concealed.

Now, as impiety had possessed the minds of almost all the people, he says, *I will visit the men who on their lees are congealed.* This may indeed be only understood of the rich, who flattered themselves in their prosperity, and feared nothing, and were thus congealed on their lees: but Zephaniah shows in the words which follow, that he had in view something more atrocious, that is, that they said that *neither good nor evil proceeded from God.* At the same time, these two things may be suitably joined together—that he reproves here their self-security, produced by wealth—and that he also accuses the careless Jews of that gross contempt of God which is afterwards mentioned. And I am disposed to take this view, that is, that the Jews, inebriated with prosperity, became hardened, as men contract hardness often by labour —and that they so collected lees through too much quietness and abundance of things, that they became wholly stupid, and could be touched by no truth made known to them. Hence in the first place the Prophet says, that God would visit with punishment a carelessness so extreme, when men not only slumbered in their prosperity, but also became congealed in their own stupidity, so as to be almost void of sense and understanding. When one addresses a dead mass, he can effect nothing: and so the Prophet compares careless men to a dead and congealed mass; for stupidity had so bound up all their senses, that they could not be either allured by the goodness of God, or terrified by his threatenings. Congealing then is nothing else but that hardness or contumacy, which is contracted by self-indulgences, and particularly when the minds of men become almost stupified.[1] And by *lees* he means sinful indulgences, which so infatuate all the senses of men, that no light nor sincerity remains.

He then mentions what they said *in their hearts*. He expresses here what that carelessness which he condemned brings with it—even that wicked men fearlessly mock God. What it is to speak in the heart, is evident from many parts of Scripture; it means to determine anything within: for though the ungodly do not openly proclaim what they determine in their minds, they yet reason within themselves, and settle this point—that either there is no God, or that he rests idly in heaven. 'Said hath the ungodly in his heart, No God is?' Why in the heart? Because shame or fear prevents men from openly avowing their impiety; yet they cherish such thoughts in the heart and assent to them. Now here is described by the Prophet the height of impiety, when he says, that men drunk with pleasures robbed God of his office as a judge, saying, that he doeth neither good nor evil. And it is probable that there were then many at Jerusalem and throughout Judea who thus insolently despised God as a judge. But Zephaniah especially speaks of the chief men; for such above all others deride God, as the giants did, and look down as from on high on his judgments. There is indeed much insensibility among the common people; but there is more madness in the pride of great men, who, trusting in their power, think themselves exempt from the authority of God.

---

[1] There is a similar passage in Jer. xlviii. 11; but the verb is different, שקט, which means to be still, to rest, to settle, while the verb here is קפא, which signifies to be condensed or to be congealed, Ex. xv. 8. But as things congealed become fixed, the verb seems to have the meaning of fixedness here; as wines on the lees, to which allusion is made, do not become congealed, the comparison seems to be, that as wine kept still on the lees increases in strength and flavour, so the Jews, settling on their dregs —their sins—became strengthened and confirmed in their wickedness and atheistic notions. But *Newcome* and *Henderson* take another view of the metaphor, and consider that "the thoughtless tranquillity of the rich is compared to the fixed unbroken surface of fermented liquors." Our version favours the former idea, as the verb is rendered "settled."—*Ed.*

But what I have just said must be borne in mind, that an unhealable impiety is described by the Prophet, when he accuses the Jews, that they did not think God to be the author either of good or of evil; because God is thus deprived of his dignity; for except he is owned as the judge of the world, what becomes of his dignity? The majesty, or the authority, or the glory of God does not consist in some imaginary brightness, but in those works which so necessarily belong to him, that they cannot be separated from his very essence. It is what peculiarly belongs to God, to govern the world, and to exercise care over mankind, and also to make a difference between good and evil, to help the miserable, to punish all wickedness, to check injustice and violence. When any one takes away these things from God, he leaves him an idol only. Since, then, the glory of God consists in his justice, wisdom, judgment, power, and other attributes, all who deny God to be the governor of the world entirely extinguish, as much as they can, his glory. Even so do heathen writers accuse Epicurus; for as he dared not to deny the existence of some god, like Diagoras and some others, he confessed that there are some gods, but shut them up in heaven, that they might enjoy there their leisure and delights. But this is to imagine a god, who is not a god. It is then no wonder that the Prophet condemns with so much sharpness the stupidity of the Jews, as they thought that neither good nor evil proceeded from God. But there was also a greater reason why God should be so indignant at such senselessness: for whence was it that men entertained such an opinion or such a delirious thought, as to deny that God did either good or evil, except that they attempted to drive God far away from them, that they might not be subject to his judgment. They therefore who seek to extinguish the distinction between right and wrong in their consciences, invent for themselves the delirious notion, that God concerns not himself with human affairs, that he is contented with his own celestial felicity, and descends not to us, and that adversity as well as prosperity happens to men by chance.

We hence see how men seek wilfully and designedly to

indulge the notion, that neither good nor evil comes from God: they do this, that they may stupify their own consciences, and thus precipitate themselves with greater liberty into sin, as though they were free to do anything with impunity, and as though there was no judge to whom an account is to be rendered.

And hence I have said, that it is the very summit of impiety when men strengthen themselves in this error, that God rests in heaven, and that whatever miseries they endure in this world happen through fortune, and that whatever good things they have are to be ascribed either to their own industry or to chance. And so the Prophet briefly shows in this passage that the Jews were past recovery, that no one might feel surprised, that God should punish with so much severity a people who had been his friends, and whom he had adopted in preference to the whole world: for he had set apart the race of Abraham, as it is well known, as his chosen and holy people. God's vengeance on the children of Abraham might have appeared cruel or extremely rigid, had it not been expressly declared that they had advanced so far in impiety as to seek to exclude God from the government of the world, and to deprive him of his own peculiar office, even that of punishing sin, of defending his own people, of delivering them from all evils, of relieving all their miseries. Since, then, they thus shut up God in heaven, and gave the governing power on earth to fortune, it was an intolerable stupidity, nay, wholly diabolical. It was therefore no wonder that God was so severely indignant, and stretched forth his hand to punish their sin, as their disease had become now incurable.

PRAYER.

Grant, Almighty God, that as almost the whole world breaks out into such excesses, that there is no moderation, no reason,—O grant, that we may learn not only to confine ourselves within those limits which thou dost approve and command, but also to delight and glory in the smallness of our portion, inasmuch as the wealth, and honours, and pleasures of the world so fascinate the hearts and minds of all, that they elevate themselves into heaven, and carry on war, as it were, avowedly with thee. Grant also to us, that in our limited portion we may be in such a way humbled under thy powerful hand, as never to doubt but that thou wilt be our deliverer even in our greatest miseries; and that ascribing to thee the power over life and death, we may feel fully assured, that whatever afflictions happen to us, proceed from thy just judgment, so that we may be led to repentance, and daily exercise ourselves in it, until we shall at length come to that blessed rest which is laid up for us in heaven, through Christ our Lord. Amen.

Lecture One Hundred and Twenty-First.

13. Therefore their goods shall become a booty, and their houses a desolation: they shall also build houses, but not inhabit *them*; and they shall plant vineyards, but not drink the wine thereof.

13. Et erit substantia eorum in direptionem, et domus eorum in vastitatem; et ædificabunt domos, neque habitabunt; et plantabunt vineas, neque bibent vinum earum.

ZEPHANIAH pursues the same subject—that God, after long forbearance, would punish his rebellious and obstinate people. Hence he says, that they were now delivered, even by God himself, into the hands of their enemies. They indeed knew that many were inimical to them; but they did not consider God's judgment, as God himself elsewhere complains—that they did not regard the hand of him who smote them. (Is. ix. 13.) Our Prophet, therefore, declares now that they were given up to destruction, and that their enemies would find no trouble nor difficulty in invading the land, since all places would be open to plunder. And he recites what is found in Lev. xxvi. 20; for the Prophets were interpreters of the law, and the only difference between Moses and them is, that they apply his general truth to their own time. The Prophet now pursues this course, as though he had said, that God had not in vain or to no purpose threatened this evil in his law; for the Jews would find by experience that this would really be the case, and that it had been truly said, that the fruit of the land, their habitations, and other comforts of life, would be transferred to others. It now follows—

14. The great day of the Lord *is* near, *it is* near, and hasteth greatly, *even* the voice of the day of the Lord: the mighty man shall cry there bitterly.

14. Propinquus dies Jehovæ magnus, propinquus et festinans valdè; vox diei Jehovæ amara (*ut alii vertunt,*) vociferabitur illic fortis (*vel*, amarum, *aut*, amarè illic vociferabitur fortis; *alii secus distinguunt*, Vox diei Jehovæ amara vociferabitur, *aut*, amarè; *postea*, illic fortis.)

The Prophet in this verse expresses more clearly what I have already stated—That God would be the author of all the evils which would happen to the Jews; for as they grew more insensible in their sins, they more and more provoked God's wrath against themselves. It is therefore no common wisdom to consider God's hand when he strikes or chastens us. This is the reason why the Prophet now calls the attention of the Jews to God, that they might not fix their minds, as it is commonly done, on men only. At the same time, he tries to shake off their torpor by declaring that the day would be terrible, and that it was also now near at hand. We indeed know that hypocrites trifle with God, except they feel the weight of his wrath, and that they protract time, and promise themselves so long a respite, that they never awake to repentance. Hence the Prophet in the first place shows, that whatever evils then impended over the Jews were not only from men, but especially from God. This is one thing; and then, in order thoroughly to touch stupid hearts, he says, that the *day would be terrible;* and lastly, that they might not deceive themselves by vain flatteries, he declares that the day was at hand. These three things must be noticed in order that we understand the Prophet's object.

But he says at the beginning of the verse, that *the great day of Jehovah was nigh.* In these words he includes the three things to which I have already referred. By calling it the *day of Jehovah*, he means, that whatever evils the Jews suffered, ought to have been ascribed to his judgment; and by calling it *the great day*, his object was to strike terror; as well as by saying, in the third place, that it was *nigh*. We hence see that three things are included in these words. But the Prophet more fully explains what might, on account of the brevity of his words, have seemed not quite clear.

Near, he says, *is the day, and quickly hastens.* Men, we know, are wont to extend time, that they may cherish their sins; for though they cannot divest themselves of every feeling as to religion, or shake it off, they yet imagine for themselves a long distance between them and God; and by such an imagination they find ease for themselves. Hence the Prophet declares *the day* to be *nigh;* and as it was hardly credible that the destruction of which he spake was near, he adds, that the day was *quickly hastening;* as though he had said, that they ought not to judge by the present state of things what God would do, for in a moment his wrath would pass through from east to west like lightning. Men need long preparation when they determine to execute their vengeance; but God has no need of much preparation, for his own power is sufficient for him when he resolves to destroy the wicked. We now, then, see why it was added by the Prophet, that the day would quickly hasten.

He now repeats that the *day of Jehovah* and *his voice would cry out bitterly.* I have stated three renderings as given by interpreters. Some read thus—" The day of Jehovah shall be bitter; there the strong shall cry aloud." This meaning is admissible, and a useful instruction may from it be elicited; as though the Prophet had said, that no courage could bring help to men, or be an aid to them, against God's vengeance. Others give this rendering, that the day would bitterly cry out, for there would be the strong, that is, the strength of enemies would break down whatever courage the Jews might have. But this second meaning seems forced; and I am disposed to adopt the third—that the voice of the day of Jehovah would bitterly cry out. And he means the voice of those who would have really to know God as a judge, whom they had previously despised; for God would then put forth his power, which had been an object of contempt, until the Jews had by experience felt it.[1]

[1] The Rabbinical punctuation has destroyed the simplicity of this passage by connecting "bitter" with the latter clause. *Jerome, Pagninus,*

As to the Prophet's design, there is no ambiguity: for he seeks here to rouse the Jews from their insensibility, who had so hardened themselves against all threatenings, that the Prophets were not able to convince them. Since, then, they had thus hardened themselves against every instruction and all warnings, the Prophet here says, that the voice of God's day would be different: for God's voice had sounded through the mouth of the Prophets, but it availed not with the deaf. An awful change is here announced; for the Jews shall then cry aloud, as the roaring of the divine voice shall then terrify them, when God shall really show that he is the avenger of wickedness—"When therefore he shall ascend his tribunal, then ye shall cry. His messengers now cry to you in vain, for ye close up your ears; ye shall cry in your turn, but it will be in vain."

But if one prefers to take it as one sentence, "The voice of the day of Jehovah, there strong, shall bitterly cry out," the meaning will be the same as to the main point. I would not, therefore, contend about words, provided we bear in mind what I have already said—that Zephaniah sets here the cry of the distressed people in opposition to the voices of the Prophets, which they had despised, yea, and for the most part, as it appears from other places, treated

Newcome, as well as the *Septuagint*, connect it with the former clause. The literal rendering of the two lines is as follows—

  The voice of the day of Jehovah *shall be* grievous;
  Roar out there (or then) shall the brave.

"The voice of the day," &c., means the voice uttered on that day, as *Drusius* explains it. מר is no doubt "bitter;" but it is often applied in scripture to express what is grievous, afflictive, or sorrowful. If we render שם, "there," it refers to Jerusalem, verse 12; but it is sometimes used as an adverb of time, "then," see Ps. xiv. 5; Neh. iii. 15. "The meaning is," says *Drusius*, "that the voice of that day, which they who excel in strength of mind and body shall utter, shall be bitter." The whole verse is remarkably concise and emphatical,—

  14. Nigh *is* the great day of Jehovah,
   Nigh and hastening quickly:
  The voice of the day of Jehovah *shall be* grievous;
  Roar out then shall the brave.

Then the following verse is not to begin, as in our version, which has been followed by *Newcome* and *Henderson*, "That day *is* a day of wrath," but thus—

  A day of wrath *shall be* that day.

This is the order of the original, and as there is no verb, it must be supplied and regulated as to its tense by the context.—*Ed.*

with ridicule. However this may have been, he indirectly condemns their false confidence, when he speaks of the strong; as though he had said, that they were strong only for their own ruin, while they opposed God and his servants; for this strength falls at length, nay, it breaks itself by its own weight, when God rises to judgment. It follows—

15. That day is a day of wrath, a day of trouble and distress, a day of wasteness and desolation, a day of darkness and gloominess, a day of clouds and thick darkness,
16. A day of the trumpet and alarm against the fenced cities, and against the high towers.

15. Dies excandescentiæ, dies ille, dies angustiæ et afflictionis, dies tumultus et vastationis, dies tenebrarum et caliginis, dies nubis et nebulæ;
16. Dies tubæ et clangoris super urbes munitas, et super arces excelsas.

The Prophet shows here how foolish they were who extenuated God's vengeance, as hypocrites and all wicked men are wont to do. Hence he accuses the Jews of madness, that they thought that the way of reconciliation would be easy to them, when they had by their perverseness provoked God to come against them as an armed enemy. For though the ungodly do not promise to themselves anything of God's favour, yet they entertain vain imaginations, as though he might with no trouble be pacified: they do not think that he will be propitious to them, and yet in the meantime they deride his vengeance. Against this kind of senselessness the Prophet now inveighs. We have stated in other places, that these kinds of figurative expressions were intended solely for this end—to constrain men to entertain some fear, for they wilfully deluded themselves: for the Prophets had to do, partly with open despisers of God, and partly with his masked worshippers, whose holiness was hypocrisy.

This, then, was the reason why he said, that that day would be *a day of wrath,* and also a *day of distress and of affliction,*[1] *of tumult and desolation,*[2] *of darkness and of thick*

[1] The original words are similar in sound and meaning; the first, צרה, comes from a verb which means to inclose, to confine, to straiten, and it may be rendered, narrowness, confinement, straitness, distress. The other, מצוקה, is oppression, as the verb means to press down, to press close.
[2] Waste or confusion is, שאה, and משואה, derived from the same root, may be rendered desolation. The two next words, "darkness" and "thick

darkness, of clouds and of mist. In short, he intended to remove from the Jews that confidence with which they flattered themselves, yea, the confidence which they derived from their contempt of God: for the flesh is secure, while it has coverts, where it may withdraw itself from the presence of God. True confidence cannot exceed moderation, that is, the confidence that is founded on God's word, for thus men come nigh to God: but the flesh wishes for no other rest but in the forgetfulness of God. And we have already seen in the Prophet Amos, (Amos v. 18,) why the day of Jehovah is painted as being so dreadful; he had, as I have said, to contend with hypocrites, who made an improper use of God's name, and at the same time slumbered in gross insensibility. Hence Amos said, "It will be a day, not of light, but of darkness; not of joy, but of sorrow. Why then do ye anxiously expect the day of the Lord?" For the Jews, glorying in being the chosen people of God, and trusting only in their false title of adoption, thought that everything was lawful for them, as though God had renounced his own authority. And thus hypocrites ever flatter themselves, as though they held God bound to them. Our Prophet does not, as Amos, distinctly express these sentiments, yet the meaning of the words is the same, and that is, that when God ascends his tribunal, there is no hope for pardon. He at the same time cuts off from them all their vain confidences; for though God excludes all escapes, yet hypocrites look here and there, before and behind, to the right hand and to the left.

The Prophet therefore intimates, that there would be everywhere darkness and thick darkness, clouds and mists, affliction and distress,—Why? because it would be the day of wrath; for God, after having borne patiently a long time with the Jews, and seen that they perversely abused his patience, would at length put forth his power. And that

---

darkness," occur in Joel ii. 2. In the same passage we have also "the day of cloudiness and of entire darkness," literally, bare or naked darkness; for the word is, ערפל, derived, as I conceive, from ער, bare, and אפל, thick darkness. There is a gradation in the words used in each line; the second word is stronger than the first.—*Ed.*

they might not set up their own strongholds against God, he says, that war was proclaimed against *the fortified cities and high citadels*. We hence see that he deprives the Jews of all help, in order that they might understand that they were to perish, except they repented, and thus return into favour with God. *It shall then be a day of the trumpet and of shouting*,¹—How ? *on all fortified cities*. For the Jews, as it is usually done, compared the strength of their enemies with their own. It was not their purpose to go forth beyond their own borders: and they thought that they would be able to resist, and be sufficiently fortified, if any foreign enemy invaded them. The Prophet laughs to scorn this notion, for God had declared war against their fortified cities. It follows—

17. And I will bring distress upon men, that they shall walk like blind men, because they have sinned against the Lord: and their blood shall be poured out as dust, and their flesh as the dung.

17. Et coarctabo hominem (*vel*, homines,) et ambulabunt tanquam cæci, quia contra Iehovam impie egerunt; et fundetur sanguis quasi pulvis ; et caro eorum erit tanquam stercora.

He confirms what I have already stated—that though other enemies, the Assyrians or Chaldeans, attacked the Jews, yet God would be the principal leader of the war. God then claims here for himself what the Jews transferred to their earthly enemies : and the Prophet has already often

¹ Rather " acclamation," the triumphant voice of conquerors. As an attempt to preserve the distinctive character of each word in this singular passage, I offer the following version—
 15. A day of extreme wrath *shall be* that day,
  A day of distress and oppression,
  A day of waste and of desolation,
  A day of darkness and of thick darkness,
  A day of cloudiness and of entire darkness;
 16. A day of the trumpet and of acclamation
  Over the cities that are inclosed,
  And over the towers which are lofty.
The word עברה, " extreme wrath," means such wrath as passes over all bounds—overflowing wrath. We are obliged to use the word darkness three times for lack of suitable terms. The first is the common darkness of the night, the second is a grosser darkness, and the third is complete darkness. The words " gloominess" and " obscurity," used by *Newcome* and *Henderson*, are not sufficiently strong, and convey not the meaning.—*Ed.*

called it the day of Jehovah; for God would then make known his power, which had been a sport to them. He therefore declares in this place, that he would *reduce man to distress,* so that the whole nation would *walk like the blind*—that, being void of counsel, they would stumble and fall, and not be able to proceed in their course: for they are said to go astray like the blind, who see no end to their evils, who find no means to escape ruin, but are held as it were fast bound. And we must ever bear in mind what I have already said—that the Jews were inflated with such pride, that they heedlessly despised all the Prophets. Since then they were thus wise in themselves, God denounces blindness on them.

He subjoins the reason, *Because they had acted impiously towards Jehovah.*[1] By these words he confirms what I have already explained—that the intermediate causes are not to be considered, though the Chaldeans took vengeance on the Jews; for there is a higher principle, and another cause of this evil, even the contempt of God and of his celestial truth; for they had acted impiously towards God. And by these words the Prophet reminds the Jews, that no alleviation was to be expected, as they had not only men hostile to them, but God himself, whom they had extremely provoked.

Hence he adds, *Poured forth shall be your blood as dust.*[2] They whom God delivered up to extreme reproach were deserving of this, because he had been despised by them. *Their flesh,*[3] he says, *shall be as dung.* Now, we know how much the Jews boasted of their pre-eminence; and God had certainly given them occasion to boast, had they made a right and legitimate use of his benefits; but as they had despised him, they deserved in their turn to be exposed to every ignominy and reproach. Hence the Prophet here lays

---

[1] The Hebrew words are literally,
   For against Jehovah have they sinned.—*Ed.*

[2] "Copiously and in contempt," says *Marckius;* "as a thing of no value," says *Grotius;* "as worthless as dust," says *Drusius.* The comparison is evidently intended to show that their blood, or their life, would be treated with contempt, and no more regarded than dust.—*Ed.*

[3] The word is לחם, usually rendered food; here it means what is fed, the carcass, the body. It is rendered "flesh" by the Septuagint.—*Ed.*

prostrate all their false boastings by which they were inflated; for they wished to be honourable, while God was despised by them. At last he adds—

18. Neither their silver nor their gold shall be able to deliver them in the day of the Lord's wrath; but the whole land shall be devoured by the fire of his jealousy: for he shall make even a speedy riddance of all them that dwell in the land.	18. Etiam argentum eorum, etiam aurum eorum, nihil proficiet ad liberandos ipsos in die excandescentiæ Jehovæ, et in igne indignationis ejus devorabitur omnis terra; quia consumptionem et quidem definitam (*vel*, horribilem, *vel*, celerem) faciet cum omnibus incolis terræ.

He repeats what he has already said—that the helps which the Jews hoped would be in readiness to prevent God's vengeance would be vain. For though men dare not openly to resist God, yet they hope by some winding courses to find out some way by which they may avert his judgment. As then the Jews, trusting in their wealth, and in their fortified cities, became insolent towards God, the Prophet here declares, that neither *gold nor silver* should be a help to them. "Let them," he says, " accumulate wealth; though by the mass of their gold and silver they form high mountains for themselves, yet they shall not be able to turn aside the hand of God, nor be able to deliver themselves,"—and why? He repeats again the same thing, that it would be *the day of wrath*. We indeed know, that the most savage enemies are sometimes pacified by money, for avarice mitigates their cruelty; but the Prophet declares here, that as God would be the ruler in that war, there would be no redemption, and therefore money would be useless: for God could by no means receive them into favour, except they repented and truly humbled themselves before him.

He therefore adds, that the land would be *devoured by the fire of God's jealousy*, or indignation. He compares God's wrath to fire; for no agreement can be made when fire rages, but the more materials there are the more will there be to increase the fire. So then the Prophet excludes the Jews from any hope of deliverance, except they reconciled themselves to God by true and sincere repentance; *for a consummation*, he says, *he will make as to all the inhabitants of the land, and one indeed very quick* or speedy.¹ In short, he means, that as the Jews had hardened themselves against every instruction, they would find God's vengeance to be such as would wholly consume them, as they would not anticipate it, but on the contrary enhance it by their pride and stupidity, and even deride it. Now follows—

CHAPTER II.

1. Gather yourselves together, yea, gather together, O nation not desired;
2. Before the decree bring forth, *before* the day pass as the chaff, before the fierce anger of the Lord come upon you, before the day of the Lord's anger come upon you.

1. Colligite vos, et colligite gens non amabilis ;
2. Antequam pariat decretum, sicut stipula transibit die, antequam veniat super eos furor iræ Iehovæ, antequam veniat super eos dies iræ Iehovæ.

THE Prophet, after having spoken of God's wrath, and shown how terrible it would be, and also how near, now exhorts the Jews to repentance, and thus mitigates the severity of his former doctrine, provided their minds were teachable. We hence learn that God fulminates in his word against men, that he may withhold his hand from them. The more severe, then, God is, when he chastises us and makes known our sins, and sets before us his wrath, the more clearly he testifies how precious and dear to him is our

---

¹ Quickness rather than terror is what is evidently meant. See ver. 14. Most agree in this respect. *Newcome* renders it "speedy," and *Henderson* "sudden." The word "riddance," for כלה, in our version, is improper. It is rendered "full end" by *Newcome*, and "consummation" by *Henderson*, and "συντέλειαν—end" by the Septuagint. The particle אך does not mean "altogether," as rendered by *Henderson*, but it is an asseveration—surely, indeed, certainly, doubtless. The את before "inhabitants" has evidently here the meaning of κατα, with regard to. It is rendered ἐπι, upon, in the Septuagint, and "with" by *Marckius* and *Newcome*. The whole verse is as follows,—

    18. Neither their silver nor their gold
        Shall be able to deliver them
        In the day of the extreme-wrath of Jehovah ;
        By the fire of his jealousy
        Shall be consumed the whole land ;
        For an end, doubtless sudden, will he make,
        As to all the inhabitants of the land.

salvation; for when he sees us rushing headlong, as it were, n to ruin, he calls us back by threatenings and chastisements. Whenever, then, God condemns us by his word, let us know that he will be propitious to us, if, touched with true repentance, we flee to his mercy; for to effect this is the design of all his reproofs and threatenings.

There follows then a seasonable exhortation, after the Prophet had spoken of the dreadfulness of God's vengeance. *Gather yourselves,* he says, *gather, ye nation not worthy of being loved.* Others read—" Search among yourselves, search;" and interpreters differ as to the root of the verb; some derive it from קשׁשׁ, *koshesh,* and others from קושׁ, *kush;* while some deduce the verb from the noun קשׁ, *kosh,* which signifies chaff or stubble. But however this may be, I consider the real meaning of the Prophet to be—" Gather yourselves, gather;" for this is what grammatical construction requires. I do not see why they who read " search yourselves," depart from the commonly received meaning, except they think that the verb gather does not suit the context; but it suits it exceedingly well. Others with more refinement read thus—" Gather the chaff, gather the chaff," as though the Prophet ridiculed the empty confidence of the people. But as I have already said, he no doubt shows here the remedy, by which they might have anticipated God's judgment, with which he had threatened them. He indeed compares them to stubble, as we find in the next verse, but he shows that still time is given them to repent, so that they might gather themselves, and not be dissipated; as though he said—" The day of your scattering is at hand; ye shall then vanish away like chaff, for ye shall not be able to stand at the breath of the Lord's wrath. But now while God withholds himself, and does not put forth his hand to destroy you, gather yourselves, that ye may not be like the chaff." There are then two parts in this passage; the first is, that if the Jews abused, as usual, the forbearance of God, they would become like the chaff, for God's wrath would in a moment scatter them; but the Prophet in the meantime reminds them that a seasonable time for repentance was still given them; for if they willingly gathered themselves, God would spare them. *Before* then *the day of Jehovah's wrath shall come; gather,* he says, *yourselves.*[1]

But the way of gathering is, when men do not vanish away in their foolish confidences, or when they do not indulge their own lusts; for whenever men give loose reins to wicked licentiousness, and thus go astray in gratifying their corrupt lusts, or when they seek here and there vain confidences, they expose themselves to a scattering. Hence the Prophet exhorts them to examine themselves, to gather themselves, and as it were to draw themselves together, that they might not be like the chaff. Hence he says—" Gather yourselves, yea, gather, *ye nation not loved."*

Some take the participle נכסף, *necasaph,* in an active sense, as though the Prophet had said that the Jews were void of every feeling, and had become wholly hardened in their stupidity. But I know not whether this can be grammatically allowed. I therefore follow what has been more approved. The nation is called not worthy of love, because it did not deserve mercy; and God thus amplifies and renders illustrious his own grace, because he was still solicitous about the salvation of those who had wilfully destroyed themselves, and rejected his favour. Though then the Jews had by their depravity so alienated themselves from God, that there was no reason why he should save them, he yet still continued to call them back to himself. It is therefore a remarkable proof of the unfailing grace of God, when he shows love to a nation wholly worthy of being hated, and is concerned for its safety.[2]

---

[1] The verb, found only in five other places—Ex. v. 7, 12; Num. xv. 32, 33; and 1 Kings xvii. 10, 12, means to collect, to gather, and not "to search," as said by *Kimchi,* and adopted by *Marckius;* nor "to bind," as rendered by *Henderson.* The import of the passage is considered by all to be an invitation to repentance, though the words are differently rendered. It is difficult to see the meaning when it is said—" Gather yourselves, yea, gather," &c, except such an assembling is meant as is recommended by Joel i. 14; the kind of gathering being well understood, it is not mentioned. " Gather yourselves," that is, to offer prayers, says *Grotius.* " Be ye assembled—συνάχθητι," is the rendering of the Septuagint.—*Ed.*

[2] כסף is found as a verb in four other places, Gen. xxxi. 30; Job xiv. 15; Ps. xvii. 12; and Ps. lxxxiv. 3. It means to be or to grow pale, either through love, as in Genesis and Job, or through hunger, as in the first

He then adds, *Before the decree brings forth.* Here the Prophet asserts his own authority, and that of God's other servants: for the Jews thought that all threatenings would come to nothing, as it is the case with most men at this day who deride every true doctrine, as though it were nothing but an empty sound. Hence the Prophet ascribes birth to his doctrine. It is indeed true, that the word decree has a wider meaning; but the Prophet does not speak here of the hidden counsel of God. He therefore calls that a decree, which God had already declared by his servants: and the meaning is, that it is not beating the air when God denounces his vengeance on sinners by his Prophets, but that it is a fixed and unchangeable decree, which shall at length be effected. But the similitude of birth is most apposite; for as the embryo lies hid in the womb, and then emerges in due time into light; so God's vengeance, though hid for a time, will yet in due season be accomplished, when God sees that men's wickedness is past a remedy. We now understand why the Prophet says, that the time was near when the decree should bring forth.

Then he says, *Pass away shall the chaff in a day.* Some read, "Before the day comes, when the stubble (or chaff) shall pass away." But I take יום, *ium*, in another sense, as meaning that the Jews shall quickly pass away as the chaff;

Psalm referred to, or through longing for God's house, as in the last, or through shame, as some—such as *Grotius, Dathius* and *Gesenius,* suppose to be the case here; and they therefore give this rendering—" O nation without shame;" or, "not ashamed." This idea is favoured by the Septuagint—" unteachable—ἀπαίδευτον." In no instance is it found in a passive sense as to the feeling through which the paleness is occasioned, and therefore "worthy of love," or "desired," cannot be its proper rendering. *Buxtorf* gives its meaning in Niphal—" desiderio affici—to be touched with or to feel a desire." Hence the person spoken of is the subject, not the object, of the desire. According, then, to the use of the verb, the rendering here is to be—" Ye nation that feels no desire," that is, for God and his law, or, "that feels no shame," that is, for its sins. The paraphrase of the *Targum* is—"not willing to be converted to the law," which corresponds with the idea which has been stated.

Marckius considers that the nation is here described as having "no desire," that is for that which was good, and that its torpidity and indifference as to religion is what is set forth. And such is the view of *Cocceius;* it had no thirst for righteousness, no desire for the kingdom of God—the mark of an unregenerated mind.—*Ed.*

the like expression we have also met in Hosea. He says then that the Jews would perish in a day, in a short time, and as it were in a moment; though they thought that they would not be for a long time conquered. *Pass away*, he says, *shall they like chaff.*[1]

Then he adds, *Before it comes, the fury of Jehovah's wrath; the day of Jehovah's wrath*, gather ye yourselves. He says first, "before it comes upon you, the fury of wrath," and then, "the day of wrath." He repeats the same thing; but some of the words are changed, for instead of the fury of wrath, he puts in the second clause, the day of wrath; as though he had said, that they were greatly deceived if they thought that they could escape, because the Lord deferred his vengeance. How so? For the day, which was nigh, though not yet arrived, would at length come. As when one trust-

---

[1] It is difficult to make the words bear this sense. Hardly a sentence has been more variously rendered. The most satisfactory solution perhaps is to regard it parenthetic, and to consider "the day" as that allowed for repentance: it was to pass away quickly, like the chaff carried away by the wind—

As the chaff passing away *will be* the day.

Both *Marckius* and *Henderson* regard this as the meaning. Then the whole verse might be thus translated—

2. Before the bringing forth of the decree,
(As the chaff passing away will be the day,)
Before it shall come upon you,
The burning of Jehovah's anger;
Before it shall come upon you,
The day of the anger of Jehovah.

Literally it is, "Before it shall not come," &c., or, "During the time when it shall not come," &c. בטרם may be rendered "while;" then the version would be—

While it shall not come upon you,
The burning of Jehovah's anger;
While it shall not come upon you,
The day of the anger of Jehovah.

There are several MSS. which omit the two first lines; but evidently without reason. They are retained in the Septuagint.

Possibly the second line may refer to the speedy execution of "the decree," that its day would pass quickly. Its birth, or its bringing forth was its commencement; and the second line may express its speedy execution: it would be carried into effect with the quickness by which the chaff is carried away by the wind—

As the chaff passing away will be *its* day.

The word עבר is, in either case, a participle, and the auxiliary verb is understood, as often is the case in Hebrew, and must partake of the tense of the context.—*Ed.*

ing in the darkness of the night, and thinking himself safe from the danger of being taken, is mistaken, for suddenly the sun rises and discovers his hiding-place; so the Prophet intimates, that though God was now still, it would yet be no advantage to the Jews: for he knew the suitable time. Though then he restrained for a time his wrath, he yet poured it forth suddenly, when the day came and the iniquity of men had become ripe.

PRAYER.

Grant, Almighty God, that as we continue in various ways to provoke thy wrath, we may at length be awakened by the blasting of that trumpet which sounds in our ears, when thou proclaimest that thou wilt be the judge of the world, and testifiest also the same so plainly in the gospel, so that we may, with our minds raised up to thee, learn to renounce all the depraved lusts of the world, and that having shaken off our torpidity, we may so hasten to repent, that we may anticipate thy judgment, and so find that we are reconciled to thee, as to enjoy thy goodness, and ever to retain the taste of it, in order that we may be enabled to renounce all the allurements and pleasures of this world, until we shall at length come to that blessed rest, where we shall be filled with that unspeakable joy, which thou hast promised to us, and which we hope for in Christ our Lord. Amen.

Lecture One Hundred and Twenty-second.

3. Seek ye the Lord, all ye meek of the earth, which have wrought his judgment; seek righteousness, seek meekness: it may be ye shall be hid in the day of the Lord's anger.

3. Quærite Jehovam omnes mansueti terræ, qui judicium ejus fecerunt (*pro* fecistis;) quærite justitiam, quærite mansuetudinem, si fortè abscondamini in die iræ Jehovæ.

HERE the Prophet turns his discourse to a small number, for he saw that he could produce no effect on the promiscuous multitude. For had his doctrine been addressed in common to the whole people, there were very few who would have attended. He would therefore have been discouraged had he not believed that some seed remained among the people, and that the office of teaching and exhorting had not been in vain committed to him by God. But he shows at the same time that the greater part were wholly given up to destruction. We now see why the Prophet especially addresses the *meek of the land;* for few undertook the yoke, though they had been already broken down by many calamities. And it hence appears that the fruit of correction was not found equal in all, for God had chastised the good and the bad, the whole people, from the least to the greatest; they had all been laid prostrate by many evils, yet the same ferocity remained, as God complains in Isaiah, that he laboured in vain in punishing that refractory nation. (Isa. i. 5.)

But we are here taught that though ministers of the word may think that they spend their labour to no purpose, while they sing to the deaf, as the proverb is, they ought not yet to depart from the course of their vocation; for there will ever be some who will really show, after a long time, that they had been divinely and wonderfully saved, so as not to perish with others. But what the Prophet had especially in view was to show, that the faithful ought not to regard what the multitude may do, or how they live; but that when God invites them to repentance, and gives them a hope of pardon, they ought without delay to come to him, that they might not perish with the rest. And it deserves to be noticed, that when God raises his voice, some harden others, and thus men lead one another into ruin. Thus it happens that all teaching becomes unsuccessful. Hence the Prophet applies a remedy, by showing how preposterous it is when some follow others; for in this way they increase the ranks of the rebellious; but that if there be any who are meek, they ought to be teachable, when God stretches forth his hand and shows that he will be propitious, provided they return to the right way.

He calls them meek who had profited under the scourges of God; for the Hebrews consider עניים, *onuim,* to be the afflicted, deriving the word from ענה, *one,* to afflict, or to be humble. But as men for the most part are not subdued except by scourges, they call, by a metaphor, עניים, *onuim,* the meek, such as have been subdued: for men grow wanton in their pleasures, and abundance commonly produces insolence; but by adversity they learn to become meek. Hence our Prophet calls those the meek of the land who were submissive to God, after having been chastised by him. For we know, that though God may smite the wicked, they yet continue to have a stiff and iron neck and a brazen front: but the faithful are tamed, as Jeremiah confesses as to himself; for he says that he was like an untamed heifer before he was chastised by God's scourges. So the Prophet directs his discourse to the few who had felt the afflicting hand of God, and had been thus humbled.[1]

He bids them to *seek Jehovah*, and yet he says that they had *wrought his judgment*. These two clauses seem inconsistent with each other; for if they had been previously alienated from God, justly might the Prophet bid them to return to the right way; but as they had devoted themselves to religion, and formed their life according to the rule of uprightness, the Prophet seems to have exhorted them without reason to seek God. But the passage is worthy of special notice; for we hence learn that even the best are roused by God's scourges to seek true religion with greater ardour than they had before done. Though then it be our object to serve God and to follow his word, yet when calamities arise and God appears as a judge, we ought to be stimulated to greater care and diligence; for it never is the case that any one of us fully performs his duty. Let us then remember, that we are roused by God whenever adversity impends over us, and when God himself shows by mani-

---

[1] *Newcome* renders the adjective "lowly," and the noun "lowliness;" but *Marckius* and *Henderson* render the first "humble," as the Septuagint do—ταπεινοι, and the second "humility." They were those who had been made humble by affliction. The design of affliction is to make us humble, submissive to God's will; and this is the effect of sanctified affliction. It is somewhat singular that the verb means to afflict and to be humble, as though affliction were needful to render us humble. The word ענוה, occurs in 2 Sam. xxii. 36, and Ps. xviii. 35, and is rendered "gentleness" in our common version, but more correctly in our Prayer-book version "loving correction." Perhaps the best rendering would be "humbling affliction;" and the idea of humbling affliction making great is very striking. The word used by the Septuagint is παιδεια—discipline; and the Vulgate is the same.—*Ed.*

fest signs that he is displeased. This is the reason why the Prophet bids the pious doers of righteousness to seek God, however much they were before devoted to what was just and upright.

There was also another reason: we know how grievously faith is tried, when the good and wicked are indiscriminately and without any difference chastised by God's hand; for the godly are then tempted to think that it avails them nothing that they have laboured sincerely to serve God; they think that this has all been in vain and to no purpose, for they are brought into the same miseries with others. As then this temptation is enough to shake even the strongest, the Prophet here exhorts the faithful to persevere, as though he had said, that in the first confusion no difference would be found between the good and the wicked as to their circumstances, for God would afflict both alike, but that the end would be different; and that there was therefore no reason for them to despond or to think it of no advantage to seek God: for he would at length really show that he approved of their integrity; as though he had said, "God will not remunerate you at the first moment; but your patience will at length find that he is a just judge, who has regard for his people, and delivers them in their extremity."

To do the judgment of God in this place is to form the life according to the righteousness of the law. The word משפט, *meshepheth*, has various meanings in Scripture. Sometimes, and indeed often, it designates the punishment which God allots to the wicked: but it frequently means equity or the rule of right living. Hence to do judgment is to observe what is righteous and just, to abstain from what is wrong and injurious. But the Prophet calls it the judgment of God, because it is what he prescribes in his word and what he approves. For we know that men blend various things, by which they would prove themselves to be just and righteous: but they deceive themselves, except they form their life especially according to what God requires. We now perceive what the Prophet means; and he afterwards defines what it is to seek God; for the latter part of the verse is added as an explanation, that the faithful might understand how God is to be sought.

For hypocrites, as soon as God invites them, accumulate many rites, and weary themselves much in things of no value. In short, they think that they have sufficiently sought God when they have performed a number of ceremonies. But by over-acting they trifle as it were with God, and thus deceive themselves. Thus we see repentance profaned. They under the Papacy prattle enough about repentance, but when they are asked to define it, they begin with contrition; and yet no displeasure at sin is mentioned by them, nor any real love of righteousness, but they talk about attrition and contrition, and then immediately they leap to confession; and this is the principal part of repentance: they afterwards come to satisfactions. Thus repentance among the Papists is nothing else but a some kind of mistaken solicitude, by which they labour to pacify God, as though they came nigh him: nay, the satisfactions of the Papacy are nothing else but obstructions between God and men.

This evil has been common in all ages. The Prophet, therefore, does not without reason define what the true and rightful way of seeking God is, and that is, when *righteousness* is sought, when *humility* is sought. By righteousness he understands the same thing as by judgment; as though he had said, " Advance in a righteous and holy course of life, for God will not forget your obedience, provided your hearts grow not faint, and ye persevere to the end." We hence see that God complains, not only when we obtrude external pomps and devices I know not what, as though he might like a child be amused by us; but also when we do not sincerely devote our life to his service. And he adds humility to righteousness; for it is difficult even for the very best of men not to murmur against God when he severely chastises them. We indeed find how much their own delicacy embitters the minds of men when God appears somewhat severe with them. Hence the Prophet, in order to check all clamours, exhorts the faithful here to cultivate humility, so that they might patiently bear the rigour by which God would try them, and might suffer themselves to be ruled by his hand. Peter had the same thing in view when he said, " Humble yourselves under the mighty hand of God." (1 Pet. v. 6.) We now then see why the Prophet requires from the faithful not only righteousness but also humility; it was, that they might with composed minds wait for the deliverance which God had promised. They were not in the interval to murmur, nor to give vent to their own perverse feelings, however severely God might treat them.

We may hence gather a profitable instruction: The Prophet does not address here men who were depraved and had wholly neglected what was just and right, but he directs his discourse to the best, the most upright, the most holy: and yet he shows that they had no other remedy, but humbly and patiently to bear the chastisement of God. It then follows that no perfection can be found among men, such as can meet the judgment of God. For were any to object and say, that they devoted themselves to righteousness, there is yet a just reason why they should humble themselves; for we are all guilty before God, and no one can clear himself, inasmuch as when any one examines his own conscience, he finds that he is not free from sin. However conscious then we may be of acting uprightly, and God himself may be a judge to us, and the Holy Spirit the witness of our true and real integrity; yet when the Lord summons us before his tribunal, let us all, from the least to the greatest, learn to confess ourselves guilty and exposed to judgment.

He afterwards adds, *If it may be* (or, *it may be*) *ye shall be concealed*[1] *in the day of Jehovah's anger*. The Prophet speaks not doubtingly, as though the faithful were uncertain as to God's favour: but he had another thing in view,—that though no hope remained as to the perceptions of men, yet the faithful would not lose their labour, if they sought God; for in their worst circumstances they would find him propitious to them and their safety secured by his kindness. Hence

---

[1] The idea is not "protected," as given by *Newcome*, but "secreted" or concealed as in a hiding-place. "Hid" is the version of *Henderson*, and also of *Marckius* —*Ed.*

we see, that the Prophet in these words points out the disastrous character of the event, but no deficiency in the love of God. Though the Lord is ready to pardon, nay, of his own self anticipates his people, and kindly invites them to himself; it is yet necessary for them to consider how wonderful is his power in preserving his elect, when all things seem desperate. *It may* then *be,* he says, when the Jews understood that all things were in a state of extreme despair: and the Prophet said this, partly that the reprobate and the perverse might know that they were to perish, and partly that the faithful might appreciate the more the favour of God, when they saw themselves delivered from death by a miracle, and found that it would be a kind of resurrection, when God became their deliverer. Hence the Prophet, in order to commend to God's children his salvation, which he offers them, and to render more illustrious God's favour, makes use of the particle אולי, *auli,* it may be. In the meantime he fulminates, as I have already said, against the reprobate, that they might understand that it was all over with them. It follows—

4. For Gaza shall be forsaken, and Ashkelon a desolation: they shall drive out Ashdod at the noonday, and Ekron shall be rooted up.

5. Woe unto the inhabitants of the sea-coasts, the nation of the Cherethites! the word of the Lord *is* against you; O Canaan, the land of the Philistines, I will even destroy thee, that there shall be no inhabitant.

4. Quia Aza derelicta erit, et Askalon in vastationem; Asdod in meridie expellent, et Ekron dissipabitur.

5. Heus habitatores funiculi maris (*vel,* regionis) gens Cretim; sermo Iehovæ contra vos Canaan, terra Philistim; et exterminabo te, ne sit habitator.

The Prophet begins here to console the elect; for when God's vengeance had passed away, which would only be for a time against them, the heathens and foreigners would find God in their turn to be their judge to punish them for the wrongs done to his people; though some think that God's judgment on the Jews is here described, while yet the Prophet expressly mentions their neighbours: but the former view seems to me more suitable,—that the Prophet reminds the faithful of a future change of things, for God would not perpetually afflict his chosen people, but would transfer his vengeance to other nations. The meaning then is—that God, who has hitherto threatened the Jews, would nevertheless be propitious to them, not indeed to all the people, for a great part was doomed to destruction, but to the remnant, whom the Lord had chosen as a seed to himself, that there might be some church remaining. For we know, that God had always so moderated the punishment he inflicted on his people, as not to render void his covenant, nor abolish the memory of Abraham's race : for this reason he was to come forth as their Redeemer.

Since then the Prophet speaks here against Gaza, and Ashkelon, and Ashdod, and Ekron, and the Philistines, and the Cretians and others, he intended no doubt to add courage to the faithful, that they might not despair of God's mercy, though they might find themselves very grievously oppressed; for he could at length put an end to his wrath, after having purged his Church of its dregs. And this admonition the faithful also need, that they may not envy the wicked and the despisers of God, as though their condition were better or more desirable. For when the Lord spares the wicked and chastens us, we are tempted to think that nothing is better than to shake off every yoke. Lest then this temptation should have assailed the faithful, the Prophet reminded them in time, that there was no reason why the heathens should flatter or congratulate themselves, when God did not immediately punish them ; for their portion was prepared for them.

He mentions Gaza first, a name which often occurs in scripture. The Hebrews called it Aza ; but as ע, *oin*, is the first letter, the Greeks have rendered it Gaza , and heathen authors have thought it to be a Persic word, and it means in that language a treasure. But this is a vain notion, for it is no doubt a Hebrew word. He then adds Ashkelon, a city nigh to Gaza. In the third place he mentions Ashdod, which the Greeks have translated Azotus, and the Latins have followed the Greeks. He names Ekron in the last place. All these cities were near to the Jews, and were not far from one another towards the Moabites and the Idumeans.[1]

He then adds, *Ho!* (or, *woe to,* הוֹי) *the inhabitants of the line of the sea.* The region of the sea he calls Galilee; and he joins the Kerethites and the Philistines. Some think that he alludes to the troops, who carried on war under David; for he had chosen his garrison soldiers from that nation, that is, from the people of Galilee, and had called them Kerethites and Philistines. But I know not whether the Prophet spoke so refinedly. I rather think, that he refers here to those heathen nations, which had been hostile to the Jews, though vicinity ought to have been a bond of kindness. Hence he includes them all in the name of Canaan: for I do not take it here, as some do, as signifying merchants; for the Prophet evidently means, that however called, they were all Canaanites, who had been long ago doomed to destruction. Since then those regions had been enemies to the Jews, the Prophet intimates that God would become the defender of his chosen people.

The word of Jehovah is against you. "God, who has hitherto threatened his own people, summons you to judgment. Think not that you will escape unpunished for hav-

---

[1] This verse, literally rendered, retains more of its poetic character,—
  4. For Gaza, forsaken shall she be,
   And Ashkelon *shall be* a desolation;
   Ashdod, at mid-day shall they drive it out,
   And Ekron shall be rooted up.
In the first and the last line there is a correspondence in the sound of the words.
The following presents another instance of the nominative case absolute,—
  5. Woe to the dwellers of the line of the sea,
   The nation of the Kerethites!
   The word of Jehovah is against you:
   Canaan, the land of the Philistines,
   I will even destroy thee, that there shall be no inhabitant.
The *line* of the sea, meaning the coast along the shore, is so called, says *Henderson,* "from the custom of using a cord or line in measuring off or dividing a territory."
Some derive "Kerethites" from כרת, to cut off, to destroy; and so they were cutters off or destroyers. They were celebrated men of war in the time of David, 2 Sam. viii. 18. "Philistines" mean emigrants, says *Henderson;* the word being derived from a verb, which signifies, in the Ethiopic language, to rove, to migrate.—*Ed.*

ing vexed his Church." For though God designed to prove the patience of his people, yet neither the Moabites, nor the rest, were excusable when they cruelly oppressed the Jews; yea, when they purposed through them to fight with God himself, the creator of heaven and earth. He afterwards adds, *There shall be no inhabitant*, for God would destroy them all. We now see that the Prophet had no other design but to alleviate the bitter grief of the faithful by this consolation,—that their miseries would be only for a time, and that God would ere long punish their enemies. It follows—

6. And the sea coast shall be dwellings *and* cottages for shepherds, and folds for flocks.	6. Et erit funiculus maris (*id est*, regio; *sed metaphorice Hebræi vocant regionem, funiculum, propter distributionem*) habitaculum caulis pastorum et septa ovium.
7. And the coast shall be for the remnant of the house of Judah; they shall feed thereupon: in the houses of Ashkelon shall they lie down in the evening: for the Lord their God shall visit them, and turn away their captivity.	7. Et erit regio reliquiis domus Jehudah, apud eos pascentur, in domibus Ascalon vesperi accubabunt; quia visitabit Jehova Deus ipsorum ipsos, et reducet captivitatem eorum.

The Prophet confirms what he has before said respecting the future vengeance of God, which was now nigh at hand to the Moabites and other neighbouring nations, who had been continually harassing the miserable Jews. Hence, he says, that that whole region would become the habitation of sheep. It is a well known event, that when any country is without inhabitants shepherds occupy it; for there is no sowing nor reaping there, but grass alone grows. Where, therefore, there is no cultivation, where no number of men are found, there shepherds find a place for their flocks, there they build sheepcots. It is, therefore, the same as though the Prophet had said, that the country would be desolate, as we find it expressed in the next verse.[1]

---

[1] The words, נות כרת רעים, are rendered by *Calvin*, "habitaculum caulis pastorum—an habitation (or a dwelling) for the sheepcots of shepherds." The *Targum* takes the two first words in the singular number; the second is evidently so, and the first may be so also: and כרת certainly does not mean sheepcots, but digging, from כרה, to dig. The reference is either to the pits dug for watering the flock, as *Piscator* thinks, or to the

He immediately adds, but for a different reason, that *the coast of the sea would be a habitation to the house of Judah.* And there is here a striking divergency from the flocks of shepherds to the tribe of Judah, which was as it were, the chosen flock of God. The Prophet then, after having said that the region would be waste and desolate, immediately adds, that it would be for the benefit of the chosen people; for the Lord would grant there to the Jews a safe and secure rest. But the Prophet confines this to the remnant; for the greater part, as we have already seen, were become so irreclaimable, that the gate of mercy was completely closed against them. The Prophet, at the same time, by mentioning a remnant, shows that there would always be some seed from which God would raise up a new Church; and he also encourages the faithful to entertain hope, so that their own small number might not terrify them; for when they considered themselves and found themselves surpassed by a vast multitude, they might have thought that they were of no account. Lest then they should be disheartened the Prophet says, that this remnant would be the object of God's care; for when he would visit the whole coast of the sea and other regions, he would provide there for the Jews a safe habitation and refuge.

That line then, he says, *shall be for the residue of the house of Judah; feed shall they in Ashkelon, and there shall they lie down in the evening;* that is, they shall find in their exile some resting-place; for we know that the Jews were not all removed to distant lands; and they who may have

subterraneous huts, or caves, dug for the purpose of shelter, as *Drusius* and *Bochart* suppose. *Junius* and *Tremelius* render the words, "sheep-cots, the delvings of shepherds;" and *Drusius*, "dwellings of the digging out of shepherds," *i. e.*, dwellings dug out by shepherds. The most literal and the easiest construction is, "dwellings, the digging of shepherds." Then the verse might be thus rendered,—
        And the line of the sea shall be dwellings,
        Dug out by shepherds, and folds for sheep.
Parkhurst quotes *Harmer,* who says, "the Eastern shepherds make use of *caves* very frequently, sleeping in them and driving their flocks into them at night. . . . . The mountains bordering on the *Syrian* coast are remarkable for the number of caves, and are found particularly in the neighbourhood of *Ashkelon.*" How fully then was this prophecy fulfilled. —*Ed.*

been hid in neighbouring places were afterwards more easily gathered, when a liberty to return was permitted them. This is what the Prophet means now, when he says, that there would be a refuge in the night to the Jews among the Moabites and other neighbouring nations.

A reason follows, which confirms what I have stated, *for Jehovah their God*, he says, *will visit them*. We hence see that the Prophet mitigates here the sorrow of exile and of that most grievous calamity which was nigh the Jews, by promising to them a new visitation of God; as though he had said, "Though the Lord seems now to rage against you, and seems to forget his own covenant, yet he will again remember his mercy, when the suitable time shall come." And he adds, *he will restore their captivity;* and he added this, that he might show that his favour would prove victorious against all hindrances. The Jews might indeed have raised this objection, "Why does not the Lord help us immediately; but he, on the contrary, allows our enemies to remove us into exile?" The Prophet here calls upon them to exercise patience; and yet he promises, that after having been driven into exile, they should again return to their country; for the Lord would not suffer that exile to be perpetual. It now follows—

| 8. I have heard the reproach of Moab, and the revilings of the children of Ammon, whereby they have reproached my people, and magnified *themselves* against their border. | 8. Audivi opprobrium Moab, et contumelias filiorum Ammon, quibus exprobrârunt populo meo, et se extulerunt contra terminum ipsorum. |

The Prophet confirms what I have just said of God's vengeance against foreign enemies. Though all the neighbouring nations had been eager in their hostility to the Jews, yet we know that more hatred, yea and more fury, had been exhibited by these two nations than by any other, that is, by the Moabites and the Ammonites, notwithstanding their connection with them by blood, for they derived their origin from Lot, who was Abraham's nephew. Though, then, that connection ought to have turned the Moabites and the Ammonites to mercy, we yet know they always infested the

Jews with greater fury than others, and as it were with savage cruelty. This is the reason why the Prophet speaks now especially of them. Some indeed take this sentence as spoken by the faithful; but the context requires it to be ascribed to God, and no doubt he reminds them that he looked down from on high on the proud vauntings of Moab which he scattered in the air, as though he had declared that it was not hidden or unknown to him how cruelly the Moabites and Ammonites raged against the Jews, how proud and inhuman they had been. And this was a very seasonable consolation. For the Jews might have been swallowed up with despair, had not this promise been made to them. They saw the Moabites and the Ammonites burning with fury, when yet they had not been injured or provoked. They also saw that they made gain and derived advantage from the calamities of a miserable people. What could the faithful think? These wicked men not only harassed them with impunity, but their cruelty and perfidy towards them was gainful. Where was God now? If he regarded his own Church, would he not have interposed? Lest then a temptation of this kind should upset the faithful, the Prophet introduces God here as the speaker,—

I have heard, he says, *the reproach of Moab; I have heard the revilings of Ammon:* "Nothing escapes me; though I do not immediately show that these things are regarded by me, yet I know and observe how shamefully the Moabites and the Ammonites have persecuted you: they at length shall find that I am the guardian of your safety, and that you are under my protection." We now apprehend the Prophet's design. Nearly the same words are used by Isaiah, ch. 16, and also by Jeremiah ch. 48: but they both pursue the subject much farther, while our Prophet only touches on it briefly, for we see that what he says is comprised in very few words. But by saying that the reproach of Moab and the revilings of the children of Ammon had come into remembrance before God, what he had in view was—that the Jews might be assured and fully persuaded that they were not rejected and forsaken, though for a time they were reproachfully treated by the wicked. The Prophet indeed takes the words reproach and revilings, in an active sense.[1]

He then adds, *By which they have upbraided my people.* God intimates here that he does not depart from his elect when the wicked spit, as it were, in their faces. There is indeed nothing which so much wounds the feelings of ingenuous minds as reproach; there is not so much bitterness in hundred deaths as in one reproach, especially when the wicked licentiously triumph, and do this with the applauding consent of the whole world; for then all difference between good and evil is confounded, and good conscience is as it were buried. But the Prophet shows here, that the people of God suffer no loss when they are thus unworthily harassed by the wicked and exposed to their reproach.

He at last subjoins that they had *enlarged over their border.* Some consider "mouth" to be understood—"they have enlarged the mouth against their border;" and the word, it is true, without any addition, is often taken in this sense; but in this place the construction is fuller, for the words על־גבולם, *ol-gebulam,* over their border, follow the verb. The Prophet means that God's wrath had been provoked by the petulancy of both nations, for they wished to break up, as it were, the borders, which had been fixed by God. The land of Canaan, we know, had been given to the Jews by an hereditary right;—"When the Most High," says Moses, "divided the nations, he set a line for Jacob." (Deut. xxxii. 8.) It is indeed true that the possessions of the nations were allotted to them by the hidden counsel of God; but there was a special reason as to his chosen people; for the Lord had made Abraham the true possessor of that land, even for ever. (Gen. xvii. 8.) Now the Moabites were confined, as it were, to a certain place; the Lord had assigned to them their own inheritance. When, therefore, they sought to go beyond and to invade the land of the Jews, God's wrath must have been kindled against them; for they thus fought, not against mortals, but against God himself; for by removing the borders fixed by him, they attempted to sub-

---

[1] That is, the reproach cast by Moab, and the revilings uttered by Ammon.—*Ed.*

vert his eternal decree. We now then understand why the Prophet says that the children of Moab and of Ammon had enlarged over the border of those who had been placed in the land of Canaan by God's hand; for they not only sought to eject their neighbours, but wished and tried to take away from God's hand that inheritance which the Lord had given to Abraham, and given, as I have said, in perpetuity.[1]

PRAYER.

Grant, Almighty God, that as thou hast been pleased to consecrate us a peculiar people to thyself, we may be mindful of such an invaluable favour, and devote ourselves wholly to thee, and so labour to cultivate true sincerity as to bear the marks of thy people and of thy holy Church: and as we are so polluted by so many of the defilements of our own flesh and of this world, grant that thy Holy Spirit may cleanse us more and more every day, until thou bringest us at length to that perfection to which thou invitest us by the voice of thy gospel, that we may also enjoy that blessed glory which has been provided for us by the blood of thy only begotten Son. Amen.

[1] There is a difference as to the meaning of the last line. *Newcome* adopts our common version,—
  And magnified *themselves* against their border.
Henderson's rendering is essentially the same—
  And carried themselves haughtily against their border.
The verb גדל is transitive and intransitive in Kal—to make great and to be great; it seems to partake of a similar character in Hiphil, as it is found here, to magnify, and to grow great or proud, and hence to exult or to triumph; and when followed by על, as here, to exult over a person or a country—see Job xix. 5; Ps. xxxv. 26; xxxviii. 17; Ezek. xxxv. 13. In these verses "to exult over" would be the best rendering; as also in 10th verse of this chapter. The idea of enlarging or extending over, as adopted by *Jerome* and *Dathius*, as well as by *Calvin*, is not countenanced by any other passage. The best rendering here is—
  And exulted over their border.
This line corresponds with the revilings of Ammon, as the preceding does with the reproach of Moab. That it was the triumphant and exulting language of Ammon is evident, because it was what was *heard*—" I have heard," &c. The particle אשר, rendered here "quibus—by which," and "wherewith" by *Newcome*, is rendered "who" by *Marckius* and *Henderson*—"who have reproached my people;" and this is the most natural construction. Some have rendered it "because."—*Ed.*

Lecture One Hundred and Twenty-third.

9. Therefore *as* I live, saith the Lord of hosts, the God of Israel, Surely Moab shall be as Sodom, and the children of Ammon as Gomorrah, *even* the breeding of nettles, and saltpits, and a perpetual desolation: the residue of my people shall spoil them, and the remnant of my people shall possess them.

10. This shall they have for their pride, because they have reproached and magnified *themselves* against the people of the Lord of hosts.

9. Propterea vivo ego, dicit Jehova exercituum, Deus Israel, quòd Moab sicuti Sodoma erit, et filii Ammon sicuti Gomorrha, productio urticæ et fodina salis, et vastitas in perpetuum: reliquiæ populi mei diripient eos, et residuum gentis meæ possidebit eos.

10. Hoc illis pro superbia sua, quia exprobrârunt et insultârunt super populum Jehovæ exercituum.

In order to cheer the miserable Jews by some consolation, God said, in what we considered yesterday, that the wantonness of Moab was known to him; he now adds, that he would visit with punishment the reproaches which had been mentioned. For it would have availed them but little that their wrongs had been observed by God, if no punishment had been prepared. Hence the Prophet reminds them that God is no idle spectator, who only observes what takes place in the world; but that there is a reward laid up for all the ungodly. And these verses are to be taken in connection, that the faithful may know that their wrongs are not unknown to God, and also that he will be their defender. But that the Jews might have a more sure confidence that God would be their deliverer, he interposes an oath. God at the same time shows that he is really touched when he sees his people so cruelly and immoderately harassed, when the ungodly seem to think that an unbridled license is permitted them. God therefore shows here, that not only the salvation of his people is an object of his care, but that he undertakes their cause as though his anger was kindled; not that passions belong to him, but such a form of speaking is adopted in order to express what the faithful could never otherwise conceive an idea of, that is, to express the unspeakable love of God towards them, and his care for them.

He then says that he *lives*, as though he had sworn by his own life. As we have elsewhere seen that he swears by his life, so he speaks now. *Live do I*, that is, "As I am God, so will I avenge these wrongs by which my people are now oppressed." And for the same reason he calls himself *Jehovah of hosts*, and the *God of Israel*. In the first clause he exalts his own power, that the Jews might know that he was endued with power; and then he mentions his goodness, because he had adopted them as his people. The meaning then is that God swears by his own life; and that the Jews might not think that this was done in vain, his power is brought before them, and then his favour is added.

Moab, he says, *shall be like Sodom, and the sons of Ammon like Gomorrah*, even *for the production of the nettle and for a mine of salt;*[1] that is, their lands should be reduced to a

---

[1] This clause is rendered differently by some. The word ממשק occurs only here. It is rendered by the *Targum* by a word which means a "deserted place," and so *Newcome* renders it, "A deserted place for the thorn;" so also do *Drusius, Grotius, Piscator,* and *Marckius*. The Septuagint have mistaken the word for "Damascus," and give a version of the whole clause wholly foreign to the context. *Henderson* thinks that the word has the same meaning with משך, to draw out, to extend, and gives this version, "A region of overrunning brambles." This is far-fetched. The word, חרול, rendered "nettle" by *Calvin, Grotius,* and others, cannot be so taken, according to *Drusius* and *Bochart*, for in Job xxx. 7, men are said to gather under it. It is found besides only in Prov. xxiv. 31. It may be rendered either a thorn or a bramble. The other part of the sentence is literally "a digging place for salt."

Moab was to be like Sodom, and Ammon like Gomorrah, not as to the *manner* of their ruin, but as to the *extent* of it. It was to be an *entire* overthrow. Their habitation was not to become a pool of water like Sodom and Gomorrah, but a place where the bramble was to grow, and salt might be dug. And it was to be "a desolation," עד־עולם, "for ages;" for the word means an indefinite time. So *Drusius* regards it here as meaning a long time. But some consider the "desolation," as having reference to the people and not to the place. If so, the rendering may be "a desolation for ever," for both these nations, as nations, were wholly obliterated. Moab and Ammon, as a separate people, are altogether extinct. The whole verse is as follows—

9. Therefore, *as* I live,
   Saith Jehovah of hosts, the God of Israel,
   Surely Moab like Sodom shall be,
   And the children of Ammon like Gomorrah,
   The desert of the thorn and the excavation of salt,
   Yea, a desolation for ages;
   The remnant of my people shall plunder them,
   And the residue of my nation shall possess them.

The two last lines refer to the children of Ammon, as the two preceding especially to Moab. The country of Moab was on the eastern side of the Dead Sea, and that of Ammon was north-east of Moab. Both were

waste, or should become wholly barren, so that nothing was to grow there but nettles, as the case is with desert places. As to the expression, the mine (*fodina*) or quarry of salt, it often occurs in scripture: a salt-pit denotes sterility in Hebrew. And the Prophet adds, that this would not be for a short time only; *It shall be* (he says) *a perpetual desolation.* He also adds, that this would be for the advantage of the Church; for *the residue of my people shall plunder them, and the remainder of my nation shall possess them.* He ever speaks of the residue; for as it was said yesterday, it was necessary for that people to be cleansed from their dregs, so that a small portion only would remain; and we know that not many of them returned from exile.

The import of the whole is, that though God determined to diminish his Church, so that a few only survived, yet these few would be the heirs of the whole land, and possess the kingdom, when God had taken vengeance on all their enemies.

It hence follows, according to the Prophet, that *this* shall be *to them for their pride.* We see that the Prophet's object is, to take away whatever bitterness the Jews might feel when insolently slandered by their enemies. As then there was danger of desponding, since nothing, as it was said yesterday, is more grievous to be borne than reproach, God does here expressly declare, that the proud triumph of their neighbours over the Jews would be their own ruin; for, as Solomon says, 'Pride goes before destruction.' (Prov. xvi. 18.) And he again confirms what he had already referred to—that the Jews would not be wronged with impunity, for God had taken them under his guardianship, and was their protector: *Because they have reproached,* he says, *and triumphed*

---

subdued and led captive by Nebuchadnezzar about four or six years after the captivity of Judah. They were afterwards partially restored, especially the children of Ammon, as Tobiah was their chief in the time of Nehemiah. Neh. iv. 3. They were "plundered," as recorded in 1 Macc. v. 35, 51, by Judas Maccabeus. Of Moab we read nothing at that time: but it appears, that for ages it has been desolate. "Not one," says *Burckhart*, the traveller, " of the ancient cities of Moab exists as tenanted by man," and he speaks of " their entire desolation." Another modern traveller, *Seetzen*, a Russian, speaking of Ammon, says, " All this country, formerly so populous, is now changed into a vast desert."—*Ed.*

over the people of Jehovah of hosts. He might have said, " over my people," as in the last verse ; but there is something implied in these words, as though the Prophet had said, that they carried on war not with mortals but with God himself, whose majesty was insulted, when the Jews were so unjustly oppressed. It follows—

11. The Lord *will be* terrible unto them: for he will famish all the gods of the earth; and *men* shall worship him, every one from his place, *even* all the isles of the heathen.	11. Terribilis Iehova super eos, quia consumpsit omnes deos terræ : et adorabit eum quisque ex loco suo, omnes insulæ gentium.

He proceeds with the same subject,—that God would show his power in aiding his people. But he calls him a *terrible* God, who had for a time patiently endured the wantonness of his enemies, and thus became despised by them : for the ungodly, we know, never submit to God unless they are constrained by his hand ; and then they are not bent so as willingly to submit to his authority; but when forced they are silent.[1] This is what the Prophet means in these words ; as though he had said, that the wicked now mock God, as they disregard his power, but that they shall find how terrible an avenger of his people he is, so that they would have to dread him. And then he compares the superstitions of the nations with true religion ; as though he had said, that this would be to the Jews as a reward for their piety, inasmuch as they worshipped the only true God, and that all idols would be of no avail against the help of God. And this was a necessary admonition ; for the ungodly seemed to triumph for a time, not only over a conquered people, but over God himself, and thus gloried in

---

[1] The word, נורא, is rendered "to be feared," by *Cocceius* and *Henderson*, and עליהם, "above them," that is, "the gods of the earth," mentioned in the next line; it being considered an instance of a pronoun preceding its noun. But this is forced; and it is not necessary. Moab and Ammon are evidently referred to ; and what is said is, that God would be terrible to them, as well as to others, for he would famish or destroy all the gods of the earth. And then in the next verse he mentions other nations. Some extend what is here said to gospel-times; but there seems no reason for this, inasmuch as God's judgment is the subject of the Prophet.—*Ed.*

their superstitious and vain inventions. The Prophet, therefore, confirms their desponding minds; for God, he says, will at length *consume all the gods of the nations.*

The verb רזה, *reze*, means strictly to make lean or to famish, but is to be taken here metaphorically, as signifying to consume. God then will famish all the inventions of the nations: and he alludes to that famine which idols had occasioned through the whole world; as though he had said, that God's glory would shortly appear, which would exterminate whatever glory the false gods had obtained among them, so that it would melt away like fatness.

He at last adds, that the remotest nations would become suppliants to God; for by saying, *adore him shall each from his place,*[1] he doubtless means, that however far off the countries might be, the distance would be no hinderance to God's name being celebrated, when his power became known to remote lands. And, for the same reason, he mentions *the islands of the nations,* that is, countries beyond the sea: for the Hebrews, as it has been elsewhere observed, call those countries islands which are far distant, and divided by the sea.[2] In short, the Prophet shows, that the redemption of the people would be so wonderful, that the fame of it would reach the farthest bounds of the earth, and constrain foreign nations to give glory to the true God, and that it would dissipate all the mists of superstition, so that idols would be exposed to scorn and contempt. It follows—

12. Ye Ethiopians also, ye *shall be* slain by my sword.	12. Etiam vos Ethiopes, interfecti gladio meo ipsi (*alii vertunt,* cum ipsis.)

The Prophet extends farther the threatened vengeance, and says, that God would also render to the Ethiopians the reward which they deserved; for they had also harassed the

---

[1] Literally—
　　And bow down to him, every one from his place,
　　Shall all the islands of the nations.

[2] "By the earth the Jews understood the great continent of all Asia and Africa, to which they had access by land; and by the isles of the sea they understood the places to which they sailed by sea, particularly all Europe. Sir I. Newton on Daniel, p. 276."—*Newcome.*

chosen people. But if God punished that nation, how could Ammon and Moab hope to escape? For how could God spare so great a cruelty, since he would visit with punishment the remotest nations? For the hatred of the Moabites and of the Ammonites, as we have said, was less excusable, because they were related to the children of Abraham. They ought, on this account, to have mitigated their fierceness: besides, vicinity ought to have rendered them more humane. But as they exceeded other nations in cruelty, a heavier punishment awaited them. Now this comparison was intended for this end—that the Jews might know that God would be inexorable towards the Moabites, by whom they had been so unjustly harassed, since even the Ethiopians would be punished, who yet were more excusable on account of their distance.

As to the words, some regard the demonstrative pronoun המה, *eme*, they, as referring to the Babylonians, and others, to the Moabites. I prefer to understand it of the Moabites, if we read, "like them," or "with them," as these interpreters consider it: for they regard the particle את, *at*, "with," or כ, *caph*, "like," to be understood, "Ye Ethiopians shall be slain by my sword like them," or with them. It would in this case doubtless apply to the Moabites. But it seems to me that the sentence is irregular, *even ye Ethiopians*, and then, *they shall be slain by my sword*. The Prophet begins the verse in the second person, summoning the Ethiopians to appear before God's tribunal; he afterwards adds in the third person, they shall be slain by my sword.[1]

God calls whatever evils were impending over the Ethiopians his sword; for though they were destroyed by the Chaldeans yet it was done under the guidance of God

---

[1] *Newcome* cuts the knot here by an emendation, by אתם, ye, for המה, they; and *Houbigant*, by תהיו, ye shall be,—"the wounded of my sword shall ye be." This is according to the Septuagint; but the former is more in accordance with the Hebrew idiom; for the pronoun is often used without the auxiliary verb. Some take המה as *ipsi* in Latin, connected with *vos*, ye yourselves. Then the rendering would be—

Also ye Cushites,
The slain of my sword shall ye yourselves be.

But what *Calvin* says is not uncommon in the Prophet, the abrupt change of persons.—*Ed.*

himself. The Chaldeans made war under his authority, as the Assyrians did, who had been previously employed by him to execute his vengeance. It follows—

| 13. And he will stretch out his hand against the north, and destroy Assyria; and will make Nineveh a desolation, *and* dry like a wilderness. | 13. Et extendet manum suam ad Aquilonem, et perdet Assyriam, et ponet Nineveni in vastitatem, desolationem instar deserti. |

The Prophet proceeds here to the Assyrians, whom we know to have been special enemies to the Church of God. For the Moabites and the Ammonites were fans only, as we have elsewhere seen, as they could not do much harm by their own strength. Hence they stirred up the Assyrians, they stirred up the Ethiopians and remote nations. The meaning, then, is, that no one of all the enemies of the Church would be left unpunished by God, as every one would receive a reward for his cruelty. He speaks now of God in the third person; but in the last verse God himself said, that the Ethiopians would be slain by his sword. The Prophet adds here, *He will extend his hand to the north;* that is, God will not complete his judgments on the Ethiopians; but he will go farther, even to Nineveh and to all the Assyrians.

Nineveh, we know, was the metropolis of the empire, before the Assyrians were conquered by the Babylonians. Thus Babylon then recovered the sovereignty which it had lost; and Nineveh, though not wholly demolished, was yet deprived of its ruling power, and gradually lost its name and its wealth, until it was reduced into a waste; for the building of Ctesiphon, as we have elsewhere seen, proved its ruin. But the Prophet, no doubt, proceeds here to administer comfort to the Jews, lest they should despair, while the Lord did not interfere. And the extension of the hand means as though he said, that his own time is known to the Lord, and that he would put forth his power when needful. Assyria was north as to Judea: hence he says, to the north will the Lord extend his hand, and will destroy Assyria; he will make Nineveh a desolation, that it may be like the desert. It follows—

14. And flocks shall lie down in the midst of her, all the beasts of the nations: both the cormorant and the bittern shall lodge in the upper lintels of it; *their* voice shall sing in the windows; desolation *shall be* in the thresholds: for he shall uncover the cedar work.

14. Et cubabunt in medio ejus greges, omnes bestiæ gentium: etiam onocrotalus, etiam noctua (*alii vertunt, pro* onocrotalo, ibin, *alii*, cuculum; *alii, pro* noctua, ericium) in postibus ejus pernoctabunt; vox cantabit in fenestra, in poste vastitas (*alii vertunt,* corvum; *sed nomen* vastitatis, *quòd postulat ratio grammaticæ, retinendum nobis est,*) quia nudavit cedrum (*vel,* contignationem.)

The Prophet describes here the state of the city and the desolation of the country. He says, that the habitation of flocks would be in the midst of the city Nineveh. The city, we know, was populous; but while men were so many, there was no place for flocks, especially in the middle of a city so celebrated. Hence no common change is here described by the Prophet, when he says, that *flocks would lie down in the middle of Nineveh;* and he adds, *all wild beasts*. For beasts, which seek seclusion and shun the sight of men, are wont to come forth, when they find a country desolate and deserted; and they range then at large, as it is the case after a slaughter in war; and when any region is emptied of its inhabitants, the wolves, the lions, and other wild beasts, roam here and there at full liberty. So the Prophet says, that wild beasts would come from other parts and remote places, and find a place where Nineveh once stood.[1] He adds that the bitterns, or the storks or the cuckoos, and similar wild birds would be there.[2] As to their various kinds, I make no laborious research; for it is enough to know the Prophet's design: besides, the Jews themselves,

---

[1] It is literally, "every wild beast of the nation,"—גוי,—"of the land," in the Septuagint. What is meant is, every wild beast that belonged to that country.—*Ed.*

[2] Both *Newcome* and *Henderson* render the two words, "the pelican and the porcupine." The former says that קאת, "pelican," comes from קאה, to vomit, because it casts up fish or water from its membranaceous bag; and קפד, "porcupine," according to *Bochart*, is from the verb, which means to cut off as by a bite, or rather, he says, from its Syriac meaning, to dread, for it is a solitary animal. See *Newcome*. But *Parkhurst* contends that it is the hedge-hog, and both the Septuagint and Vulgate render it so.

What *Calvin* translates "in postibus ejus," בכפתריה, is rendered by *Newcome*, "in the carved lintels thereof," by *Henderson*, "in her capitals," and by *Parkhurst*, "in her door-porches," *i.e.* when thrown down.—*Ed.*

who boldly affirm that either the bittern or the stork is meant, yet adduce nothing that is certain. What, in short, this description means, is—that the place, which before a vast multitude of men inhabited, would become so forsaken, that wild beasts and nocturnal birds would be its only inhabitants.

But we must bear in mind what I have stated, that all these things were set before the Jews, that they might patiently bear their miseries, understanding that God would become their defender. For this is the only support that remains for us under very grievous evils, as Paul reminds us in the first chapter of the Second Epistle to the Thessalonians; for he says, that the time will come when the Lord shall give to us relief and refreshment, and that he will visit our adversaries with punishment.

The Prophet mentions especially Nineveh, that the Jews might know that there is nothing so great and splendid in the world which God does not esteem of less consequence than the salvation of his Church, as it is said in Isaiah, "I will give Egypt as thy ransom." So God threatens the wealthiest city, that he might show how much he loved his chosen people. And the Jews could not have attributed this to their own worthiness; but the cause of so great a love depended on their gratuitous adoption. It afterwards follows—

15. This *is* the rejoicing city that dwelt carelessly, that said in her heart, I *am*, and *there is* none besides me: how is she become a desolation, a place for beasts to lie down in! every one that passeth by her shall hiss, *and* wag his hand.	15. Hæc urbs exultabunda, quæ sedebat confidenter, quæ dicebat in corde suo, Ego et non præter me amplius: quomodo facta est in vastationem, cubile animalibus? Quisquis transierit (*vel*, omnis viator) super eam sibilabit, agitabit manum suam.

He seems to have added this by way of anticipation, lest the magnificent splendour of the city Nineveh should frighten the Jews, as though it were exempt from all danger. The Prophet therefore reminds them here, that though Nineveh was thus proud of its wealth, it could not yet escape the hand of God; nay, he shows that the greatness, on account of which Nineveh extolled itself, would be the cause of its ruin; for it would cast itself down by its own pride: as a wall, when it swells, will not long stand; so also men, when they inwardly swell, and vent their own boastings, burst; and though no one pushes them down, they fall of themselves. Such a destruction the Prophet denounces on the Ninevites and the Assyrians.

This, he says, *is the exulting city, which sat in confidence.* Isaiah reprobates in nearly the same words the pride of Babylon: but what Isaiah said of Babylon our Prophet justly transfers here to Nineveh. But he no doubt had respect to the Jews, and exhibits Nineveh in its state of ruin, lest the power of that city should dazzle their eyes; for we are seized with wonder, when anything grand and splendid presents itself to us. Here then Zephaniah makes a representation of Nineveh and sets it before the Jews: "Behold," he says, "ye see this city full of exultation; ye also see that it rests as in a state of safety; for it is conscious of no fear; it regards itself exempt from the common lot of men, as though it was built in the clouds. This city," he says, "is above all others celebrated; but let not frail and evanescent splendour terrify you; for God will doubtless in his own time overthrow it and reduce it to nothing."

Let us also in the meantime observe what I have lately referred to,—that the cause of the ruin of Nineveh is described, which was, that it had promised to itself a perpetuity in the world. But let us remember, that in this city is presented to us an example, which belongs in common to all nations,—that God cannot endure the presumption of men, when inflated by their own greatness and power, they do not think themselves to be men, nor humble themselves in a way suitable to the condition of men, but forget themselves, as though they could exalt themselves above the heavens.

But it is necessary to examine the words: Nineveh *said in her heart, I, and besides me no other.* By these words the Prophet means, that Nineveh was so blinded by its splendour that it now defied every change of fortune. Had Babylon spoken thus, it would have been no wonder, for it had taken from Nineveh its sovereignty. But we see that the same pride infatuates people as well as superior kings; for each thinks himself to be great alone, and when he compares himself with others, he looks on them as far below him, as though they were placed beneath his feet. Thus then the Prophet shows in few words what was the cause of the ruin of Nineveh: it thought that its condition on the earth was fixed and perpetual. If then we desire to be protected by God's hand, let us bear in mind what our condition is, and daily, yea, hourly prepare ourselves for a change, except God be pleased to sustain us. Our stability is to depend only on the aid of God, and from consciousness of our infirmity, to tremble in ourselves, lest a forgetfulness of our state should creep in.

He afterwards adds, *How has it become a desolation?* The Prophet accommodates his words to the capacities of men: for the ruin of Nineveh might have appeared incredible. Hence the Prophet by a question rouses the minds of the faithful, that they might not doubt the truth of what God declared, for he would work in an extraordinary manner. This *how* then intimates, that the Jews ought not to be incredulous, while thinking that Nineveh was on all sides fortified, so as to prevent the occurrence of anything disastrous: for God would, in a wonderful manner and beyond what is usual, overthrow it. *How, then, has it become a desolation, a resting-place for beasts?*

He then subjoins, *Every one who passes by will hiss and shake his hand.* The Prophet seems to point out the future reproach of Nineveh, and to confirm also by a different mode of speaking what he had before said, that its ruin would be wonderful; for the shaking of the hand and hissing are marks of reproach: "Behold Nineveh, which so much flattered itself! we now see only its sad ruins." The Prophet, I have no doubt, means here by hissing and the shaking of the hand, that Nineveh would become an ignominious spectacle to all people: and the same mode of speaking often occurs in the Prophets. "All shall hiss at thee;" that is, I will make thee a reproach and a disgrace. Then the Prophet, as I have already said, still declares the same truth—that the ruin of Nineveh would be like a miracle; for all those who pass by would be amazed; as though he had said, "Behold, they will hiss—What is this? and then they will shake the hand—What can be firm in this world? We see the principal seat of empire demolished, and differing nothing from a desert." We now perceive the meaning of the Prophet.

As this doctrine is also necessary for us at this day, we must notice the circumstances to which we have referred. If, then, our enemies triumph now, and their haughtiness is intolerable, let us know, that the sooner the vengeance of God will overtake them; if they are become insensible in their prosperity, and secure, and despise all dangers, they thus provoke God's wrath, and especially if to their pride and hardness they add cruelty, so as basely to persecute the Church of God, to spoil, to plunder, and to slay his people, as we see them doing. Since then our enemies are so wanton, we may see as in a mirror their near destruction, such as is foretold by the Prophet: for he spoke not only of his own age, but designed to teach us, by the prophetic spirit, how dear to God is the safety of his Church; and the future lot of the ungodly till the end of the world will no doubt be such as Nineveh is described here to have been—that though they swell with pride for a time, and promise themselves every success against the innocent, God will yet put a stop to their insolence and check their cruelty, when the proper time shall come. I shall not to-day begin the third chapter, for it contains a new subject.

PRAYER.

Grant, Almighty God, that as thou triest us in the warfare of the cross, and arousest most powerful enemies, whose barbarity might justly terrify and dishearten us, were we not depending on thine aid,—O grant, that we may call to mind how wonderfully thou didst in former times deliver thy chosen people, and how seasonably thou didst bring them help, when they were oppressed and entirely overwhelmed, so that we may learn at this day to flee to thy protection, and not doubt, but that when thou becomest propitious to us, there is in thee sufficient power to preserve us, and to lay prostrate our enemies, how much soever they may now exult and think to triumph above the heavens, so that they may at length know by experience that they are earthly and frail creatures, whose life and condition is like the mist which soon vanishes: and may we learn to aspire after that blessed eternity, which is laid up for us in heaven by Christ our Lord. Amen.

CHAPTER III.

Lecture One Hundred and Twenty-fourth.

1. Woe to her that is filthy and polluted, to the oppressing city!	1. Væ pollutæ et inquinatæ, urbi direptrici (*vel*, fraudatrici.)
2. She obeyed not the voice; she received not correction; she trusted not in the Lord; she drew not near to her God.	2. Non audivit ad vocem; non suscepit disciplinam (*vel*, correctionem;) in Iehova non est confisa; ad Deum suum non appropinquarit.

The Prophet speaks here again against Jerusalem; for first, the Jews ought ever to have been severely reproved, as they were given to many sins; and secondly, because there was always there some seed which needed consolation: and this has been the way pursued, as we have hitherto seen, by all the Prophets. But we must also bear in mind, that the books now extant were made up of prophetic addresses, that we might understand what was the sum of the doctrine delivered.

The Prophet here makes this charge against the Jews, that they were *polluted and become filthy.* And he addresses Jerusalem, where the sanctuary was; and it might therefore seem to have been superior to other cities; for God had not in vain chosen that as the place for his worship. But the Prophet shows how empty and fallacious was any boasting of this kind; for the city which God had consecrated for himself had polluted itself with many sins. The Prophet seems to allude to the ancient rites of the law, which, though many, had been prescribed, we know, by God, that the people might observe a holy course of life: for the ceremonies could not of themselves wash away their filth; but the people were instructed by these external things to worship God in a holy and pure manner. As then they often washed themselves with water, and as they carefully observed other rites of outward sanctity, the Prophet derides their hypocrisy, for they did not regard the real design of the ceremonies. Hence he says, that they were polluted, though in appearance they might be deemed the most pure; for they were defiled as to their whole life.[1]

He adds that the city was היונה, *eiune*, some render it the city of dove, or, a dove; for the word has this meaning: and they take it metaphorically for a foolish and thoughtless city, as we find it to be so understood in Hos. vii. 11; where Ephraim was said to be a dove, because the people were void of reason and knowledge, and of their own accord exposed themselves to traps and snares. Some then consider this place to have this meaning,—that Jerusalem, which ought to have been wise, was yet wholly fatuitous and foolish. But it may be easily gathered from the context, that the Prophet means another thing, even this,—that Jerusalem was given to plunder and fraud; for the verb ינה, *ine*, signifies to defraud and to take by force what belongs to another; and it means also to circumvent as well as to plunder. He

---

[1] The first word, מוראה, is rendered "rebellious" by *Newcome* and *Henderson*. The *Vulgate* is nearly the same, "provocatrix—provoking." The verb is מרא, once in *Hiphil* in Job xxxix. 8; and to take it to be the same with מרה, to rebel, is gratuitous. The context in Job shows its idea to be that of raising up or swelling; and *Parkhurst* very properly renders the participle here, swelling, arrogant, insolent; and this notion entirely corresponds with the character given of the city in the next verse; being arrogant, it did "not hear the voice" of God. The verse may be rendered thus—

    Woe to the arrogant and polluted,
    The city, which is an oppressor!

Then follows a specification as to her conduct,—

    She has not hearkened to the voice,
    She has not received instruction;
    In Jehovah has she not trusted,
    To her God has she not drawn nigh.

To "obey the voice," as given in our version and by *Newcome*, is not quite correct; she was too arrogant even to hear or attend to the voice. "Correction," as in our version, and by *Calvin*, is rendered "instruction" by *Newcome* and *Henderson*; for מוסר has often this meaning. The *Septuagint* have παιδείαν—discipline. But the same phrase occurs in ver. 7, where the word necessarily means instruction, by way of warning, communicated by the example of others.—*Ed.*

therefore means no doubt, that Jerusalem was a city full of every kind of iniquity, as he had before called it a polluted city; and then he adds an explanation.

The Prophet in the first verse seems to have in view the two tables of the law. God, we know, requires in the law that his people should be holy; and then he teaches the way of living justly and innocently. Hence when the Prophet called Jerusalem a polluted city, he meant briefly to show that the whole worship of God was there corrupted, and that no regard for true religion flourished there; for the Jews thought that they had performed all their duty to God, when they washed away their filth by water. Such was the extremely foolish notion which they entertained: but we know and they ought to have known that the worship of God is spiritual. He afterwards adds, that the *city was rapacious*, under which term he includes every kind of injustice.

It follows, *She heard not the voice,* she *received not correction.* The Prophet now explains and defines what the pollution was of which he had spoken: for true religion begins with teachableness; when we submit to God and to his word, it is really to enter on the work of worshipping him aright. But when heavenly truth is despised, though men may toil much in outward rites, yet their impiety discovers itself by their contumacy, inasmuch as they suffer not themselves to be ruled by God's authority. Hence the Prophet shows, that whatever the Jews thought of their purity at Jerusalem, it was nothing but filth and pollution. He says, that they were unteachable, because they did not hear the Prophets sent to them by God.

This ought to be carefully noticed; for without this beginning many torment themselves in the work of serving God, and do nothing, because obedience is better than sacrifice. If, then, we wish our efforts to be approved by God, we must begin with faith; for except the word of God obtains credit with us, whatever we may offer to him are mere human inventions. It is, in the second place, added, that they did not receive correction; and this was no superfluous addition. For when God sees that we are not submissive, and that we do not willingly come to him when he calls us, he strengthens his instruction by chastisements. He allures us at first to himself, he employs kind and gentle invitations; but when he sees us delaying, or even going back, he begins to treat us more roughly and more severely: for teaching without the goads of reproof would have no effect. But when God teaches and reproves in vain, it then appears that our disposition is wicked and perverse. So the Prophet intended here to show the wickedness of his people as extreme, by saying, that they *heard not the voice nor received correction;* as though he had said, that the wickedness of his people was unhealable, for they not only rejected the doctrine of salvation, when offered, but also obstinately rejected all warnings, and would not bear any correction.

But we must bear in mind, that the Prophet had to do with that holy people whom God had chosen as his peculiar treasure. There is therefore no reason why those who profess the name of Christians at this day should exempt themselves from this condemnation; for our condition is not better than the condition of that people. Jerusalem was in an especial manner, as we have already said, the sanctuary, as it were, of God: and yet we see how severely the Prophet reproves Jerusalem and all its inhabitants. We have no cause to flatter ourselves, except we willingly submit to God, and suffer ourselves to be ruled by his word, and except we also patiently bear correction, when his teaching takes no suitable effect, and when there is need of sharp goads to stimulate us.

He afterwards adds, that it *did not trust in the Lord, nor draw nigh to its God.* The Prophet discovers here more clearly the spring of impiety—that Jerusalem placed not the hope of salvation in God alone; for from hence flowed all the mass of evils which prevailed; because if we inquire how it is that men burn with avarice, why they are insatiable, and why they wantonly defraud and plunder one another, we shall find the cause to be this—that they trust not in God. Rightly then does the Prophet mention this here, among other pollutions at Jerusalem, as the chief—that it did not put its trust in God. The same also is the cause and origin of all superstitions; for if men felt assured that God alone is enough for them, they would not follow here and there their own inventions. We hence see that unbelief is not only the mother of all the evil deeds by which men wilfully wrong and injure one another, but that it is also the cause of all superstitions.

He says, in the last place, that it *did not draw nigh to God.* The Prophet no doubt charges the Jews that they wilfully departed from God when he was nigh them; yea, that they wholly alienated themselves from him, while he was ready to cherish them, as it were, in his own bosom. This is indeed a sin common to all who seek not God; but Jerusalem sinned far more grievously, because she would not draw nigh to God, by whom she saw that she was sought. For why was the law given, why was adoption vouchsafed, and in short, why had they the various ordinances of religion, except that they might join themselves to God? 'And now Israel,' said Moses, 'what does the Lord thy God require of thee, except to cleave to him?' God thus intended his law to be, as it were, a sacred bond of union between him and the Jews. Now when they wandered here and there, that they might not be united to him, it was a diabolical madness. Hence the Prophet here does not only accuse the Jews of not seeking God, but of withdrawing themselves from him; and thus they were ungovernable. The Lord sought to tame them; but they were like wild beasts. It now follows—

3. Her princes within her *are* roaring lions; her judges *are* evening wolves; they gnaw not the bones till the morrow.

3. Principes ejus in medio ejus, leones rugientes; judices ejus lupi vespertini, non lacerant ad manè (*alii* non differunt, *nempe ossa comminuere; sed* גרם, *propriè significat,* conterere *vel,* frangere: *ergo de ossibus loquitur Propheta, quod scilicet non expectarent usque ad mane, ut ipsa contererent dentibus; sed præ fame, vel potius rabie prædam statim lacerarent; imo etiam contererent ossa dentibus.*)

The Prophet now explains what we have stated respecting plunder and fraud. He confirms that he had not without reason called Jerusalem היונה, *eiune,* a rapacious city, or one given to plunder; for the princes were like lions and the judges like wolves. And when he speaks of judges, he does not spare the common people; but he shows that all orders were then corrupt: for though no justice or equity is regarded by the people, there will yet remain some shame among the judges, so as to retain the people at least within some limits, that an extreme licentiousness may not prevail: but when robbery is practised in the court of justice, what can be said of such a city? We hence see that the Prophet in these words describes an extreme confusion: *The princes of Jerusalem*, he says, *are lions*. And we have elsewhere similar declarations; for the Prophets, when it was their object to condemn all from the least to the greatest, did yet direct their discourse especially to the judges.

And this is worthy of being noticed, for there was then no Church of God, except at Jerusalem. Yet the Prophet says, that the judges, and prophets, and priests, were all apostates. What comfort could the faithful have had? But we hence see that the fear of God had not wholly failed in his elect, and that they firmly and with an invincible heart contended against all offences and trials of this kind. Let us also learn to fortify ourselves at this day with the same courage, so that we may not faint, however much impiety may everywhere prevail, and all religion may seem extinct among men.

But we may also hence learn, how foolishly the Papists pride themselves in their vain titles, as though they thought that God was bound as it were to them, because they have bishops and pastors. But the Prophet shows, that even those who performed the ordinary office of executing the laws could yet be the wicked and perfidious despisers of God. He also shows, that neither prophets nor priests ought to be spared; for when God sets them over his Church, he gives them no power to tyrannize, so that they might dare to do anything with impunity, and not be reproved. For though the priesthood under the law was sacred, we yet see that it was subject to correction. So let no one at this day claim for himself a privilege, as though he was exempt from all instruction and reproof, while occupying a high station among the people of God.

He distinguishes between princes and judges; and the reason is, because the kingdom was as yet standing. So the courtiers, who were in favour and authority with the king, drew a part of the spoil to themselves, and the judges devoured another part. Though Scripture often makes no difference between these two names, yet I doubt not but he means by שׂרים, *sherim*, princes, the chiefs who were courtiers; and he calls them שפטים, *shephthim*, judges, who administered justice. And he says that the judges were evening wolves, that is, hungry, for wolves become furious in the evening when they have been roaming about all day and have found nothing. As their want sharpens the savageness of wolves, so the Prophet says that the judges were hungry like evening wolves, whose hunger renders them furious. And for the same purpose he adds, that they *broke not the bones in the morning;* that is, they waited not till the dawn to break the bones;[1] for when they devoured the flesh they also employed their teeth in breaking the bones, because their voracity was so great. We now apprehend the Prophet's meaning. It afterwards follows—

4. Her Prophets *are* light *and* treacherous persons: her priests have polluted the sanctuary, they have done violence to the law.	4. Prophetæ ejus leves (*vel*, futiles,) viri transgressionum; sacerdotes ejus polluerunt sanctum (*vel*, sanctuarium,) sustulerunt legem.

The Prophet again reverts to the pollution and filth of which he has spoken in the first verse. He shows that he had not without reason cried against the polluted city; for

---

[1] This is the explanation of *Grotius, Mede* and *Henderson*. The latter's version is—"They gnaw no bones in the morning;" *i. e.*, all is devoured in the night. *Newcome*, adopting the conjecture of *Houbigant*, supposes the true reading to be ידמו, and gives this rendering—"They wait not until the morning," which seems to have no meaning in this connection. What *Cocceius* proposes is more probable—"Who have not gnawed in the morning;" and on this account they were exceedingly voracious in the evening. But the idea of our common version is very appropriate; it implies that they were like wild beasts prowling all night, and carrying as it were their prey to their dens, that they might devour it there in the morning. This is the view taken by *Henry*. "They devour the flesh," says Adam *Clarke*, "in the night, and gnaw the bones, and extract the marrow afterwards."—*Ed.*

though the Jews used their washings, they could not yet make themselves clean in this manner before God, as the whole of religion was corrupted by them.

He says that *the Prophets were light.* He alone speaks here, and he condemns the many. We hence see that there is no reason why the ungodly should allege their great number, when God by his word accuses them, as the Papists do at this day, who deny it to be right in one or two, or few men, to speak against their impiety, however bad the state of things may be; there must be the consent of the whole world, as though the Prophet was not alone, and had not to contend with a great many. It is indeed true that he taught at the same time with the Prophet Jeremiah, as we have elsewhere seen; but yet hardly two or three did then discharge faithfully their office of teaching; and from this and other places we learn that the false Prophets, relying on their number, were on that account bolder. But Zephaniah did not for this reason cease to cry against them. However much then the false Prophets raged against him, and terrified him by the show of their number, he still exercised his liberty in condemning them. So at this day, though the whole world should unite in promoting impiety, there is yet no reason why the few should be disheartened when observing the worship of God perverted; but they ought on the contrary to encourage themselves by this example, and strenuously to resist thousands of men if necessary; for no union formed by men can possibly lessen the authority of God.

It now follows that they were *men of transgressions.* What we render "light," others render "empty;" (*vacuos;*) but the word פוחזים, *puchezim,* means strictly men of nought, and also the rash, and those who are void of judgment as well as of all moderation. In short, it is the same as though the Prophet had said that they were stupid and blind; and he says afterwards that they were fraudulent, than which there is nothing more inconsistent with the Prophetic office. But Zephaniah shows that the whole order was then so degenerated among the people, that the thickest darkness prevailed among those very leaders whose office it was to bring forth the light of celestial truth. And he makes a concession by calling them Prophets. The same we do at this day when we speak of Popish bishops. It is indeed certain that they are unworthy of so honourable a title; for they are blinder than moles, so that they are far from being overseers. We also know, that they are like brute beasts; for they are immersed in their lusts: in short, they are unworthy to be called men. But we concede to them this title, in order that their turpitude may be more apparent. The Prophet did the same, when he said, that the Jews did not draw nigh to their God; he conceded to them what they boasted; for they ever wished to be regarded as the holy and peculiar people of God: but their ingratitude did hence become more evident, because they went back and turned to another object, when God was ready to embrace them, as though they designedly meant to show that they had nothing to do with him. It is then the same manner of speaking, that Zephaniah adopts here, when he says, that the Prophets were light and men of transgressions.[1]

He then adds, *The priests have polluted the holy place.* The tribe of Levi, we know, had been chosen by God; and those who descended from him, were to be ministers and teachers to others: and for this reason the Lord in the law

---

[1] Her prophets are light, *they are* treacherous men.—*Newcome.*
Her prophets are vainglorious, hypocritical men.—*Henderson.*
The word rendered "light," occurs once as a verb in Gen. xlix. 4; and means evidently to "overflow" as a river, and not "unstable," as in our version. It is applied as a participle in Judges ix. 4, to designate persons overflowing in wickedness, dissolute, licentious, dissipated; and as a noun in Jer. xxiii. 32, to set forth the licentious conduct of the false prophets, who like the priests under the Papacy, were given to lasciviousness, and "committed adultery with their neighbours' wives," Jer. xxix. 23. See also Jer. xxiii. 14. As Zephaniah was cotemporary with Jeremiah, his description of the Prophets is thus seen to be the same, "Her Prophets are licentious," or lascivious.

Men of dissimulations or deceits, אנשי בגדות, signify, that under the pretence of telling the truth, they delivered what was false; or in the words of Jeremiah, they "caused the people to err by their lies," while they pretended to deliver true messages from God: so that Jer. xxiii. 32, contains an explanation of this clause. "Deceiving men" would perhaps be the best rendering. Though they were licentious, yet they deceived men, and made them to believe that they were true Prophets. They were impostors, and notwithstanding their immoral character, they persuaded deluded men that they were true and faithful.—*Ed.*

ordered the Levites to be dispersed through the whole country. He might indeed have given them as to the rest, a fixed habitation; but his will was, that they should be dispersed among the whole population, that no part of the land should be without good and faithful ministers. The Prophet now charges them, that they had polluted the holy place. By the word, קדש, *kodash*, the Prophet means whatsoever is holy; at the same time he speaks of the sanctuary. Moreover, since the sanctuary was as it were the dwelling-place of God, when the Prophets speak of divine worship and religion, they include the whole under the word, Temple, as in this place. He says then that the sanctuary was polluted by the priests, and then that they took away or subverted the law.[1]

We here see how boldly the Prophet charges the priests. There is then no reason why they who are divinely appointed over the Church should claim for themselves the liberty of doing what they please; for the priests might have boasted of this privilege, that without dispute everything was lawful for them. But we see that God not only calls them to order by his Prophets, but even blames them more than others, because they were less excusable. Now the Papists boast, that the clergy, even the very dregs collected from the filthiest filth, cannot err; which is extremely absurd; for they are not

---

[1] The word, קדש, as *Calvin* intimates, does not specifically mean the sanctuary, but holiness, or, as *Henderson* renders it, "what is sacred," or holy. Both our version and *Newcome* improperly render it "the sanctuary." The explanation of what is meant may be found in Ezek. xxii. 26. The word for sanctuary is מקדש. See Ezek. xxiii. 38, 39.

The words, חמסו תורה, have been taken to mean,—either, "They violated the law," as the words are rendered in Ezek. xxii. 26, that is, transgressed it by acting contrary to it; or, "They perverted the law," forcing it, as it were, out of its plain meaning by subtle glosses. The *Septuagint* render the verb ηθετησαν—set aside or abolished, in Ezekiel, and here ασεβουσι—act impiously. "Transgressed," says *Grotius;* "Do violence to," say *Piscator* and *Drusius*, that is, by wresting its words. It occurs much oftener as a noun than as a verb, and it commonly means a wrong or injustice done in an outrageous and violent manner. According to this general idea, we may render the phrase here, "they have outraged the law," either by their conduct, or by their comments. It was in either case a wrong done to the law, that was enormous, passing all reason and decency. So that to transgress, or to violate, or to do violence to, or to pervert the law, does not convey the full meaning.—*Ed.*

better than the successors of Aaron. But we see what the Prophet objects now to them,—that they *subverted the law:* he not only condemns their life, but says also, that they were perfidious towards God; for they strangely corrupted the whole truth of religion. The Papists confess, that they indeed can sin, but that the sin dwells only in their moral conduct. They yet seek to exempt themselves from all the danger of going astray. Though the Levitical priests were indeed chosen by the very voice of God, we yet see that they were apostates. But God confirms the godly, that they might not abandon themselves to impiety, though they saw their very leaders going astray, and rushing headlong into ruin. For it behoved the faithful to fortify themselves with constancy, when the priests not only by their bad conduct withdrew the people from every fear of God, but also perverted every sound doctrine; it behoved, I say, the faithful to remain then invincible. Though then at this day those who hold the highest dignity in the Church neglect God and even despise every celestial truth, and thus rush headlong into ruin, and though they attempt to turn God's truth into falsehood, yet let our faith continue firm; for John has not without reason declared, that it ought to be victorious against the whole world. (1 John v. 4.) It follows—

5. The just Lord *is* in the midst thereof; he will not do iniquity: every morning doth he bring his judgment to light, he faileth not; but the unjust knoweth no shame.

5. Iehova justus in medio ejus, non faciet iniquitatem: mane, mane judicium suum proferet in lucem, non deficiet: neque tamen cognoscet iniquus pudorem.

Here the Prophet throws back against hypocrites what they were wont to pretend, when they sought wickedly to reject every instruction and all warnings; for they said, that God dwelt in the midst of them, like the Papists at the present day, who raise up this as their shield against us,—that the Church is the pillar of the truth. Hence they think that all their wicked deeds are defended by this covering. So the Jews at that time had this boast ever on their lips,— "We are notwithstanding the holy people of God, and he dwells in the midst of us, for he is worshipped in the Temple, which has been built, not according to men's will, but by his command; for that voice proceeded not from earth, but came from heaven, 'This is my rest for ever, here will I dwell.'" (Ps. cxxxii. 14.) Since then the Jews were inflated with this presumption, the Prophet concedes what they claimed, that God dwelt among them; but it was for a far different purpose, which was, that they might understand, that his hand was nigh to punish their sins. This is one thing.

Jehovah is in the midst of them; "Granted," he says; "I allow that he dwells in this city; for he has commanded a temple to be built for him on Mount Sion, he has ordered a holy altar for himself; but why does God dwell among you, and has preferred this habitation to all others? Surely, he says, *he will not do iniquity*. Consider now what the nature of God is; for when he purposed to dwell among you, he certainly did not deny himself, nor did he cease to be what he is. There is therefore no reason for you to imagine, as though God intended, for the sake of those to whom he bound himself, to throw aside his own justice, or intended to pollute himself by the defilements of men." He warns the Jews, that they absurdly blended these things together. *God* then *who dwells in the midst of you, will not do iniquity;* that is, "He will not approve of your evil deeds; and though he may for a time connive at them, he will not yet bear with them continually. Do not therefore foolishly flatter yourselves, as though God were the approver of your wickedness."

Some apply this to the people,—that they ought not to have done iniquity; but this is a strained exposition, and altogether foreign to the context. Most other interpreters give this meaning, that God is just and will do no iniquity, for he had sufficient reasons for executing his vengeance on a people so wicked. They hence think, that the Prophet anticipates the Jews, lest they murmured, as though the Lord was cruel or too rigid. He will not do iniquity, that is, "Though the Lord may inflict on you a most grievous punishment, yet he cannot be arraigned by you as unjust; and ye in vain contend with him, for he will ever be found to be a righteous judge." But this also is a very frigid explanation. Let us bear in mind what I have already said,—that the Prophet here, by way of irony, concedes to the Jews, that God dwelt among them, but afterwards brings against them what they thought was a protection to them,—"God dwells in the midst of you; I allow it, he says; but is not he a just God? Do not then dream that he is one like yourselves, that he approves of your evil deeds. God will not do iniquity; ye cannot prevail with him to renounce himself, or to change his own nature. Why then does God dwell in the midst of you? *In the morning, in the morning,* he says, *his judgment will he bring forth to light;* the Lord will daily bring forth his judgment." How this is to be understood, we shall explain to-morrow.

PRAYER.

Grant, Almighty God, that inasmuch as thou hast deigned to favour us with an honour so invaluable, as to adopt us for a holy people to thee, and to separate us from the world,—O grant, that we may not close our eyes against the light of thy truth, by which thou showest to us the way of salvation; but may we with true docility follow where thou callest us, and never cast away the fear of thy majesty, nor mock thee with frivolous ceremonies, but strive sincerely to devote ourselves wholly to thee, and to cleanse ourselves from all defilements, not only of the flesh, but also of the spirit, that by thus seeking true holiness, we may aspire after and diligently labour for that heavenly perfection, from which we are as yet far distant; and may we in the meantime, relying on the favour of thy only-begotten Son, lean on thy mercy; and while depending on it, may we ever grow up more and more into that true and perfect union, reserved for us in heaven, when we shall be made partakers of thy glory, through Christ our Lord. Amen.

Lecture One Hundred and Twenty-fifth.

WE began yesterday to explain the passage, where the Prophet says, that God dwelt at Jerusalem, but that he was notwithstanding just, and could not possibly associate with the ungodly and the wicked, because he changes not his nature to suit the humour of men.

It now follows, *In the morning, in the morning, his judgment will he bring forth to light:* by which words he means, either that God would be the avenger of wickedness, which seems to escape, as it were, his eyes, while he delays his punishment, or that he is ready to restore his people, whenever they are attentive to instruction. If the former view be approved, the sense will be this,—that hypocrites foolishly flatter themselves, when God spares them; for he will suddenly ascend his tribunal that he may visit them with punishment. Some however choose to apply this to the judgments executed on the Gentiles, of which the Jews had not once nor twice been reminded, but often, that they might in time repent. But there is no doubt but that the Prophet refers here to a judgment belonging to the Jews.

Let us now see whether this judgment is pronounced or inflicted. It would not ill suit the passage to understand it of the vengeance which God was hastening to execute, for the Jews were worthy of what had been severely threatened, because they falsely professed his name; and while they absurdly boasted that he dwelt among them, they withdrew themselves very far from him. It is however no less suitable to refer this to teaching, so that the Prophet thus enhanced the sin of the people, because they had hardened themselves after so many and so constant warnings, which continually sounded in their ears, as God elsewhere complains, that though he rose early, and indeed daily, this solicitude had been without its fruit. The verb in the future tense will thus signify a continued act, for God ceased not to exhort to repentance those wretched beings who had ears which were deaf. And this view strikingly corresponds with what immediately follows, that he *fails not;* for such a perseverance was a proof of unwearied mercy, when God continued to send Prophets one after the other.

He now adds, *The wicked knows no shame.* He means what he has just referred to—that the people had become so hardened in their wickedness that they could not be reformed, either by instruction or by threats, or by the scourges of God.

If we refer judgment to teaching, which I approve, the meaning will be—that though God, by making known daily his law, kindled as it were a lamp, which discovered all evils, yet the ungodly were not ashamed. But if we understand it, as they say, of actual judgment, the meaning will be in substance the same—that the ungodly repented not, though the hand of God openly appeared; and though he rose to judgment, yet he says they knew not what it was to feel ashamed. As to the main subject there is no ambiguity; for the Prophet means only that the people were past recovery; for though God proved himself a judge by manifest evidences, and even by his own law, they yet felt no shame, but went on in their wicked courses. The word judgment, in the singular number, seems to have been put here in the sense of a rule, by which men live religiously and justly, and a rule which ought to make men ashamed.[1] It now follows—

6. I have cut off the nations: their towers are desolate; I made their streets waste, that none passeth by: their cities are destroyed, so that there is no man, that there is none inhabitant.	6. Excidi gentes; vastatæ sunt arces earum; perdidi vicos earum, ut nemo transeat; vastatæ sunt urbes earum, ut non sit vir, non sit qui habitet.
7. I said, Surely thou wilt fear me, thou wilt receive instruction; so their dwelling should not be cut off, howsoever I punished them: but they rose early *and* corrupted all their doings.	7. Dixi, certè timebis me, suscipies disciplinam; et non excidetur habitatio ejus, quicquid visitavi super eam: certè properarunt, corruperunt omnia studia sua.

Here the Prophet shows in another way that there was no hope for a people, who could not have been instructed

---

[1] The verbs here are in the future tense, but evidently express, as *Calvin* observes, a continued act. The same is exactly the case in *Welsh;* the verbs are in the future tense, but are understood as expressing a present act or a continued act, or what is continually or habitually done. In English the present must be adopted—

    The righteous Jehovah *is* in the midst of her,
    He doeth no injustice:
    Every morning his judgment
    He bringeth to light—it fails not;
    Yet the unjust knoweth no shame.

"Injustice" in the second, and "unjust" in the fifth line, come from the same root. "Judgment" here is what God judges and determines to be right and just; and it is set forth here as the sun rising every day from morning to morning, and as never failing to appear.—*Ed.*

by the calamities of others, to seek to return to God's favour. For God here complains that he had in vain punished neighbouring nations, and made them examples, in order to recall the Jews to himself. Had they been of a sane mind they might have been led, by their quiet state, while God spared them, to consider what they had deserved—"If this is done in the green tree, what at length will be done in the dry?" They might then have thought within themselves, that a most grievous calamity was at hand, except they anticipated God's wrath, which had grown ripe against them; and God also testified that he intended by such examples to stay the judgment which he might have already justly executed on them. As they then even hastened it, it is evident that their wickedness was past remedy. This is the sum of the whole.

He says first, I *have cut off nations;* by which words he shows that he warned the Jews to repent, not only by one example, but by many examples; for not one instance only of God's wrath had appeared, but God had on all sides manifested himself to be a judge, in inflicting punishment on one nation after another. Since then they had been so often warned, we may hence learn that they were wholly blinded by their wickedness.

He now enhances the atrocity of the punishment inflicted, and says, that *citadels had been demolished and streets cut off, that no one passed through;* and then, that *cities had been reduced to solitude, so that there was no inhabitant.* For when punishment is of an ordinary kind, it is wont, for the most part, to be disregarded; but when God showed, by so remarkable proofs, that he was displeased with the nations, that is, with the ignorant, who in comparison with the Jews were innocent, how could such an instance as this be disregarded by the Jews, whom God thus recalled to himself, except that they were of a disposition wholly desperate and irreclaimable? We now then see why the Prophet enlarges on the punishments which, having been inflicted on the nations, ought to have been considered by the Jews.[1]

[1] This verse, literally rendered, is as follows,—
I have cut off nations;
Desolate are become their towers;

He now subjoins the object which God had in view, *I said, Surely thou wilt fear me.* Here God assumes the character of man, as he does often elsewhere: for he does not wait for what is future, as though he was doubtful; but all things, as we know, are before his eyes. Hence God was not deceived, as though something had happened beyond his expectation; but as I have already said, he undertakes here the character of man; for he could not otherwise have sufficiently expressed how inexcusable the Jews were who had despised all his warnings. For what was God's design when he punished the heathens, one nation after another, except that the Jews might be awakened by the evils of others, and not provoke his wrath against themselves? Paul makes use of the same argument. " On account of these things,' he says, ' the wrath of God comes upon all the unbelieving.' (Rom. i. 17.) Inasmuch as men for the most part deceive themselves by self-flatteries and cherish with extreme indulgence their own wickedness, Paul says, that the wrath of God comes on the unbelieving: and it is a singular proof of God's love, that he does not immediately assail us, but sets before us the examples of others. As when any one lays hold of his servant in the presence of his son, and punishes him severely, the son must be moved by the sight, except he be wholly an abandoned character: however, in such a case the father's love manifests itself; for he withholds his hand from his son and inflicts punishment on the servant, and this for the benefit of his son, that he may learn wisdom by what another suffers. God declares in this place that he had done the same; but he complains that it had been without benefit, for the Jews had frustrated his purpose.

It may be here asked, whether men so frustrate God that he looks for something different from what happens. I have

> I have made solitary their streets, without a passenger;
> Deserted are become their cities,
> Without a man, without an inhabitant.

It is not the *destruction* of the towers, streets, and cities, that is here intended, but their *desolation*. The nations being cut off, then the towers became desolate, the streets empty, and the cities forsaken. The last line but one is literally—" Hunted have been their cities," so that no man was left behind.—*Ed.*

already said, that God speaks after the manner of men, and in a language not strictly correct: and hence we ought not here to enter or penetrate into the secret purpose of God, but to be satisfied with this reason,—that if we profit nothing when God warns us either by his word or by his scourges, we are then equally guilty, as though he was deceived by us: and hence also the madness of those is reproved, who are unwilling to ascribe anything to God but what is conveyed in these common forms of speech: God says, that he wills the salvation of all, (1 Tim. ii. 4;) hence there is no election, which makes a distinction between one man and another; but the Lord leaves the whole human race to their free-will, so that every one may provide for himself as he pleases; otherwise the will of God must be twofold. So unlearned men vainly talk; and such not only show their ignorance in religion, but are also wholly destitute of common sense. For what is more absurd than to conclude, that there is a twofold will in God, because he speaks otherwise with us than is consistent with his incomprehensible majesty? God's will then is one and simple, but manifold as to the perceptions of men; for we cannot comprehend his hidden purpose, which angels adore with reverence and humility. Hence the Lord accommodates himself to the measure of our capacities, as this passage teaches us with sufficient clearness. For if we receive what the fanatics imagine, then God is like man, who hopes well, and finds afterwards that he has been deceived: but what can be more alien to his glory? We hence see how these insane men not only obscure the glory of God, but also labour, as far as they can, to reduce his whole essence to nothing. But this mode of speaking ought to be sufficiently familiar to us,—that God justly complains that he has been deceived by us, when we do not repent, inasmuch as he invites us to himself, and even stimulates us, *I said, Surely thou wilt fear me.*

This word *said*, ought not then to be referred to the hidden counsel of God, but to the subject itself, and that is, that it was time to repent. "Who would not have hoped but that you would have returned to the right way? When the next house was on fire, how was it possible for you to sleep, except ye were extremely stupid? And when so many examples were presented before your eyes without any advantage, it is evident that there is no more any hope of repentance." Thou, then, wilt fear me; that is, "God might have hoped for some amendment, though he had not yet touched you even with his smallest finger; for ye beheld, while in a tranquil state, how severely he punished the contempt of his justice as to the heathens." He uses a similar language in Isaiah v. 4, 'My vine, what have I done to thee? or what could I have done to thee more than what I have done? I expected thee to bring forth fruit; but, behold, thou hast brought forth wild grapes.' God in that passage expostulates with the Jews as though they had by their perfidiousness deceived him. But we know, that whatever happens was known to him before the creation of the world: but, as I have already said, the fact itself is to be regarded by us, and not the hidden judgment of God.

He afterwards adds, *Thou wilt receive correction;* that is, thou wilt be hereafter more tractable: for monstrous is our stupidity, when we fear not God's vengeance; when yet it evidently appears that we are warned, as I have already said, to repent, by all the examples of judgments which are daily presented to us. But if we proceed in our wickedness, what else is it but to kick against the goad, as the old proverb is? In short, we here see described an extreme wickedness and obstinacy, which admitted of no remedy.

Hence the Prophet adds again, *And cut off should not be her habitation, howsoever I might have visited her;* that is, though the Jews had already provoked me, so that the punishment they have deserved was nigh; yet I was ready to withdraw my hand and to forgive them, if they repented: not that God ever turns aside from his purpose, for there is no shadow of turning in him; but he sets before them the fact as it was; for the subject here, as I have said, is not respecting the secret purpose of God, but we ought to confine ourselves to the means which he employs in promoting our salvation. God had already threatened the Jews for many years; he had as yet deferred to execute what he had threatened. In the meantime his wrath had been manifested through the whole neighbourhood; the heathen nations had suffered the severest judgments. God here declares, that he had been so lenient to his people as to give time to repent; and he complains that he had delayed in vain, for they had gone on in their wickedness, and had mocked, as it were, his patience. When, therefore, he says, *Cut off should not* be her habitation, *howsoever I might have visited her*, or have visited her, he pursues still the same mode of speaking, that is, that he was prepared to forgive the Jews, though he had before destined them to destruction; not that he, as to himself, would retract that sentence; but that he was still reconcileable, if the Jews had been touched by any feeling of repentance.[1]

He at last adds, *Surely*, (some render it *but*,) *surely they have hastened*. The verb שכם, *shecam*, means properly to rise early, but is to be taken metaphorically in the sense of hastening; as though he had said, "They run headlong to

---

[1] The last clause has been variously rendered. There is no assistance from the Septuagint, as the whole text is very different. *Marckius*, after *Drusius*, connects it, not with the preceding, but with the following line, in this sense, that how much soever God had punished the city, yet its inhabitants were the more bent to corrupt their ways. But the words can hardly admit of this meaning. *Henderson* supposes כ to be understood before כל, and gives this rendering of the two lines—
    That her habitation might not be cut off,
    According to all that I had appointed concerning her.
Newcome differs as to the last line—
    After all *the punishment with* which I had visited her.
None of these are satisfactory. *Grotius*, taking the sense of the *Targum*, seems to have given the best meaning. He says that פקד, followed by על, means sometimes to appoint or constitute, and refers to 2 Chron. xxxvi. 23, "All the *good* which I have appointed to her," or promised; but he unnecessarily supposes "shall come" to be understood; for the word, "all which," may be considered to be in apposition with "habitation." I give the following version of this whole verse—
    I said, "Surely thou wilt fear me,
    Thou wilt receive instruction;"
    Then cut off should not be her habitation—
    All that I have committed to her:
    Yet they rose up early, they corrupted all their doings.
To rise up early is a Hebrew phrase, which means a resolved and diligent attention to a thing. The import of the line is, that they with full-bent purpose and activity corrupted all their doings.—*Ed.*

corrupt their ways." God had said that he had been indulgent to them for this end—that he might lead them by degrees to repentance: now he complains, that they on the contrary had run another way, when they saw that he suspended his judgments, as though it was their designed object to accelerate his wrath. Thus they hastened to corrupt their ways. The meaning, then, is—that this people were not only irreclaimable in their obstinacy, but that they were also sottish and presumptuous, as though they wished to hasten the judgment, which the Lord was ready for a time to defer. It now follows—

8. Therefore wait ye upon me, saith the Lord, until the day that I rise up to the prey: for my determination *is* to gather the nations, that I may assemble the kingdoms, to pour upon them mine indignation, *even* all my fierce anger: for all the earth shall be devoured with the fire of my jealousy.

8. Propterea expectate me, dicit Jehova, usque ad diem quo surgam ad prædam; quia judicium meum (*hoc est*, decretum est mihi,) ut colligam gentes, ut congregem regna; ut effundam super ipsa (regna, *vel*, super ipsas gentes) indignationem meam, totum furorem iræ meæ; quia igne zeli (*vel*, indignationis meæ) vorabitur tota terra.

God here declares that the last end was near, since he had found by experience that he effected nothing by long forbearance, and since he had even found the Jews becoming worse, because he had so mercifully treated them. Some think that the address is made to the faithful, that they might prepare themselves to bear the cross; but this view is foreign to the subject of the Prophet: and though this view has gained the consent of almost all, I yet doubt not but that the Prophet, as I have now stated, breaks out into a complaint, and says, that God would not now deal in words with a people so irreclaimable.

Look for me, he says; that is, "I am now present fully prepared: I have hitherto endeavoured to turn you, but your hearts have become hardened in depravity. But inasmuch as I have lost all my labour in teaching, warning, and exhorting you, even when I presented to you examples on every side among heathen nations, which ought to have stimulated you to repentance, and inasmuch as I have effected nothing, it is now all over with you—*Look for me:*

I shall no more contend with you, nor is there any ground for you to hope that I shall any more send Prophets to you." *Look then for me, until I shall rise*—for what purpose? *to the prey.* Some render the word לְעַד, *laod*, for ever; but the Prophet means, that God was so offended with the contumacy of the people, that he would now plunder, spoil and devour, and forget his kindness, which had been hitherto a sport to them—" I shall come as a wild beast; as lions rage, lacerate, tear, and devour, so also will I now do with you; for I have hitherto too kindly and paternally spared you." We hence see that these things are not to be referred to the hope and patience of the godly; but that God on the contrary does here denounce final destruction on the wicked, as though he had said—" I bid you adieu; begone, and mind your own concerns; for I will no longer contend with you; but I shall shortly come, and ye shall find me very different from what I have been to you hitherto." We now see that God, as it were, repudiates the Jews, and threatens that he would come to them with a drawn sword; and at the same time he compares himself to a savage and cruel wild beast.

He afterwards adds—*For my judgment is;* that is, I have decreed to *gather all nations.* We have elsewhere spoken of this verb אָסַף, *asaph;* it is the same in Hebrew as the French *trousser.* It is then my purpose to *gather,* that is, to heap together into one mass *all nations,* to *assemble the kingdoms,* so that no corner of the earth may escape my hand. But he speaks of all nations and kingdoms, that the Jews might understand that his judgment could no longer be deferred; for if a comparison be made between them and heathen nations, judgment, as it is written, is wont to begin with the house of God, (1 Pet. iv. 17;) and further, they were less excusable than the unbelieving, who went astray, which is nothing strange, in darkness, for they were without the light of truth. God then threatens nations and kingdoms, that the Jews might know that a most dreadful punishment was impending over their heads, for they had surpassed all others in wickedness and evil deeds.[1] He afterwards adds—

---

[1] This verse is considered by *Newcome* and *Henderson* to be addressed to the godly, to encourage them at the approaching calamities, while *Piscator*,

9. For then will I turn to the people a pure language, that they may all call upon the name of the Lord, to serve him with one consent.	9. Certè tunc convertam ad populos labium purum, ut invocent omnes nomen Jehovæ, ut serviant ei humero uno.

The Prophet now mitigates the asperity of his doctrine, which might have greatly terrified the godly; nay, it might have wholly disheartened them, had no consolation been applied. God then moderates here what he had previously threatened; for if the Prophet had only said this—"My purpose is to gather all the nations, and thus the whole earth shall be devoured by the fire of indignation," what could the faithful have concluded but that they were to perish with the rest of the world? It was therefore necessary to add something to inspire hope, such as we find here.

We must at the same time bear in mind what I have reminded you of elsewhere—that the Prophet directs his discourse one while to the faithful only, who were then few in number, and that at another time he addresses the multitude indiscriminately; and so when our Prophet threatens, he regards the whole body of the people; but when he proclaims the favour of God, it is the same as though he turned his eyes

---

Grotius, *Marckius* and *Dathius*, agree with *Calvin* that it is an awful warning to the wicked Jews, spoken of in the preceding verse. Differing somewhat from *Calvin*, they regard the "nations" and "kingdoms" to be the Babylonians, who were composed of various nations and kingdoms, and "upon them" to be the Jews, and "the whole land" to be that of Judea. This view, no doubt, is the most consistent with the context. The objection made by *Henderson*, that the words *expect*, or *wait for me*, are ever used in a good sense, seems to have no force, for these words by themselves can mean neither what is good nor what is bad, the whole depends on the context. The verb חבה simply means to tarry, to wait—μενειν. The word "therefore" seems to connect this with the preceding verse, and there is nothing in the foregoing part of the chapter that alludes to the godly. Besides, the words which follow "wait for me" explain them, as will be seen by the following literal rendering of the whole verse—

> 8. Therefore wait for me, saith Jehovah,
> For the day of my rising to the prey!
> For my purpose is to gather nations,
> To assemble kingdoms,
> In order to pour on them my indignation,
> All the heat of my anger;
> For by the fire of my jealousy
> Shall be consumed the whole land.

The "fire of God's jealousy" sufficiently proves that what is meant is the land of Judea. (See ch. i. 18.)—*Ed.*

towards the faithful only, and gathered them into a place by themselves. As for instance, when a few among a people are really wise, and the whole multitude unite in hastening their own ruin, he who has an address to make will make a distinction between the vast multitude and the few; he will severely reprove those who are thus foolish, and live for their own misery; and he will afterwards shape his discourse so as to suit those with whom he has not so much fault to find. Thus also the Lord changes his discourse; for at one time he addresses the ungodly, and at another he turns to the elect, who were but a remnant. So the Prophet has hitherto spoken by reproofs and threatenings, for he addressed the whole body of the people; but now he collects, as I have said, the remnant as it were by themselves, and sets before them the hope of pardon and of salvation.

Hence he says, *But then*[1] (for I take כִּי, *ki*, as an adversative) *will I turn to the people a pure lip*. God intimates that he would propagate his grace wider, after having

---

[1] כִּי אָז, " For then," *Henderson;* " Surely then," *Newcome;* " Postea vero—but afterwards," *Dathius* and *Grotius*. And *Newcome* says, that אָז is used here largely, for " afterwards." It refers to the time after the execution of the judgments previously mentioned.

" The pure lip" is evidently not the language which God would adopt in addressing the nations, but the language they would adopt in addressing him. What is meant is a pure heart; what gives utterance to the heart is mentioned for the heart itself; as the " shoulder" is afterwards used for the service that is rendered to God.

The verb הָפַךְ, to turn, means to change the form, condition, or course of a thing, conveying perhaps here the idea, that the pure lip is substituted for that which is impure: " I will give them as a change, instead of what they have, a pure lip." Μεταστρεψω—" I will change," Sept. and Sym.; στρεψω—" I will turn," Aq. and Theod. It is rendered " reddam" and " restituam" by *Drusius* and *Grotius*.

Newcome, following the conjecture of *Houbigant*, reads אֶשְׁפֹּךְ, " I will pour out," contrary to all the ancient versions, and without the countenance of a single MS.

Though the word, עַמִּים, peoples, most frequently means the nations, yet there are instances in which it means the people of Israel, inasmuch as they were composed of various tribes. See 1 Kings xxii. 28; Joel ii. 6. And if we render the verb, " restore," with *Drusius* and *Grotius*, then we must adopt this meaning. Eleven MSS. have " and," וְ, before the verb to " serve:" and as there is no preposition before " shoulder," we may render the verse—

> But I will then restore to the people a pure lip,
> That they may, all of them, call on the name of Jehovah,—
> And one shoulder, that they may serve him.—*Ed.*

cleansed the earth; for he will be worshipped not only in Judea, but by foreign nations, and even by the remotest. For it might have been objected, "Will God then extinguish his name in the world? For what will be the state of things when Judea is overthrown and other nations destroyed, except that God's name will be exposed to reproach! It will nowhere be invoked, and all will outvie one another in blasphemies against him." The Prophet meets this objection, and says, that God has in his own hand the means by which he will vindicate his own glory; for he will not only defend his Church in Judea, but will also gather into it nations far and wide, so that his name shall be everywhere celebrated.

But he speaks first of a pure lip, *I will turn*, he says, *to the nations a pure lip*. By this word he means, that the invocation of God's name is his peculiar work; for men do not pray through the suggestion of the flesh, but when God draws them. It is indeed true, that God has ever been invoked by all nations; but it was not the right way of praying, when they heedlessly cast their petitions into the air: and we also know, that the true God was not invoked by the nations; for there was no nation then in the world which had not formed for itself some idol. As then the earth was full of innumerable idols, God was not invoked except in Judea only. Besides, though the unbelieving had an intention to pray to God, yet they could not have prayed rightly, for prayer flows from faith. God then does not without reason promise, that he would turn pure lips to the nations; that is, that he would cause the nations to call on his name with pure lips. We hence then learn what I have stated—that God cannot be rightly invoked by us, until he draws us to himself; for we have profane and impure lips. In short, the beginning of prayer is from that hidden cleansing of the Spirit of which the Prophet now speaks.

But if it be God's singular gift, to turn a pure lip to the nations, it follows that faith is conferred on us by him, for both are connected together. As God then purifies the hearts of men by faith, so also he purifies their lips that his name may be rightly invoked, which would otherwise be profaned by the unbelieving. Whenever they pretend to call on God's name, it is certain that it is not done without profanation.

As to the word *all*, it is to be referred to nations, not to each individual; for it has not been that every one has called on God; but there have been some of all nations, as Paul also says in the first chapter of the first Epistle to the Corinthians: for in addressing the faithful, he adds, 'With all who call on the name of the Lord in every place'—that is, not only in Judea; and elsewhere he says, 'I would that men would stretch forth hands to heaven in every place.' (1 Tim. ii. 8.)

He afterwards adds, *That they may serve him with one shoulder;* that is, that they may unitedly submit to God in order to do him service; for to serve him with the shoulder is to unite together, so as to help one another. The metaphor seems to have been derived from those who carry a burden; for except each assists, one will be overpowered, and then the burden will fall to the ground. We are said then to serve God with one shoulder when we strive by mutual consent to assist one another. And this ought to be carefully noticed, that we may know that our striving cannot be approved by God, except we have thus the same end in view, and seek also to add courage to others, and mutually to help one another. Unless then the faithful thus render mutual assistance, the Lord cannot approve of their service.[1]

We now see how foolishly they talk who so much extol free-will and whatever is connected with it: for the Lord demands faith as well as other duties of religion; and he requires also from all, love and the keeping of the whole law. But he testifies here that his name cannot be invoked, as the lips of all are polluted, until he has consecrated them, cleansing by his Spirit what was before polluted: and he shows also that men will not undertake the yoke, unless he joins them together, so as to render them willing. I must not proceed farther.

---

[1] The expression " with one shoulder" is rendered by the Septuagint, " under one yoke"—ὑπὸ ζυγὸν ἵνα. The idea is that of oxen drawing together. To serve God under one yoke, is to do the same service unitedly. " A metaphor," says *Newcome*, " from the joint efforts of yoked beasts."—*Ed.*

PRAYER.

Grant, Almighty God, that since it is the principal part of our happiness, that in our pilgrimage through this world there is open to us a familiar access to thee by faith,—O grant, that we may be able to come with a pure heart to thy presence: and when our lips are polluted, O purify us by thy Spirit, so that we may not only pray to thee with the mouth, but also prove that we do this sincerely, without any dissimulation, and that we earnestly seek to spend our whole life in glorifying thy name, until being at length gathered into thy celestial kingdom, we may be truly and really united to thee, and be made partakers of that glory, which has been procured for us by the blood of thy only-begotten Son. Amen.

Lecture One Hundred and Twenty-sixth.

10. From beyond the rivers of Ethiopia my suppliants, *even* the daughters of my dispersed, shall bring mine offering.

10. Trans fluvios Ethiopiæ supplicantes mihi (*vel*, supplices mei;) filia dispersorum meorum offerent munus meum (*hoc est*, mihi; *nam* ՚ *affixum accipitur loco pronominis* ՚אל.)

INTERPRETERS agree not as to the meaning of this verse; for some of the Hebrews connect this with the former, as though the Prophet was still speaking of the calling of the Gentiles. But others, with whom I agree, apply this to the dispersed Jews, so that the Prophet here gives hope of that restoration, of which he had before spoken. They who understand this of the Gentiles, think that Atharai and Phorisai are proper names. But in the first place, we cannot find that any nations were so called; and then, if we receive what they say, these were not separate nations, but portions of the Ethiopians; for the Prophet does not state the fact by itself, that Atharai and Phorisai would be the worshippers of God; but after having spoken of Ethiopia, he adds these words: hence we conclude, that the Prophet means this,— that they would return into Judea from the farthest region of the Ethiopians to offer sacrifices to God. And as he mentions the daughter of the dispersion, we must understand this of the Jews, for it cannot be applied to the Ethiopians.

And this promise fits in well with the former verse: for the Prophet spoke, according to what we observed yesterday, of the future calling of the Gentiles; and now he adds, the Jews would come with the Gentiles, that they might unite together, agreeing in the same faith, in the true and pure worship of the only true God. He had said, that the kingdom would be enlarged, for the Church was to be gathered from all nations: he now adds, that the elect people would be restored, after having been driven away into exile.

Hence he says, *Beyond the rivers of Ethiopia shall be my suppliants:* for עתר, *otar,* means to supplicate; but it means also sometimes to be pacified, or to be propitious; and therefore some take עתרים, *otarim,* in a passive sense, "they who shall be reconciled to God;" as though he had said, "God will at length be propitious to the miserable exiles, though they have been cast away beyond the rivers of Ethiopia: they shall yet again be God's people, for he will be reconciled to them." As David calls Him the God of his mercy, because he had found him merciful and gracious, (Ps. lix. 18,) so also in this place they think that the Jews are said to be the עתרי, the reconciled of Jehovah, because he would be reconciled to them. But this exposition is too forced: I therefore retain that which I have stated,—that some suppliants would come to God from the utmost parts of Ethiopia, not the Ethiopians themselves, but the Jews who had been driven there.

To the same purpose is what is added, *The daughter of my dispersed;* for פוץ, *puts,* means to scatter or to disperse.[1] Hence by the daughter of the dispersed he means the gathered assembly of the miserable exiles, who for a time were considered as having lost their name, so as not to be counted as the people of Israel. These then *shall again offer to me a gift,* that is, they are to be restored to their country, that they may there worship me after their usual manner. Now

---

[1] It is more consonant with the style of the Prophets to render the clauses apart, as *Calvin* does, than as it is done in our version, and by *Newcome* and *Henderson.* The auxiliary verb, as is often the case, is to be understood in the first clause,—

From beyond the rivers of Cush *shall be* my suppliants;
The daughter of my dispersed shall bring my offering.

though this prophecy extends to the time of the Gospel, it is yet no wonder, that the Prophet describes the worship of God such as it had been, accompanied with the ceremonies of the Law. We now then perceive what Zephaniah means in this verse,—that not only the Gentiles would come into the Church of God, but that the Jews also would return to their country, that they might together make one body. It follows,—

| 11. In that day shalt thou not be ashamed for all thy doings, wherein thou hast transgressed against me: for then I will take away out of the midst of thee them that rejoice in thy pride, and thou shalt no more be haughty because of my holy mountain. | 11. In die illo non erubesces ob omnia facta tua, quibus prævaricata es contra me; quia tunc auferam è medio tui qui exultant superbia tua; et non adjicies ad superbiendum posthac (*hoc est*, non adjicies superbire) in monte sanctitatis meæ. |

Here the Prophet teaches us, that the Church would be different, when God removed the dross and gathered to himself a pure and chosen people: and the Prophet stated this, that the faithful might not think it hard that God so diminished his Church that hardly the tenth part remained; for it was a sad and a bitter thing, that of a vast multitude a very few only remained. It could not then be, but that the ruin of their brethren greatly affected the Jews, though they knew them to be reprobate. We indeed see how Paul felt a sympathy, when he saw that his own nation were alienated from God. (Rom. ix. 1.) So it was necessary that some consolation should be given to the faithful, that they might patiently bear the diminution of the Church, which had been previously predicted. Hence the Prophet, that he might moderate their grief, says, that this would be for their good; for in this manner the reproaches were to be removed, by which the Jewish name had been polluted, and rendered abominable.

Thou shalt not be ashamed, he says, *for the sins by which I have been offended*. Why? For thou shalt be cleansed; for it is God's purpose to reserve a few, by whom he will be purely worshipped. Some think that he does not speak here of the remission of sins, but on the contrary, of a pure and holy life, which follows regeneration; as though he had said, "There will be no reason any more for thee to be ashamed of thy life; for when I shall chasten you, ye will then fear me, and your correction will be conducive to a newness of life: since then your life will not be the same as formerly, and since my glory shall shine forth among you, there will be no cause why ye should be ashamed." But this is a strained view, and cannot be accommodated to the words of the Prophet; for he says, *Thou shalt no more be ashamed of the sins by which thou hast transgressed against me.* We hence see that this cannot be otherwise applied than to the remission of sins. But the last clause has led interpreters astray, for the Prophet adds, *For I will take away from the midst of thee those who exult:* but the Prophet's design, as I have stated, was different from what they have supposed; for he shows that there was no reason for the Jews to lament and deplore the diminution of the Church, because the best compensation was offered to them, which was, that by this small number God would be purely served. For when the body of the people was complete, it was, we know, a mass of iniquity. How then could Israel glory in its vast number, since they were all like the giants carrying on war against God? When now God collects a few only, these few would at length acknowledge that they had been preserved in a wonderful manner, in order that religion and the true worship of God should not be extinguished in the earth.

We now perceive the Prophet's design; but I will endeavour to render this clearer by a comparison: Suppose that in a city licentiousness of life so prevails that the people may seem to be irreclaimable; when it happens that the city itself falls away from its power and pristine state, or is in some other way reformed, not without loss, and is thus led to improve its morals, this would be a compensation to the good, and would give courage to the godly and ease their grief, so that they would patiently submit, though the city had not the same abundance, nor the same wealth and enjoyments. How so? because they who remained would form a body of people free from reproach and disgrace. When disease is removed from the human body, the body itself is necessarily weakened; and it is sometimes necessary to amputate a member, that the whole body may be preserved. In this case there is a grievous diminution; but as there is no other way of preserving the body, the remedy ought to be patiently sustained. In a similar manner does the Prophet now speak of the city Jerusalem: *Thou shalt not be ashamed of the sins by which thou hast transgressed against me.* How so? Because they were to be separated from the profane and gross despisers of God; for as long as the good and the evil were mixed together, it was a reproach common to all. Jerusalem was then a den of robbers; it was, as it were, a hell on earth; and all were alike exposed to the same infamy, for the pure part could not be distinguished, as a mass of evil prevailed everywhere. The Prophet now says, "Thou shalt not be ashamed of thy former infamy." Why? "Because God will separate the chaff from the wheat, and will gather the wheat; ye shall be, as it were, in the storehouse of God; the chosen seed shall alone remain; there will be such purity, that the glory of the Lord shall shine forth among you: ye shall not therefore be ashamed of the disgraceful deeds by which ye are now contaminated."

We now apprehend the meaning of the words. But it may seem strange that the Prophet should say, that sins should be covered by oblivion, which the Jews ought indeed to have thought of often and almost at all times, according to what Ezekiel says, 'Thou wilt then remember thy ways, and be ashamed,' (Ezek. xxxvi. 61;) that is, when God shall be pacified. Ezekiel says, that the fruit of repentance would be, that the faithful, covered with shame, would condemn themselves. Why so? Because the reprobate proceed in their wicked courses, as it were, with closed eyes, and as it has been previously said, they know no shame: though God charges them with their sins, they yet despise and reject every warning with a shameless front; yea, they kick against the goads. Since it is so, justly does Ezekiel say, that shame would be the fruit of true repentance, according to what Paul also says in the sixth chapter to the Romans, "Of which ye are now ashamed." He intimates, that when they were sunk in their unbelief, they were so given to shameful deeds, that they perceived not their abomination. They began therefore to be ashamed, when they became illuminated. The Prophet seems now to cut off this fruit from repentance : but what he says ought to be otherwise understood, that is, that the Church would be then free from reproach ; for the reprobate would be separated, all the filth would be taken away, when God gathered only the remnant for himself; for in this manner, as it has been said, the wheat would be separated from the chaff. *Thou shalt not then be ashamed in that day of evil deeds ; for I will take away from the midst of thee those who exult.* He shows how necessary the diminution would be; for all must have perished, had not God cut off the putrid members. How severe soever then and full of pain the remedy would be, it ought yet to be deemed tolerable ; for the Church, that is the body, could not otherwise be preserved.

But it may be again objected—That the Church is cleansed from all spots, inasmuch as the reprobate are taken away ; for he says, *Thou shalt not be ashamed* of the evil deeds *by which thou hast sinned,* literally, *against me,* that is, by which thou hast transgressed against me. God here addresses, it may be said, the faithful themselves: He then does not speak of the evil deeds of those whom the Lord had rejected. But the answer is easy : When he says, that the Church had sinned, he refers to that mixture, by which no distinction is made between the wheat and the chaff. We may say that a city is impious and wicked, when the majority so much exceeds in number the good, that they do not appear. When therefore among ten thousand men there are only thirty or even a smaller number who are anxious for a better state of things, the whole number will be generally counted wicked on account of the larger portion, for the others are hid, and, as it were, covered over and buried. Justly then and correctly does Zephaniah declare, that the Jews had transgressed against God ; for in that mixed multitude the elect could not have been distinguished from the reprobate. But he now promises that there would be a distinction, when God took away the proud, who exulted in vain boasting. For he says, *I will take away from the midst of thee those who exult in thy pride.*

Some render the word in the abstract, "the exultations of thy pride:" but the term עליזים, found here, is never in construction rendered exultations. It is therefore no doubt to be understood of men. He then names the pride of the people; and yet he addresses the elect, who were afterwards to be gathered. What does this mean? even what we have already stated, that before the Church was cleansed from her pollution and filth, there was a common exultation and insolence against God; for these words were everywhere heard—"We are God's holy people, we are a chosen race, we are a royal priesthood, we are a holy inheritance." (Ex. xix. 6.) Since, then, these boastings were in the mouth of them all, the Prophet says, that it was the pride of the whole people. *I will* then *take away*, he says, *from the midst of thee those who exult in thy pride.*[1]

He afterwards adds, *Thou shalt no more add to take pride in my holy mountain.* Here the Prophet points out the main spring of the evil, because the Jews had hardened themselves in a perverse self-confidence, as they thought that all things were lawful for them, inasmuch as they were God's chosen people. Jeremiah also in a similar manner represents their boasting as false, when they pretended to be the temple of God. (Jer. vii. 4.) So our Prophet condemns this pride,

---

[1] This may be rendered, "Those who exult in thy exaltation:" the Targum has it, "in thy glory." This "glory" or "exaltation," as explained in the next verse, was Mount Sion. There was a preeminence, but it was made an object of unholy boasting. The paraphrase of *Henderson*, "thy proud exulters," completely leaves out the character of their exultation. The whole verse may be thus rendered,—

In that day thou shalt not be ashamed of thy doings,
By which thou hast transgressed against me;
For then will I remove from the midst of thee
Those who exult in thy exaltation;
And thou shalt no more be elevated
On account of the mount of my holiness.

The word גאות means exaltation or glory in a good as well as in a bad sense. See Ps. xciii. 1; Is. xii. 5. What they exulted in was in itself good, but they exulted only in an outward privilege, without connecting it with God, as many have done in all ages. This is the essence of Pharisaism. *Vatablus* and *Drusius* regard the word as having this sense here.—*Ed.*

because they concealed their sins under the shadow of the temple, and thought it a sufficient defence, that God dwelt on Mount Sion. To show, then, that the people were unhealable, without being cleansed from this pride, the Prophet says, *I will take away those who exult*—How did they exult? *in thy pride:* and what was this pride? that they inhabited the holy mount of God, besides which there was no other sanctuary of God on earth. As then they imagined that God was thus bound to them, they insolently despised all admonitions, as though they were exempt from every law and restraint. *Thou shalt not then add to take pride in my holy mountain.*

We now then see how careful we ought to be, lest the favours of God, which ought by their brightness to guide us to heaven, should darken our minds. But as we are extremely prone to arrogance and pride, we ought carefully to seek to conduct ourselves in a meek and humble manner, when favoured with God's singular benefits; for when we begin falsely to glory in God's name, and to put on an empty mask to cover our sins, it is all over with us; inasmuch as to our wickedness, to our contempt of God, and to other evil lusts and passions, there is added perverseness, for we persevere in our course, as it were, with an iron and inflexible neck. Thus, indeed, it happens to all hypocrites, who elate themselves through false pretences as to their connection with God. It follows—

12. I will also leave in the midst of thee an afflicted and poor people, and they shall trust in the name of the Lord.	12. Et residuum faciam in medio tui populum afflictum et pauperem; et sperabunt in nomine Iehovæ.
13. The remnant of Israel shall not do iniquity, nor speak lies; neither shall a deceitful tongue be found in their mouth: for they shall feed and lie down, and none shall make *them* afraid.	13. Residuum Israel non perpetrabunt iniquitatem (*hoc est,* reliquæ; *ad verbum est,* residuum; *sed quia nomen est collectivum, ideo mutatur numerus,*) et non loquentur mendacium, et non invenietur in ore ipsorum lingua dolosa (*vel,* lingua fraudis;) quoniam ipsi pascentur et accubabunt; et nemo erit exterrens.

Here the Prophet pursues the same subject—that God would provide for the safety of his Church, by cutting off the majority of the people, and by reserving a few; for his purpose was to gather for himself a pure and holy Church, as the city had previously been full of all uncleanness. It ought, then, to have been a compensation to ease their grief, when the godly saw that God would be propitious to them, though he had treated them with great severity. And we must bear in mind what I have before stated—that the Church could not have been preserved without correcting and subduing that arrogance, which arose from a false profession as to God. Zephaniah takes it now as granted, that pride could not be torn away from their hearts, except they were wholly cast down, and thus made contrite. He then teaches us, that as long as they remained whole, they were ever proud, and that hence it was necessary to apply a violent remedy, that they might learn meekness and humility; which he intimates when he says, *that the residue of the people would be humble and afflicted;* for if they had become willingly teachable, there would have been no need of so severe a correction. In short, though the faithful lament that God should thus almost annihilate his Church, yet in order that they might not murmur, he shows that this was a necessary remedy. How so? because they would have always conducted themselves arrogantly against God, had they not been afflicted. It was, therefore, needful for them to be in a manner broken, because they could not be bent. *I will*, then, he says, *make the residue an afflicted and a poor people.*

The word, עֲנִי, *oni*, means humble; but as he adds the word דַּל, *dal*, poor, he no doubt shows that the Jews could not be corrected without being stripped of all the materials of their glorying.[1] They were, indeed, extremely wedded to

---

[1] The first word, עֲנִי, means one made humble by distress, or affliction, the humbled, rather than the humble. The second word, דַּל, is one exhausted, or reduced in number, or reduced to poverty. *Newcome* renders it "lowly," but improperly. *Jerome* has "pauperem et egenum—poor and needy;" the Septuagint, "πραὺν καὶ ταπεινόν—meek and humble;" *Marckius*, "afflictum et attenuatum—afflicted and diminished." Perhaps the best rendering would be, "a people humbled and reduced." The idea of being "afflicted" or distressed, is excluded by what is expressed at the end of the next verse, and also that of being "poor" in a worldly respect. The reference seems to be to a humbled state of mind, occasioned by calamities, and to a reduced number—a remnant.

"I will leave" for השארתי, as in our version, is not its full meaning. It

their boastings; yea, they were become hardened in their contempt of God. He therefore says, that this fruit would at last follow, that they would *trust in the Lord,* that is, when he had laid them prostrate.

This verse contains a most useful instruction: for first we are taught that the Church is subdued by the cross, that she may know her pride, which is so innate and so fixed in the hearts of men, that it cannot be removed, except the Lord, so to speak, roots it out by force. There is then no wonder that the faithful are so much humbled by the Lord, and that the lot of the Church is so contemptible; for if they had more vigour, they would soon, as is often the case, break out into an insolent spirit. That the Lord, then, may keep his elect under restraint, he subdues and tames them by poverty. In short, he exercises them under the cross. This is one thing.

We must also notice the latter clause, when he says, *They shall trust in the Lord,* that is, those who have been reduced to poverty and want. We hence see for what purpose God deprives us of all earthly trust, and takes away from us every ground of glorying; it is, that we may rely only on his favour. This dependence ought not, indeed, to be extorted from us, for what can be more desirable than to trust in God? But while men arrogate to themselves more than what is right, and thus put themselves in the place of God, they cannot really and sincerely trust in him. They indeed imagine that they trust in God, when they ascribe to him a part of their salvation; but except this be done wholly, no trust can be placed in God. It is hence necessary that they who ascribe to themselves even the smallest thing, should be reduced to nothing: and this is what the Prophet means. Let us further know, that men do not profit under God's scourges, except they wholly deny themselves, and forget their own power, which they falsely imagine, and recumb on him alone.

But the Prophet speaks of the elect alone; for we see that many are severely afflicted, and are not softened, nor do

means to reserve as a remnant. "I will cause to remain," or, "I will reserve," would be the proper rendering.—*Ed.*

they put off their former hardihood. But the Lord so chastises his people, that by the spirit of meekness he corrects in them all pride and haughtiness. But by saying, *They shall trust in the name of Jehovah,* he sets this trust in contrast with the pride which he had previously condemned. They indeed wished to appear to trust in the name of God, when they boasted of Mount Sion, and haughtily brought forward the adoption by which they had been separated from heathen nations; but it was a false boasting, which had no trust in it. To trust, then, in the name of Jehovah is nothing else than sincerely to embrace the favour which he offers in his word, and not to make vain pretences, but to call on him with a pure heart and with a deep feeling of penitence.

For the same purpose he adds, *The residue of Israel shall no more work iniquity nor speak falsehood; nor shall there be found a deceitful tongue in their mouth.* The Prophet continues the same subject—that the Church is not to be less esteemed when it consists only of a few men; for in the vast number there was great filth, which not only polluted the earth by its ill savour, but infected heaven itself. Since then Jerusalem was full of iniquities, as long as the people remained entire, the Prophet adduces this comfort—that there was no reason for sorrow, if from a vast number as the sand of the sea, and from a great multitude like the stars, God would only collect a small band; for by this means the Church would be cleansed. And it was of great importance that the filth should be cleansed from God's sanctuary; for what could have been more disgraceful than that the holy place should be made the lodging of swine, and that the place which God designed to be consecrated to himself, should be profaned? As then Jerusalem was the sanctuary of God, ought not true religion to have flourished there? But when it became polluted with every kind of filth, the Prophet shows that it ought not to have seemed grievous that the Lord should take away that vast multitude which falsely boasted that they professed his name. *They shall not* then *work iniquity*.

Under one kind of expression he includes the whole of a

righteous life, when he says, *They shall not speak falsely, nor will there be found a deceitful tongue.* It is indeed sufficient for the practice of piety or integrity of life to keep the tongue free from frauds and falsehood ; but as it cannot be that any one will abstain from all frauds and falsehood, except he purely and from the heart fears God, the Prophet, by including the whole under one thing, expresses under the word *tongue* what embraces complete holiness of life.

It may be now asked, whether this has ever been fulfilled. It is indeed certain, that though few returned to their own country, there were yet many hypocrites among that small number ; for as soon as the people reached their own land, every one, as we find, was so bent on his own advantages, that they polluted themselves with heathen connections, that they neglected the building of the temple, and deprived the priests of their tenths, that they became cold in the worship of God. With these things they were charged by Haggai, Zechariah, and Malachi. Since these things were so, what means this promise, that there would be no iniquity when God had cleansed his Church? The Prophet speaks comparatively ; for the Lord would so cleanse away the spots from his people that their holiness would then appear more pure. Though then many hypocrites were still mixed with the good and real children of God, it was yet true that iniquity was not so prevalent, that frauds and falsehood were not so rampant among the people as they were before.

He afterwards adds, *For they shall feed and lie down, and there will be none to terrify them.* He mentions another benefit from God—that he will protect his people from all wrongs when they had repented. We must ever bear in mind what I have stated—that the Prophet intended here to heal the sorrow of the godly, which might have otherwise wholly dejected their minds. That he might then in some measure alleviate the grief of God's children, he brings forward this argument—" Though few shall remain, it is yet well that the Lord will cleanse away the filth of the holy city, that it may be justly deemed to be God's habitation, which was before the den of thieves. It is not then a loss to you, that few will dwell in the holy land, for God will be a faithful guardian of your safety. What need then is there of a large multitude, except to render you safe from enemies and from wild beasts? What does it signify, if God receives you under his protection, under the condition that ye shall be secure, though not able to resist your enemies? Though one cannot defend another, yet if God be your protector, and ye be made to live in peace under the defence which he promises, there is no reason why ye should say, that you have suffered a great loss, when your great number was made small. It is then enough for you to live under God's guardianship; for though the whole world were united against you, and ye had no strength nor defence yourselves, yet the Lord can preserve you; *there will be no one to terrify you.*

And this argument is taken from the law; for it is mentioned among other blessings, that God would render safe the life of his people; which is an invaluable blessing, and without which the life of men, we know, must be miserable; for nothing is more distressing than constant fear, and nothing is more conducive to happiness than a quiet life: and hence to live in quietness and free from all fear, is what the Lord promises as a chief blessing to his people.

PRAYER.

Grant, Almighty God, that since the depravity of our nature is so great, that we cannot bear prosperity without some wantonness of the flesh immediately raging in us, and without becoming even arrogant against thee,—O grant, that we may profit under the trials of the cross; and when thou have blest us, may we with lowly hearts, renouncing our perverseness, submit ourselves to thee, and not only bear thy yoke submissively, but proceed in this obedience all our life, and so contend against all temptations as never to glory in ourselves, and feel also convinced, that all true and real glory is laid up for us in thee, until we shall enjoy it in thy celestial kingdom, through Christ our Lord. Amen.

Lecture One Hundred and Twenty-seventh.

14. Sing, O daughter of Zion; shout, O Israel; be glad and rejoice with all the heart, O daughter of Jerusalem.
15. The Lord hath taken away thy judgments, he hath cast out thine enemy: the king of Israel, *even* the Lord, *is* in the midst of thee: thou shalt not see evil any more.

14. Exulta filia Sion (*vel*, jubila;) exulta Israel; gaude et exulta toto corde filia Ierusalem.
15. Abstulit Iehova judicia tua, purgando avertit inimicos tuos; rex Israel Iehova in medio tui; non videbis malum amplius.

THE Prophet confirms what he has been teaching, and encourages the faithful to rejoice, as though he saw with his eyes what he had previously promised. For thus the Prophets, while encouraging the faithful to entertain hope, stimulate them to testify their gratitude, as though God's favour was already enjoyed. It is certain, that this instruction was set before the Jews for this purpose,—that in their exile and extreme distress they might yet prepare themselves to give thanks to God, as though they were already, as they say, in possession of what they had prayed for. But we must remember the design of our Prophet, and the common mode of proceeding which all the Prophets followed; for the faithful are exhorted to praise God the same as if they had already enjoyed his blessings, which yet were remote, and seemed concealed from their view.

We now then perceive what the Prophet meant in encouraging the Jews to praise God: he indeed congratulates them as though they were already enjoying that happiness, which was yet far distant: but as it is a congratulation only, we must also bear in mind, that God deals so bountifully with his Church as to stimulate the faithful to gratitude; for we pollute all his benefits, except we return for them, as it has been stated elsewhere, the sacrifice of praise: and as a confirmation of this is the repetition found here, which would have otherwise appeared superfluous. "Exult, daughter of Sion, shout, be glad; rejoice with all thine heart, daughter of Jerusalem."[1]

---
[1] To give the words their specific meaning, they may be thus rendered,—
   Cry aloud thou daughter of Zion,
   Shout ye Israel;

But the Prophet was not thus earnest without reason; for he saw how difficult it was to console the afflicted, especially when God manifested no evidence of hope according to the perception of the flesh; but his purpose was by this heap of words to fortify them, that they might with more alacrity struggle with so many hard and severe trials.

He then adds, that God had *taken away the judgments* of Zion. By judgments, he means those punishments which would have been inflicted if it had been the Lord's purpose to deal according to strict justice with the Jews, as when any one says in our language, *J'ai brulé tous tes procés*. He intimates then that God would no more make an enquiry as to the sins of his people. The word, משפט, *meshiphath*, we know, has various meanings in Hebrew; but in this place, as I have said, it means what we call in French, *Toutes procedures*. In short, God declares that the sins of his people are buried, so that he in a manner puts off his character as a judge, and remits his own right, so that he will no more contend with the Jews, or summon them, as they say, to trial. *Jehovah* then *will take away thy judgments.*[1]

Then follows an explanation, *By clearing he hath turned aside all enemies;*[2] for we know that war is one of God's judgments. As then God had punished the Jews by the Assyrians, by the Egyptians, by the Chaldeans, and by other heathen nations, he says now, that all enemies would be turned away. It hence follows, that neither the Assyrians nor the Chaldeans had assailed them merely through their own inclination, but that they were, according to what has been elsewhere stated, the swords, as it were, of God.

> Rejoice and exult with all thine heart,
> Thou daughter of Jerusalem.

The first two lines encourage the fullest expression of feelings, loud crying, and shouting like a trumpet; and then is set forth the character of these feelings; they were to be those of joy and exultation. Our version, *Newcome* and *Henderson*, render the second line correctly, but not the first; and "Be glad and rejoice" are too feeble to express what the third line contains: for the exhortation is to "rejoice" and to "exult." It was to be the loud cry of joy, and the shouting of exultation or triumph.—*Ed.*

[1] Turned aside hath Jehovah thy judgments.—*Ed.*
[2] The words are, פנה איבך, "he hath turned away thine enemy." Many copies have איביך, "thine enemies;" but it may be regarded as the poetical singular.—*Ed.*

It afterwards follows, *The king of Israel is Jehovah in the midst of thee.* Here the Prophet briefly shows, that the sum of real and true happiness is then possessed, when God declares, that he undertakes the care of his people. God is said to be in the midst of us, when he testifies that we live under his guardianship and protection. Properly speaking, he never forsakes his own; but these forms of speech, we know, are to be referred to the perception of the flesh. When the Lord is said to be afar off, or to dwell in the midst of us, it is to be understood with reference to our ideas: for we think God to be then absent when he gives liberty to our enemies, and we seem to be exposed as a prey to them; but God is said to dwell in the midst of us when he protects us by his power, and turns aside all assaults. Thus, then, our Prophet now says, that God will be in the midst of his Church; for he would really and effectually prove that he is the guardian of his elect people. He had been indeed for a time absent, when his people were deprived of all help, according to what Moses expresses when he says, that the people had denuded themselves, because they had renounced God, by whose hand they had been safely protected, and were also to be protected to the end. (Exod. xxxii. 25.)

He lastly adds, *Thou shalt not see evil.* Some read, " Thou shalt not fear evil," by inserting , *iod;* but the meaning is the same: for the verb, to see, in Hebrew is, we know, often to be taken in the sense of finding or experiencing. *Thou shalt* then *see no evil;* that is, God will cause thee to live in quietness, free from every disturbance. If the other reading, " Thou shalt not fear evil," be preferred, then the reference is to the blessing promised in the law; for nothing is more desirable than peace and tranquillity. Since then this is the chief of temporal blessings, the Prophet does not without reason say, that the Church would be exempt from all fear and anxiety, when God should dwell in the midst of it, according to what he says in Ps. xlvi. It now follows—

| 16. In that day it shall be said to Jerusalem, Fear thou not. *and to* Zion, Let not thine hands be slack. | 16. In die illa dicitur Jerosolymæ, Ne timeas; Sion, ne pigrescant (*vel*, solvantur, *nam* רפה *significat* lentum esse, *vel*, remissum, *vel*, dissolutum; ne *ergo* pigrescant) manus tuæ. |

17. The Lord thy God in the midst of thee *is* mighty; he will save, he will rejoice over thee with joy; he will rest in his love, he will joy over thee with singing.

17. Iehova Deus tuus in medio tui fortis servabit; exultabit (*vel,* gaudebit) super te in lætitia; quiescet (silebit *ad verbum, vel,* quietus erit) in amore suo; exultabit super te cum jubilatione.

The Prophet proceeds still to confirm the same truth, but employs a different mode of speaking. It shall, he says, be then said everywhere to Zion, *Fear not, let not thine hands be let down,* &c. For these words may no less suitably be applied to the common report or applause of all men, than to the prophetic declaration; so that the expression, " It shall be said," may be the common congratulation, which all would vie to offer. The import of the whole is, that Jerusalem would be so tranquil that either the Prophets, or all with common consent would say, " Thou enjoyest thy rest: for God really shows that he cares for thee; there is therefore no cause for thee hereafter to fear." For there is expressed here a real change: since the Jews had been before in daily fear, the Prophet intimates, that they would be so safe from every danger, as to be partakers of the long-wished-for rest, with the approbation even of the whole world. Hence, *it shall* be said—by whom? either by the Prophets, or by common report: it makes no great difference, whether there would be teachers to announce their state joyful and prosperous, or whether all men would, by common consent, applaud God's favour, when he had removed from his people all wars, troubles, and fears, so as to make them live in quietness.

It shall then *be said to Jerusalem, fear not; Sion! let not thine hands be relaxed.* By saying " Fear not, and let not thine hands be relaxed," he intimates, that all vigour is so relaxed by fear, that no member can perform its function. But by taking a part for the whole, he understands by the word hands, every other part of the body; for by the hands men perform their works. Hence in Scripture the hands often signify the works of men. The meaning then is—that God's Church would then be in such a state of quietness as to be able to discharge all its duties and transact its concerns peaceably and orderly. And it is what we also know by experience, that when fear prevails in our hearts we are as it were lifeless, so that we cannot raise even a finger to do anything: but when hope animates us, there is a vigour in the whole body, so that alacrity appears everywhere. The Prophet, no doubt, means here, that God thus succours his elect, not that they may indulge in pleasures, as is too often the case, but that they may, on the contrary, strenuously devote themselves to the performance of their duties. We ought therefore to notice the connection between a tranquil state and diligent hands; for, as I have said, God does not free us from all trouble and fear, that we may grow torpid in our pleasures, but that we may, on the contrary, be more attentive to our duty. *Sion, then! let thine hands be no more torpid*—Why?

Jehovah, he says, *in the midst of thee strong, will save.* He repeats what he had said, but more fully expresses what might have appeared obscure on account of its brevity. He therefore shows here more at large the benefit of God's presence—that God will not dwell idly in his Church, but will be accompanied with his power. For what end? To save. We hence see that the word גבור, *gebur*, ascribed to God, is very emphatical; as though he had said, that God would not be idle while residing in the midst of his Church, but would become its evident strength. And it is worthy of notice, that God exhibits not himself as strong that he may terrify his elect, but only that he may become their preserver.

He afterwards adds, *He will rejoice over thee with gladness.* This must be referred to the gratuitous love of God, by which he embraces and cherishes his Church, as a husband his wife whom he most tenderly loves. Such feelings, we know, belong not to God; but this mode of speaking, which often occurs in Scripture, is thus to be understood by us; for as God cannot otherwise show his favour towards us and the greatness of his love, he compares himself to a husband, and us to a wife. He means in short—that God is most highly pleased when he can show himself kind to his Church.

He confirms and shows again the same thing more clearly,

He will be at rest (or silent) *in his love.* The proper meaning of חרש, *charesh,* is to be silent, but it means here to be at rest. The import is, that God will be satisfied, as we say in French, *Il prendra tout son contentement;* as though he had said, that God wished nothing more than sweetly and quietly to cherish his Church. As I have already said, this feeling is indeed ascribed to God with no strict correctness; for we know that he can instantly accomplish whatever it pleases him: but he assumes the character of men; for except he thus speaks familiarly with us, he cannot fully show how much he loves us. God then shall be at rest in his love; that is, "It will be his great delight, it will be the chief pleasure of thy God when he cherishes thee: as when one cherishes a wife most dear to him, so God will then rest in his love." He then says, *He will exult over thee with joy.*[1]

These hyperbolic terms seem indeed to set forth something inconsistent; for what can be more alien to God's glory than to exult like man when influenced by joy arising from love? It seems then that the very nature of God repudiates these modes of speaking, and the Prophet appears as though he had removed God from his celestial throne to the earth. A heathen poet says,—

> Not well do agree, nor dwell on the same throne,
> Majesty and love. (*Ovid. Met.* Lib. ii. 846-7.)

God indeed represents himself here as a husband, who

---

[1] This is a very remarkable passage. Perhaps the more literal version would be the following,—
16. In that day he will say to Jerusalem, "Fear thou not;
    Sion! relaxed let not thy hands be:
17. Jehovah thy God in the midst of thee is mighty; he will save;
    He will rejoice over thee with joy;
    He will renew *thee* in his love,
    He will exult over thee with acclamation."

The verb יאמר is rendered as above by the Septuagint, ιςιι, meaning the Lord. The last line but one is according to the Septuagint and the Syriac; and this sense has been adopted by *Houbigant, Dathius,* and *Newcome.* There is the difference only of one letter, ד for ר, which are very like. The law of parallelism is in favour of this meaning. The verse contains four lines: there is an evident correspondence of meaning in the second and the last line; and so there is between the first and the third according to the preceding version, but not otherwise. The word rendered "acclamation" is a noun from the verb רנה, to cry aloud, used at the beginning of verse 14.—*Ed.*

burns with the greatest love towards his wife; and this does not seem, as we have said, to be suitable to his glory; but whatever tends to this end—to convince us of God's ineffable love towards us, so that we may rest in it, and being weaned as it were from the world, may seek this one thing only, that he may confer on us his favour—whatever tends to this, doubtless illustrates the glory of God, and derogates nothing from his nature. We at the same time see that God, as it were, humbles himself; for if it be asked whether these things are suitable to the nature of God, we must say, that nothing is more alien to it. It may then appear by no means congruous, that God should be described by us as a husband who burns with love to his wife: but we hence more fully learn, as I have already said, how great is God's favour towards us, who thus humbles himself for our sake, and in a manner transforms himself, while he puts on the character of another. Let every one of us come home also to himself, and acknowledge how deep is the root of unbelief; for God cannot provide for our good and correct this evil, to which we are all subject, without departing as it were from himself, that he might come nigher to us.

And whenever we meet with this mode of speaking, we ought especially to remember, that it is not without reason that God labours so much to persuade us of his love, because we are not only prone by nature to unbelief, but exposed to the deceits of Satan, and are also inconstant and easily drawn away from his word: hence it is that he assumes the character of man. We must, at the same time, observe what I have before stated—that whatever is calculated to set forth the love of God, does not derogate from his glory; for his chief glory is that vast and ineffable goodness by which he has once embraced us, and which he will show us to the end.

What the Prophet says of *that day* is to be extended to the whole kingdom of Christ. He indeed speaks of the deliverance of the people; but we must ever bear in mind what I have already stated—that it is not one year, or a few years, which are intended, when the Prophets speak of future redemption; for the time which is now mentioned began when the people were restored from the Babylonian captivity, and continues its course to the final advent of Christ. And hence also we learn that these hyperbolic expressions are not extravagant, when the Prophets say, "Thou shalt not afterwards fear, nor see evil:" for if we regard the dispersion of that people, doubtless no trial, however heavy, can happen to us, which is not moderate, when we compare our lot with the state of the ancient people; for the land of Canaan was then the only pledge of God's favour and love. When, therefore, the Jews were ejected from their inheritance, it was, as we have said elsewhere, a sort of repudiation; it was the same as if a father were to eject from his house a son, and to repudiate him. Christ was not as yet manifested to the world. The miserable Jews had an evidence, in figures and shadows, of that future favour which was afterwards manifested by the gospel. Since, then, God gave them so small an evidence of his love, how could it be otherwise but that they must have fainted, when driven far away from their land? Though the Church is now scattered and torn, and seems little short of being ruined, yet God is ever present with us in his only-begotten Son: we have also the gate of the celestial kingdom fully opened. There is, therefore, administered to us at all times more abundant reasons for joy than formerly to the ancient people, especially when they seemed to have been rejected by God. This is the reason why the Prophet says, that the Church would be lessened by calamities, when God again gathered it. But that redemption of the people of Israel ought at this day to be borne in mind by us; for it was a memorable work of God, by which he intended to afford a perpetual testimony that he is the deliverer of all those who hope in him. It follows—

18. I will gather *them that are* sorrowful for the solemn assembly, *who are* of thee, *to whom* the reproach of it *was* a burden.

18. Afflictos à tempore (*vel*, pro tempore, *vel*, ad tempus, *ut alii vertunt*) congregabo qui ex te erunt: onus (*vertunt quidam, sed active videtur accipere Propheta potius*, qui sistinuerunt *ergo*) super eam opprobrium.

He proceeds here with the same subject, but in different words; for except some consolation had been introduced, what the Prophet has hitherto said would have been frigid;

for he had promised them joy, he had exhorted the chosen of God to offer praise and thanksgiving; but they were at the same time in a most miserable state. It was hence necessary to add this declaration respecting the exiles being gathered.

But he says *at the time*. Some read, "in respect to time;" but this is obscure and strained. Others render it, "at the time;" but it means strictly "from the time;" though מ, *mem*, may sometimes be rendered as a particle of comparison. Interpreters do not seem to me rightly to understand the Prophet's meaning: for I do not doubt but that he points out here the fixed time of deliverance, as though he had said, "I will again gather thine afflicted, and those who have endured thy reproach." When? at the time, ממועד, *memuod;* that is, at the determined or fixed time: for מועד, *muod*, is not taken in Hebrew for time simply, but for a predetermined time, as we say in French, *Un terme préfix*. *I will* then *gather thine afflicted*, but not soon. Our Prophet then holds the faithful here somewhat in suspense, that they might continue in their watchtower, and patiently wait for God's help; for we know how great is our haste, and how we run headlong when we hope for anything; but this celerity, according to the old proverb, is often delay to us. Since, then, men are always carried away by a certain heat, or by too much impetuosity, to lay hold on what may happen, the Prophet here lays a restraint, and intimates that God has his own seasons to fulfil what he has promised, that he will not do so soon, nor according to the will of men, but when the suitable time shall come. And this time is that which he has appointed, not what we desire.

He then adds, *Who have sustained reproach for her.* In this second clause the Prophet no doubt repeats the same thing; but at the same time he points out, not without reason, their condition—that the Jews suffered reproach and contumely at the time of their exile, and that on account of being the Church; that is, because they professed to worship their own God; for on account of his name the Jews were hated by all nations, inasmuch as their religion was different from the superstitions of all heathens. It could not hence be, but that the unbelieving should vex them with many reproaches, when they were carried away into exile, and scattered in all directions.[1]

He had said before, "I will gather the afflicted;" but he now adds, "I will gather those who have sustained reproach." I have stated that some read, "A burden upon her is reproach;" but no sense can be elicited from such words. The Prophet does here no doubt obviate a temptation which awaited God's children, who would have to experience in exile what was most grievous to be borne; for they were to be exposed to the taunts and ridicule of all nations. Hence he seasonably heals their grief by saying, that though for a time they would be laughed at by the ungodly, they would yet return to their own country; for the Lord had resolved to gather them. But we must ever remember what I have said—that God would do this in his own time, when he thought it seasonable. It follows—

---

[1] This verse presents considerable difficulties, and has been variously rendered. The Septuagint and the Targum differ as much from one another, as they do from the Hebrew. None regard the former as at all suitable; but some, as *Grotius* and *Dathius*, take the meaning of the latter, though to reconcile it with the Hebrew is difficult. *Marckius* seems to have given the most probable meaning—

    Remotos à festivitate collegi,
    Ex te sunt, onus super eam opprobrium.
    Those driven away from festivity have I gathered,
    From thee they are—a burden on her *is* reproach.

The word נוגי, he derives from הגה. In this case it is literally, "my driven away," or, "my removed" ones. מועד is assembling or meeting, as well as a fixed time or season; and the assembling was that on festal days: it may therefore be rendered, "festivals." "From thee" is "Sion" in verse 16. Instead of "on her," more than ten copies, as well as the Targum, have "on thee," עליך; but an abrupt change of person is of frequent occurrence in the Prophets.

Following the sense of the Targum, we may, perhaps, give the following version—

    The grieved for the festivals have I gathered from thee;
    They were a burden on thee, a reproach.

The paraphrase of the Targum, as given by *Dathius*, is the following—

    Those who among thee have impeded the seasons of thy festivity,
    I will expel from thee; wo to them who have carried arms against thee, and loaded thee with reproaches.

The "grieved for the festivals" were those who disliked them, who grudged the offerings that were to be made. The words are in the past tense, but future as to what is said; for the Prophets declare things as exhibited to them in a vision.—*Ed.*

19. Behold, at that time I will undo all that afflict thee: and I will save her that halteth, and gather her that was driven out; and I will get them praise and fame in every land where they have been put to shame.

19. Ecce ego conficiens omnes oppressores tuos (qui te humiliant, *ad verbum*) in tempore illo; et servabo claudicantem, et reducam expulsam, ad faciendum eos in laudem et nomen in terra opprobrii ipsorum.

He confirms here what I have referred to in the last verse—that God would overcome all obstacles, when his purpose was to restore his people. On this the Prophet, as we have said, dwells, that the Jews might in their exile sustain themselves with the hope of deliverance. As, then, they could not instantly conceive what was so incredible according to the perceptions of the flesh, he testifies that there is sufficient power in God to subdue all enemies.

At that time, he says, he repeats what had been stated before—that his people must wait as long as God pleases to exercise them under the cross; for if their option had been given to the Jews, they would have willingly continued at their ease; and we know how men are wont to exempt themselves from every trouble, fear, and sorrow. As therefore men naturally desire rest and immunity from all evil, the Prophet here exhorts the faithful to patience, and shows, that it cannot be that God will become their deliverer, except they submit to his chastisement; "at that time" then. It is ever to be observed, that the Prophet condemns that extreme haste which usually takes hold of men when God chastises them. However slowly then and gradually God proceeds in the work of delivering his own, the Prophet shows here, that there was no reason for them to despair, or to be broken down in their spirits.[1]

He then subjoins, that he would *save the halting, and restore the driven away*. By these words he means, that though

---

[1] The first clause in this verse is amended by *Newcome* and some others in conformity with the Septuagint: but this is a very unsafe process. *Henderson's* version is—
Behold, I will deal with all thine oppressors at that time. "Deal," עשה; "interficiam—I will slay," *Vulg.*; "conficiam—I will make an end," *Drusius*; but to "deal with," or "act against," is the literal rendering. More is implied than what is expressed, which is often the case with words used in every language.—*Ed.*

the Church would be maimed and torn, there would yet be nothing that could hinder God to restore her: for by the halting and the driven away he understands none other than one so stripped of power as wholly to fail in himself. He therefore compares the Church of God to a person, who, with relaxed limbs, is nearly dead. Hence, when we are useless as to any work, what else is our life but a languor like to death? But the Prophet declares here, that the seasonable time would come when God would relieve his own people: though they were to become prostrate and fallen, though they were to be scattered here and there, like a torn body of man, an arm here and a leg there, every limb separated; yet he declares that nothing could possibly prevent God to gather his Church and restore it to its full vigour and strength. In short, he means that the restoration of the Church would be a kind of resurrection; for the Lord would humble his people until they became almost lifeless, so as not to be able to breathe: but he would at length gather them, and so gather them that they would not only breathe but be replenished with such new vigour as though they had received no loss. I cannot finish the whole to-day.

PRAYER.

Grant, Almighty God, that as we are at this day so scattered on account of our sins, and even they who seem to be collected in thy name and under thy authority, are yet so torn by mutual discords, that the safety of thy Church hangs as it were on a thread, while in the meantime thine enemies seek with savage cruelty to destroy all those who are thine, and to obliterate thy gospel,—O grant, that we may live in quietness and resignation, hoping in thy promises, so that we may not doubt, but that thou in due time wilt become our deliverer: and may we so patiently bear to be afflicted and cast down by thee, that we may ever raise up our groans to heaven so as to be heard through the name of thy Son, until being at length freed from every contest, we shall enjoy that blessed rest which is laid up for us in heaven, and which thine only-begotten Son has procured for us. Amen.

Lecture One Hundred and Twenty-eighth.

WE stopped yesterday at the latter clause of the last verse but one of the Prophet Zephaniah, where God promises that the Jews, who had been before not only obscure, but also exposed to all kinds of reproaches, would again become illustrious; for to give them for a name and for a praise, is no other thing than to render them celebrated, that they might be, as they say, in the mouth of every one.

And he says, *in the land of their shame*, or reproach; for they had been a mockery everywhere; as the unbelieving thought that they deluded themselves with a vain hope, because they boasted that God, under whose protection they lived, would be their perpetual guardian, though they were driven away into exile. Hence an occasion for taunt and ridicule was given. But a change for the better is here promised; for all in Assyria and Chaldea would have to see that this was a people chosen by God; so that there would be a remarkable testimony among all nations, that all who trust in God are by no means disappointed, for they find that he is faithful in his promises. The last verse follows—

20. At that time will I bring you *again*, even in the time that I gather you: for I will make you a name and a praise among all people of the earth, when I turn back your captivity before your eyes, saith the Lord.

20. In tempore illo reducam vos, in tempore illo colligam vos; quia ponam vos in nomen et laudem per cunctos populos terræ, (*vel*, inter cunctos populos terræ,) quum reducam captivitates vestras in oculis vestris, dicit Jehova.

He repeats the same things, with some change in the words; and not without reason, because no one then thought that the Jews, who were cast as it were into the grave, would ever come forth again, and especially, that they would be raised unto such dignity and unto so elevated an honour. As then this was not probable, the Prophet confirms his prediction—*I will restore you*, says God, *I will gather you, even because I have given you a name;* that is, it is my resolved and fixed purpose to render you celebrated: but here again are laid down the words we have already noticed.

He afterwards adds—*When I shall restore your captivities.* The plural number is to be noticed; and not rightly nor prudently is what has been done by many interpreters, who have rendered the word in the singular number; for the Prophet mentions "captivities" designedly, as the Jews had not only been driven into exile, but had also been scattered through various countries, so that they were not one captive people, but many troops of captives. Hence his purpose was to obviate a doubt; for it would not have been enough that one captivity should be restored, except all who had been dispersed were collected into one body by the wonderful power of God. And hence he adds *before your eyes,* that the Jews might be convinced that they should be eye-witnesses of this miracle, which yet they could hardly conceive, without raising up their thoughts above the world.

THE

COMMENTARIES OF JOHN CALVIN

ON THE

PROPHET HAGGAI.

CALVIN'S PREFACE TO HAGGAI.

AFTER the return of the people, they were favoured, we know, especially with three Prophets, who roused their fainting hearts, and finished all predictions, until at length the Redeemer came in his appointed time. During the time of THE BABYLONIAN EXILE the office of teaching was discharged among the captives by EZEKIEL, and also by DANIEL; and there were others less celebrated; for we find that some of the Psalms were then composed, either by the Levites, or by some other teachers. But these two, EZEKIEL and DANIEL, were above all others eminent. Then EZRA and NEHEMIAH followed them, the authority of whom was great among the people; but we do not read that they were endued with the Prophetic gift.

It then appears certain that three only were divinely inspired to proclaim the future condition of the people.

DANIEL had before them foretold whatever was to happen till the coming of Christ, and his Book is a remarkable mirror of God's Providence; for he paints, as on a tablet, three things which were to be fulfilled after his death, and of which no man could have formed any conjecture. He has given even the number of years from the return of the people to the building of the Temple, and also to the death of Christ. But we must come to the other witnesses, who confirmed the predictions of Daniel. The Lord raised up three witnesses—HAGGAI, ZECHARIAH, and MALACHI.[1]

The first[2] condemned the sloth of the people; for, being intent on their own advantages, they all neglected the building of the Temple; and he shows that they were deservedly suffering punishment for their ingratitude; for they despised God their Deliverer, or at least honoured him less than they ought to have done, and deprived him of the worship due to him. He then encouraged them to hope for a complete restoration, and showed that there was no reason for them to be disheartened by difficulties, and that though they were surrounded by enemies, and had to bear many evils, and were terrified by threatening edicts, they ought yet to have entertained hope; for the Lord would perform the work which he had begun—to restore their ancient dignity to his people, and Christ also would at length come to secure the perfect happiness and glory of the Church.

This is the sum of the whole. I now come to the words.

---

[1] " Prophecy ceased with these Prophets until the time of Christ. For it was God's purpose, by this *famine of the word*, (according to the prophetic language,) to render the Jews more desirous (*appetentiores*) of the Messiah, who was to surpass all the Prophets in the power of doing miracles."—*Grotius*.

[2] " We know nothing of the parentage of Haggai. He was probably born in Babylon during the captivity. He was sent particularly to encourage the Jews to proceed with the building of the temple, which had been interrupted for about *fourteen* years."—*Adam Clark*.

COMMENTARIES

ON

THE PROPHET HAGGAI

CHAPTER I.

1. In the second year of Darius the king, in the sixth month, in the first day of the month, came the word of the Lord by Haggai the Prophet unto Zerubbabel the son of Shealtiel, governor of Judah, and to Joshua the son of Josedech, the high priest, saying—

1. Anno secundo Darii regis, mense sexto, die primo mensis, datus fuit sermo Jehovæ in manum Chaggai Prophetæ ad Zerubbabel, filium Sealtiel, ducem Jehudah, et ad Jehosuah, filium Jehosadak, sacerdotem magnum, dicendo—

THE Prophet mentions here the year, the month, and the day in which he began to rouse up the people from their sloth and idleness, by the command of God; for every one studied his own domestic interest, and had no concern for building the Temple.

This happened, he says, *in the second year of Darius the king.* Interpreters differ as to this time; for they do not agree as to the day or year in which the Babylonian captivity began. Some date the beginning of the seventy years at the ruin which happened under Jeconiah, before the erasing of the city, and the destruction of the Temple. It is, however, probable, that a considerable time had passed before Haggai began his office as a Prophet; for Babylon was taken twenty years, or little more, before the death of king Cyrus; his son Cambyses, who reigned eight years, succeeded him. The third king was Darius, the son of Hystaspes, whom the Jews will have to be the son of Ahasuerus by Esther; but no credit is due to their fancies; for they hazard any bold notion in matters unknown, and assert anything that may come to their brains or to their mouths; and thus they deal in fables, and for the most part without any semblance of truth. It may be sufficient for us to understand, that this Darius was the son of Hystaspes, who succeeded Cambyses, (for I omit the seven months of the Magi; for as they crept in by deceit, so shortly after they were destroyed;) and it is probable that Cambyses, who was the first-born son of Cyrus, had no male heir. Hence it was that his brother being slain by the consent of the nobles, the kingdom came to Darius. He, then, as we may learn from histories, was the third king of the Persians. Daniel says, in the fifth chapter, that the city of Babylon had been taken by Cyrus, but that Darius the Mede reigned there.

But between writers there is some disagreement on this point; though all say that Cyrus was king, yet Xenophon says, that Cyaxares was ever the first, so that Cyrus sustained only the character, as it were, of a regent. But Xenophon, as all who have any judgment, and are versed in history, well know, did not write a history, but fabled most boldly according to his own fancy; for he invents the tale that Cyrus was brought up by his maternal grandfather, Astyages. But it is evident enough that Astyages had been conquered in war by Cyrus.[1] He says also that Cyrus married a wife a considerable time after the taking of Babylon, and that she was presented to him by his uncle Cyaxares, but that he dared not to marry her until he returned to Persia, and his father Cambyses approved of the marriage. Here Xenophon fables, and gives range to his own invention, for it was not his purpose to write a history. He is a very fine writer, it is true; but the unlearned are much mistaken who think that he has collected all the histories of the world. Xenophon is a

---

[1] " According to the opinions of Plato and Cicero, the Cyropædia of Xenophon was a moral romance; and these venerable philosophers suppose, that the historian did not so much write what Cyrus had been, as what every true, good, and virtuous monarch ought to be."—*Lemprière's Class. Dict.*

highly approved philosopher, but not an approved historian; for it was his designed object fictitiously to relate as real facts what seemed to him most suitable. He fables that Cyrus died in his bed, and dictated a long will, and spoke as a philosopher in his retirement; but Cyrus, we know, died in the Scythian war, and was slain by the queen, Tomyris, who revenged the death of her son; and this is well known even by children. Xenophon, however, as he wished to paint the image of a perfect prince, says that Cyrus died in his bed. We cannot then collect from the *Cyropædia*, which Xenophon has written, anything that is true. But if we compare the historians together, we shall find the following things asserted almost unanimously:—That Cambyses was the son of Cyrus; that when he suspected his younger brother he gave orders to put him to death; that both died without any male issue; and that on discovering the fraud of the Magi,[1] the son of Hystaspes became the third king of the Persians. Daniel calls Darius, who reigned in Babylon, the Mede; but he is Cyaxares. This I readily admit; for he reigned by sufferance, as Cyrus willingly declined the honour. And Cyrus, though a grandson of Astyages, by his daughter Mandane, was yet born of a father not ennobled; for Astyages, having dreamt that all Asia would be covered by what proceeded from his daughter, was easily induced to marry her to a stranger. When, therefore, he gave her to Cambyses, his design was to drive her to a far country, so that no one born of her should come to so great an empire: this was the advice of the Magi. Cyrus then acquired a name and reputation, no doubt, only by his own efforts; nor did he venture at first to take the name of a king, but suffered his uncle, and at the same time his father-

---

[1] The account of the Magi is briefly this:—Cyrus had two sons, Cambyses and Smerdis. When Cambyses ascended the throne, suspecting the fidelity of his brother, he caused him to be secretly put to death. This was known to some of the Magi. On the death of Cambyses, one of them, named Smerdis, who resembled the deceased prince, was by the Magi declared king, under the pretence of being the brother of Cambyses. The imposition was detected, and seven of the nobles of Persia dethroned him after six months' reign, and one of themselves, Darius Hystaspes, was made king, in the year before Christ 521.—*Ed.*

in-law, to reign with him; and yet he was his colleague only for two years; for Cyaxares lived no longer than the taking of Babylon.

I come then now to our Prophet: he says, *In the second year of Darius* it was commanded to me by the Lord to reprove the sloth of the people. We may readily conclude that more than twenty years had elapsed since the people began to return to their own country.[1] Some say thirty or forty years, and others go beyond that number; but this is not probable. Some say that the Jews returned to their country in the fifty-eighth year of their captivity; but this is not true, and may be easily disproved by the words of Daniel as well as by the history of Ezra. Daniel says in the ninth chapter that he was reminded by God of the return of the people when the time prescribed by Jeremiah was drawing nigh. And as this happened not in the first year of Darius, the son of Hystaspes, but about the end of the reign of Belshasar before Babylon was taken, it follows that the time of the exile was then fulfilled. We have also this at the beginning of the history, 'When seventy years were accomplished, God roused the spirit of Cyrus the king.' We hence see that Cyrus had not allowed the free return of the people but at the time predicted by Jeremiah, and according to what Isaiah had previously taught, that Cyrus, before he was born, had been chosen for this work: and then God began openly to show how truly he had spoken before the people were driven into exile. But if we grant that the people returned in the fifty-eighth year, the truth of prophecy will not appear. They therefore speak very thoughtlessly who say that the Jews returned to their country before the seventieth year; for thus they subvert, as I have said, every notion of God's favour.

Since then seventy years had elapsed when Babylon was taken, and Cyrus by a public edict permitted the Jews to return to their country, God at that time stretched forth his hand in behalf of the miserable exiles; but troubles did

---

[1] *Adam Clark* says, that it was in the *sixteenth* year after their return from Babylon.—*Ed.*

afterwards arise to them from their neighbours. Some under the guise of friendship wished to join them, in order to obliterate the name of Israel; and that they might make a sort of amalgamation of many nations. Then others openly carried on war with them; and when Cyrus was with his army in Scythia, his prefects became hostile to the Jews, and thus a delay was effected. Then followed Cambyses, a most cruel enemy to the Church of God. Hence the building of the Temple could not be proceeded with until the time of this Darius, the son of Hystaspes. But as Darius, the son of Hystaspes, favoured the Jews, or at least was pacified towards them, he restrained the neighbouring nations from causing any more delay as to the building of the Temple. He ordered his prefects to protect the people of Israel, so that they might live quietly in their country and finish the Temple, which had only been begun. And we may hence conclude that the Temple was built in forty-six years, according to what is said in the second chapter of John;[1] for the foundations were laid immediately on the return of the people, but the work was either neglected or hindered by enemies.

But as liberty to build the Temple was given to the Jews, we may gather from what our Prophet says, that they were guilty of ingratitude towards God; for private benefit was by every one almost exclusively regarded, and there was hardly any concern for the worship of God. Hence the Prophet now reproves this indifference, allied as it was with ungodliness: for what could be more base than to enjoy the country and the inheritance which God had formerly promised to Abraham, and yet to make no account of God, nor of that special favour which he wished to confer—that of dwelling among them? An habitation on mount Sion had been chosen, we know, by God, that thence might come forth

---

[1] The reference in John ii. 19, 20, seems to have been made not to the time in which it was built then, but to the time in which it was built or rebuilt by Herod the Great. For this temple was finished in the sixth year of Darius (see Ezra vi. 15,) and about twenty-one years after the edict of Cyrus. The return from Babylon was before Christ 536, and the temple was finished in 515. It was about four years in building under Darius.—*Ed.*

the Redeemer of the world. As then this business was neglected, and each one built his own house, justly does the Prophet here reprove them with vehemence in the name and by the command of God. Thus much as to the time. And he says in the *second* year of Darius, for a year had now elapsed since liberty to build the Temple had been allowed them; but the Jews were negligent, because they were too much devoted to their own private advantages.

And he says, that *the word was given by his hand to Zerubbabel, the son of Shealtiel, and to Joshua, the son of Josedech.* We shall hereafter see that this communication had a regard without distinction to the whole community; and, if a probable conjecture be entertained, neither Zerubbabel nor Joshua were at fault, because the Temple was neglected; nay, we may with certainty conclude from what Zechariah says, that Zerubbabel was a wise prince, and that Joshua faithfully discharged his office as a priest. Since then both spent their labours for God, how was it that the Prophet addressed them? and since the whole blame belonged to the people, why did he not speak to them? why did he not assemble the whole multitude? The Lord, no doubt, intended to connect Zerubbabel and Joshua with his servant as associates, that they three might go forth to the people, and deliver with one mouth what God had committed to his servant Haggai. This then is the reason why the Prophet says, that he was sent to Zerubbabel and Joshua.

Let us at the same time learn, that princes and those to whom God has committed the care of governing his Church, never so faithfully perform their office, nor discharge their duties so courageously and strenuously, but that they stand in need of being roused, and, as it were, stimulated by many goads. I have already said, that in other places Zerubbabel and Joshua are commended; yet the Lord reproved them and severely expostulated with them, because they neglected the building of the Temple. This was done, that they might confirm by their authority what the Prophet was about to say: but he also intimates, that they were not wholly free from blame, while the people were thus negligent in pursuing the work of building the Temple.

Zerubbabel is called the son of Shealtiel: some think that son is put here for grandson, and that his father's name was passed over. But this seems not probable. They quote from the Chronicles a passage in which his father's name is said to be Pedaiah: but we know that it was often the case among that people, that a person had two names. I therefore regard Zerubbabel to have been the son of Shealtiel. He is said to have been the governor[1] of Judah; for it was necessary that some governing power should continue in that tribe, though the royal authority was taken away, and all sovereignty and supreme power extinguished. It was yet God's purpose that some vestiges of power should remain, according to what had been predicted by the patriarch Jacob, 'Taken away shall not be the sceptre from Judah, nor a leader from his thigh, until he shall come;' &c. (Gen. xlix. 10.) The royal sceptre was indeed taken away, and the crown was removed, according to what Ezekiel had said, 'Take away the crown, subvert, subvert, subvert it,' (Ezek. xxi. 26, 27;) for the interruption of the government had been sufficiently long. Yet the Lord in the meantime preserved some remnants, that the Jews might know that that promise was not wholly forgotten. This then is the reason why the son of Shealtiel is said to be the governor of Judah. It now follows—

2. Thus speaketh the Lord of hosts, saying, This people say, The time is not come, the time that the Lord's house should be built.

3. Then came the word of the Lord by Haggai the prophet, saying,

2. Sic dicit Iehova exercituum, dicendo, Populus isti dicunt (*hoc est*, dicit,) Non venit tempus domui Iehovæ ad ædificandum.

3. Et datus fuit sermo Iehovæ in manu Chaggai Prophetæ, dicendo,

---

[1] פחה; it is a word current in several languages, Chaldee, Persic, &c. *Parkhurst* derives it from פה, to extend. *Theod. Aq.* and *Sym.* render it ἡγούμενον, governor. He is called Sheshbazzar in Ezra v. 14; and Cyrus is said to have made him פחה, governor or deputy. It is the name of a person endued with authority by a sovereign. Zerubbabel, זרבבל, has been derived from זר, a stranger, and בבל, Babylon, a stranger or sojourner at Babylon. It deserves to be noticed, that the civil governor is put here before the chief priest; and we find from Ezra that it was to the civil governor that Cyrus delivered the holy vessels of the temple. See Ezra v. 14.—*Ed.*

4. *Is it* time for you, O ye, to dwell in your ceiled houses, and this house *lie* waste?

4. An tempus vobis, ut habitatis vos in domibus vestris tabulatis, et domus hæc deserta?

They who think that seventy years had not passed until the reign of Darius, may from this passage be easily disproved: for if the seventy years were not accomplished, an excuse would have been ready at hand,—that they had deferred the work of building the Temple; but it was certain, that the time had then elapsed, and that it was owing to their indifference that the Temple was not erected, for all the materials were appropriated to private uses. While then they were thus taking care of themselves and consulting their own interest, the building of the Temple was neglected. That the Temple was not built till the reign of Darius, this happened, as we have said, from another cause, because the prefects of king Cyrus gave much annoyance to the Jews, and Cambyses was most hostile to them. But when liberty was restored to them, and Darius had so kindly permitted them to build the Temple, they had no excuse for delay.

It is however probable that they had then many disputes as to the time; for it may have been, that they seizing on any pretext to cover their sloth, made this objection,—that many difficulties had occurred, because they had been too precipitate, and that they had thus been punished for their haste, because they had rashly undertaken the building of the Temple: and we may also suppose that they took another view of the time as having not yet come, for easily might this objection occur to them,—"It is indeed true that the worship of God is deservedly to be preferred to all other things; but the Lord grants us this indulgence, so that we are allowed to build our own houses; and in the meantime we attend to the sacrifices. Have not our fathers lived many ages without a Temple? God was then satisfied with a sanctuary: there is now an altar erected, and there sacrifices are offered. The Lord then will forgive us if we defer the building of the Temple to a suitable time. But in the meantime every one may build his own house, so that afterwards the Temple may at leisure be built more sumptuously." However this may have been, we find that true which I have often stated,—that the Jews were so taken up with their own domestic concerns, with their own ease, and with their own pleasures, that they made very little account of God's worship. This is the reason why the Prophet was so greatly displeased with them.

He declares what they said, *This people say, The time is not yet come to build the house of Jehovah.*[1] He repeats here what the Jews were wont to allege in order to disguise their sloth, after having delayed a long time, and when they could not, except through consummate effrontery, adduce anything in their own defence. We however see, that they hesitated not to promise pardon to themselves. Thus also do men indulge themselves in their sins, as though they could make an agreement with God and pacify him with some frivolous things. We see that this was the case then. But we may also see here, as in a mirror, how great is the ingratitude of men. The kindness of God had been especially worthy of being remembered, the glory of which ought to have been borne in mind to the end of time: they had been restored from exile in a manner beyond what they had ever expected. What ought they to have done, but to have devoted themselves entirely to the service of their deliverer? But they built, no, not even a tent for God, and sacrificed in the open air; and thus they wilfully trifled with God. But at the same time they dwelt at ease in houses elegantly fitted up.

And how is the case at this day? We see that through a remarkable miracle of God the gospel has shone forth in our time, and we have emerged, as it were, from the abodes below. Who does now rear up, of his own free-will, an altar to God? On the contrary, all regard what is advantageous only to themselves; and while they are occupied with their own concerns, the worship of God is cast aside; there is no care, no zeal, no concern for it; nay, what is worse, many make gain of the gospel, as though it were a lucrative business. No wonder then, if the people have so basely disre-

---

[1] The words literally are,—
    This people say, Not come is the time,
    The time for the house of Jehovah to be built.—*Ed.*

garded their deliverance, and have almost obliterated the memory of it. No less shameful is the example witnessed at this day among us.

But we may hence also see how kindly God has provided for his Church; for his purpose was that this reproof should continue extant, that he might at this day stimulate us, and excite our fear as well as our shame. For we also thus grow frigid in promoting the worship of God, whenever we are led to seek only our own advantages. We may also add, that as God's temple is spiritual, our fault is the more atrocious when we become thus slothful; since God does not bid us to collect either wood, or stones, or cement, but to build a celestial temple, in which he may be truly worshipped. When therefore we become thus indifferent, as that people were thus severely reproved, doubtless our sloth is much more detestable. We now see that the Prophet not only spoke to men of his age, but was also destined, through God's wonderful purpose, to be a preacher to us, so that his doctrine sounds at this day in our ears, and reproves our torpor and ungrateful indifference: for the building of the spiritual temple is deferred, whenever we become devoted to ourselves, and regard only what is advantageous to us individually. We shall go on with what follows to-morrow.

PRAYER.

Grant, Almighty God, that as we must carry on a warfare in this world, and as it is thy will to try us with many contests,— O grant, that we may never faint, however extreme may be the trials which we shall have to endure: and as thou hast favoured us with so great an honour as to make us the framers and builders of thy spiritual temple, may every one of us present and consecrate himself wholly to thee: and, inasmuch as each of us has received some peculiar gift, may we strive to employ it in building this temple, so that thou mayest be worshipped among us perpetually; and especially, may each of us offer himself wholly as a spiritual sacrifice to thee, until we shall at length be renewed in thine image, and be received into a full participation of that glory, which has been attained for us by the blood of thy only-begotten Son. Amen.

Lecture One Hundred and Twenty-ninth.

WHEN the Prophet asks, whether the time had come for the Jews to dwell in splendid and well furnished houses, and whether the time had not come to build the Temple, he intimates, that they were trifling in a very gross manner with God; for there was exactly the same reason for building the Temple as for building the city. How came they to be restored to their country, but that God performed what he had testified by the mouth of Jeremiah? Hence their return depended on the redemption promised to them: it was therefore easy for them to conclude, that the time for building the Temple had already come; for the one could not, and ought not to have been separated from the other, as it has been stated. He therefore upbraids them with ingratitude, for they sought to enjoy the kindness of God, and at the same time disregarded the memorial of it.

And very emphatical are the words, when he says, *Is it time for you to dwell in houses?*[1] For there is implied a comparison between God, whose Temple they set no value on, and themselves, who sought not only commodious, but sumptuous dwellings. Hence the Prophet inquires, whether it was consistent that mortal men, who differ not from worms, should possess magnificent houses, and that God should be without his Temple. And to the same purpose is what he adds, when he says, that their *houses* were *boarded;* for ספונים, *saphunim*, means in Hebrew what we express by *Cambrisees*.[2] Since then they were not satisfied with what

---

[1] There is a double pronoun, העת לכם אתם, "Is it time for you, *even* you," or, "you yourselves?" The Welsh often use two pronouns in this way, for the sake of emphasis. The rendering is very flat, as in our version, and adopted by *Henderson*, "Is it time for you, O ye?" &c. *Houbigant*, who always amends, proposes אתה, to come, "Is the time come for you?" &c. This is suitable, but without authority. *Dathius* suggests עתה, now, "Is it now time for you?" &c. This conjecture also would suit the place, but it is no more than a conjecture. There is no doubt an emphasis is intended by the repetition.—*Ed*.

[2] It is rendered "wainscoted" by *Henderson;* "κοιλοστάθμοις—ceiled," by the *Sept.*; "ωροφωμένοις—roofed," by *Aquila*. It was the custom in the east, says *Parkhurst*, to cover or line the roof with boards or wainscot.—*Ed*.

was commodious, without splendour and luxury being added, it was extremely shameful for them to rob God at the same time of his Temple, where he was to be worshipped. It now follows—

5. Now therefore thus saith the Lord of hosts; Consider your ways.	5. Et nunc sic dicit Iehova exercituum, Adjicite cor vestrum ad vias vestras ;
6. Ye have sown much, and bring in little; ye eat, but ye have not enough; ye drink, but ye are not filled with drink; ye clothe you, but there is none warm; and he that earneth wages earneth wages *to put it* into a bag with holes.	6. Seminâstis multum, et intulistis parum ; comedere, et non ad satietatem ; bibere, et non ad ebrietatem ; vestire, et non ad calorem cuique ; et qui colligit mercedem, colligit mercedem in sacculum perforatum.

Here the Prophet deals with the refractory people according to what their character required; for as to those who are teachable and obedient, a word is enough for them; but they who are perversely addicted to their sins must be more sharply urged, as the Prophet does here; for he brings before the Jews the punishments by which they had been already visited. It is commonly said, that experience is the teacher of fools; and the Prophet has this in view in these words, *apply your hearts to your ways;*[1] that is, "If the authority of God or a regard for him is of no importance among you, at least consider how God deals with you. How comes it that ye are famished, that both heaven and earth deny food to you? Besides, though ye consume much food, it yet does not satisfy you. In a word, how is it that all things fade away and vanish in your hands? How is this? Ye cannot otherwise account for it, but that God is displeased with you. If then ye will not of your own accord obey God's word, let these judgments at least induce you to repent." It was to apply the heart to their ways, when they acknowledged that they were thus famished, not by chance, but that the curse of God urged them, or was suspended

---

[1] Literally it is, "Set your heart on your ways." An idiomatic phrase, but very expressive. They were to fix their attention on their conduct, not merely to take a glance, but seriously and steadily to reflect on their ways.

over their heads. He therefore bids them to receive instruction from the events themselves, or from what they were experiencing; and by these words the Prophet more sharply teaches them; as though he had said, that they profited nothing by instruction and warning, and that it remained as the last thing, that they were to be drawn by force while the Lord was chastising them.

He says that they had *sown much*, and that *small was the produce*. They who render the clause in the future tense, wrest the meaning of the Prophet: for why did he say, apply your heart to your ways, if he only denounced a future punishment? But, as I have already stated, he intimates, that they very thoughtlessly champed the bridle, for they perceived not that all their evils were inflicted by God's hand, nor did they regard his judgment as righteous. Hence he says, that they had sowed much, and that the harvest had been small; and then, that they *ate* and were *not satisfied;* that they *drank* and had not their *thirst quenched;* that they *clothed themselves* and were *not warmed.* How much soever they applied those things which seemed necessary for the support of life, they yet availed them nothing. And God, we know, does punish men in these two ways—either by withdrawing his blessings, by rendering the earth arid and the heavens dry; or by making the abundant produce unsatisfying and even useless. It often happens that men gather what is sufficient for support, and yet they are always hungry. It is a kind of curse, which appears very evident when God takes away their nourishing power from bread and wine, so that they supply no support to man. When therefore fruit, and whatever the earth produces for the necessities of man, give no support, God proves, as it were by an outstretched arm, that he is an avenger. But the other curse is more frequent; that is, when God smites the earth with drought, so that it produces nothing. But our Prophet refers to both these kinds of evils. Behold, he says, *Ye have sown much and ye gather little;* and then he says, "Though ye are supplied with the produce of wine and corn, yet with eating and drinking ye cannot satisfy yourselves; nay, your very clothes do not make you warm."

They might have had a sure hope of the greatest abundance, had they not broken off the stream of God's favour by their sins. Were they not then extremely blind this experience must have awakened them, according to what is said in the first chapter of Joel.

He says at the end of the verse, *He who gains wages, gains them for a perforated bag.* By these words he reminds them, that the vengeance of God could not only be seen in the sterility of the earth, and in the very hunger of men, who by eating were not satisfied; but also in their work, for they wearied themselves much without any profit, as even the money cast into the bag disappeared. Hence he says, even your work is in vain. It was indeed a most manifest proof of God's wrath, when their money, though laid up, yet vanished away.[1]

We now see what the Prophet means: As his doctrine appeared frigid to the Jews and his warnings were despised, he treats them according to the perverseness of their disposition. Hence he shows, that though they disregarded God and his Prophets, they were yet sufficiently taught by his judgments, and that still they remained indifferent. He therefore goads them, as though they were asses, that they might at length acknowledge that God was justly displeased with them, and that his wrath was conspicuous in the sterility of the land, as well as in everything connected with their life; for whether they did eat or abstained from food, they were hungry; and when they diligently laboured and gathered wages, their wages vanished, as though they had cast them into a perforated bag. It follows—

---

[1] There seems to be an irregularity in the construction of the whole verse. Literally it is as follows—

    Ye have sown much, but the coming in *is* little;
    There is eating, but not to satisfaction;
    They drink, but not to fulness;
    There is clothing, but there is no warmth in it;
    And earn does the earner for a perforated bag.

This change in the mode of construction takes away the monotony which would have otherwise appeared. The words הבא, אכול, and לבוש, are not infinitives, as some suppose, but participles used as nouns; which is often the case in Hebrew, as well as in Welsh, and often too in English, such as teaching, drinking, clothing, &c.—*Ed.*

7. Thus saith the Lord of hosts; Consider your ways.	7. Sic dicit Iehova exercituum, Ponite cor vestrum super vias vestras:
8. Go up to the mountain, and bring wood, and build the house; and I will take pleasure in it, and I will be glorified, saith the Lord.	8. Ascendite in montem et afferte lignum, et ædificate domum (*vel,* hanc domum;) et propitius ero in ea (*vel,* mihi placebit in ea;) et glorificabor, dicit Iehova.

The Prophet now adds, that since the Jews were thus taught by their evils, nothing else remained for them but to prepare themselves without delay for the work of building the Temple; for they were not to defer the time, inasmuch as they were made to know, that God had come forth with an armed hand to vindicate his own right: for the sterility of which he had spoken, and also the famine and other signs of a curse, were like a drawn sword in the hand of God; by which it was evident, that he intended to punish the negligence of the people. As God then had been robbed of his right, he not only exhorted the people by his Prophets, but also executed his vengeance on this contempt.

This is the reason why the Prophet now says, *Apply your heart,* and then adds, *Go up to the mountain, bring wood,* &c. And this passage strikingly sets forth why God punished their sins, in order that they might not only perceive that they had sinned, but that they might also seek to amend that which displeased God. We may also, in the second place, learn from what is said, how we are to proceed rightly in the course of true repentance. The beginning is, that our sins should become displeasing to us; but if any of us proceed no farther, it will be only an evanescent feeling: it is therefore necessary to advance to the second step; an amendment for the better ought to follow. The Prophet expresses both here: He says first, *Lay your heart on your ways;* that is, "Consider whence comes this famine to you, and then how it is that by labouring much ye gain nothing, except that God is angry with you." Now this was what wisdom required. But he again repeats the same thing, "Lay your heart on your ways," that is, "Not only that sin may be hated by you, but also that this sloth, which has hitherto offended God and provoked his wrath, may be changed into strenuous activity." Hence he says, *Go up to the mountain, and bring wood, and let the house be builded.*

If any one is at a loss to know why the Prophet insists so much on building the Temple, the ready answer is this—that it was God's design to exercise in this way his ancient people in the duties of religion. Though then the Temple itself was of no great importance before God, yet the end was to be regarded; for the people were preserved by the visible Temple in the hope of the future Christ; and then it behoved them always to bear in mind the heavenly pattern, that they might worship God spiritually under the external symbols. It was not then without reason that God was offended with their neglect of the temple; for it hence clearly appeared, that there was no care nor zeal for religion among the Jews. It often was the case that they were more sedulous than necessary in external worship, and God scorned their assiduity, when not connected with a right inward feeling; but the gross contempt of God in disregarding even the external building, is what is reprehended here by the Prophet.

He afterwards adds, *And I will be propitious in it*, or, I will take pleasure in it. Some read, "It will please me;" and they depart not from the real meaning of the verb: for רצה, *retse*—is to be acceptable. But more correct, in my view, is the opinion of those who think that the Prophet alludes to the promise of God; for he had said, that he would on this condition dwell among the Jews, that he might hear their prayers, and be propitious to them. As, then, the Jews came to the Temple to expiate their sins, that they might return to God's favour, it is not without reason that God here declares that he would be propitious in that house. ' If any one sin,' said Solomon, ' and entering this house, shall humbly pray, do thou also hear from thy heavenly habitation.' (1 Kings viii. 30.) We further know that the covering of the ark was called the propitiatory, because God there received the suppliant into favour. This meaning, then, seems the most suitable—that the Prophet says, that if the Temple was built, God would be there propitious. But it was a proof of extreme impiety to think that they could prosper while God was adverse to them: for whence could they hope for happiness, except from the only fountain of all blessings, that is, when God favoured them and was propitious to them? And how could his favour be sought, except they came to his sanctuary, and thence raise up their minds by faith to heaven? When, therefore, there was no care for the Temple, it was easy to conclude that God himself was neglected, and regarded almost with scorn. We then see how emphatically this was added, *I will be propitious there*, that is, in the Temple; as though he had said, "Your infirmity ought to have reminded you that you have need of this help, even of worshipping me in the sanctuary. But as I gave you, as it were, a visible mirror of my presence among you, when I ordered a Temple to be built for me on mount Sion, when ye despise the Temple, is it not the same as though I was rejected by you?"

He then adds, *And I shall be glorified, saith Jehovah.* He seems to express the reason why he should be propitious; for he would then see that his glory was regarded by the Jews. At the same time, this reason may be taken by itself, and this is what I prefer.[1] The Prophet then employs two goads to awaken the Jews: When the Temple was built, God would bless them; for they would have him pacified, and whenever they found him displeased, they might come as suppliants to seek pardon; this was one reason why it behoved them

---

[1] The whole verse may be thus rendered—
    Ascend the mountain, for ye have brought wood;
    And build the house, that I may delight in it,
    That I may be glorified, saith Jehovah.

The ו, *vau*, here in two instances may have the meaning of *ut*, that; but before הבאתם, a verb in the perfect tense, it must be rendered "for," or, "as;" and the clause seems to be a parenthesis. The ו, *vau*, is not conversive when preceded by a verb in the imperative mood, as it appears from the end of the verse. The mount was not Libanus, as many have supposed, but Sion, where wood had been previously brought, but was not used. See Ezra iii. 7. As to the verb רצה, followed by ב, it means to approve, to be pleased with, or to take pleasure or delight in, a thing. See 1 Chron. xxix. 3; Ps. cxlvii. 10; Mic. vi. 7. Probably the best rendering of the two last lines is the following—
    And build the house, and I shall delight in it
    And render *it* glorious, saith Jehovah.

To take the last verb in a causative sense is more consistent with the tenor of the passage. This is the meaning given by the Targum, and is adopted by *Dathius.—Ed.*

strenuously to undertake the building of the Temple. The second reason was, that God would be glorified. Now, what could have been more inconsistent than to disregard God their deliverer, and so late a deliverer too? But how God was glorified by the Temple I have already briefly explained; not that it added anything to God; but such ordinances of religion were then necessary, as the Jews were as yet like children. It now follows—

| 9. Ye looked for much, and, lo, *it came* to little; and when ye brought *it* home, I did blow upon it. Why? saith the Lord of hosts. Because of mine house that *is* waste, and ye run every man unto his own house. | 9. Respexistis ad multum, et ecce parum; et intulistis ad domum, et sufflavi in illud: cur hoc? dicit Iehova exercituum: Propter domum meam quæ est deserta, et vos curritis (*vel*, addicti estis quisque domi suæ) quisque in domum suam. |

Here the Prophet relates again, that the Jews were deprived of support, and that they in a manner pined away in their distress, because they robbed God of the worship due to him. He first repeats the fact, *Ye have looked for much, but behold little*. It may happen that one is contented with a very slender portion, because much is not expected. They who are satisfied with their own penury are not anxious though their portion of food is but scanty, though they are constrained to feed on acorns. Those who are become hardened in enduring evils, do not seek much; but they who desire much, are more touched and vexed by their penury. This is the reason why the Prophet says, Ye have looked for much, and, behold, there was but little; that is, "Ye are not like the peasants, who satisfy themselves with any sort of food, and are not troubled on account of their straitened circumstances; but your desire has led you to seek abundance. Hence ye seek and greedily lay hold on things on every side; but, behold, it comes to little."

In the second place he adds, *Ye have brought it home*. He farther mentions another kind of evil—that when they gathered wine, and corn, and money, all these things immediately vanished. *Ye have brought it home, and I have blown upon it.* By saying that they brought it home, he intimates that what they had acquired was laid up, that it might be preserved safely; for they who had filled their storehouses, and wine-cellars, and bags, thought that they had no more to do with God. Hence it was that profane men securely indulged themselves; they thought that they were beyond the reach of danger, when their houses were well filled. God, on the contrary, shows that their houses became empty, when filled with treasures and provisions. But he speaks still more distinctly—that he had *blown* upon them, that is, that he had dissipated them by his breath: for the Prophet did not deem it enough historically to narrate what the Jews had experienced; but his purpose also was to point out the cause, as it were, by the finger. He therefore teaches us, that what they laid in store in their houses did not without a cause vanish away; but that this happened through the blowing of God, even because he cursed their blessing, according to what we shall hereafter see in the Prophet Malachi.

He then adds, *Why is this? saith Jehovah of hosts.* God here asks, not because he had any doubts on the subject, but that he might by this sort of goading rouse the Jews from their lethargy,—"Think of the cause, and know that my hand is not guided by a blind impulse when it strikes you. You ought, then, to consider the reason why all things thus decay and perish." Here again is sharply reproved the stupidity of the people, because they attended not to the cause of their evils; for they ought to have known this of themselves.

But God gives the answer, because he saw that they remained stupified—*On account of my house*, he says, *because it is waste.*[1] God here assigns the cause; he shows that though no one of them considered why they were so famished, the judgment of his curse was yet sufficiently manifest, on account of the Temple remaining a waste. *And you*, he says, *run, every one to his own house.* Some read, "You take delight, every one in his own house;" for it is

---

[1] This is the literal rendering—" On account of my house, because it is waste." אשר is not "which" here, for it is followed by הוא, "it;" but a conjunction, "because." The word *quod*, in Latin, admits of two similar meanings.—*Ed.*

the verb רצה, *retse*, which we have lately noticed; and it means either to take pleasure in a thing, or to run. Every one, then, runs to his house, or, Every one delights in his house. But it is more suitable to the context to give this rendering, "Every one runs to his house." For the Prophet here reminds the Jews that they were slow and slothful in the work of building the Temple, because they hastened to their private houses. He then reproves here their ardour in being intent on building their own houses, so that they had no leisure to build the Temple. This is the hastening which the Prophet blames and condemns in the Jews.[1]

We may hence learn again, that they had long delayed to build the sanctuary after the time had arrived: for, as we have mentioned yesterday, they who think the Jews returned in the fifty-eighth year, and that they had not then undergone the punishment denounced by Jeremiah, are very deluded; for they thus obscure the favour of God; nay, they wholly subvert the truth of the promises, as though they had returned contrary to God's will, through the permission of Cyrus, when yet Isaiah says, that Cyrus would be the instrument of their promised redemption. (Is. xlv. 5.) Surely, then, Cyrus must have been dead before the time was fulfilled! and in that case God could not have been the redeemer of his people. Therefore Eusebius, and those who agree with him, did thus most absurdly confound the order of time. It now follows—

---

[1] The first word in this verse, פנה, is evidently a participle noun; similar instances we find in verse 6. The verse, literally rendered, is as follows—
  Looking for much, and behold little!
  And you brought *it* home, and I blew upon it:
  On what account this, saith Jehovah of hosts?
  On account of my house, because it is waste,
  And ye *are* running, each to his own house.

The first line is put in an absolute form, as is sometimes the case in Hebrew; "There has been," or some such words being understood. Both the Targum and the Septuagint read היה instead of הנה, which would be more suitable to the word which follows, which has ל before it. The line would then be—
  There has been looking for much, but it came to little.

The "blowing" seems to be a metaphor taken from scorching wind, blowing on vegetation, and causing it to wither. The last line may be thus rendered—
  And ye *are* delighted, each with his own house.—*Ed.*

10. Therefore the heaven over you is stayed from dew, and the earth is stayed *from* her fruit.	10. Propterea prohibiti super vos sunt cœli à rore, et terra à proventu suo prohibita est.
11. And I called for a drought upon the land, and upon the mountains, and upon the corn, and upon the new wine, and upon the oil, and upon *that* which the ground bringeth forth, and upon men, and upon cattle, and upon all the labour of the hands.	11. Et vocavi siccitatem super terram, et super montes, et super triticum, et super mustum (*aut*, vinum,) et super omne quod profert terra, et super hominem, et super animal, et super omnem laborem manuum.

He confirms what the last verse contains—that God had made it evident that he was displeased with the people because their zeal for religion had become cold, and, especially, because they were all strangely devoted to their own interest and manifested no concern for building the Temple. Hence, he says, *therefore the heavens* are shut up and *withhold the dew;* that is, they distil no dew on the earth: and he adds, that the earth was closed that it produced no fruit; it yielded no increase, and disappointed its cultivators. As to the particle על־כן, *ol-can*, we must bear in mind what I have stated, that God did not regard the external and visible Temple, but rather the end for which it was designed; for it was his will then that he should be worshipped under the ceremonies of the law. When, therefore, the Jews offered mutilated, lame, or diseased sacrifices, they manifested impiety and contempt of God. It is yet true, that it was the same thing as to God; but he had not commanded sacrifices to be offered to him for his own sake, but that by such services they might foster true religion. When, therefore, he says now, that he punished their neglect of the Temple, we ought ever to regard that as a pattern of heavenly things, so that we may understand that the coldness and indifference of the Jews were reproved; because it hence evidently appeared that they had no care for the worship of God.

With respect to the withholding of dew and of produce, we know that the Prophets took from the law what served to teach the people, and accommodated it to their own purposes. The curses of the law are general. (Deut. xi. 17.) It is therefore the same thing as though the Prophet had said, that what God had threatened by Moses was really fulfilled. It ought not to have been to them a new thing, that whenever heaven denied its dew and rain it was a sign of God's wrath. But as, at this day, during wars, or famine, or pestilence, men do not regard this general truth, it is necessary to make the application : and godly teachers ought wisely to attend to this point, that is, to remind men, according to what the state of things and circumstances may require, that God proves by facts what he has testified in his word. This is what is done by our Prophet now, *withheld have the heavens the dew and the earth its produce.*[1]

In a word, God intimates, that the heavens have no care to provide for us, and to distil dew so that the earth may bring forth fruit, and that the earth also, though called the mother of men, does not of itself open its bowels, but that the heavens as well as the earth bear a sure testimony to his paternal love, and also to the care which he exercises over us. God then shows, both by the heavens and the earth, that he provides for us; for when the heavens and

---

[1] *Calvin* seems to have overlooked עליכם, "on your account." The verse is—
    Therefore, on your account, withheld have the heavens from dew,
    And the earth has withheld its produce.

The verb כלא, to restrain, to keep back, to withhold, is used here twice, and in the first line in an intransitive sense, and in the second in a transitive sense, as it is often the case in other languages, when the same verb is both neuter and active.

The 11th verse is passed by without any particular remarks. The word חרב is rendered "siccitas—drought," as *Jerome* does, and also our version, as well as *Newcome* and *Henderson*; but *Grotius* and also *Marckius* very justly observe, that it means here "waste," or "desolation," it being the same word as is applied to God's house in verse 9. They left his house a waste; by a just retribution he had brought or called for a waste on the land, &c. The contrast is so evident that it cannot be denied. The ideal meaning of the word is to be waste or desolate : it is then applied to various things which produce desolation, the sword, drought, pestilence, &c.; but it is used here in its primary sense, and the contrast is very striking: "My house has been left waste ; I have caused a waste to come upon every thing else." The verse may be thus rendered—
    And I have called for a waste
    On the land and on the mountains,
    And on the corn and on the wine and on the oil,
    And on whatever the ground produces,
    And on man and on the cattle,
    And on all the labour of the hands.—*Ed.*

the earth administer and supply us with the blessings of God, they thus declare his love towards us. So also, when the heaven is, as it were, iron, and when the earth with closed bowels refuses us food, we ought to know that they are commissioned to execute on us the vengeance of God. For they are not only the instruments of his bounty, but, when it is necessary, God employs them for the purpose of punishing us. This is briefly the meaning.

PRAYER.

Grant, Almighty God, that since thou kindly and graciously invitest us to thyself, we may not wait until thou stimulatest us with goads, but cast aside our sloth and run quickly to thee. And when our torpor so possesses us as to render punishment necessary, permit us not to harden ourselves; but being at length effectually warned, may we return to the right way, and strive so to render all we do approved by thee, that we may find a door opened to thy grace and favour: and being made partakers of those blessings, by which thou affordest a taste of that goodness which we shall enjoy in heaven, may we ever aspire thither, and be satisfied with the abundant blessings which we daily and even continually receive from thine hand, in such a manner as not to be detained by this world; but may we, with minds raised up to heaven, ever tend upwards, and labour for that perfect happiness which is there laid up for us by Christ our Lord. Amen.

Lecture One Hundred and Thirtieth.

12. Then Zerubbabel the son of Shealtiel, and Joshua the son of Josedech, the high priest, with all the remnant of the people, obeyed the voice of the Lord their God, and the words of Haggai the prophet, as the Lord their God had sent him, and the people did fear before the Lord.

12. Et audivit Zerubbabel, filius Sealtiel, et Jehosua, filius Jehosadak, sacerdos magnus, et omnes reliquiæ populi vocem Iehovæ Dei sui, et ad verba Chaggai Prophetæ; quemadmodum miserat ipsum Iehova Deus eorum; et timuerunt populus à conspectu Iehovæ.

THE Prophet here declares that his message had not been without fruit, for shortly after the whole people prepared themselves for the work. And he names both Zerubbabel and Joshua; for it behoved them to lead the way, and, as it were, to extend a hand to others. For, had there been no leaders, no one of the common people would have pointed out the way to the rest. We know what usually happens when a word is addressed indiscriminately to all the people: they wait for one another. But when Joshua and Zerubbabel attended to the commands of the Prophet, the others followed them: for they were dominant, not only in power, but also in authority, so that they induced the people willingly to do their duty. One was the governor of the people, the other was the high priest; but the honesty and faithfulness of both were well known, so that the people spontaneously followed their example.

And this passage teaches us that though God invites all to his service, yet as any one excels in honour or in other respects, so the more promptly he ought to undertake what is proposed by the authority of God. Our Prophet, no doubt, meant to point out this due order of things, by saying, that he was heard first by Zerubbabel and Joshua, and then by the whole people.

But as all had not returned from exile, but a small portion, compared with that great number, which, we know, had not availed themselves of the kindness allowed them—this is the reason why the Prophet does not simply name the people, but *the remnant of the people,* שארית העם, *sharit eom.* As also the gift of prophecy had been for a long time more rare, and few appeared among the people who had any decided evidence of their call, such as Samuel, Isaiah, David, and others possessed, the Prophet, for this reason, does here more carefully commend and honour his own office: he says that the people attended to *the voice of Jehovah*—How? By attending, he says, *to the words of Haggai the Prophet, inasmuch as Jehovah their God had sent him.* He might have said more shortly that his labour had not been without fruit; but he used this circuitous mode of speaking, that he might confirm his own call; and he did this designedly, because the people had for a long time been without the opportunity of hearing God's Prophets, for there were none among them.

But Haggai says nothing here but what belongs in common to all teachers in the Church: for we know that men are not sent by divine authority to speak that God himself may be silent. As then the ministers of the word derogate nothing from the authority of God, it follows that none except the only true God ought to be heard. It is not then a peculiar expression, which is to be restricted to one man, when God is said to have spoken by the mouth of Haggai; for he thus declared that he was God's true and authorized Prophet. We may therefore gather from these words, that the Church is not to be ruled by the outward preaching of the word, as though God had substituted men in his own place, and thus divested himself of his own office, but that he only speaks by their mouth. And this is the import of these words, *The people attended to the voice of Jehovah their God, and to the words of Haggai the Prophet.* For the word of God is not distinguished from the words of the Prophet, as though the Prophet had added anything of his own. Haggai then ascribed these words to himself, not that he devised anything himself, so as to corrupt the pure doctrine which had been delivered to him by God, but that he only distinguished between God, the author of the doctrine, and his minister, as when it is said, "The sword of God and of Gideon," (Jud. vii. 20,) and also, "The people believed God and Moses his servant." (Ex. xiv. 31.) Nothing is ascribed to Moses or to Gideon apart from God; but God himself is placed in the highest honour, and then Moses and Gideon are joined to him. In the same sense do the Apostles write, when they say, that "it had pleased the Holy Spirit" and themselves. (Acts xv. 22.)

And hence it is evident how foolish and ridiculous are the Papists, who hence conclude that it is lawful for men to add their own inventions to the word of God. For the Apostles, they say, not only alleged the authority of the Holy Spirit, but also say, that it seemed good to themselves. God then does not so claim, they say, all things for himself, as not to leave some things to the decision of his Church, as though indeed the Apostles meant something different from what our Prophet means here; that is, that they truly and faithfully delivered what they had received from the Spirit of God.

It is therefore a mode of speaking which ought to be carefully marked, when we hear, that the voice of God and the words of Haggai were reverently attended to by the people.—Why? *Inasmuch*, he says, *as God had sent him;* as though he had said, that God was heard when he spoke by the mouth of man. And this is also worthy of being noticed, because many fanatics boast, that they show regard to the word of the Lord, but are unwilling to give credit to men, as that would be even preposterous; and they pretend, that in this way what belongs to the only true God is transferred to creatures. But the Holy Spirit most easily reconciles these two things—that the voice of God is heard when the people embrace what they hear from the mouth of a Prophet. Why so? because it pleases God thus to try the obedience of our faith, while he commits to man this office. For if the Lord was pleased to speak himself, then justly might men be neglected: but as he has chosen this mode, whosoever reject God's Prophets, clearly show that they despise God himself. There is no need of inquiring here, why it is that we ought to obey the word preached or the external voice of men, rather than revelations; it is enough for us to know that this is the will of God. When therefore he sends Prophets to us, we ought unquestionably to receive what they bring.

And Haggai says also expressly, that he was *sent* by the God of Israel; as though he had said, that the people had testified their true piety when they acknowledged God's Prophet in his legitimate vocation. For he who clamorously objects, and says that he knows not whether it pleases God or not to send forth men to announce his word, shows himself to be wholly alienated from God: for it ought to be sufficiently evident to us that this is one of our first principles.

He afterwards adds, that *the people feared before Jehovah.*[1] Haggai confirms here the same truth—that the

---

[1] This clause may be thus rendered,—
   And fear him did the people on account of Jehovah.
   This comports better with the previous clause, that Jehovah had sent him. The ו affixed to "fear" is a pronoun, otherwise the verb is plural;

people received not what they heard from the mouth of mortal man, otherwise than if the majesty of God had openly appeared. For there was no ocular view of God given; but the message of the Prophet obtained as much power as though God had descended from heaven, and had given manifest tokens of his presence. We may then conclude from these words, that the glory of God so shines in his word, that we ought to be so much affected by it, whenever he speaks by his servants, as though he were nigh to us, face to face, as the Scripture says in another place. It now follows—

13. Then spake Haggai the Lord's messenger, in the Lord's message unto the people, saying, I *am* with you, saith the Lord.
14. And the Lord stirred up the spirit of Zerubbabel the son of Shealtiel, governor of Judah, and the spirit of Joshua the son of Josedech, the high priest, and the spirit of all the remnant of the people; and they came and did work in the house of the Lord of hosts, their God.

13. Et dicit Chaggai, legatus Iehovæ in legatione Iehovæ, dicendo (*vel,* dicens) populo, Ego vobiscum sum, dicit Iehova.
14. Et excitavit Iehova spiritum Zerubbabel, filii Sealtiel, ducis Jehudah, et spiritum Jehosuæ, filii Jehozadak, sacerdotis magni, et spiritum omnium reliquiarum (*hoc est,* totius residuæ multitudinis) populi; et venerunt et fecerunt opus in templo (in domo, *ad verbum*) Iehovæ exercituum Dei sui.

The Prophet tells us here, that he had again roused the leaders as well as the common people; for except God frequently repeats his exhortations, our alacrity relaxes. Though then they had all attended to God's command, it was yet necessary that they should be strengthened by a new promise: for men can be encouraged, and their indifference can be corrected, by no other means, to such a degree, as when God offers and promises his help. This, then, was the way in which they were now encouraged, *I am with you.* And experience sufficiently shows, that we never really and from the heart obey, except when we rely on his promises and hope for a happy success. For were God only to call us to our work, and were our hope doubtful, all our zeal would doubtless die away. We cannot then devote our ser-

and "people" seldom, if ever, has a verb in the plural number. To fear sometimes means to respect, to reverence: the people honoured him as God's servant, by obeying his message.—*Ed.*

vices to God, except he supports and encourages us by promises. We also see, that it is not enough that God should speak once, and that we should once receive his word, but there is need that he should rouse us again and again; for the greatest ardour grows cold when no goads are applied.

And the Prophet makes known again his vocation, for he says, that *he spake in the message of Jehovah*, for he was his *messenger*. The word מלאך, *malak*, means a messenger; and as angels are called מלאכים, *melakim*, some foolish men have thought that Haggai was one of the celestial angels, clothed with the form of man: but this is a most frivolous conjecture; for priests, we know, are honoured with this title in the second chapter of Malachi, and God in many other places calls his Prophets messengers or ambassadors. There is, therefore, no doubt but that Haggai meant simply to testify, that he brought forward nothing presumptuously, but was a faithful dispenser of the word; for he knew that he was sent by God; and that he might attain attention, he was able justly to testify that his message came from heaven.

Hence he says, that he spake as a *messenger of Jehovah in the message of Jehovah;* that is, he spoke according to his calling, and not as a private individual, but as one who derived his authority from heaven, and could call to order the whole people; for he was to give way neither to the chief priest nor to Zerubbabel the ruler of the people, inasmuch as he was superior to them on this account, because he had a message which had been committed to him by God.[1] We now then understand the design of the Prophet.

And we hence learn that there is no dignity which

---

[1] The verse literally is—
    Then said Haggai, the messenger of Jehovah in the messages of
      Jehovah to the people, saying,
    I am with you, saith Jehovah.

The word for "messages" is in the plural number, preceded by the preposition ב. Why commentators have generally rendered it in the singular number, does not appear. Haggai is expressly said to be God's messenger in, or with regard to, the messages or communications he made to the people. To connect the word, as some do, with "said," hardly gives a meaning, except the clause be rendered, as it is done by *Newcome*, "by the message of Jehovah," that is, by his command; but then a plural word is made singular.—*Ed.*

exempts us from obedience common to all, when God's word is addressed to us. Doubtless Joshua the high priest was superior to all the rest in matters of religion, and he was the chief angel or messenger of the God of hosts; and yet he refused not to submit himself to God's Prophet, for he understood that he was in a special manner appointed by God to this office. Zerubbabel, the governor of the people, followed also his example. Let us, then, know that God's word is proclaimed under this condition, that no eminence, either in honour or in dignity, exempts us, as it were, by a sort of privilege, from the obligation of receiving it.

The Prophet at length adds, that the people hastened quickly to the work, because God had given encouragement to them all. He had lately spoken of the fruit of his doctrine; but he now declares that his voice had not so penetrated into the hearts of all, as though it had been of itself efficacious, but that it had been connected with the hidden influence of the Spirit.

And this passage is remarkable; for the Prophet includes both these things—that God allows not his word to be useless or unfruitful—and yet that this proceeds not from the diligence of men, but from the hidden power of the Spirit. The Prophet, then, did not fail in his efforts; for his labour was not in vain, but brought forth fruit. At the same time, that that saying might remain true, 'He who plants and he who waters is nothing,' (1 Cor. iii. 7,) he says, that the Israelites were ready for the work, because the Lord roused them; *Jehovah*, he says, *stirred up the spirit of Zerubbabel, the spirit of Joshua, and of the whole people*. It is not right to restrict the influence of the Spirit to one thing only, as some do, who imagine that the Israelites were confirmed in their good resolution, as they say, having before spontaneously obeyed the word of God. These separate, without reason, what ought to be read in the Prophet as connected together. For God roused the spirit of Zerubbabel and of the whole people; and hence it was that they received the message of the Prophet, and were attentive to his words. Foolishly, then, do they imagine that the Israelites were led by their own free-will to obey the word of

God, and then that some aid of the Holy Spirit followed, to make them firmly to persevere in their course. But the Prophet declared, in the first place, that his message was respectfully received by the people; and now he explains how it was, even because God had touched the hearts of the whole people.[1]

And we ought to notice the expression, when it is said that the *spirit* of Zerubbabel and of all the people was *stirred up*. For much sloth, we know, prevailed, especially among the multitude. But as to Zerubbabel and Joshua, they were, as we have said, already willing, but delayed until the coldness under which they laboured was reproved. But the Prophet here simply means, that they became thus obedient through the hidden impulse of God, and also that they were made firm in their purpose. God does not form new souls in us, when he draws us to his service; but changes what is wrong in us: for we should never be attentive to his word, were he not to open our ears; and there would be no inclination to obey, were he not to turn our hearts; in a word, both will and effort would immediately fail in us, were he not to add his gift of perseverance. Let us, then, know that Haggai's labours produced fruits, because the Lord effectually touched the hearts of the people; for we indeed know that it is his special gift, that the elect are made disciples, according to that declaration, 'No one comes to me, except my Father draw him.' (John vi. 24.) It is therefore said that they *came and did the work in the house of Jehovah.*

---

[1] It is sometimes the case, that a doctrine is illegitimately drawn from a passage, and then that it is unfairly opposed. The building of the Temple had nothing to do with the first movement of the spiritual life: and therefore to draw an argument from the willingness of the people to undertake that work in favour of free-will in the great business of salvation, is by no means legitimate. It would have been, then, better to deny the application, than to turn the passage from its regular course. But we shall not do violence to the passage, if we render the ו at the beginning of this verse, "Thus," and refer "the stirring up" to the threatening and the promise previously announced. The object seems not to have been to set forth the direct influence of the Spirit on the minds of the people, but to show the effect produced on them by the message conveyed to them from the Lord by the Prophet. God stirs up the minds of men both by his word and by his Spirit, both outwardly and inwardly. The former may more properly be meant here.—*Ed.*

We may also hence learn, that no one is fit to offer sacrifices to God, or to do any other service, but he who has been moulded by the hidden operation of the Spirit. Willingly, indeed, we offer ourselves and our all to God, and build his temple; but whence is this voluntary action, except that the Lord subdues us, and thus renders us teachable and obedient? It is afterwards added—

| 15. In the four and twentieth day of the sixth month, in the second year of Darius the king. | 15. In die vicesimo quarto mensis sexti, anno secundo Darii regis. |

The Prophet mentions even the time when they commenced the building of the temple. Three-and-twenty days interposed between the first message and the beginning of the work. It hence appears how ignorant he was who divided the chapters, having begun the second chapter at this verse, where the Prophet shows, as it were by his finger, how much was the distance between the day in which he began to exhort the people, and the success of which he speaks. He then simply tells us here when the Temple began to be built—that is, in the second year of Darius the king, and in the twenty-fourth day of the sixth month. He had previously said that a message was given to him in the second year of Darius the king, and in the sixth month, and on the first day. Then from that day to the twenty-fourth the people delayed; not that they disregarded the command of the Prophet, but because it was not so easy a thing to persuade them all, that they might unanimously undertake the work. Though then the promptitude of the people is commended, we must yet observe that there was some mixture of weakness; for the effect of the doctrine did not appear till the twenty-fourth day.[1] It afterwards follows—

---

[1] The reasons assigned here for a different division is by no means satisfactory. The fact is that this verse necessarily belongs to the last of the previous chapter, as it specifies the time when the people began the work as there mentioned; and what follows this verse is another message, and at another time. The usual division is no doubt the best.

CHAPTER II.

1. In the seventh *month*, in the one and twentieth *day* of the month, came the word of the Lord by the prophet Haggai, saying,

2. Speak now to Zerubbabel the son of Shealtiel, governor of Judah, and to Joshua the son of Josedech, the high priest, and to the residue of the people, saying,

3. Who *is* left among you that saw this house in her first glory? and how do ye see it now? *is it* not in your eyes in comparison of it as nothing?

4. Yet now be strong, O Zerubbabel, saith the Lord; and be strong, O Joshua, son of Josedech, the high priest; and be strong, all ye people of the land, saith the Lord, and work: for I *am* with you, saith the Lord of hosts:

5. *According to* the word that I covenanted with you when ye came out of Egypt, so my spirit remaineth among you: fear ye not.

1. In septimo et vicesimo uno mensis (*hoc est*, septimo mense, vicesima prima die mensis) fuit sermo Iehovæ in manu Chaggai Prophetæ, dicendo,

2. Dic nunc ad Zerubbabel, filium Sealtiel, ducem Jehudah, et ad Jehosuah, filium Jehosadak, sacerdotem magnum, et ad reliquias populi, dicendo,

3. Quis in vobis superstes (*vel*, residuus, *ad verbum*) qui viderit domum hanc in gloria sua priore, et quam vos videtis hanc nunc, annon præ illa sicut nihilum in oculis vestris?

4. Et nunc (*vel*, nunc tamen) fortis sis Zerubbabel, dicit Iehova, et fortis sis Jehosuah, fili Jehosadak, sacerdos magne, et fortis sis omnis populus terræ, dicit Iehova, et operamini, quia ego vobiscum, dicit Iehovah exercituum,

5. Secundum verbum quod pepigi vobiscum dum egressi estis ex Egypto; et spiritus meus stabit (*vel*, perseverabit) in medio vestri, ne timeatis.

The Prophet now states another reason why he had been sent by God, in order that he might obviate a temptation which might have hindered the work that was begun. We have seen that they were all stirred up by the celestial spirit to undertake the building of the Temple. But as Satan, by his many arts, attempts to turn back the godly from their course, so he had devised a reason by which the desire of the people might have been checked. Inasmuch as the old people, who had seen the splendour of the former temple, considered this temple no better than a cottage, all their zeal evaporated; for, as we have said, without a promise there will continue in men no ardour, no perseverance. Now we know what had been predicted by Ezekiel, and what all the other Prophets had testified, especially Isaiah, who had spoken highly of the excellency of the Church, and shown that it was to be superior to its ancient state. (Isaiah xxxiii. 21.) Besides, Ezekiel describes the form of the Temple, and states its dimensions. (Ezek. xli. 1.) As then the faithful had learnt from these prophecies that the new Temple would be more splendid than the ancient, they were in danger, not only of becoming cold in the business, but also of being wholly discouraged, when they perceived that the new Temple in no respect reached the excellency and grandeur of the ancient Temple. And these things are described at large by Josephus.

But we may easily conclude, from the words of the Prophet, that there was then a danger lest they should lay aside the work they had begun, except they were encouraged by a new exhortation. And he says that this happened in the seventh month, and on the first day of the month.

Here arises a question, How was it that they so soon compared the new with the old building. Seven or eight days had passed since the work was begun: nothing, doubtless, could have been then constructed, which might have afforded a ground of comparison. It seems then strange, that the Prophet had been so soon sent to them. An answer to this will be easily found, if we bear in mind that what I have stated at the beginning of the first chapter, that the foundations of the Temple had been previously laid, but that there had been a long interruption: for the people had turned to their own private concerns, and all had become so devoted to their own advantages, that they neglected the building of the Temple. For it is wholly a false notion, that the people had returned from exile before the appointed time, and it has been sufficiently refuted by clear proofs; for scripture expressly declares, that both Cyrus and Darius had been led by a divine impulse to allow the return of the people. Hence, when the Jews returned to their country, they immediately began to build the Temple; but afterwards, as I have said, either avarice, or too anxious a desire for their own private benefit, laid hold on their minds. As then the building of the Temple had been for some time neglected, they were again encouraged, as our Prophet has shown to us. They had now hardly applied their hands to the work, when, through the artifice of Satan, such suggestions as these crept in—" What are ye doing, ye miserable men!

Ye wish to build a Temple to your God; but what sort of Temple will it be? Certainly it will not be that which all the Prophets have celebrated. For what do we read in Isaiah, Jeremiah, and Ezekiel? Have not all these testified that the Temple which would be rebuilt after our return from Babylonian exile would be more splendid than the other? But we now build a shed. Surely this is done without authority. We do not then fight under the guidance of God; and it would be better for us to leave off the work; for our service cannot be approved of God, except it be founded on his Word. And we see how far this Temple comes short of what God has promised."

We now hence learn, that it was not without reason that Haggai was sent on the eighth day to recover the people from their indifference. And hence also we may learn how necessary it is for us to be constantly stimulated; for Satan can easily find out a thousand impediments, by which he may turn us aside from the right course, except God often repeats his exhortations to keep us awake. Eight days only had elapsed, and the people would have ceased from their work, had not Haggai been sent to encourage them again.

Now the cause of this cessation, which the Prophet designed to obviate and to remove, ought to be especially noticed. The people had before ceased to work, because they were immoderately devoted to their own interest, which was a proof of base ingratitude and of profane impiety: for those who had no care for building the Temple were most ungrateful to God; and then their impiety was intolerable, inasmuch as they sought boarded houses to dwell in, being not content with decent houses without having them adorned, while the Temple was left, as it were, a wilderness. But the cause was different, when Haggai was sent the second time; for their indifference then arose from a good principle and a genuine feeling of religion. But we hence see what a subtle contriver Satan is, who not only draws us away openly from God's service, but insinuates himself in a clandestine manner, so as to turn us aside, under the cover of zeal, from the course of our vocation. How was it that the people became negligent after they had begun the work?

even because it grieved the old men to see the glory of the second, so far inferior to the first Temple. For though the people animated themselves by the sound of trumpets, yet the old among them drowned the sound by their lamentations. Whence was this? even because they saw, as I have said, that this Temple was in no way equal to the ancient one; and hence they thought that God was not as yet reconciled to them. Had they said, that so great an expense was not necessary, that God did not require much money to be laid out, their impiety should have been openly manifested; but when they especially wished that the splendour of the Temple would be such, as might surely prove that the restoration of the Church was come, such as had been promised by all the Prophets, we doubtless perceive their pious feeling.

But we are thus reminded, that we ought always to beware of the intrigues of Satan, when they appear under the cover of truth. When, therefore, our minds are disposed to piety, Satan is ever to be feared, lest he should stealthily suggest to us what may turn us aside from our duty; for we see that some leave the Church because they require in it the highest perfection. They are indignant at vices which they deem intolerable, when they cannot be corrected: and thus, under the pretext of zeal, they separate themselves and seek to form for themselves a new world, in which there is to be a perfect Church; and they lay hold on those passages in which the Holy Spirit recommends purity to the Church, as when Paul says, that it was purchased by Christ, that it might be without spot or wrinkle. As then these are inflamed with a zeal so rigid that they depart from God himself and violate the unity of the Church; so also there are many proud men who despise the Church of God, because it shines not forth among them in great pomp; and they think that God does not dwell in the midst of us, because we are obscure and of no great importance, and also because they regard our few number with contempt.

In all these there is some appearance of piety. How so? Because they would have God to be revered, so that they would have the whole world to be filled with the fear of his majesty; or they would have much wealth to be gathered, so that sumptuous offerings might be made. But, as I have already said, Satan thus cunningly insinuates himself; and hence we ought to fear his intrigues, lest, under plausible pretences, he should dazzle our eyes. But the best way of caution is to regard what God commands, and so to rely on his promises as to proceed steadily in our course, though the accomplishment of the promises does not immediately correspond with our desires; for God designedly keeps us in suspense in order to try our faith. Though then he may not as yet fulfil what he has promised, let it yet be our course to attempt nothing rashly, while we are obeying his command. It will then be our chief wisdom, by which we may escape all the crafts of Satan, simply to obey God's word, and to exercise our hope so as patiently to wait the seasonable time, when he will fulfil what he now promises.

PRAYER.

Grant, Almighty God, that as we are not only alienated in mind from thee, but also often relapse after having been once stirred up by thee, either into perverseness, or into our own vanity, or are led astray by various things, so that nothing is more difficult than to pursue our course until we reach the end of our race,— O grant that we may not confide in our own strength, nor claim for ourselves more than what is right, but, with our hearts raised above, depend on thee alone, and constantly call on thee to supply us with new strength, and so to confirm us that we may persevere to the end in the discharge of our duty, until we shall at length attain the true and perfect form of that temple which thou commandest us to build, in which thy perfect glory shines forth, and into which we are to be transformed by Christ our Lord. Amen.

Lecture One Hundred and Thirty-first.

THE Prophet, after having declared why it was necessary to add new stimulants, now exhorts Zerubbabel and Joshua, and also the people, to be courageous, and thus to proceed with the work. And he again repeats what he had said, that the Lord was with them; *I am with you,* he says. Now this one thing is enough for us, that is, when God declares that he is with us; for his aid, we know, is stronger than the whole world, however Satan may on every side attempt to resist us.

He also adds, that his *Spirit would be in the midst* of them; and then he says, that there was no reason for them to *fear.* By his Spirit God means the power by which he strengthened their minds, that they might not give way to their trials, or, that fear might not hinder them. And what is particular is joined to what is general; for God is present with his own in various ways: but he especially shows, that he is present when, by his Spirit, he confirms weak minds. He then bids them all to be of a courageous mind. This is one thing. But he also shows whence this courage proceeded; for he sustained them by his Spirit when they were growing faint, or when they were not able to resist fears. The Prophet reminds them by these words, that courage was to be sought from God.

We hence learn that what belongs to our calling and duty is not required from us as though we were able to perform everything; but when the Lord, according to his own right, commands, he offers the help of his Spirit; and thus we ought to connect the promise of grace with the precept, of which foolish men take no notice, who deduce free will from what is commanded: for they thus reason—that it is in vain to require from us what is above our ability, and that as God requires us to form our life according to the rule of the highest perfection, it is therefore in our power to perform the highest justice. But the Prophet here, in the first place, exhorts Joshua and Zerubbabel, and the whole people, to be courageous, and then, he immediately adds, that the *Spirit* of God *would be in the midst* of them; as though he had said, that there was no reason for them to despond, though they had not sufficient strength in themselves; for courage was to be sought from the Spirit of God, who would dwell among them. In short, the Prophet teaches us that the faithful are so to strive as not to arrogate anything to themselves, but to offer themselves to be ruled by the Lord, that he may supply them with weapons as well as with strength, and thus conquer in them ; for though the victory is ascribed to us it is yet certain that God conquers in us.

He then adds, *According to the word;* for so I render the particle אֵת, *at.* They who think that the Jews are here reminded that it was their duty to obey God, and purely to serve him, and truly to keep his law, according to what he had commanded them when he brought them out of the land of Egypt, far depart from the design of the Prophet ; for the Prophet pursues the same subject ; and in the latter clause he confirms what I have just mentioned—that the *Spirit* of God *would be in the midst of them.* He therefore shows that he promises nothing new, but what God had formerly engaged to give to their fathers. If any one prefers taking the particle אֵת, *at,* in an explicative sense, I do not object ; for the meaning would be the same—that this is the word which he had promised.[1] The object of the Prophet is by no means doubtful ; for he means to teach us that God is faithful and constant in his promises, and that the Jews would find this to be the case, for he would perform what he had formerly promised to their fathers : *The word,* he says, *which I had covenanted with you when I brought you out of Egypt.* For the Prophets were wont to remind the faithful of the ancient covenant, that they might gain more credit to their special prophecies. We indeed know that whatever God had

---

[1] This is the most approved manner. There is no instance in which it means "according." It may be rendered—"This *is* the word," &c. There were two things which were intended to dispel their fear—the covenant made with the fathers, and the Spirit of God—the spirit of prophecy, "standing," or existing among them. The Chaldee Paraphrase is—"My Prophets are teaching among you." The verse may be thus translated—

This *is* the word which I covenanted with you
At your coming forth from Egypt,
And my Spirit *is* continuing among you; fear not.

Junius and *Tremelius* render the אֵת, "with," and the verse thus—

With the word (*i. e.,* having the word) which I covenanted with you
When ye came forth from Egypt,
And with my Spirit standing among you, fear not.

Henderson considers "the word," and "my Spirit," to be nominatives to the particle "standing," or rather to the auxiliary verb which is to be understood before it, and that "standing" is in the singular number, on account of the nearer nominative "my Spirit." *Newcome* follows our version, and views אֵת as a preposition—"according to."—*Ed.*

promised to the Jews, was founded on their first adoption. When, therefore, the Prophets brought forward the ancient covenant, it was the same as though they led the Jews back to the fountain itself; for the promises, which now and then occurred, were like streams which flowed from the first spring, even their gratuitous covenant.

We now then see why an express mention is made of the ancient compact which God had made with the chosen people at their departure out of Egypt.

It must also be observed, that God became then the Redeemer of his people, in order to be their eternal Father, and thus to be the perpetual guardian of their safety. Hence the design of what the Prophet says is to show that their fathers were not formerly redeemed, that their children might reject God, but that he might continue his favour to his people to the end. But the ultimate issue is to be found in Christ, that is, the full accomplishment; for God does not cease to show kindness in him to his chosen people, but performs much more fully and abundantly what he had previously exhibited under types and shadows. For whatever he conferred on his ancient Church, was, as it were, a prelude of his vast bounty, which was at length made known by the coming of Christ.

We now clearly apprehend what the Prophet meant: For he upbraided the Jews for their stupidity, because they did not consider that their fathers were formerly delivered from Egypt, that God might defend them to the end. Hence he bids them maturely to examine the design and character of the covenant which God made at their departure from Egypt; for he entered into covenant with them, that he might be their Redeemer, and confer on them the fulness of all blessings. Since it is so, he says, the time is now come when God will perform what he then promised to your fathers; and whatever faithfulness ye have hitherto found in God, ought to be applied for this end—that ye may feel assured that ye have been now restored to your country, in order that he might re-establish his Church, and that ye might not continue in that low condition, which now depresses your minds. As then ye ought to look for that fulness of happiness which God formerly promised, either his covenant is void and he unfaithful, or ye ought with cheerfulness and alacrity to proceed with the work. It follows—

6. For thus saith the Lord of hosts; Yet once, it *is* a little while, and I will shake the heavens, and the earth, and the sea, and the dry *land;*	6. Quia sit dicit Iehova exercituum, Adhuc unum modicum hoc, et ego commovebo cœlos et terram et mare et aridam;
7. And I will shake all nations, and the desire of all nations shall come: and I will fill this house with glory, saith the Lord of hosts.	7. Et commovebo omnes gentes, et venient, desiderium omnium gentium; et implebo domum hanc gloriâ, dicit Iehova exercituum.
8. The silver *is* mine, and the gold *is* mine, saith the Lord of hosts.	8. Meum argentum, et meum aurum, dicit Iehova exercituum.
9. The glory of this latter house shall be greater than of the former, saith the Lord of hosts; and in this place will I give peace, saith the Lord of hosts.	9. Major erit gloria domus hujus secundæ (posterioris, *ad verbum,*) quàm prioris dicit Iehova exercituum: et in loco hoc dabo pacem, dicit Iehova exercituum.

Here the Prophet expresses more clearly, and confirms more fully, what I have said—that God would in time bring help to the miserable Jews, because he would not disappoint the assurance given to the fathers. This declaration, then, depends on the covenant before mentioned; and hence the causative particle is used, *For thus saith Jehovah of hosts, as yet a small one it is,* or, yet shortly, *I will fill this house with glory.* The expression "a small thing," most interpreters apply to time. Yet there are those who think the subject itself is denoted. The more received opinion is, that it means a small duration, a short time, because God would soon make a change for the better. "Though then there does not as yet appear the accomplishment of the promises, by which ye have hitherto supported your faith and your hope, yet after a short time God will really prove that he has spoken nothing falsely to you."

There are yet some, as I have said, who think that the matter itself is denoted by the Prophet, even that the Temple did not yet appear in splendour before the eyes of men, *a small one it is,* that is, "Ye see not indeed a building such as that was, before the Assyrians and the Chaldeans took possession of the city; but let not your eyes remain fixed on the appearance of this Temple." Let then *this small one as yet* pass by; but in a short time *this house will be filled with glory.*

With regard to the main object, it was the Prophet's design to strengthen the minds of the godly, that they might not think that the power of God was inefficient, though he had not as yet performed what they had hoped. In short, they were not to judge by present appearances of what had been previously said of their redemption. We said yesterday that the minds of the godly were heavily depressed, because the Prophets had spoken in high terms of the Temple as well as of the kingdom: the kingdom was as yet nothing; and the temple was more like a shed than what might have been compared in glory with the former Temple. It was hence necessary for the Prophet to meet this objection; and this is the reason why he bids them to overlook the present appearance, and to think of the glory which was yet hidden. *As yet*, he says, *it is a small one;* that is, "There is no reason for you to despair, though the grandeur of the Temple does not as yet appear to be so great as you have conceived; but, on the contrary, let your minds pass over to that restoration which is still far distant. *As yet* then *a small one it is; and I will move the heavens and the earth.*[1]

In a word, God here bids them to exercise patience, until he should put forth the ineffable power of his hand to restore fully his Church; and this is what is meant by the shaking of the heaven and the earth.

But this is a remarkable passage. The Jews indeed, who

---

[1] Our common version is no doubt the best, and is materially followed by *Newcome*, *Henderson*, and many others. Retaining the tense of the passage, I would render the clause thus,
    Yet once, shortly *will it be*,
    And I will shake, &c.
" Shortly *will* it *be*," מעט היא (shortly it) may be taken as a parenthesis. It is not given by the Septuagint, nor by Paul in Heb. xii. 27.
   Yet once *more, in* a short time,—*Newcome*.
   Yet once, within a little,—*Henderson*.
The shaking of the heavens, earth, sea, and dry land is explained, according to the common manner of the Prophets, in the next verse, by shaking of all nations: the material world is named in the first instance, while its inhabitants are intended. So *Henderson* very properly renders the ו at the beginning of the seventh verse, " Yea."—*Ed.*

are very absurd in everything connected with the kingdom of Christ, pervert what is here said by the Prophet, and even reduce it to nothing. But the Apostle in Heb. xii. reminds us of what God means here. For this passage contains an implied contrast between the law and the gospel, between redemption, just mentioned here, and that which was to be expected, and was at length made known by the coming of Christ. God, then, when he redeemed his people from Egypt, as well as from Babylon, moved the earth: but the Prophet announces here something greater—that God would shake the heaven and the earth. But that the meaning of the Prophet may appear more evident, each sentence must be examined in order.

He says first, *this once, shortly*. I am inclined to apply this to time, that I may not depart from what is commonly received. But there is no reason for us to contend on the subject, because it makes little or no difference as to the main point. For we have said that what the Prophet had in view was to show that the Jews were not to fix their eyes and their minds on the appearance of the Temple at the time: "Allow," he says, "and give place to hope, because your present state shall not long remain; for the Lord will shake the heaven and the earth; think then of God's power, how great it is; does he not by his providence rule both the earth and the heaven? And he will shake all things above and below, rather than not to restore his Church; he will rather change the appearance of the whole world, than that redemption should not be fully accomplished. Be not then unwilling to be satisfied with these preludes, but know what God's power can do: for though it may be necessary to throw the heaven and the earth into confusion, yet this shall be done, rather than that your enemies should prevent that full restoration, of which the Prophets have so often spoken." But the Apostle very justly says, that the gospel is here set in contrast with the law; for God exhibited his wonderful power, when the law was promulgated on mount Sinai; but a fuller power shone forth at the coming of Christ, for then the heaven, as well as the earth, was shaken. It is not, then, without reason that the Apostle concludes that God speaks now to us from heaven, for his majesty appears more splendid in the gospel than formerly in the law: and hence we are less excusable, if we despise him now speaking in the person of his only-begotten Son, and thus speaking to show to us that the whole world is subject to him.

He then adds, *I will move all the nations, and they shall come.* After having mentioned the heaven and the earth, he now shows that he would arrest the attention of all mortals, so as to turn them according to his will, in any way it may please him: *Come,* he says, *shall* all nations—How? because I shall shake them. Here again the Prophet teaches us that men come not to Christ except through the wonderful agency of God. He might have spoken more simply, "I will lead all nations," as it is said elsewhere; but his purpose was to express something more, even that the impulse by which God moves his elect to betake themselves to the fold of Christ is supernatural. Shaking seems a forcible act. Lest men, then, should obscure the power of God, by which they are roused that they may obey Christ, and submit to his authority, it is here by the Prophet expressed by this term, in order that they might understand that the Lord does not work in an usual or common manner, when they are thus changed.

But it must be also observed, that men are thus powerfully, and in an extraordinary or supernatural manner influenced, so that they follow spontaneously at the same time. The operation of God is then twofold; for it is first necessary to shake men, that they may unlearn their whole character, that is, that forgetting their former nature, they may willingly receive the yoke of Christ. We indeed know how great is our perverseness, and how untameable we are, until God subdues us by his Spirit. There is need in such a case of a violent shaking. But we are not forced to obey Christ, as lions and wild beasts are, who indeed yield, but still retain their inward ferocity, and roar, though led in chains and subdued by scourges and beatings. We are not, then, so shaken, that our inward rebellion remains in us; but we are shaken, so that our disposition is changed, and we receive willingly the yoke of Christ. This is the reason why the Prophet says, *I will shake all nations, and they shall come;* that is, there will be indeed a wonderful conversion, when the nations who previously despised God, and regarded true religion and piety with the utmost hatred, shall habituate themselves to the ruling power of God: and they *shall come,* because they shall be so drawn by his hidden influence, that the obedience they shall render will be voluntary. We now perceive the meaning of the Prophet.

He afterwards adds, *The desire of all nations.* This admits of two explanations. The first is, that nations shall come and bring with them everything that is precious, in order to consecrate it to the service of God; for the Hebrews call whatever is valuable a desire; so that under this term they include all riches, honours, pleasures, and everything of this kind. Hence some render the passage thus, " I will shake all nations, and come shall the desire of all nations." As there is a change of number, others will have ב, *beth,* or מ, *mem,* to be understood, "They shall come with what they desire;" that is, the nations shall not come empty, but shall gather all their treasures to be a holy oblation to God. But we may understand what he says of Christ, *Come shall the desire of all nations, and I will fill this house with glory.* We indeed know that Christ was the expectation of the whole world, according to what is said by Isaiah. And it may be properly said, that when the desire of all nations shall come, that is, when Christ shall be manifested, in whom the wishes of all ought to centre, the glory of the second Temple shall then be illustrious; but as it immediately follows, *Mine is the silver, and mine is the gold,* the more simple meaning is that which I first stated—that the nations would come, bringing with them all their riches, that they might offer themselves and all their possessions as a sacrifice to God.

It is, then, better to read what follows as an explanation, *Mine is the silver, mine is the gold, saith Jehovah;* that is, " I have not through want of money deferred hitherto the complete building of the Temple; for what can hinder me from amassing gold and silver from all quarters? Should it so please me, I could in a short time build a Temple by all the wealth of the world. Is it not indeed in my power to create mountains of gold and silver, by which I might erect for myself a Temple? Ye hence see that wealth is not wanting to me to build the Temple which I have promised; but the time is not arrived. Therefore they who believe the preceding predictions, ought to wait and to look forward, until the suitable time shall come." This is the import of the passage.[1]

He at length declares that *the glory* of the second *Temple* would be *greater* than that of *the first*, and that there would be *peace in that place*. As to the words there is nothing obscure; but we ought especially to attend to what is said.

It must, indeed, be first observed, that what is said here of the future glory of the Temple is to be applied to the excellency of those spiritual blessings which appeared when Christ was revealed, and are still conspicuous to us through faith; for ungodly men are so blind that they see them not. And this we must bear in mind, lest we dream like some gross interpreters, who think that what is here said was in part fulfilled when Herod reconstructed the Temple. For though that was a sumptuous building, yet there is no doubt

[1] Many have been the criticisms on this clause, both as to its grammatical construction and as to the import of the word rendered "desire." The verb "come" is plural, and the word for "desire" is singular. The easiest solution, and countenanced by the Septuagint, where the word is rendered τὰ ἐκλεκτὰ—" choice things," is to consider חמדת as a plural, the ו being omitted. This would remove the grammatical anomaly, and the sentiment, as *Calvin* says, would be more consonant with the context.

And come shall the choice things of all nations.

There is no ground for the objection which *Bishop Chandler* states, that to "come" is in this case an improper expression; for there are other similar instances. See Josh. vi. 12; Is. lx. 5. It is also applied to trees, Is. lx. 13; and to incense, Jer. vi. 20.

Newcome takes the word as a plural, but applies it as *deliciæ* in Latin to a person, and refers to Dan. ix. 23; where Daniel is called חמודות, rendered in our version "greatly beloved."

The version of *Henderson* is the following—

And the things desired by all nations shall come.

He considers that they are the blessings of the kingdom of Christ, and thinks that the Prophet refers to the general expectation which pervaded the world of some better state of things, and especially of some deliverer.

But the most tenable is the view of *Calvin*, which has been held by *Kimchi, Drusius, Vitringa*, and others.—*Ed.*

but that it was an attempt of the Devil to delude the Jews, that they might cease to hope for Christ. Such was also, probably, the craft of Herod. We indeed know that he was only a half-Jew. He professed himself to be one of Abraham's children; but he accommodated his habits, we know, to those of the Jews, only for his own advantage. That they might not look for Christ, this delusive and empty spectacle was presented to them, so as almost to astound them. Though this, however, may not have entered into the mind of Herod, it is yet certain that the Devil's design was to present to the Jews this deceptive shade, that they might not raise up their thoughts to look for the coming of Christ, as the time was then near at hand.

God might, indeed, immediately at the beginning have caused a magnificent temple to be built: as he had allowed a return to the people, so he might have given them courage, and supplied them with materials, to render the latter Temple equal or even superior to the Temple of Solomon. But Cyrus prohibited by an edict the Temple to be built so high, and he also made its length somewhat smaller. Why was this done? and why also did Darius do the same, who yet liberally helped the Jews, and spared no expense in building the Temple? How was it that both these kings, though guided by the Spirit of God, did not allow the Temple to be built with the same splendour with which it had been previously erected? This did not happen without the wonderful counsel of God; for we know how gross in their notions the Jews had been, and we see that even the Apostles were entangled in the same error; for they expected that the kingdom of Christ would be no other than an earthly one. Had then this Temple been equally magnificent with the former, and had the kingdom become such as it had been, the Jews would have acquiesced in these outward pomps; so that Christ would have been despised, and God's spiritual favour would have been esteemed as nothing. Since, then, they were so bent on earthly happiness, it was necessary for them to be awakened; and the Lord had regard to their weakness, by not allowing a splendid Temple to be built. But in suffering a counterfeit Temple to be built by Herod, when the manifestation of Christ was nigh, he manifested his vengeance by punishing their ingratitude, rather than his favour; and I call it counterfeit, because its splendour was never approved by God. Though Herod spent great treasures on that building, he yet profaned rather than adorned the Temple. Foolishly, then, do some commemorate what Helena, queen of Adiabenians, had laid out, and think that thus a credit is in some measure secured to this prophecy. But it was on the contrary Satan who attempted to deceive by such impostures and crafts, that he might draw away the minds of the godly from the beauty of the spiritual Temple.

But why does the Prophet mention gold and silver? He did this in conformity with what was usual and common; for whenever the Prophets speak of the kingdom of Christ, they delineate or describe its splendour in figurative terms, suitable to their own age. When Isaiah foretells the restoration of the Church, he declares that the Church would be all gold and silver, and whatever glittered with precious stones; and in ch. lx. he especially sets forth the magnificence of the Temple, as though nations from all parts were to bring for sacrifice all their precious things. But Isaiah speaks figuratively, as all the other Prophets do. So then what we read of gold and of silver ought to be so explained as to be applied mystically to the kingdom of Christ; as we have already observed respecting Mal. i. 11—'They shall offer to me, saith the Lord, pure sacrifices from the rising to the setting of the sun.' What are these sacrifices? Are heifers yet to be offered, or lambs, or other animals? By no means; but we must regard the spiritual character of the priesthood; for as the gold of which the Prophet now speaks, and the silver, ought to be taken in a spiritual sense; for since Christ has appeared in the world, it is not God's will to be served with gold and silver vessels; so also there is no altar on which victims are to be sacrificed, and no candlestick; in a word, all the symbols of the law have ceased. It hence follows that the Prophet speaks of the spiritual ornaments of the Temple. And thus we perceive how the glory of the second Temple is to be greater than that of the first.

It then follows, that God *would give peace in this place;*

as though he had said that it would be well with the Jews if they only waited patiently for the complete fulfilment of redemption. But it must be observed, that this peace was not so evident to them that they could enjoy it according to the perception of the flesh; but it was that kind of peace of which Paul speaks, and which, he says, exceeds all understanding. (Phil. iv. 7.) In short, the people could not have comprehended what the Prophet teaches here respecting the future splendour of the Temple, except they leaped over all the obstacles which seemed to obstruct the progress of complete redemption; and so it was ever necessary for them to have recourse to this truth—*yet a little while;* as though he said that they were patiently to endure while God was exercising their faith: but that the time would come, and that shortly, when the Lord would fill that house with glory—that is, when Christ would bring with him all fulness of glory; for though they were to gather the treasures of a thousand worlds into one mass, such a glory would yet be corruptible; but when God the Father appeared in the person of his own Son, he then glorified indeed his Temple; and his majesty shone forth so much that there was nothing wanting to a complete perfection.

PRAYER.

Grant, Almighty God, that since we are by nature extremely prone to superstition, we may carefully consider what is the true and right way of serving thee, such as thou dost desire and approve, even that we offer ourselves spiritually to thee, and seek no other altar but Christ, and relying on no other priest, hope to be acceptable and devoted to thee, that he may imbue us with the Spirit which has been fully poured on him, so that we may from the heart devote ourselves to thee, and thus proceed patiently in our course, that with minds raised upwards we may ever go on towards that glory which is as yet hid under hope, until it shall at length be manifested in due time, when thine only-begotten Son shall appear with the elect angels for our final redemption. Amen.

Lecture One Hundred and Thirty-second.

10. In the four and twentieth *day* of the ninth *month*, in the second year of Darius, came the word of the Lord by Haggai the prophet, saying,

11. Thus saith the Lord of hosts; Ask now the priests *concerning* the law, saying,

12. If one bear holy flesh in the skirt of his garment, and with his skirt do touch bread, or pottage, or wine, or oil, or any meat, shall it be holy? And the priests answered and said, No.

13. Then said Haggai, If *one that is* unclean by a dead body touch any of these, shall it be unclean? And the priests answered and said, It shall be unclean.

14. Then answered Haggai, and said, So *is* this people, and so *is* this nation before me, saith the Lord; and so *is* every work of their hands; and that which they offer there *is* unclean.

10. Vicesimo quarto noni (mensis, *subaudiendum,*) anno secundo Darii, fuit sermo Iehovæ ad Chaggai Prophetam, dicendo,

11. Sic dicit Iehova exercituum, Interroga Sacerdotes de Lege, dicendo,

12. Si sustulerit vir (quispiam) carnem sanctam in ala vestis suæ, et tetegerit ala sua panem, et coctionem, et vinum, et oleum, et quodvis edulium, an sanctificabitur? Et responderunt Sacerdotes et dixerunt, Non.

13. Et dixit Chaggai, Si tetegerit pollutus in anima omne hoc, an polluetur? Responderunt Sacerdotes, et dixerunt, Polluetur.

14. Et respondit Chaggai et dixit, Sic populus iste, et sic gens ista in conspectu meo, dicit Iehova: et sic omne opus manuum ipsorum, et quod obtulerint i'lic, pollutum erit.

THOUGH interpreters seem to perceive the meaning of the Prophet, yet no one really and clearly expresses what he means and intends to teach us: nay, they adduce nothing but what is jejune and frigid; for they refer all these things to this point,—that sacrifices were not acceptable to God before the people had begun to build the Temple, but that from that time they were pleasing to God, because the people, in offering sacrifices in a waste place, proved by such negligence that they disregarded the command of God: but when their hands were applied to the work, God was appeased, and thus he began to accept their sacrifices which before he had rejected. This is, indeed, a part of what is meant, but not the whole; and the Prophet's main object seems to me to be wholly different. He has been hitherto exhorting the people to build the Temple; he now exhorts them to build from a pure motive, and not to think that they had done everything when the Temple assumed a fine appearance before the eyes of men, for God required something else. Hence, I have no doubt but that the Prophet intended here to raise up the minds of the people to the spiritual worship of God.

It was, indeed, necessary diligently to build the Temple, but the end was also to be regarded; for God never cared for external ceremonies; nor was he delighted with that building as men are with their splendid houses. As the Jews absurdly ascribed these gross feelings to God, the Prophet here shows why so strict a command had been given as to the building of the Temple; and the reason was,—that God might be worshipped in a pure and holy manner.

I will repeat again what I have said, that the explanation may be more familiar to you. When the people neglected the building of the Temple, they manifested their impiety and their contempt of Divine worship: for what was the cause of their delay and tardiness, except that each of them regarded nothing but just his own private interest? Now, when all of them strenuously undertook the work of building the Temple, their industry was indeed laudable, for it was a proof of their piety: but when the people thought that God required nothing more than a splendid Temple, it was manifest superstition: for the worship of God, we know, is corrupted when it is confined to external things; for, in this manner God is transformed into a nature not his own: as he is a Spirit, so he must be spiritually worshipped by us. Whosoever then obtrudes on him only external pomps in order to pacify him, most childishly trifles with him. This second part, in my view, is what the Prophet now undertakes to handle. From the seventh to the ninth month they had been diligently engaged in the work which the Lord had commanded them to do: but men, as we know, busy themselves with external things and neglect spiritual worship; hence it was necessary to join what is said here, that the people might understand, that it was not enough to satisfy God, though they spared neither expense nor labour in building the Temple; but that something greater was required, even to worship God in it in a pure and holy manner. This is the design of the whole passage. But we must first examine the Prophet's words, and then it will be easier to gather the whole import of his doctrine.

He says then that he was ordered by God, *on the twenty-fourth day of the month,* in the same year, *in the second year of Darius,* to *ask the priests concerning the law.*[1] Haggai is not bid to inquire respecting the whole law, but only that the priests should answer a question according to the Word of God, or the doctrine of the law according to what is commonly said—" What is law, is the question :" for it was not allowed to the priests to allege anything they pleased indiscriminately; but they were only interpreters of the law. This is the reason why God bids his Prophet to inquire what the law of Moses defines as to the ceremony mentioned here. And the design was, that the people, being convinced as to the legal ceremonies, might not contend nor clamour, but acknowledge that all works are condemned as sinful which flow not from a pure and sincere heart.

Haggai asks first, *If a man takes holy flesh*—that is, some part of the sacrifice,—if any one takes and carries it in a sleeve or skirt, that is, in any part of his vestment, and then touches bread, or oil, or any eatable thing, will anything connected with that holy flesh be sanctified by mere touch? *The priests answer, No.* Here also interpreters grossly mistake: for they take "sanctified" as meaning "polluted," altogether falsely; for there is here a twofold question proposed—Whether holy flesh sanctifies anything it may touch? and then, whether an impure and a polluted man contaminates whatever he may touch? As to the first question, the priests wisely and truly answer, that there is no such efficacy in sacrifices, as that they can sanctify what they may touch: and this is true. The second definition is also most proper, that whatever is touched by an unclean man is polluted, as the law everywhere declares.

The Prophet then accommodates this to his present case, *So,* he says, *is this people, and this nation, and the work of their hands.* For as long as they are polluted, however they

---

[1] This clause is literally rendered by *Newcome*—" Ask now the law from the priests;" or, according to the order of the words, " Ask now from the priests the law "—*Ed.*

may spend money in sacrifices, and greatly weary themselves in worshipping God, not only is their labour vain, but whatever they offer is polluted, and is an abomination only. We now understand the words of the Prophet, and so we may now consider the subject.

But before I speak generally of the present subject, I shall first notice what the Prophet says here, that he *inquired respecting the law;* for it was not allowed to the priests to allege anything they pleased. We indeed know, that they had advanced into such licentiousness, as arbitrarily to demand what God had never commanded, and also to forbid the people what was lawful, the use of which had been permitted by God's law. But Haggai does not here allow such a liberty to the priests; he does not ask what they thought, but what was required by the law of the Lord. And this is worthy of being noticed; for it is a pernicious evil to exercise an arbitrary control over the conscience. And yet the devil has ever corrupted the worship of God, and the whole system of religion, under the pretence of extolling the authority of the Church. It is indeed true, that the sacerdotal office was very honourable and worthy of respect; but we must ever take heed lest men assume too much, and lest what is thoughtlessly conceded to them should deprive God of what belongs to him; as the case is, we know, under the Papacy. When the Pope seeks to show that all his commands ought without any dispute to be obeyed, he quotes what is found in Deut. xvii. 8—' If a question arises about the law, the high priest shall judge between what is sacred and profane.' This is indeed true; but was it permitted to the high priest to disregard God's law, and foolishly to allege this or that according to his own judgment? Nay, the priest was only an interpreter of the law. Whenever then God bids those pastors to be heard whom he sets over his Church, his will is, as it has been before stated, that he himself should be heard through their mouth. In short, whatever authority is exercised in the Church ought to be subjected to this rule—that God's law is to retain its own pre-eminence, and that men blend nothing of their own, but only define what is right according to the Word of the

Lord. Now this is by the way; I come now to the main point.

The priests answered, that neither flesh, nor oil, nor wine, was sanctified by touching a piece or part of a sacrifice. Why? because a sacrifice sanctifies not things unclean, except by way of expiation; for this, we know, was the design of sacrifices—that men who were polluted might reconcile themselves to God. A right answer was then given by the priests, that unclean flesh or unclean oil is not sanctified by the touch of holy flesh. Why? because the flesh itself was not dedicated to God for this end—to purify what was unclean by a mere touch. Yet, on the other hand, it is most true, that when a man was unclean he polluted whatever he touched. It is commonly thought, that he is said to be unclean in his soul who had defiled himself by touching a corpse; but I differ from this. The word soul is often taken in the law for man himself—'The soul that eats of what died of itself is polluted; the soul that touches a corpse is polluted.' (Lev. xvii. 15.) Hence he is here said to be polluted in his soul, who had an outward uncleanness, as we say in French, *Pollu en sa personne*. Whosoever then is unclean pollutes by touch only whatever might have been otherwise clean; and the conclusion sufficiently proves that this is the purport of this passage.[1] I have said enough of what the design of the Prophet is, but the subject must be more fully explained.

We know how heedlessly men are wont to deal with God; for they trifle with him like children with their puppets. And this presumption has been condemned, as it is well known, even by heathens. Hardly a Prophet could have inveighed more severely against this gross superstition than Persius, who compares sacrifices, so much thought of by all,

---

[1] The words are טְמֵא־נֶפֶשׁ, polluted of soul; or polluted soul. When pollution by a carcase or a dead body is meant, the preposition לְ is put before נֶפֶשׁ. See Numb. v. 2; ix. 6, 7, 10. A polluted person seems to be intended here, without any reference to the way in which he became so: and this is sufficient for the purpose of the Prophet. *Theodoret* takes this sense—ἀκάθαρτόν τινα—"an unclean person." But most agree with our version: so do *Jerome, Dathius, Newcome, Henderson*, and others—"the polluted by a dead body."—*Ed.*

to puppets, and shows that other things are required by God, even

> A well ordered condition and piety of soul, and an inward purity
> Of mind, and a heart imbued with generous virtue.[1]

He means then that men ought to be imbued with true holiness, and that inwardly, so that there should be nothing fictitious or feigned. He says that they who are such, that is, who have imbibed the true fear of God, do rightly serve him, though they may bring only a crumb of incense, and that others only profane the worship of God, though they may bring many oxen; for whatever they think avails to cover their filth is polluted by new and repeated filth. And this is what has been expressed by heathen authors: another poet says,—

> An impious right hand does not rightly worship the celestials.[2]

So they spoke according to the common judgment of natural knowledge. As to the Philosophers, they ever hold this principle—that no sacrifice is rightly offered to God except the mind be right and pure. But yet the Philosophers, as well as the Poets, adopted this false notion, by which Satan beguiled all men, from the least to the greatest—that God is pacified by ceremonies: hence have proceeded so many expiations, in which foolish men trusted, and by which they thought that God would be propitious to them, though they obstinately continued daily to procure for themselves new punishments, and, as it were, avowedly to carry on war with God himself.

They admit at this day, under the Papacy, this principle —that the true fear of God is necessary, as hypocrisy contaminates all the works of men; nor will they indeed dare to commend those who seek feignedly and triflingly to satisfy God, when they are filled with pride, contempt, and impiety. And yet they will never receive what the Prophet says here —that men not only lose all their labour, but also contract new pollution, when they seek to pacify God by their sacri-

---

[1] Compositum jus, fasque animi, sanctosque recessus
Mentis, et incoctum generoso pectus honesto.—*Per. Sat.* ii. 74.
[2] Non bene celestes impia dextra colit.

fices, unaccompanied by inward purity. For whence is that partial righteousness which the Papists imagine? For they say, that if one does not keep the whole law, yet obedience in part is approved by God; and nothing is more common among them than this expression, partial righteousness. If then an adulterer refrains from theft, and lays out in alms some of his wealth, they will have this to be charity, and declare it to be acceptable. Though it proceeds from an unclean man, it is yet made a covering, which is deemed sufficient in some way or another to pacify God. Thus the Papists seek, without exercising any discrimination, to render God bound to them by their works, though they may be full of all uncleanness. We hence see that this error has not sprung up to-day or yesterday for the first time; but it is inherent in the bones and marrows of men; for they have ever thought that their services please God, though they may be unclean themselves.

Hence this definition must be borne in mind—that works, however splendid they may appear before our eyes, are of no value or importance before God, except they flow from a pure heart. Augustine has very wisely explained this in his fourth book against Julian. He says, that it would be an absurd thing for the faithful to judge of works by the outward appearance; but that they ought to be estimated according to the fountain from which they proceed, and also according to their design. Now the fountain of works I consider to be integrity of heart, and the design or end is, when the object of men is to obey God and to consecrate their life to him. Hence then we learn the difference between good and evil works, between vices and virtues, that is, from the inward state of the mind, and from the object in view. This is the subject of the Prophet in the first clause; and he drew an answer from the priests, which was wholly consistent with the law; and it amounted to this, that no work, however praised and applauded by the world, is valued before God's tribunal, except it proceeds from a pure heart.

Now as to the second part, it is no less difficult to convince men of its truth—that whatever they touch is contaminated, when they are themselves unclean; and yet this is what

God had plainly made known to the Jews: and the priests hesitated not nor doubted, but immediately returned an answer, as though the matter was well known—that an unclean man contaminates whatever thing he touches. But when we come to apply the subject, men then reject what they had been clearly taught; nay, what they are forced to confess, until they see the matter brought home to them, and then they begin to accuse God of too much rigour: "Why is this, that whatever we touch is polluted, though we might have some defilement? Are not our works still deserving of some praise, as they are good works?" And hence also is the common saying, That works, which are in their kind good, are always in a measure meritorious, and though they are without faith, they yet avail to merit the gift of faith, inasmuch as they are in themselves praiseworthy, as chastity, liberality, sobriety, temperance, beneficence, and all almsgiving. But God declares that these virtues are polluted, though men may admire them, and that they are only abominable filth, except the heart be really cleansed and purified. Why so? because nothing can flow from an impure and polluted fountain but what is impure and polluted.

It is now easy to understand how suitably the Prophet had led the priests and the whole people to see this difference. For if he had abruptly said this to them—that no work pleased God, except the doer himself had been cleansed from every defilement, there would have arisen immediately many disputations: "Why will God reject what is in itself worthy of praise? When one observes chastity, when another liberally lays out a part of his property, when a third devotes himself wholly to promote the good of the public, when magnanimity and firmness shine forth in one, when another cultivates the liberal arts—are not these such virtues as deserve some measure of praise!" Thus a great clamour would have been raised among the people, had not Haggai made this kind of preface—that according to the law what is unclean is not sanctified by the touch of holy flesh, and also that whatever is touched by an unclean person is polluted. What the law then prescribed in its rituals silenced all those clamours, which might have immediately arisen among the people. Moreover, though ceremonies have now ceased and are no longer in use, yet what God has once declared still retains its force—that whatever we touch is polluted by us, except there be a real purity of heart to sanctify our works.

Let us now inquire how our works please God: for no one is ever found to be pure and perfect, as the most perfect are defiled with some vices; so that their works are always sprinkled with some spots and blemishes, and contract some uncleanness from the hidden filth of their hearts. In answer to this, I say first, that all our works are corrupt before God and abominable in his sight, for the heart is naturally corrupt: but when God purifies our hearts by faith, then our works begin to be approved, and obtain praise before him; for the heart is cleansed by faith, and purity is diffused over our works, so that they begin to be pleasing to God. For this reason Moses says, that Abel pleased God with his sacrifices, "The Lord had respect to Abel and to his gifts." (Gen. iv. 4.) Had Moses said only, that the sacrifices of Abel were approved by God, he would have spoken unadvisedly, or at least obscurely; for he would have been silent on the main thing. But he begins with the person, as though he had said, that Abel pleased God, because he worshipped him with an upright and sincere heart. He afterwards adds, that his sacrifices were approved, for they proceeded from the true fear of God and sincere piety. So Paul, when speaking of the real keeping of the law, says, that the end of the law is love from a pure heart and faith unfeigned. (1 Tim. i. 5.) He shows then that no work is deemed right before God, except it proceeds from that fountain, even faith unfeigned, which is always connected with an upright and sincere heart. This is one thing.

Secondly, we must bear in mind how God purifies our hearts by faith. There is indeed a twofold purification: He first forms us in his image, and engraves on us true and real fear, and an obedient disposition. This purity of the heart diffuses itself over our works; for when we are imbued with true piety, we have no other object but to offer ourselves and all we have to God. Far indeed are they who are hypocrites and profane men from having this feeling; nay, they are wholly alienated from it: they offer liberally their own things to God, but they wish to be their own masters; for a hypocrite will never give up himself as a spiritual sacrifice to God. We hence see how faith purifies our hearts, and also purifies our works: for having been regenerated by the Spirit of God, we offer to him first ourselves and then all that we have. But as this purgation is never found complete in man, it is therefore necessary that there should come an aid from gratuitous acceptance. Our hearts then are purified by faith, because God imputes not to us that uncleanness which remains, and which defiles our works. As then God regards with gracious acceptance that purity which is not as yet perfect, so he causes that its contagion should not reach to our works. When Abel offered sacrifices to God, he was indeed perfect, inasmuch as there was nothing feigned or hypocritical in him: but he was a man, we know, encompassed with infirmity. It was therefore necessary for his remaining pollution to have been purified by the grace of Christ. Hence it was that his sacrifices were accepted: for as he was accepted, so God graciously received whatever proceeded from him.

We now then see how men, while in a state of nature, displease God by their works, and can bring nothing but what is corrupt, filthy, and abominable. We farther see how the children of God, after having been renewed by his Spirit, come pure to him and offer him pure sacrifices: they come pure, because it is their object to devote themselves to God without any dissimulation; but as this devotedness is never perfect, God supplies the defect by a gratuitous imputation, for he embraces them as his servants in the same manner as though they were entirely formed in all righteousness. And in the same way he approves of their works, for all their spots are wiped away, yea, those very spots, which might justly prevent all favour, were not all uncleanness washed away by the blood of Christ, and that through faith.

We hence learn, that there is no ground for any one to

deceive himself with vain delusions, by attempting to please God with great pomp: for the first thing of which the Prophet treats here is always required, that is, that a person must be pure in his heart, that inward purity must precede every work. And though this truth meets us everywhere in all the Prophets, yet as hypocrisy dazzles our eyes and blinds all our senses, it ought to be seriously considered by us; and we ought to notice in an especial manner not only this passage but other similar passages where the Prophets ridicule the solicitude of the people, when they busied themselves with sacrifices and outward observances, and neglected the principal thing—real purity of heart.

We must also take notice of what the Prophet says in the last verse, that *so was every work of their hand and whatever they offered*.[1] It seems apparently a hard matter, that the very sacrifices were condemned as polluted. But it is no wonder that fictitious modes of worship, by which profane men dishonour God, should be repudiated by him; for they seek to transform him according to their own fancy, as though he might be soothed by playthings or such trifles. It is therefore a most disgraceful mockery when men deal thus with God, offering him only external ceremonies, and disregarding his nature: for they make no account of spiritual worship, and yet think that they please him. We must then, in a word, make this remark—that the Prophet teaches us here, that it is not enough for men to show obedience to God, to offer sacrifices, to spend labour in building the Temple, except these things were rightly done—and how

---

[1] The literal rendering of the verse would be as follows,—
    Then answered Haggai and said,—
    Such *is* this people and such *is* this nation,
    Before me, saith Jehovah;
    Yea, such *is* every work of their hands,
    And what they offer there, polluted it is.

The Prophet seems to have pointed to the altar on which they offered their sacrifices, when he says, "What they offer there." Both *Newcome* and *Henderson* are evidently wrong in rendering the passage in the past tense. The last verb is future, used, as it is often, as a present. So we render it in Welsh, *yr hyn a aberthant yna;* but we understand it as a present act. We may notice here what is often the character of the Prophetic style; the two last lines explain more particularly what the two first contain.—*Ed.*

rightly? by a sincere heart, so there should be no dissimulation, no duplicity.

PRAYER.

Grant, Almighty God, that inasmuch as we come from our mother's womb wholly impure and polluted, and afterwards continually contract so many new defilements,—O grant that we may flee to the fountain which alone can cleanse us. And as there is no other way by which we can be cleansed from all the defilements of the flesh, except we be sprinkled by the blood of thy only-begotten Son, and that by the hidden power of thy Spirit, and thus renounce all our vices,—O grant that we may so strive truly and sincerely to devote ourselves to thee, as daily to renounce more and more all our evil affections, and to have nothing else as our object, but to submit our minds and all our affections to thee, by really denying ourselves, and to exercise ourselves in this strenuous effort as long as we are in this world, until we attain to that true and perfect purity, which is laid up for us in thine only-begotten Son, when we shall be fully united to him, having been transformed into that glory into which he has been received. Amen.

Lecture One Hundred and Thirty-third.

15. And now, I pray you, consider from this day and upward, from before a stone was laid upon a stone in the temple of the Lord:

16. Since those *days* were, when *one* came to an heap of twenty *measures*, there were *but* ten: when *one* came to the pressfat for to draw out fifty *vessels* out of the press, there were *but* twenty.

17. I smote you with blasting and with mildew and with hail in all the labours of your hands; yet ye *turned* not to me, saith the Lord.

18. Consider now from this day and upward, from the four and twentieth day of the ninth *month*, even from

15. Et nunc ponite quæso (*vel,* agedum) super cor vestrum à die hac et suprà, antequam poneretur lapis super lapidem in templo Iehovæ:

16. Ante hæc quum veniret quis ad acervum viginti, fuit decem; quum veniret ad torcular ut hauriret quinquaginta è torculari, fuit summa viginti.

17. Percussi vos orientali vento (*vel,* urente) et rubigene, et grandine in omni opere manuum vestrarum (*alii vertunt,* et omne opus, *sed malè, et potius hic debet resolvi quemadmodum dictum est,* in omni ergo opere) et vos non ad me, dicit Iehova.

18. Ponite quæso super cor vestrum à die hac et suprà, à die vicesimo quarto noni mensis, à die quo

| the day that the foundation of the Lord's temple was laid, consider *it.* | fundatum fuit templum Iehovæ, ponite super cor vestrum. |
| 19. Is the seed yet in the barn? yea, as yet the vine, and the fig tree, and the pomegranate, and the olive tree, hath not brought forth: from this day will I bless *you.* | 19. An adhuc semen in horreo? et adhuc vitis, et ficus, et malusgranata, et arbor olivæ non protulit; à die hac benedicam vobis. |

I AM under the necessity of joining all these verses together, for the Prophet treats of the same thing: and the import of the whole is this—that the Lord had then openly punished the tardiness of the people, so that every one might have easily known that they acted very inconsistently in attending only to their private concerns, so as to neglect the Temple. The Prophet indeed speaks here in a homely manner to earthly men, addicted to their own appetites: had they really become wiser, or made greater progress in true religion, he might have addressed them differently, and would have no doubt followed the rule mentioned by Paul, 'We speak wisdom among those who are perfect.' (1 Cor. ii. 6.) But as they had their thoughts fixed on meat and drink, and were intent on their private advantages, the Prophet tells them what they could comprehend—that God was angry with them, and that the proofs of his curse were evident, as the earth did not produce fruit, and they themselves were reduced to want. We hence perceive the object of the Prophet: but I shall run over the words, that the subject may become more evident.

Lay it, he says, *on your heart.* Here the Prophet indirectly condemns their insensibility, as they were blind in things quite manifest; for he does not here direct their thoughts to heaven, nor announce deep mysteries, but only speaks of food and daily support. Since God, then, impressed clear marks of his wrath on their common sustenance, it was an intolerable stupidity in them to disregard these. And the Prophet often repeats the same thing, in order to shame the Jews; for their tardiness being so often reproved, ought to have made them ashamed. *Lay it on the heart,* he says; that is, Consider what I am going to say; *from this day and heretofore,*[1] he says, *before a stone*

[1] *Supra,* מעלה; "upward," *Newcome;* "backward," *Henderson;* "for-

was laid on a stone; that is, from that day when I began to exhort you to build the Temple, consider what has happened to this very day.

ward," *Secker.* The last refers to 1 Sam. xvi. 13, and xxx. 25, as the only places besides here and in verse 18, where it is applied to time: and clearly in Samuel it means "forward," or hereafter. It means the same when applied to age, Num. i. 20, and when applied to place, Deut. xxviii. 43.

If we retain this meaning, we must consider this verse, and its repetition in verse 18, as the commencement of a sentence, which is completed at the end of verse 19, as intervening clauses. Then the passage would be as follows—

15. And now take, I pray, notice;
    From this day and forward,
    From the time of setting a stone on a stone
    In the Temple of Jehovah,
16. From the time you came to a heap of twenty,
    And it was ten,
    And came to the vat to draw fifty measures,
    And there were twenty;
17. I smote you with blight, and with mildew,
    And with hail, even all the work of your hands;
    But ye *turned* not to me, saith Jehovah;—
18. Take, I pray, notice;
    From this day and forward,
    From the twenty-fourth day of the ninth *month*,
    From the day in which was founded
    The Temple of Jehovah;—take notice;
19. Is yet the seed in the granary?—
    And as yet the vine and the fig tree,
    And the pomegranate and the olive, it hath not borne;—
    From this day will I bless *you*.

I prefer "Take notice," or, "mark," to "consider," as the meaning of שימו לבבכם, "set or fix your heart." In favour of "your" instead of "their" in verse 16, there are three MSS.; and it is more consistent with the context. The expression literally is, "From your being to come," *i.e.* from the time in which you came, and found out the deficiency. "Fifty measures;" פורה is rendered by the Septuagint μετρητὰς—"baths;" by *Jerome,* "Lagenas—flagons." The word means here evidently a vessel to measure the wine from the vat; what quantity it contained is not known. It is here in the singular number, while the numeral, "fifty," is in the plural; which is a Hebrew idiom, very similar to what it is in Welsh, *deg mesur a deugain,* which literally in English is, "ten measure and forty." In verse 17, "even all the work of your hands," is in apposition with "you," and explanatory of it, according to what we often find in the Prophets; for by "you" was meant their "work," and not themselves personally. "But ye *turned* not to me," literally, "But ye not to me;" perhaps the meaning is, "Ye ascribed it not to me," that is, the judgment previously mentioned, or, "Ye attended not to me:" but the verb שבתם is commonly thought to be understood. See Amos iv. 9. The question in verse 19 is to be taken negatively, to correspond with the negative declaration in what follows.
—*Ed.*

Then he adds, Before ye began, he says, to build the Temple, was it not that every one who came to a heap of twenty measures found only ten? that is, was it not, that when the husbandmen expected that there would be twenty measures in the storehouse or on the floor, they were disappointed? because God had dried up the ears, so they yielded not what they used to do; for husbandmen, by long experience, can easily conjecture what they may expect when they see the gathered harvest; but this prospect had disappointed the husbandmen. God, then, had in this case given proofs of his curse. Farther, when any one came to the vat, and expected a large vintage, had he not also been disappointed? for instead of fifty casks he found only twenty.

He afterwards adds, *I have smitten you with the east wind:* for שדפון, *shidaphun*, is to be taken for a scorching wind; and the east wind proved injurious to Judea by its dryness. So also ירקון, *irkun*, is mildew, or a moist wind, from which mildew proceeds; for we know that corn, when it has much wet, contracts mildew when the sun emits its heat. As to the meaning of the Prophet there is no ambiguity, for he intended to teach them that they were in various ways visited, that they might clearly perceive that God was displeased with them. He then mentions the *hail:* for when famine happens only from the cold or from the heat, it may be ascribed to chance or to the stars: but when God employs various scourges, we are then constrained to acknowledge his wrath, as though he were determined to awaken us. This is the reason why the Prophet records here various kinds of judgments. And he says, *In every work of your hands.* Some read, "And every work," &c., which is improper; for they were not smitten in their own bodies, but in the produce of the earth. Then he adds, *And you* returned *not to me,* that is, "During the whole of that time I effected nothing, while I was so often and in such various ways chastising you. And yet what good has the obduracy of your hearts done you? ye have not returned to me."

Lay it, he says, *on your heart from this day, and heretofore,* &c. He repeats what he had said, even from the twenty-fourth day of the ninth month. We have seen before, that the Prophet was sent on that day to reprove the people for their sins. *Lay it* then *on your heart,* he says, *from this day,* &c. We see how emphatical is this repetition, because in things evident the Jews were so insensible that their want and famine could not touch them: and we know that there is no sharper goad to stimulate men than famine. Since then the Lord snatched away their food from their mouth, and they remained inattentive to such a judgment, it was a sure evidence of extreme stupidity. It is on this account that the Prophet often declares, that the Jews were extremely insensible; for they did not consider the judgments of God, which were so manifest. He now subjoins, *Is there yet seed in the barn?* Jerome reads, "in the bud;" and the probable reason why he thus rendered the word was, that he thought that the clauses would not correspond without giving the meaning of bud to מגורה, *megure;* but, as I think, he was mistaken. The Hebrews propose what I cannot approve, for some of them read the sentence as an affirmation, "For there is seed in the barn;" because they dared not to commit the seed to the ground in their state of want. And others read it as a question, as though he had said, that the time of harvest was far off, and that what they had remaining was so small that it was not enough to support them. But, in my judgment, the "seed" refers not to what had been gathered, but to what had been sown. I therefore doubt not but that he speaks of God's blessing on the harvest which was to come after five months, to which I shall presently refer. Some, indeed, render the words in the past tense, as though the Prophet had said, that the Jews had already experienced how great the curse of God was; but this is a forced view. The real meaning of the Prophet is this, *Is there yet seed in the barn?* that is, "Is the seed, as yet hid in the ground, gathered?"

He then adds affirmatively, *neither the vine, nor the fig tree, nor the pomegranate, nor the olive had yet produced any thing;* for it was the ninth month of the year; and the beginning of the year, we know, was in the month of March. Though then they were nearly in the midst of winter, they remained uncertain as to what the produce would be. In the month of November no opinion could be formed, even by the most skilful, what produce they were to expect. As then they were still in suspense, the Prophet says, that God's blessing was in readiness for them. What he had in view was, to show that he brought a sure message from God; for he speaks not of a vintage the prospect of which had already appeared, nor of a harvest when the ears had already made their appearance. As then there was still danger from the hail, from scorching winds, and also from rains and other things injurious to fruit and produce of the land, he says, that the harvest would be most abundant, the vintage large, that, in a word, the produce of the olive and the fig tree would be most exuberant. The truth of the prophecy might now be surely known, when God fulfilled what he had spoken by the mouth of his servant. I now return to the subject itself.

As I have before observed, the Prophet deals with the Jews here according to their gross disposition: for he might in a more refined manner have taught the godly, who were not so entangled with, or devoted to, earthly concerns. It was then necessary for him to speak in a manner suitable to the comprehension of the people, as a skilful teacher who instructs children and those of riper age in a different manner. And he shows by evidences that the Jews were unthankful to God, for they neglected the building of the Temple, and every one was diligently and earnestly engaged in building his own house. He shows by proofs their conduct,—How? Whence has it happened, he says, that at one time your fruit has been destroyed by mildew, at another by heat, and then by the hail, except that the Lord intended thus to correct your neglect? It then follows, that you are convicted of ingratitude by these judgments; for you have neglected God's worship, and only pursued your own private advantages. This is one thing.

The latter clause contains a promise; and by it the instruction given was more confirmed, when the people saw that things suddenly and unexpectedly took a better turn. They had been for many years distressed with want of sustenance; but, when fruitfulness of a sudden followed, did not this change manifest something worthy of their consideration? especially when it was foretold before it happened, and before any such thing could have been foreseen by human conjectures? We see then, that the Prophet dwells on two things,—he condemns the Jews for their neglect, and proves that they were impious and ungrateful towards God, for they disregarded the building of the Temple; and then, in order to animate them and render them more active in the work they had begun, he sets before them, as I have said, what had taken place. God had, indeed, abundantly testified, by various kinds of punishment, that he was displeased with them: but when he now promises that he would deal differently with them, there hence arises a new and a stronger evidence.

But some one may here raise an objection and say, that these evidences are not sure or unvaried; since it often happens, that when people devote themselves faithfully to the service of God they are pressed down by adverse events; yea, that God very often designedly tries their faith by withholding from them for a time his blessing. But the answer to this may be readily given: I indeed allow that it often happens that those who sincerely and from the heart serve God, are deprived of earthly blessings, because God intends to elevate their minds to the hope of eternal reward. God then designedly withdraws his blessing often from the faithful, that they may hunger and thirst in this world, as though they lost all their labour in serving him. But it was not the Prophet's design to propound here an evidence of an unvarying character, as he counted it sufficient to convince the Jews by experience, that nothing prevented them from acknowledging that their avarice displeased God, except their extreme stupidity. The Prophet then does here reprove their insensibility; for, while they greatly laboured in enriching themselves, they did not observe that their labour was in vain, because God from heaven poured his curse on them. This then might have been easily known by them had they not hardened themselves in their vices. And what the Prophet testifies here respecting the fruitful produce of wine, and corn, and oil, and of other things, was still, as I have said, a stronger confirmation.

Now, if any one objects again and says—that this was of no value, because a servile and mercenary service does not please God: to this I answer—that God does often by such means stimulate men, when he sees them to be extremely tardy and slothful, and that he afterwards leads them by other means to serve him truly and from the heart. When therefore any one obeys God, only that he may satisfy his appetite, it is as though one laboured from day to day for the sake of wages, and then disregards him by whom he has been hired. It is certain that such a service is counted as nothing before God; but he would have himself to be generously worshipped by us; and he loves, as Paul says, a cheerful giver. (2 Cor. vi. 7.) But as men, for the most part, on account of their ignorance, cannot be led at first to this generous state of mind, so as to devote themselves willingly to God, it is necessary to begin by using other means, as the Prophet does here, who promises earthly and daily sustenance to the Jews, for he saw that they could not immediately, at the first step, ascend upwards to heaven; but it was not his purpose to stop short, until he elevated their minds higher. Let us then know, that this was only the beginning, that they might learn to fear God and to expect whatever they wanted from his blessing, and also that they might shake off their stupor, under which they had previously laboured. In short, God deals in one way with the rude and ignorant, who are not yet imbued with true religion; and he deals in another way with his own disciples, who are instructed in sound doctrine. When I say that the Prophet acted thus towards the Jews, I speak not of the whole nation; but I regard what we have observed at the beginning of this book—that the Jews cared for nothing then but to build their own houses, and that there was no zeal for religion among them. As then the recollection of God was nigh buried among them, the Temple being neglected, and every one's anxiety being concentrated in building his own house, we hence learn how grossly earthly their affections were. It is therefore no wonder that the Prophet treated them in the manner stated here. Let us proceed—

20. And again the word of the Lord came unto Haggai in the four and twentieth *day* of the month, saying,

21. Speak to Zerubbabel, governor of Judah, saying, I will shake the heavens and the earth:

22. And I will overthrow the throne of kingdoms, and I will destroy the strength of the kingdoms of the heathen; and I will overthrow the chariots, and those that ride in them; and the horses and their riders shall come down, every one by the sword of his brother.

23. In that day, saith the Lord of hosts, will I take thee, O Zerubbabel, my servant, the son of Shealtiel, saith the Lord, and will make thee as a signet: for I have chosen thee, saith the Lord of hosts.

20. Et fuit (postea fuit) sermo Iehovæ secundò ad Chaggai vicesimo quarto mensis, dicendo,

21. Dic ad Zerubbabel, ducem Iehudah, dicendo, Ego concutiam cœlos et terram;

22. Et evertam solium regnorum, et perdam robur regnorum gentium; et evertam quadrigam et sessores ejus; et descendent equi et sessores eorum, quisque in gladio fratris sui.

23. In die illa, dicit Iehova exercituum, sumam te Zerubbabel, fili Sealtiel, serve mi, dicit Iehova; et ponam te quasi annulum, quia elegi te, dicit Iehova exercituum.

The Prophet now proceeds still farther; for there is here a really gratuitous and spiritual promise, by which God affirms that he will have a care for his people to the end. He does not now speak of wine and corn, in order to feed the hungry; but he shows that he would be an eternal Father to that people; for he could not and would not forget the covenant he made with their fathers. There is no doubt but he points out Christ in the person of Zerubbabel, as we shall presently see. So that it is right to distinguish this prophecy from the last; for God has before shown, that the worship which the Jews had for a time disregarded was pleasing to him, as a reward was in readiness, and also that he was offended with the negligence previously reproved, as he had inflicted manifest punishment, not once, nor for a short time, but for many years, and in various ways. What then does follow? In this second prophecy he addresses Zerubbabel, and promises to be a Saviour to the people under his authority.

With regard to these words, some think that a continued

act is signified when he says, " I shake the heavens and the earth ;" and they give this explanation—" That though it belongs to me to shake the heaven and the earth, and I am wont to subvert kingdoms, yet I will render firm the sacred kingdom which I have raised among my people." But this view is very frigid: and we see even from this chapter what is meant by the shaking of the heaven and of the earth, of which mention is made. The Apostle also rightly interprets this passage, when he teaches us, that this prophecy properly belongs to the kingdom of Christ. (Heb. xii. 26.) There is therefore no doubt, but that the Prophet means here something special, when he introduces God as saying, " Behold, I shake the heavens and the earth." God then does not speak of his ordinary providence, nor simply claim to himself the government of the heaven and of the earth, nor teach us that he raises on high the humble and the low, and also brings down the high and the elevated; but he intimates, that he has some memorable work in contemplation, which, when done, would shake men with fear, and make heaven and earth to tremble. Hence, the Prophet no doubt intended here to lead the Jews to the hope of that redemption, some prelude of which God had then given them; but its fulness could not as yet be seen—nay, it was hid from the view of men: for who could have expected such a renovation of the world as was effected by the coming of Christ ? When the Jews found themselves exposed to the wrongs of all men, when so small a number returned, and there was no kingdom and no power, they thought themselves to have been as it were deceived. Hence the Prophet affirms here, that there would be a wonderful work of God, which would shake the heaven and the earth. It is therefore necessary that this should be applied to Christ ; for it was, as it were, a new creation of the world, when Christ gathered together the things scattered, as the Apostle says, in the heaven and in the earth. (Col. i. 20.) When he reconciled men to God and to angels, when he conquered the devil and restored life to the dead, when he shone forth with his own righteousness, then indeed God shook the heaven and the earth ; and he still shakes them at this day, when the gospel is preached;

for he forms anew the children of Adam after his own image. This spiritual regeneration then is such an evidence of God's power and grace, that he may justly be said to shake the heaven and the earth. The import of the passage is, that it behoved the Jews to form a conception in their minds of something greater than could be seen by their eyes; for their redemption was not yet completed.

Hence he subjoins—*I will overthrow the throne of kingdoms; I will destroy the strength of the kingdoms of the nations; and I will overthrow the chariot and him who sits in it; come down shall the horses and their riders; every one shall fall by the sword of his brother.* He confirms here the former sentence—that nothing would be an hinderance that God should not renew his Church. And rightly he adds this by way of anticipation; for the Jews were surrounded on all sides by inveterate enemies; they had as many enemies as they had neighbours; and they were hated even by the whole world. How then could they emerge into that dignity which was then promised to them, except God overturned the rest of the world? But the Prophet here meets this objection, and briefly shows that God would rather that all the nations should perish, than that his Church should remain in that dishonourable state. We then see that the Prophet here means no other thing than that God would overcome all those impediments, which Satan and the whole world may throw in the way, when it is his purpose to restore his Church.

We now perceive the Prophet's design, and we also perceive the application of his doctrine. For whenever impediments and difficulties come in our way, calculated to drive us to despair, when we think of the restoration of the Church, this prophecy ought to come to our minds, which shows that it is in God's power, and that it is his purpose to overturn all the kingdoms of the earth, to break chariots in pieces, to cast down and lay prostrate all riders, rather than to allow them to prevent the restoration of his Church.

But in the last verse the Prophet shows why God would do this—even that Zerubbabel might prosper together with the whole people. Hence he says—*In that day, saith Jeho-*

vah, I will take thee, Zerubbabel, and will set thee as a signet, for I have chosen thee. As we have before said, God addresses Zerubbabel here, that in his person he might testify that he would bless the people whom he intended to gather under that sacred leader; for though Zerubbabel never had a kingdom, nor ever wore a crown, he was yet of the tribe of Judah; and God designed that some spark of that kingdom should exist, which he had raised in the family of David. Since, then, Zerubbabel was at that time a type of Christ, God declares here that he would be to him as a signet—that is, that his dignity would be esteemed by him. This comparison of a signet is found also in other places. It is said in Jer. xxii. 24—" Though this Coniah were a signet on my right hand I would pluck him thence." But here God says that Zerubbabel would be to him a signet—that is, "Thou shalt be with me in high esteem." For a sealing signet is wont to be carefully preserved, as kings seek in this way to secure to themselves the highest authority, so that more trust may be placed in their seal than in the greatest princes. The meaning, then, of the similitude is, that Zerubbabel, though despised by the world, was yet highly esteemed by God. But it is evident that this was never fulfilled in the person of Zerubbabel. It hence follows that it is to be applied to Christ. God, in short, shows, that that people gathered under one head would be accepted by him; for Christ was at length to rise, as it is evident, from the seed of Zerubbabel.

But this reason is to be especially noticed—*Because I have chosen thee.* For God does not here ascribe excellencies or merits to Zerubbabel, when he says that he would hold him in great esteem; but he attributes this to his own election. If, then, the reason be asked why God had so much exalted Zerubbabel, and bestowed on him favours so illustrious, it can be found in nothing else but in the goodness of God alone. God had made a covenant with David, and promised that his kingdom would be eternal; hence it was that he chose Zerubbabel after the people had returned from exile; and this election was the reason why God exalted Zerubbabel, though his power at that time was but small. We indeed know that he was exposed to the contempt of all nations; but God invites here the attention of the faithful to their election, so that they might hope for more than what the perception of the flesh could conceive or apprehend; for what he has decreed cannot be made void; and in the person of Zerubbabel he had determined to save a chosen people; for from him, as it has been said, Christ was to come.

PRAYER.

Grant, Almighty God, that as we are still restrained by our earthly cares, and cannot ascend upward to heaven with so much readiness and alacrity as we ought—O grant, that since thou extendest to us daily so liberal a supply for the present life, we may at least learn that thou art our Father, and that we may not at the same time fix our thoughts on these perishable things, but learn to elevate our minds higher, and so make continual advances in thy spiritual service, until at length we come to the full and complete fruition of that blessed and celestial life which thou hast promised to us, and procured for us by the blood of thy only-begotten Son. Amen.

END OF THE COMMENTARIES ON HAGGAI.

A TRANSLATION

OF

CALVIN'S VERSION

OF

THE PROPHECIES OF HABAKKUK,
ZEPHANIAH, AND HAGGAI,

AS MODIFIED BY

HIS COMMENTARIES.

A TRANSLATION

OF

CALVIN'S VERSION

OF

THE BOOK OF HABAKKUK.

CHAPTER I.

1 THE burden which Habakkuk the Prophet saw:

2 How long, Jehovah, shall I cry,
   And thou wilt not hear?
   And cry aloud to thee of violence,
   And thou wilt not save?
3 Why showest thou me iniquity,
   And makest me to see trouble?
   And *why* are violence and plunder in my sight,
   And he who excites strife and contention? (19)
4 Therefore dissolved is the law,
   And judgment does not continually go forth;
   For the wicked surrounds the just,
   Therefore go forth does perverted judgment. (21)

5 Look ye among the Gentiles and see,
   And be astonished, be astonished;
   For a work will I work in your days,
   Which ye will not believe, though it be told you:
6 For behold, I will rouse the Chaldeans—
   A nation bitter and hasty,
   Which shall march through the breadths of the earth,
   To possess habitations not its own:

⁷ Terrible and fearful *shall* it *be*,
   From itself shall its judgment and its dignity proceed:
⁸ And swifter than leopards *shall be* its horses,
   And fiercer than the evening wolves;
   And numerous shall be its horsemen;
   And its horsemen from far shall come,
   They shall fly as an eagle hastening to devour: (30)
⁹ The whole *of it* for booty shall come;
   The aspect of their faces will be like the east-wind;
   And he will gather captives like the sand:
¹⁰ And at kings he will laugh,
   And princes *shall be* a scorn to him:
   Every fortress he will scorn,
   He will gather dust and take it:
¹¹ Then will he change his spirit,
   And pass through and act impiously,
   Ascribing this his power to his god. (37)

¹² Art not thou, Jehovah, from the beginning, my God?
   My holy One! we shall not die:
   Thou, Jehovah, for judgment hast set him;
   And thou strong One, for correction hast established him.
¹³ Pure art thou of eyes, so as not to behold evil,
   And on trouble thou canst not look:—
   Why lookest thou on transgressors,
   And takest no notice, when the ungodly devours
   One more righteous than himself?
¹⁴ Thou makest man like the fish of the sea,
   Like the reptile, which is without a leader: (46)
¹⁵ The whole by his hook will he draw up,
   Collect into his drag, and gather into his net;
   He will therefore rejoice and exult: (48)
¹⁶ Hence sacrifice will he to his drag,
   And incense will he offer to his net;
   For through them fat *will be* his portion,
   And his meat *will be* rich.—
¹⁷ Shall he therefore extend his drag,
   And continue to slay the nations,
   So as not to spare *them?*

CHAPTER II.

1 On my watch-tower will I stand,
And set myself on a citadel;
And I will watch to see what he may say to me,
And what I may answer to the reproof given me.—
2 Then answer me did Jehovah and said,—

"Write the vision, and make it plain on tables,
That run may he who reads it;
3 For yet the vision shall be for an appointed time,
And will speak at the end, and will not deceive:
If it tarry, wait for it; (66)
For coming it will come, and will not delay.
4 Behold the elated! not right is his soul within him;
But the just, by his faith shall he live." (72)

5 Yea, truly! as by wine, transgress does the proud man,
And he will not rest; (87)
For he enlarges as the grave his soul,
And is like to death, and is not satisfied;
Yea, he collects to himself all nations,
And heaps together for himself all the people.
6 Shall not all these take up against him a parable,
And against him an enigmatical taunt, and say,—

"Ho! he multiplies what is not his own! how long!
And he accumulates on himself thick clay!
7 Shall they not suddenly rise up who shall bite thee,
And awake, who shall torment thee?
And shalt not thou become tramplings to them?
8 As thou has spoiled many nations,
Spoil thee shall all the remnant of the people,
On account of men's blood, and of violence
To the land, to the city and to all its inhabitants.

9 Ho! he covets an evil covetousness to his house,

In order to set on high his nest,
That he may keep himself from the hand of evil!
10 Thou hast provided shame for thine own house,
By cutting off many nations,
And thou hast sinned against thine own soul."

11 For the stone from the wall shall cry,[1]
And the wood from the chamber shall answer it,—

[1] *Calvin* makes here a change in the discourse; but the whole to the end of the chapter may be viewed as the parable or the taunt mentioned in verse 6, and the particle Ho! may be retained instead of Wo. The taunt seems to have been formed so as to have been especially suitable to be used by the Jews.

By regarding the passage in this light, we can understand the sudden change of person in verse 16, if the proposed emendation be disapproved; for we see the same in the former portions of the "taunt." See 6 and 7, and also 9 and 10. That the reader may see the whole of this passage, containing the "taunt," in the light in which I am now fully inclined to regard it, it shall be presented to him complete:—

 6. Will not these, every one of them,
  Raise up a proverb concerning him,
  And a taunt, enigmas for him, and say,—

  "Ho! He increases what is not his! how long!
  And he accumulates on himself thick clay!—
 7. Will they not suddenly rise up—thy biters,
  And awake—thy tormentors,
  And thou become booties to them?
 8. For thou hast spoiled many nations,
  And spoil thee shall all the remnant of the people,
  On account of men's blood, and of violence
  To the land, to the city, and to all its inhabitants."

 9. "Ho! he has coveted an evil covetousness to his house,
  To set on high his nest,
  In order to save himself from the hand of evil!—
 10. Thou hast consulted shame to thine house,
  By cutting off many nations
  And by sinning against thine own soul :
 11. For the stone—from the wall it cries,
  And the beam—from the woodwork it answers it,—
 12. 'Ho! he builds a town by blood,
  And sets up a city by oppression!'—
 13. Shall nothing *be*, lo! from Jehovah of hosts?
  Yea, labour shall the people for the fire,
  And nations—for vanity shall they weary themselves:
 14. For filled shall be the earth
  With the knowledge of the glory of Jehovah,
  Like the waters which spread over the sea."

 15. "Ho! he gives drink to his neighbour!—

12 " Ho! he builds a town by blood,
And sets up a city by iniquity!"
13 Behold, shall nothing be from Jehovah of hosts?
Hence labour shall the people in the fire,
And weary themselves in vain;
14 For filled shall be earth
With the knowledge of the glory of Jehovah,
As the waters cover the sea.

15 Wo to him who gives his friend drink!—
Uniting thy heat, thou makest *them* also to drink,
That thou mayest look on their nakedness.   (112)
16 Thou art filled with shame for the sake of glory;
Drink thou also, and be thou uncovered:
Poured forth to thee shall be the cup of Jehovah's right
  hand,

> Thou addest thy bottle and also strong drink,
> In order to look on their nakedness!
> 16. Thou hast been filled with reproach rather than with glory:
> Drink thou also, and be uncovered;
> Come round to thee shall the cup
> Of the right hand of Jehovah;
> And shameful spewing shall be on thy glory:
> 17. For the violence done to Lebanon—it shall overwhelm thee,
> And the plunder of beasts—it shall rend thee;
> On account of men's blood, and of violence
> To the land, to the city, and to all its inhabitants."
> 18. "What avails the graven image!
> For its graver—he forms it—
> Even the molten image and the teacher of falsehood:
> Yea, trust in it does the former of its form,
> After having made dumb idols!
> 19. Ho! he saith to the wood, 'Arise, Awake;'
> To the dumb stone, 'It will teach?'
> Behold it! covered it is with gold and silver,
> Yet there is no spirit within it!
> But Jehovah is in his holy temple:
> Silent at his presence let the whole earth be."

The "taunt" *may* be deemed as terminating at the end of the 17th verse; but I regard it as continuing to the end of the chapter. The word "neighbour," in the 15th verse, is a collective singular, meaning every neighbour: hence "their" at the end of the verse. The same may be said of "image" in verse 18, which means every image or images, as "idols" are mentioned afterwards. Such are common instances in the Prophets. "It will teach," in verse 19, most evidently refers to "the dumb stone"—the idol; for it is expressly called "the teacher of falsehood" in verse 17.—*Ed.*

And shameful spewing *shall be* on thy glory:
17 For overwhelm thee shall the violence done to Lebanon,
And the spoiling of beasts, which terrified them;
On account of men's blood, and of violence
To the land, to the city, and to all its inhabitants.

18 What avails the graven image?
For graven it hath its framer,
Even the molten image and the teacher of falsehood;
For trust does the framer in his own work,
When he makes dumb idols. (122)
19 Wo to him who saith to wood, "Awake;"
And "Arise," to a dumb stone;—it will teach:
Behold, it is covered with gold and silver;
And *there is* no spirit in the midst of it. (124)
But Jehovah is in his holy Temple:
Silent at his presence let the whole earth be.

CHAPTER III.

¹ The prayer of Habakkuk the Prophet respecting ignorances:

² Jehovah! I heard thy voice, and was terrified;
Jehovah! thy work in the midst of the years, revive it;
In the midst of the years, make it known;
In wrath *thy* mercy remember. (137)

³ God! from Teman he came;
And the holy One from mount Paran: Selah:
Cover the heaven did his glory;
Of his praise full was the earth:
⁴ And brightness,—as the light it was;
Horns,—from his hands they were; (143)
And there was the hiding of his strength:
⁵ Before his face walked the pestilence,
And come forth did burning coals at his feet:
⁶ He stood, and he measured the earth;

He looked, and he dissolved nations;
Yea, shattered were perennial mountains,
Bent down were hills of antiquity;
The ways of ages were his.

7 For iniquity saw I the tents of Chusan; (150)
Tremble did the curtains of the land of Madian.

8 Wert thou angry with rivers, O Jehovah?
Was thine indignation against rivers?
Was thy wrath against the sea?
For thou didst ride on thy horses,
Thy chariots *were* salvation.
9 Quite bare was made thy bow:
The oaths to the tribes *was thy* word: Selah: (155)
With rivers didst thou cleave the earth.
10 See thee did mountains, they fell down;
The stream of waters passed away;
Utter its voice did the deep,
On high did it raise its hands. (158)

11 The sun *and* moon stood still *in their* habitation;
At the light of thy arrows did they proceed,
At the brightness of the glittering of thy spear. (160)

12 In wrath didst thou tread on the land,
In anger didst thou thresh the nations:
13 Go forth didst thou for the salvation of thy people,
For *their* salvation, with thy Christ:
Strike didst thou the head
From the house of the wicked,
Making bare the foundation even to the neck: (164)
14 Smite didst thou with his own staffs
The head of his villages:
They rushed as a whirlwind to drive me away;
Their joy was to devour the poor in secret:
15 A way hast thou made in the sea for thy horses,
Through the heap of great waters. (168)

¹⁶ I heard,—and tremble did my bowels,
  At *thy* voice quiver did my lips ;
  Enter did rottenness into my bones,
  And within me I made a great noise ;
  That I might rest in the day of affliction,
  When he ascends against the people,
  Who shall cut them off. (171)
¹⁷ For the fig-tree shall not flourish,
  And no fruit shall be on the vines,
  Fail shall the produce of the olive,
  And the fields shall not bring forth food ;
  Cut off from the fold shall be the flock,
  And there shall be no ox in the stalls :
¹⁸ But I—in Jehovah will I exult,
  I will rejoice in the God of my salvation :
¹⁹ Jehovah, the Lord, is my strength ;
  And he will set my feet as those of hinds,
  And on my high places will he make me to walk —
  To the leader on my beatings.

A TRANSLATION
OF
CALVIN'S VERSION
OF
THE BOOK OF ZEPHANIAH.

CHAPTER I.

1 THE word of Jehovah, which came to Zephaniah, the son of Cushi, the son of Gedaliah, the son of Amariah, the son of Hizkiah, in the days of Josiah, the son of Amon, king of Judah.

2 By removing I will remove all things
From the face of the land, saith Jehovah;
I will remove man and beast;
3 And I will remove the bird of heaven,
And the fishes of the sea:
And stumblingblocks shall be to the ungodly!
And I will cut off man
From the face of the land, saith Jehovah: (190)
4 Yea, I will extend my hand upon Judah,
And upon all the inhabitants of Jerusalem;
And will cut off from this place the remnants of Baal,
The name of *its* worshippers with the priests;
5 And those who worship,
On *their* roofs, the host of heaven;
And those who worship and swear by Jehovah,
And swear by their own king;
6 And who turn back from following Jehovah,

And who seek not Jehovah,
And do not inquire of him.

⁷ Be silent at the presence of the Lord Jehovah!
For nigh is the day of Jehovah;
Yea, prepared hath Jehovah a sacrifice,
He hath prepared his guests:
⁸ And it shall be in the day of Jehovah's sacrifice,
That I will visit the princes and the king's sons,
And all who wear foreign apparel;
⁹ And I will visit all those
Who dance on the threshold in that day,
Who fill the house of their masters
By means of rapine and fraud. (204)

¹⁰ And there shall be in that day, saith Jehovah,
The voice of crying from the fish-gate,
And howling from the second *gate*,
And great breach from the hills. (212)
¹¹ Howl ye, inhabitants of the lower part,
For exterminated are the people of traffic,
Cut off are all loaded with money.

¹² And it shall be in that day,
That I will search Jerusalem with candles,
And visit the men, congealed on their lees,
Who say in their hearts,—
"Good will not Jehovah do,
Nor will he do evil:"
¹³ And their substance shall be a spoil,
And their house a waste;
And houses shall they build and not inhabit;
And plant shall they vineyards,
And shall not drink the wine of them.

¹⁴ Nigh is the great day of Jehovah,
Nigh and hastening quickly;
The voice of Jehovah's day
Will cry out bitterly,—then will he be strong; (222)

15 A day of wrath *shall be* that day,
   A day of distress and of affliction,
   A day of tumult and of desolation,
   A day of darkness and of thick darkness,
   A day of clouds and of mist;
16 A day of trumpet and of shouting
   Over the fortified cities
   And over the lofty citadels.
17 And I will straiten men,
   And they shall walk as the blind,
   Because they have done wickedly against Jehovah;
   And poured out shall be their blood as dust,
   And their flesh shall be as dung.
18 Even their silver and their gold shall not avail
   To deliver them, in the day of Jehovah's wrath;
   And by the fire of his indignation
   Shall their land be consumed;
   For a consummation, and a speedy one,
   Will be made of all the inhabitants of the land.

CHAPTER II.

1 Gather yourselves, gather,
   Ye nation, not worthy of being loved;
2 Before the decree brings forth,—
   (As chaff shall they pass away in a day)
   Before it comes upon you,
   The fury of Jehovah's anger,—
   Before it comes upon you,
   The day of the anger of Jehovah. (232)
3 Seek Jehovah all ye meek of the land,
   Who his judgment have sought;
   Seek righteousness, seek humility,
   It may be that ye shall be concealed
   In the day of Jehovah's anger.

4 For Gaza, it shall be forsaken,
   And Ashkelon shall be a waste;

Ashdod shall they at mid-day drive out,
And Ekron shall be rooted up.
⁵ Ho! the inhabitants of the line of the sea,
The nation of the Cherethites!
The word of Jehovah is against you;
Canaan! the land of the Philistines!
I will also exterminate thee,
That there may be no inhabitant:
⁶ And the coast of the sea shall be a habitation
For sheepcots of shepherds and folds for sheep; (242)
⁷ And that coast shall be
For the residence of the house of Judah;
Among them shall they feed;
In the houses of Ashkelon
Shall they in the evening lie down;
For visit them shall Jehovah their God,
And he will restore their captivity.

⁸ Heard have I the reproach of Moab,
And the revilings of the children of Ammon;
By which they have upbraided my people;
And they have extended themselves over their border: (247)
⁹ Therefore *as* I live,
Saith Jehovah of hosts, the God of Israel,—
Surely Moab like Sodom shall be,
And the children of Ammon like Gomorrah,
A soil for the nettle and a mine for salt,
And a waste for ever;
The residue of my people shall plunder them,
And the remnant of my nation shall possess them.
¹⁰ This shall be to them for their pride;
Because they have reproached,
And exulted over the people of Jehovah of hosts.
¹¹ Terrible will Jehovah be to them;
For he will consume all the gods of the earth,
And worship him shall each from his place,
All the islands of the nations.—
¹² Ye also Ethiopians!—
Slain by my sword shall they be.

¹³ And extend will he his hand to the north,
   And he will destroy Assyria,
   And set Nineveh a waste,
   A desolation like the desert:
¹⁴ And lie down within it shall flocks,
   All the beasts of the nations;
   Even the bittern and the owl
   Shall on its pillars pass the night;
   A voice shall sing in the window,
   In the door-way there shall be desolation,
   For he will make bare the cedar.
¹⁵ This is the exulting city!
   Which sat in confidence,
   Which said in her heart,—
   " I am, and there is besides me no other."
   How is she become a waste,
   A resting-place for beasts!
   Every one who shall pass by
   Will hiss at her, he will shake his hand.

CHAPTER III.

¹ Wo to the polluted and the filthy—
   The city which is an oppressor! (261)
² She has not attended to the voice,
   She has not received correction,
   In Jehovah has she not trusted,
   To her God she has not drawn nigh!
³ Her princes within her are roaring lions,
   Her judges, the wolves of the evening;
   They break not the bones in the morning!
⁴ Her Prophets are vain, men of deceits; (268)
   Her Priests have polluted what is holy,
   They have subverted the law. (269)

⁵ Jehovah is just in the midst of her,
   He will not do iniquity;
   Every morning his judgment

He brings to light,—he fails not:
Yet the unjust knoweth no shame.
⁶ I have cut off nations,
Waste have become their citadels,
I have destroyed their streets,
So that no one passes through;
Wasted have become their cities,
That there is not a man, not an inhabitant: (275)
⁷ I said, "surely, thou wilt fear me,
Thou wilt receive instruction;"
Then cut off should not be her habitation,
However I might have visited her:—(279)
Truly! they have hastened,
They have corrupted all their doings!
⁸ Therefore look for me, saith Jehovah,
Till the day when I shall rise up for the prey;
For my purpose is,
To gather nations, to assemble kingdoms,
That I may pour upon them my wrath,
The whole fury of mine anger;
For with the fire of my indignation
Shall be devoured the whole earth. (281)

⁹ But I will then turn to the people a pure lip,
That they may all call on the name of Jehovah,
That they may serve him with one consent. (283)
¹⁰ Beyond the rivers of Ethiopia shall be my suppliants;
The daughter of my dispersed shall bring mine offering.
¹¹ In that day thou shalt not be ashamed
On account of all thy doings,
By which thou hast transgressed against me;
For then will I remove from the midst of thee
Those who rejoice in thy pride,
And thou shalt not take pride any more
In my holy mountain. (292)
¹² And I will cause to remain in the midst of thee,
A people afflicted and poor;
And they shall trust in the name of Jehovah.
¹³ The remnant of Israel shall not do iniquity,

And they shall not speak falsehood,
And not found in their mouth
Shall be a deceitful tongue;
And they shall feed and lie down,
And there shall be none to terrify *them*.

14 Exult thou daughter of Sion,
Exult thou Israel;
Rejoice, exult with thy whole heart,
Thou daughter of Jerusalem: (299)
15 Removed has Jehovah thy judgments,
He has turned aside thine enemies;
The King of Israel, Jehovah, is in the midst of thee,
Thou shalt see evil no more.

16 In that day it shall be said to Jerusalem, Fear not;
Sion! relaxed let not thine hands be.
17 Jehovah thy God is in the midst of thee,
He is strong, he will save;
He will exult over thee with joy,
He will rest in his love, (304)
He will exult over thee with triumph.
18 The afflicted, at the appointed time,
Will I gather,—who shall be of thee;
Who sustained for her reproach. (308)
19 Behold, I will destroy all thine oppressors at that time,
And I will save the halting,
And restore the driven away,
To make them a praise and a name
In the land of their reproach.
20 At that time will I restore you,
At that time will I gather you;
For I will make you a name and a praise
Among all the nations of the earth;
When I shall restore your captivities,
Before your eyes, saith Jehovah.

END OF NEW TRANSLATION OF ZEPHANIAH.

A TRANSLATION
OF
CALVIN'S VERSION
OF
THE BOOK OF HAGGAI.

CHAPTER I.

1 IN the second year of Darius the king, in the sixth month, on the first day of the month, came the word of Jehovah by Haggai the Prophet, to Zerubbabel, the son of Shealtiel, the governor of Judah, and to Joshua, the son of Josedech, the high priest, saying—

2 Thus saith Jehovah of hosts, saying—
This people say, "The time is not come
To build the house of Jehovah."

3 Then came the word of Jehovah,
By Haggai, the Prophet, saying—
4 " Is it time for you
To dwell yourselves in your boarded houses,
And this house a waste!"

5 And now thus saith Jehovah of hosts,—
Apply your heart to your ways:
6 Ye have sown much, and brought in little;
Ye have eaten, and were not satisfied;

Ye have drank, and were not replenished ;
Ye have clothed yourselves, and were not warmed ;
And he who gains wages,
Gains wages for a perforated bag. (330)

⁷ Thus saith Jehovah of hosts,—
Apply your heart to your ways ;
⁸ Ascend unto the mountain and bring wood,
And build the house ;
And I will be *to you* propitious in it,
And glorified shall I be, saith Jehovah. (333)

⁹ Ye have looked for much, but behold little !
And ye brought it home, and I blew on it :
Why is this ? saith Jehovah ;
On account of my house, because it is waste,
And ye run, each of you to his own house.
¹⁰ Therefore restrained over you
Are the heavens from dew ;
And the earth from producing is restrained :
¹¹ Yea, I have called for drought
On the land and on the mountains,
And on the corn and the wine and the oil,
And on everything which the earth produces,
On man and on beast,
And on every labour of the hands. (338)

¹² And Zerubbabel, the son of Shealtiel, and Joshua, the son of Josedech, the high priest, and all the residue of the people, attended to the voice of Jehovah, their God, and to the words of Haggai, the Prophet, as Jehovah their God had sent him ; and the people feared Jehovah. ¹³ Then said Haggai, the messenger of Jehovah, according to Jehovah's message, saying to the people, " With you am I," saith Jehovah. ¹⁴ And Jehovah stirred up the spirit of Zerubbabel, the son of Shealtiel, the governor of Judah, and the spirit of Joshua, the son of Josedech, the high priest, and the spirit of all the people ; and they came and carried on the work in the Temple of Jehovah of hosts, their God,

¹⁵ on the twenty-fourth day of the sixth month, in the second year of Darius the king.¹

CHAPTER II.

¹ In the seventh month, and on the twenty-first day, came the word of Jehovah to Haggai, the Prophet, saying,—
² Speak now to Zerubbabel, the son of Shealtiel, the governor of Judah, and to Joshua, the son of Josedech, the high-priest, and to all the residue of the people, saying,—

³ Who among you is alive,
  Who saw this house in its former glory,
  And how do ye see it now?
  Is it not to that as nothing in your eyes?
⁴ Yet now strong be thou Zerubbabel, saith Jehovah;
  And strong be thou Joshua,
  The son of Josedech, the high priest,
  And strong be all the people of the land;
  And work, for with you am I,
  Saith Jehovah of hosts,
⁵ According to the word I covenanted with you,
  When ye came forth from Egypt,
  And my Spirit shall be
  In the midst of you, fear ye not. (354)

⁶ For thus saith Jehovah of hosts,—
  Yet for a little while shall be this,
⁷ And I will shake the heavens and the earth,
  Also the sea and the dry land:
  Yea, I will shake all nations,
  And come shall the choice things of all nations;
  And I will fill this house with glory,
  Saith Jehovah of hosts:

---

¹ What is said in a Note in p. 347 does not apply to what *Calvin* says. He refers not, as I inadvertently apprehended, to the present division of the chapter, but to that adopted in the Septuagint; for this verse in that version forms the beginning of the next chapter.—*Ed.*

⁸ Mine the silver and mine the gold,
  Saith Jehovah of hosts:
⁹ Greater shall be the glory
  Of this latter house than that of the former,
  Saith Jehovah of hosts;
  And in this place will I give peace,
  Saith Jehovah of hosts.

¹⁰ On the twenty-fourth of the ninth *month*, in the second year of Darius, came the word of Jehovah to Haggai, the Prophet, saying,—¹¹ Thus saith Jehovah of hosts, Ask the priests respecting the law, saying,—¹² If a man carry holy flesh in the skirt of his garment, and with his skirt touch bread, or pottage, or wine, or oil, or any eatable, shall it be made holy? And the priests answered and said, No. ¹³ Then said Haggai, If any one polluted in his person touch any of these things, shall it be polluted? The priests answered and said, It shall be polluted. ¹⁴ Then answered Haggai, and said,—

  So is this people, and so is this nation,
  In my sight, saith Jehovah;
  And so is every work of their hands,
  And what they offer,—it is polluted.

¹⁵ And now I pray, lay it to heart,—
  From this day and beyond it,
  Before a stone was laid on a stone
  In the temple of Jehovah,—
¹⁶ Before this time, when one came
  To a heap of twenty, there were but ten *measures*,
  When he came to the vat to draw fifty,
  There were from the vat but twenty *vessels:*
¹⁷ I smote you with blasting and mildew and hail,
  As to every work of your hands;
  And ye turned not to me, saith Jehovah.

¹⁸ Lay it, I pray, to your heart,—
  From this day and beyond it,

From the twenty-fourth day of the ninth month,
From the day the temple of Jehovah was founded;—
Lay it to your heart,—
19 Is there now seed in the barn?
And as yet the vine and the fig tree,
And the pomegranate and the olive,
Have produced nothing;—
From this day will I bless you. (378)

20 And the word of Jehovah came again to Haggai, on the twenty-fourth of the month, saying,—21 Speak to Zerubbabel, the governor of Judah, saying,—

22 I will shake the heavens and the earth,
And will overthrow the throne of kingdoms,
And destroy the strength of the kingdoms of the nations;
Yea, I will overthrow chariots and their riders,
And down shall come the horses and their riders,
Every one by the sword of his brother:
23 In that day, saith Jehovah of hosts,
I will take thee Zerubbabel,
The son of Shealtiel, my servant, saith Jehovah,
And I will make thee as a signet,
For I have chosen thee, saith Jehovah of hosts.

www.ingramcontent.com/pod-product-compliance
Lightning Source LLC
Chambersburg PA
CBHW052138300426
44115CB00011B/1437